THE DYNAMICS OF ACTION

"Behavior we can observe, consciousness we can observe with some difficulty, but the inner dynamics of the mental process must be inferred rather than observed. Even so, psychology is in no worse case than the other sciences. They all seek to understand what goes on below the surface of things, to form conceptions of the inner workings of things that shall square with the known facts and make possible the prediction of what will occur under given conditions. A dynamic psychology must utilize the observations of consciousness and behavior as indications of the 'workings of the mind'; and that, in spite of formal definitions to the contrary, is what psychologists have been attempting to accomplish since the beginning."

ROBERT S. WOODWORTH in *Dynamic Psychology* (1918)

"When detailed evidence of neurophysiology and histology is considered, the conclusion becomes inevitable that the nonsensory factor in cerebral action must be more consistently present and of more dominating importance than reluctant psychological theory has ever recognized. Instead of a joker to occasionally confuse the student of behavior, nonsensory activities appear in every fall of the cards and must make up a large share of the deck. . . . So there really is a rational basis for postulating a central neural factor that modifies the action of a stimulus. The theoretical problem now is to discover the rules by which it operates. At first glance this is a problem for the neurophysiologist only. But look closer, much of the evidence, from which these rules must be worked out, is psychological or behavioral."

DONALD O. HEBB in *Organization of Behavior* (1949)

THE
DYNAMICS OF ACTION

JOHN W. ATKINSON & DAVID BIRCH

The University of Michigan

John Wiley & Sons, Inc.

New York · London · Sydney · Toronto

To Mary Jane and Dorothy

PREFACE

In this book we have attempted to reconstruct the theory of motivation. We begin with analysis of a simple change in activity—the kind of shift from one activity to another that is a central characteristic of the molar stream of behavior constituting the life of an individual. A simple change of activity implies that there has been a change in the relative strength, or dominance relationship, of the behavioral tendencies that motivate particular actions. To explain how these changes in the strength of particular tendencies come about during an interval of time is the main business of a theory of motivation.

Our theoretical account begins with the assumption of inertia applied to the behavioral tendencies that motivate actions. The idea is Freud's premise that the wish persists until it is expressed either directly or in some substitute activity. The conceptual scheme that is advanced redefines the functional significance of the stimuli and the responses of traditional behavior theory. It treats familiar topics—the initiation of an activity, the persistence of an activity, choice—as interrelated aspects of a change of activity. It develops the logical interrelatedness of these and other behavioral measures in the study of motivation: intensity, operant level, and time spent in an activity. And it specifies what constitutes the study of individual differences in personality in relation to the processes of motivation and action.

Neither of us could have written *The Dynamics of Action* by himself. It is the product of a theoretical dialogue that began early in the 1950's. During the past eight years, our interaction in joint teaching, research, and systematic discussion has had this book as its explicit aim. The book is the concretization of our theoretical discussion.

We have a common commitment to the development of a psychology of motivation, and we also share an understanding of the need for theory that has the twin virtues of scope and precision. Thus it has been an easy matter for us to appreciate the promise inherent in our joining complementary backgrounds, substantive interests, and special talents in this collaborative venture. We have each been teacher and student, creator and critic, optimist and skeptic in the course of this work. Our roles have varied as we have come back to each thorny issue again and again in successive years.

If the accident of alphabetical listing of our names corresponds to anything, it is the time order in which we have shared the initiative and made our most significant individual contributions. To put this theoretical missile into orbit required two stages. The first was a sustained thrust to overcome the inertia of traditional views and the attraction of familiar concepts. The second, once we had come free from the hold of habitual schemes, required the guidance and direction to be found in a refined and elaborated mathematical statement that only one of us had the requisite skill to write.

Our conception of the dynamics of action involves three interrelated motivational processes: instigation of action, resistance to action, and consummation in action. These processes are dealt with mathematically, but the dynamics of action is not intended to be a mathematical model of motivation. We did not take an abstract mathematical system and use it as a representation of motivation. Therefore, no mathematical structure specifically dictated relationships within the theory. Instead, we have taken our ideas about motivational processes, phrased them in the language of mathematics, and used mathematical operations to derive consequences. Mathematics has been a vehicle for us, one that could take us from where we start to where we want to go. Fairly early we decided on a theory that is continuous in nature rather than discrete, deterministic rather than probabilistic. We made tentative beginnings in the other directions but turned away from them because of a preference for a deterministic theory and the convenience of a theory that is based on continuous functions. Development of these theoretical alternatives could prove interesting and perhaps valuable.

Our views concerning the relationships of thought to action and learning to motivation are less well developed than other aspects of our conceptual scheme. Yet we have gone far enough to be able to introduce the plausible alternatives concerning the functional significance of conscious thought within the framework of the dynamics of action. And though we have given most attention to the problem of motivation (that is, the contemporaneous determinants of behavior which we consider logically prior to the problem of learning), we have nevertheless tried to show how principles of learning can be phrased in terms of the language of a theory of motivation.

Throughout the book we are primarily concerned with exposition of a conceptual analysis of the problem of motivation, the development of several basic principles, and the elaboration of their behavioral implications. The book is written for both mathematically trained and untrained readers. We have tried it on both in our graduate courses in motivation. Mathematical description of the dynamics of action is always coupled with verbal descriptions of the details of the motivational process as conceived, and the most complicated mathematical issues are held for notes at the end of the chapters. Hopefully the blow-by-blow verbal accounts will give life and substance to the simpler algebraic statements. There is, we believe, no substitute for the clarity in specification inherent in mathematical description of complex interrelated processes. Our book defines a level of aspiration for the field of motivation and one that should be reflected in the curriculum specifications of graduate training.

Our intention is to provide a new and hopefully heuristic guide for future approaches to the interrelated behavioral problems of motivation. We aim, at the very least, to awaken active interest in the development of theory about the temporal aspect of behavioral processes—the systematic changes that occur as a function of what happens during intervals of time.

We have had to make what we considered best guesses at many points. That is the price of even trying to develop a scheme that will have both scope and coherence. It is the price of recognizing that the whole complex theory of behavior, and not merely some limited hypothesis, is put to the test in any empirical research. It is the price of not having expert knowledge of the literature in all of the related subfields of motivation where such literature may exist.

The cost of guessing is to be wrong on some or many points. We anticipate this. Our guesses might have been different if we had chosen to take the time for thorough and intensive searches of literature. But when faced with the choice of committing time to review of evidence or pushing ahead with the construction of a coherent framework for thought about motivation, we invariably chose the latter. The self-corrective process of science is a community enterprise. Therefore, let this work be treated as the opening statement in a new dialogue that awaits the reply of experimental inquiry on many points.

We appreciate the suggestions and criticisms of our students in Psychology 742 and 842 since 1961, some of which have no doubt had a significant effect on the direction of our thought but which cannot, at this late date, be identified as to source. Our preliminary discussions of the relation of thought to action were sharpened as a result of several seminar discussions of an earlier version of the manuscript with our colleagues in philosophy, Professors Richard B. Brandt and Alvin I. Goldman, and with Professor Dorwin Cartwright. In addition to participating in these discussions near the end, Professor Cartwright helped substantially at the very beginning to establish a programmatic guide which was our starting point (see Atkinson and Cartwright, 1964; Atkinson, 1964, pps. 298–314). For a short while we proceeded as a troika until his other commitments made that impossible. To him, particularly, and to other, unnamed colleagues who commented on portions of the manuscript, we are, indeed, very grateful.

Our sustained time involvement in this work, particularly during summers when most of the writing was accomplished, was made possible by grants to one or both of us by the National Science Foundation for experimental and conceptual analysis related to some aspect of the work (GS-9 from 1962–66, GS-1399 from 1966–69, G-19217 from 1962–64, and GB-2910 from 1964–67) and, in the final stages, by a Special Research Fellowship from Public Health Service in 1969–1970.

Miss Camille Buda deserves our hearty thanks. She mastered the arts of deciphering the cryptic scribbles of manuscripts written by one and severely edited by the other, of typing then retyping the intricate equations embroidered liberally with esoteric subscripts, of redoing work that seemed done because the authors had misgivings, second thoughts, and even—occasionally—better thoughts. All this was done with commendable speed, precision, and detached good humor, touched with some very legitimate skepticism about the ultimate worth of this aspect of her work during the past four years.

And thanks, too, to David and Billy and Tom and Becky, who helped read the proofs.

Finally, to our wives who have experienced vicariously the thrill of the conception, the monotony of the eight-year gestation, the pain of the labor, the dread of possible miscarriages, and now—the joy of the actual birth, to them we dedicate the book.

Permissions to quote or reprint earlier published material were kindly granted by authors and the following publishers: American Psychological Association, Columbia University Press, and John Wiley & Sons, Inc.

JOHN W. ATKINSON
DAVID BIRCH

Amsterdam and Ann Arbor
January 1970

CONTENTS

THE DYNAMICS OF ACTION

CHAPTER 1

THE FUNDAMENTAL PROBLEM: A CHANGE OF ACTIVITY

The behavioral life of an individual is a constant flux of activity. There are no behavioral vacuums except when the individual is literally inactive and unconscious—yet still alive in a medical sense—as in the case of extreme illness or after a severe blow on the head. Otherwise, his behavioral life (which constitutes the subject matter of psychology) is, as Barker (1963) has described it: a continuous stream characterized by change from one activity to another without pause from birth until death.

If an observer is to explain behavior, he first must be able to identify and describe what the subject is doing at a particular time. There is no more basic problem (see Barker, 1963). If the subject of study is human, this preliminary task often will require taking into account the individual's own descriptions of the otherwise covert activities called thought. Thought and action, together, constitute the stream of activity—the behavior that is grist for the psychologist's explanatory mill.

Many everyday activities of people in social situations and of lower animals in their natural habitats are more difficult to describe adequately than the movements of particular rocks in a landslide. Yet general observation of these activities and the conditions surrounding them often will suggest causal links to the behavioral scientist who seeks to identify the underlying principles of behavior. These activities frequently can be interpreted more meaningfully within his causal scheme than by conventional wisdom. But observation of these complexly determined activities will rarely provide a proving ground for systematic proposals about the determinants of action. The observation of the behavior of rocks in a landslide would never provide an adequate test of the basic principles of motion. Precision in the theoretical account of behavior must come from the observation of activities under well-controlled experimental conditions. This allows an adequate identification and description of what is happening at a particular time and the measurement of fundamental characteristics of the stream of behavior.

The questions of traditional interest that concern the motivation of

1

behavior are questions about the contemporaneous determinants of activities. What factors account for the selection, initiation, intensity, persistence, and cessation of a particular activity? The answers we propose in subsequent chapters will depart in significant ways from the traditional analysis of motivation. We have attempted to overcome some fundamental conceptual obstacles in the traditional scheme of thought. But any comparison of our proposals concerning the determinants of behavior with current views should be undertaken only after the ideas and implications of our conceptual scheme have been expounded. Consequently, in this book we invite suspended judgment until there has been an opportunity to scan the domain of behavior with a new set of conceptual spectacles.

We shall begin as if approaching the task of conceptual analysis of the determinants of behavior for the first time, asking again: *What is required to account for the observable characteristics of molar behavior?* This question immediately leads us back another step to the task of identifying the fundamental characteristics of molar behavior that require some kind of theoretical explanation. The chapters of the book proceed from relatively simple matters, in terms of which our basic assumptions and concepts are introduced and clarified, to the complexities of behavior which any theory must confront. We ask the reader to assume certain simple and ideal conditions at the outset and then later to consider the more typical, complicated conditions of actual behavior. Our intention in the initial chapters is a dogmatic exposition of our views. Later, we shall begin to introduce the qualifications and to consider the proposals that are being advanced in relation to traditional problems and issues concerning motivation and action. Our limited aim throughout is the exposition of a conceptual scheme that departs in significant ways from the traditional analysis of motivation. The task of the systematic critical analysis of the adequacy of this scheme in relation to each of the different empirical problems it may illuminate in a new way is left for the future because we doubt that currently available evidence on many points is always adequate, given some new specifications as to what should be taken into account, and because we do not know enough about certain problems to do the job definitively at this time. We view this work, and we hope the reader will be willing to view it that way too, as another opening statement for the kind of dialogue between conceptual and experimental analysis that characterizes the evolution of a science. Some of the reasons for taking a fresh view of old problems have been set forth elsewhere (Atkinson and Cartwright, 1964; Atkinson, 1964).

An Initial Premise

At the outset, let us try to approach the task of conceptual analysis of molar behavior naively instead of being explicitly guided by the basic premises, elements, and implications of a theory (for example, S-R behavior theory) that has already evolved in one or another of the traditional orientations toward the subject. The untutored observation of behavior suggests, as an initial premise, that *the subject of study is constantly active.* It is always doing something that a psychologist must consider as engaging in an activity, even when it is sleeping.

In considering sleeping an activity like eating, reading, listening to music, or exploring, we are struck by certain similarities: (a) under certain conditions, the opportunity to sleep is pursued as an end; (b) like other activities, it is sometimes more enjoyable than at other times; (c) like other activities, it is sometimes easily interrupted and sometimes not depending on the situations, etc. Freud stressed the importance of viewing sleeping as an activity that could be preserved by the compatible activity of dreaming when there was a threat of interruption. When an individual is actually unconscious, that is, not alive in a behavioral sense, it is impossible to engage his attention to say nothing of producing a shift in the gross nature of his activity. But sleepers can be aroused by a call to some other activity, and they often show the same signs of irritation that accompany interruption of some other enjoyable activity.

A Principle of Action

The individual whom we observe, whether human or lower animal, is already doing something whenever we begin to observe him. This *initial activity,* the activity already in progress—whatever it may be, is an expression of the dominant behavioral tendency in that individual at the time. An animal eating is expressing a tendency to eat. A professor working at his desk is expressing a tendency to do this work. A woman chatting over morning coffee is expressing a dominant tendency, perhaps a tendency to engage in affiliative activity with her neighbor. The tendency expressed in the initial activity is designated T_A in our discussion, and the activity sustained by it is designated activity A. The tendency sustaining activity in progress (T_A) is, by definition, either the subject's only active tendency to behave at that particular time—a possibility that we consider most unlikely—or it is his dominant tendency, that is, the strongest among a set of tendencies to engage in different and mutually incompatible activities any one of which would be expressed in behavior if there were not a stronger competitor.

The representation of ongoing activity as an expression of the dominant behavioral tendency in the individual is captured in a simple *Principle of Action:* the occurrence of a particular activity A at any given moment $\Leftrightarrow T_A > T_B, T_C, \ldots$.

Thus, at the outset, we conceive the activity in progress (whether it be overt and visible to the external observer or covert and made known to him only by the report of the subject) to be less than a full expression of what the individual is then motivated to do. The activity in progress expresses the dominant tendency at the time or, to be very precise, it expresses the dominant tendency and also any other tendencies to undertake activities that are compatible with the dominant one and with each other. For now, let us consider all activities as incompatible.

The Primitive Observation: A Change of Activity

As we continue to observe the individual who is already engaging in activity A, whether it be a child playing with a toy, a rat grooming in the start box of a maze, or a student trying to solve an arithmetic problem, we shall notice some time later—as the clock continues to tick—that activity A is no longer occurring. It has ceased, and another activity, activity B, has been initiated in its place. The child has ceased playing with the toy and is now walking to the kitchen; the rat has ceased grooming and is now sniffing in the corner of the start box; the student has ceased working on the arithmetic problem and is now talking to his friend.

We can employ the simple Principle of Action to describe what has happened during this interval of observation. Activity A continued as long as $T_A > T_B, T_C, \ldots$. But the cessation of activity A and the initiation of activity B means that now $T_B > T_A, T_C, \ldots$. *The observation of a change in activity implies a change in the dominance relations among the behavioral tendencies of the individual.* The change in activity occurs when a previously subordinate tendency attains the dominant position in the hierarchy of tendencies that constitute the state of motivation of the individual at the time.

It is important to remember that we are presently assuming that activities A and B are incompatible, that is, they cannot both occur at the same time. Here, at the outset of our discussion, we confront a potential complication for the analysis, namely, the simultaneous occurrence of *compatible* activities. We assume that an individual would, if he could, simultaneously undertake all of the different activities that he is motivated to undertake. There would then be no need to distinguish activities and tendencies in a theory of behavior. But the individual cannot do this. He is so constructed that he cannot simultaneously express all of his tendencies. The incompatibility of various activities, that is, the impossibility of playing golf and sculpting at the same time, or of simultaneously reading a novel and solving calculus problems, etc., is what defines the need for a theory of action that accounts for selectivity in behavior at a particular time. In this chapter, and until the topic of compatible activities has been discussed more fully (Chapter 3), we shall limit our inquiry to the fate of tendencies to engage in activities that are mutually incompatible.

The fundamental problem of choice, which a theory of action should illuminate, occurs when an individual, already engaging in one activity, "decides" to initiate some other activity instead. Psychologists sometimes are prepared to identify, to observe, and to measure only the initiation of one particular activity (for example, a rat leaving the start box of a maze). At other times (for example, as at the first two-way choice point in the maze), they are prepared to observe and to record choice between two or more specified alternatives. But in each case the subject may face a decision that involves many more alternative action tendencies and may even express some of them in behavior before he initiates the activity that the observer is prepared to record. Viewed in this light, the study of choice among two or more alternatives and the study of the initiation of some designated activity may be said to differ in method, but both involve the same fundamental problem—a change in activity.

When the ongoing activity A ceases and a new activity B is initiated, in other words, when there is a change in activity, a change in the hierarchy of tendencies is implied. Specifically, the change in the hierarchy is such that, at least, T_A and/or T_B has changed in strength. This may be understood clearly by recalling from the Principle of Action that if activity A is occurring at time 1 and activity B is initiated at time 2, it follows that $T_A > T_B$, $T_C, \ldots$ at time 1 and $T_B > T_A, T_C, \ldots$ at time 2. From this we know that the relationship between T_A and T_B has shifted from $T_A > T_B$ to $T_B > T_A$. The strength of the other tendencies $T_C, T_D, \ldots$ may have also changed, but we have no way of knowing this. However, the fact that activity B, instead of activity $C, D, \ldots$, has replaced activity A does tell us that $T_C, T_D, \ldots$ remained weaker than T_A during the interval of observation and that they were weaker than T_B at the time of the change in activity.

A more detailed look at the change in the relative strengths of T_A and T_B during the interval of observation immediately reveals two important bits of information. No matter how dramatic and complex the alterations in the strengths of T_A and T_B may have been, we know that T_A must have remained stronger than T_B throughout the interval (otherwise activity A would not have continued). Furthermore, we know that one of five patterns of change in the relative strength of T_A and T_B must have occurred: T_B became stronger while T_A remained constant, became weaker, or became stronger but less rapidly than T_B; or T_B remained constant while T_A became weaker; or T_B became weaker but less rapidly than T_A.

These several possibilities, any one of which would account for the observed change in activity, are shown graphically in Figure 1.1. The straight lines shown in Figure 1.1 describe the changes in the strength of T_A and T_B during the interval of observation $(t_{B/A})$[1] as if these changes occurred at the

---

[1] The time taken to initiate activity B given initial activity A.

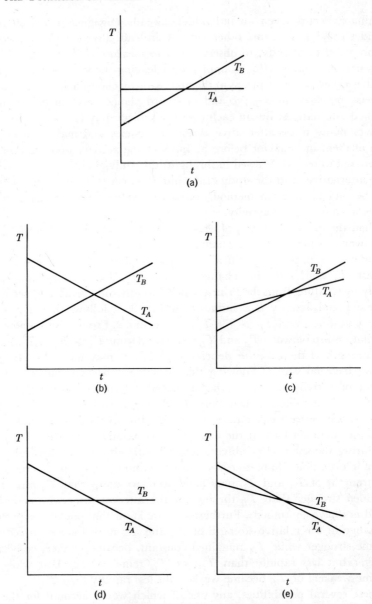

FIGURE 1.1   Schematic representation of the five patterns of changes in the strength of tendency of T_A and T_B from time 1 to time 2 that would result in a change from activity A to activity B.

same rate throughout the interval. In other words, they do not take into account any complexities or irregularities in the changing strengths of T_A and T_B from the beginning to the end of the interval in which the change of activity was observed. The observer, of course, has no direct information about the specific trends of the paths taken by the strength of T_A and T_B from a change in activity. Nevertheless, the changes in the strength of the tendencies portrayed in Figure 1.1 are instructive. We can use them to write an expression for the time required to change from one activity to another. This simple algebraic expression helps to identify the factors responsible for the change and how soon it will occur.

Time to Change from One Activity to Another

Let us use the symbol α to stand for the rate of change in the strength of T_A and the symbol β to stand for the rate of change of T_B during the interval of time that begins with an observation that activity A is in progress and that ends with an observation that activity B has just supplanted activity A. The average change in strength of each tendency per unit of time (that is, the rate of change) can be written

$$\alpha = \frac{T_{A_F} - T_{A_I}}{t_{B/A}} \quad \text{and} \quad \beta = \frac{T_{B_F} - T_{B_I}}{t_{B/A}}$$

where T_{A_F} and T_{B_F} represent the final strengths of T_A and T_B (that is, their magnitudes at the end of the interval of observation) and T_{A_I} and T_{B_I} represent the initial strengths of the two tendencies (that is, their magnitudes at the beginning of the interval of observation). The symbol $t_{B/A}$ which is used to denote the duration of the interval of observation that terminates with the initiation of activity B is a reminder that this temporal interval is the traditional measure of the latency of activity B.

With this notation, we can easily identify the determinants of the final strengths of the two tendencies: $T_{A_F} = T_{A_I} + \alpha \cdot t_{B/A}$ and $T_{B_F} = T_{B_I} + \beta \cdot t_{B/A}$. These equations describe the straight lines in Figure 1.1 and say only that the final strength of a tendency is equal to its initial strength plus the average change in its strength per unit of time multiplied by the interval of time over which that average change occurs. If, as we have assumed, the change in activity occurs when the dominance relation between the two tendencies shifts to $T_B > T_A$, we can set $T_{B_F} = T_{A_F}$ and solve for $t_{B/A}$.[2]

---

[2] The expression $T_{B_F} = T_{A_F}$, for all intents and purposes, is equivalent to $T_{B_F} = T_{A_F} + \Delta$, where Δ has a magnitude only great enough to produce the inequality $T_B > T_A$ responsible for the observed change in activity.

The result of these operations is shown in Equation 1.1:

$$t_{B/A} = \frac{T_{A_I} - T_{B_I}}{\beta - \alpha} \tag{1.1}$$

Equation 1.1 represents the basic empirical equation for a simple change in activity. Translated into words it says that the time required for a change from activity A to activity B $(t_{B/A})$ is directly proportionate to the difference between the initial strengths of the two tendencies $(T_{A_I} - T_{B_I})$ and inversely proportionate to the difference in the rates of change of the two tendencies during the interval of observation $(\beta - \alpha)$.

The numerator of Equation 1.1 must be positive, since activity A is initially in progress. Hence, it is easily seen that the time required for a change in activity will be greater the greater the magnitude of the initial difference in strengths of the two tendencies. The five possibilities for changes in activity depicted in Figure 1.1 can be recovered from Equation 1.1 by appropriate assignment of values to α and β. If $\alpha = 0$ and $\beta > 0$ we have pattern a; if $\alpha < 0$ and $\beta > 0$, pattern b; if $\alpha > 0$, $\beta > 0$ and $\beta > \alpha$, pattern c; if $\alpha < 0$ and $\beta = 0$, pattern d; and if $\alpha < 0$, $\beta < 0$, and $\beta > \alpha$, pattern e. For each of these patterns, and only for these patterns, the value of $t_{B/A}$ is positive and finite.

It is informative and very helpful for subsequent discussion of the empirical determinants of a change in activity to see that Equation 1.1 can be rewritten in two additional forms without changing its meaning. Instead of using the parameters T_{A_I}, T_{B_I}, β and α, we may write the basic equation describing the time to change from one activity to another in terms of the parameters T_{A_F}, T_{B_I}, and β. This yields Equation 1.2:

$$t_{B/A} = \frac{T_{A_F} - T_{B_I}}{\beta} \tag{1.2}$$

and by using the parameters T_{A_I}, T_{B_F}, and α, we end up with Equation 1.3:

$$t_{B/A} = \frac{T_{B_F} - T_{A_I}}{\alpha} \tag{1.3}$$

Since Equations 1.2 and 1.3 are merely alternative forms of Equation 1.1, all three expressions have the same meaning. Yet one form may be simpler or more instructive than another on different occasions, depending on which parameters of a change in activity are to receive particular attention. Equation 1.2, for example, draws attention to the final strength of the tendency sustaining an activity in progress (T_{A_F}), the initial strength of the tendency to undertake some alternative activity (T_{B_I}), and the rate of change in the strength of this latter tendency (β) during the interval of observation $(t_{B/A})$.[3]

DETERMINANTS OF CHANGE IN THE STRENGTH OF AN ACTION TENDENCY

Inherent in the observation of a change in activity is the implication that there has been a change in the strength of one or another *action tendency* during the interval of observation. These changes must be attributable to something that has occurred during the interval of observation. *What has occurred during the interval of observation that could be identified as the source or cause of the changes in the strength of action tendencies?*

Two possibilities are suggested by the fact that the individual has been exposed to the stimulation of his immediate environment and has been engaged in a particular activity during the interval of observation. A second principle, next to be developed, is a specification of how these two familiar empirical events, commonly called stimulus and response, relate to changes in the strength of tendencies to undertake various activities. But before turning to this explanatory principle, we must clarify what is meant by an action tendency.

We employ the term *action tendency*, or more briefly tendency, to represent an active impulse to do something. Thus an action tendency is analogous to

---

[3] Capturing, as they do, the most fundamental relationships in the theory of action, Equations 1.1, 1.2, and 1.3 are potentially of great use in sorting out the effects of various empirical antecedents on the time required for a simple change of activity. For example, Equation 1.1 asserts that those antecedents that have their effects exclusively on the initial strengths of two tendencies will affect the numerator of the equation, but the ones which relate to processes that determine the rates of change in the strength of the tendencies during the interval of observation will affect the denominator. As a specific illustration of this point, we may consider the familiar problem of the form of the relationship between time of food privation and the magnitude of previous food reward in determining the latency of a response previously rewarded with food. For reasons later to be developed, the theory of action presented here suggests that the effect of food privation is to increase the initial strength of tendencies to engage in food-seeking and eating activities (that is, T_{B_I}) and the effect of magnitude of food reward during training is on the process controlling the change in the strength of tendency to undertake food-seeking and eating activities (that is, β). If we assume that T_{A_I} and α, parameters of the ongoing activity, are unaffected by food deprivation and the previous food reward and, thus, are constants, it is easily derived from Equation 1.1 that deprivation and magnitude of reward should combine nonadditively to determine both latency of response and speed of response (reciprocal latency), but additively when these two measures are transformed to logarithms (see Birch, 1961).

Many empirical questions of this type are amenable to investigation by using Equation 1.1 together with the theory and methods of conjoint measurement (Luce and Tukey, 1964; Krantz, 1964; Tversky, 1967), but we shall not pause to pursue them nor shall we attempt to organize existing research findings in terms of the equation at this time.

the *reaction potential* of Hullian Theory (Hull, 1943), to the *excitatory tendency* in Spence's reformulation of S-R behavior theory (Spence, 1956), to what Tolman once called the *performance vector* (Tolman, 1955). We have chosen this particular term, tendency, in part because it was suggested long ago by Woodworth (1918, 1921), among others, as suitable for the kind of "motivology" he realized a complete psychology would require when he first confronted the problems of "the dynamics of behavior," and in part because this particular term has not already been given some special technical meaning in a previously formulated theory of behavior that would cause misleading connotations in the present context. We mean to give the term, *tendency*, a precise technical meaning and to specify its functional role in the determination of behavior.

The Basic Assumption

Unlike most formal behavior theories of the past, which explicitly or implicitly require the immediate presence of a stimulus to elicit, arouse, support, or sustain an impulse to undertake a particular activity, we now explicitly depart from the S-R tradition in beginning the explanation of behavior with this assumption: *A behavioral tendency, once it has been aroused, will persist in its present state until acted on by some force that either increases or decreases its strength.* In other words, we begin with the assumption of inertia applied to behavioral tendencies. It attempts to capture the fundamental insight of Freud (which was, in turn, included in the theory of Lewin) that a wish or intention, once aroused, will persist until it is expressed in behavior and satisfied.

One might phrase the basic assumption negatively to appreciate what a conservative scientific assumption it is. The observation of a change in activity implies a change in the dominance relations among behavioral tendencies. We mean to begin by eschewing the idea that tendencies can change in strength spontaneously. Some influence must cause the change in the strength of a tendency.

The assertion that tendencies have the property of inertia also introduces the concept of *force* (borrowed and modified from Lewinian theory) as the factor that is responsible for changes in the strength of a tendency. There are two types of "psychological" or "behavioral" forces that influence an action tendency. The ones that function to increase the strength of a tendency are called *instigating forces*. The ones that function to decrease the strength of a tendency are called *consummatory forces*.

The symbol F_X will be used to represent the instigating force for any activity X. When it is important to specify that the source of an instigating force is a stimulus S, the symbol $_SF_X$ will be employed. Consummatory force represents the effect on an action tendency of the individual of his expressing

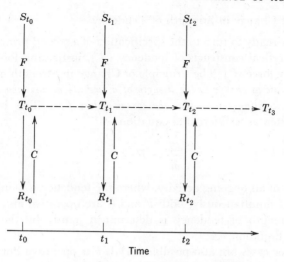

FIGURE 1.2 A rephrasing of the traditional S-O-R paradigm introduced by Woodworth (1918) showing the functional significance of the instigating force (F) of a stimulus, the consummatory force of the response (C) and the behavioral tendency (T) which is assumed to persist in its present state until influenced by forces.

the tendency in an activity; accordingly, the technical symbol for the consummatory force of any activity X will be C_X.

The proposed theory of action views both stimuli and responses as determinants of behavior: stimuli as sources of instigating forces and responses as sources of consummatory forces, but in a way that suggests a reformulation of the traditional S-O-R paradigm that was introduced by Woodworth (1918). The new S-O-R paradigm, as shown in Figure 1.2, includes a new conception of the functional significance of both stimulus and response in relation to the tendencies which govern behavior.

The stimulus situation, as here conceived, functions to enhance, selectively, the strength of certain behavioral tendencies. At the beginning of a time interval, there may be an inertial tendency to engage in a particular activity (T_{X_I} in Figure 1.2). The instigating force ($_sF_X$) of a stimulus can increase the strength of that tendency. If the tendency is dominant, as suggested in Figure 1.2, it will determine the activity or response (R_X), and the consummatory force of that response (C_X) will function to reduce the strength of the tendency.

The instigating and consummatory processes go on in time. Time is filled with stimuli and responses (or activities) that have the capacity to change the strength of action tendencies and, thus, to alter the dominance relationships among the tendencies that govern the activity of the individual.

A Principle of Change in Strength of Tendency

We are now ready to turn to the specification of a second principle, armed with the theoretical constructs of tendency (T), instigating force (F), and consummatory force (C). The Principle of Change in Strength of Tendency is stated: *the rate of change in the strength of a tendency at any moment in time is equal to the instigating force minus the consummatory force*. This is most conveniently written as a differential equation:

$$\frac{dT}{dt} = F - C \tag{1.4}$$

In the case of an ongoing activity, where the tendency is being instigated and expressed simultaneously, both F and C are operative and, hence, the change in strength of tendency is determined jointly by the two forces according to Equation 1.4.

Two simpler cases are also possible: (1) If F is operative but C is not, as when a tendency is influenced by the instigating force of some environmental stimulus to which the individual is exposed but that tendency is not dominant and so is not then being expressed in the appropriate activity, we have

$$\frac{dT}{dt} = F \tag{1.5}$$

and (2) if C is operative but F is not, as when no instigating force to undertake the activity is produced by the immediate environment but the tendency is nevertheless dominant and so is then being expressed in behavior, we have

$$\frac{dT}{dt} = -C \tag{1.6}$$

Because these two cases are simpler and help to illuminate the functions of F and C in changing the strength of tendencies, we shall deal with them first.

The Effect of an Instigating Force

Consider the case in which a tendency is under the influence of an instigating force but not a consummatory force (that is, where $dT/dt = F$). The concept of an instigating force arising from exposure to a stimulus to produce an increase in the strength of a tendency is suggested by the frequent observation of a change in behavior shortly after some significant change in the environmental stimulus. For example, a child will sometimes leave the table at which he has been eating very soon after he hears a call to play by a friend. We conceive the call of the friend as the source of a strong instigating force to play. Exposure to that stimulus increases the strength of the tendency to play. The child leaves the table because exposure to the instigating force to play has boosted the strength of his tendency to play to the point where it dominates the tendency sustaining the initial ongoing activity of eating. Often a single call by the friend is not sufficient to make the child leave the table, but several calls are. Hence, we need to take account of the effect of repeated exposures to the instigating force of a stimulus.

We do not say that a stimulus *elicits* the response. Instead, we conceive of a stimulus as the source of an instigating force, the nature and strength of which is typically determined by the past experience of the individual. The instigating force of a stimulus is capable of producing a certain amount of increase in the strength of the tendency to undertake an activity as long as the individual is exposed to it. The more frequent the exposure to the instigating force, or the longer the duration of exposure, the greater will be the magnitude of the change in the strength of the tendency.

This conception of the effect of a stimulus is represented in the case where $dT/dt = F$. Integrating this differential equation and solving for the constant of integration yields

$$T = T_I + F \cdot t \tag{1.7}$$

Equation 1.7 is to be read: the strength of a tendency (T) at the end of any arbitrary period of time is equal to the initial strength of the tendency (T_I) at the beginning of that time period plus the product of the magnitude of instigating force (F) and the duration of exposure to that instigating force (t).

Figure 1.3 shows examples of the several ways in which a tendency might increase over a time interval under the conditions of the first case, where the individual is exposed to an instigating force but the tendency affected is not being expressed in behavior. When exposure to a stimulus with fixed magnitude of instigating force is continuous over the time interval, we get the effect shown in Figure 1.3a. When an individual is exposed to a stimulus repeatedly at regular intervals, with a constant and brief duration of exposure each time, we obtain the result shown in Figure 1.3b. When exposure is again of constant and brief duration but occurs irregularly in the time period, we might have the result shown in Figure 1.3c. Figures 1.3a, 1.3b, and 1.3c might represent, respectively, the instigating force of the background hum of conversation from a coffee room next door to where one is trying to work, the ringing of a telephone, and a friend calling a child to play while the latter is eating dinner. In each example, the strength of the tendency increases at a fixed rate that is equal to the magnitude of the instigating force of the stimulus during the time of exposure. The strength of the tendency then persists unchanged between exposures (the assumption of inertia) until the next application of the instigating force.

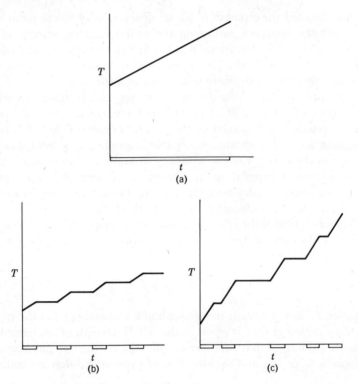

FIGURE 1.3   Examples of the growth in a tendency over a time period t when the tendency is being instigated but not expressed for (*a*) continuous exposure to a stimulus, (*b*) periodic, interrupted exposure to a stimulus, and (*c*) irregular, interrupted exposure to a stimulus.

The Effect of a Consummatory Force

Our first case has given us a special view of the operation of F on the strength of a tendency. We now consider our second case (when a tendency is being expressed in an activity but there is no instigating force for that activity) to take a comparable special look at the operation of C, the consummatory force, on the strength of an action tendency. The change in the strength of the tendency now arises only from the consummatory force, and it is in a negative direction (that is, $dT/dt = -C$). Thus the change constitutes a reduction in the strength of an action tendency.

The concept of the consummatory force of an activity is suggested by numerous instances in which activities cease and give way to other activities even though one cannot find stimuli that might be considered the obvious sources of strong instigating forces for other activities in the immediate environment. For example, an animal that eats in a relatively constant and barren environment will sooner or later cease eating and commence doing something else. Of course, the relatively barren environment may function as an instigating force and produce an increase in the strength of some other tendency which, as a result, becomes dominant and interrupts the expression of the tendency to eat. But more likely, according to traditional wisdom and traditional psychological theory, it is the activity of eating itself that is primarily responsible for the change in dominance relationships among the tendencies. In accord with this interpretation, we assume that the activity of eating has functioned as a consummatory force to reduce the tendency to eat that is expressed in the activity of eating.

The idea that engaging in an activity can reduce the tendency to engage in that activity is rooted in the traditional distinction between so-called consummatory activities and preparatory—or instrumental activities (Sherrington, 1906). Psychologists have found this idea useful and have maintained a qualitative distinction between instrumental (preparatory) and consummatory activities. We do not. We assume that *all* activities, the ones customarily referred to as instrumental, as well as the ones customarily referred to as consummatory produce consummatory force. The consummatory force always functions to reduce the strength of the tendency that is expressed in the activity. However, we do assume that there are very substantial *quantitative* differences in the consummatory force of different activities and of the same activity on different occasions. The *magnitude* of consummatory force (C) is presumed to depend on the *kind* of activity that is undertaken and the *intensity* of that activity.

Let us first consider the effect of the *kind* of activity on consummatory force. Both running to the food cup and eating the food can function to reduce the tendency that a rat is expressing in the behavior, but eating has the more pronounced and obvious effect. Both trying to solve a puzzle and getting the solution can reduce the tendency that a child is expressing, but getting the solution, that is, success, has the more dramatic consummatory effect.

Activities are viewed as differing in their consummatory value (c), that is, in the degree to which the particular kind of activity can reduce the strength of a particular tendency. The eating of salted nuts versus the eating of cheesecake constitutes a difference in *kind* of activity that is represented as a difference in consummatory value for the tendency to eat. One lick of a certain concentration of sucrose solution might have more or less consummatory value than one lick of a weaker or stronger sucrose solution. Throwing a ring over a peg from 15 feet away might have greater consummatory value (for the tendency to achieve) than throwing a ringer from one foot.

The consummatory value of an activity does not, by itself, account for the consummatory force of the activity. We must also consider the *intensity* of an activity. Consummatory force, which determines the rate of reduction in the strength of a tendency at any specified moment, depends on both the consummatory value of the kind of activity that is in progress and the intensity with which that activity is occurring. Greater intensity of activity implies greater consummatory force. *The intensity of an activity is assumed to be directly proportionate to the strength of the tendency expressed in the activity.* Thus the determinants of the consummatory force of an activity that is occurring can be simply summarized:

$$C = c \cdot T \tag{1.8}$$

It is often very difficult to measure the intensity of an activity. How can one measure the depth of concentration of an artist or scientist at work? In some cases, however, a fairly adequate measure may be obtainable. Consider a rat licking a sucrose solution from a tube suspended at the side of its cage. One lick of that particular solution of sucrose has a fixed consummatory value. But the strength of the tendency to lick the solution, as stated earlier, is assumed to account for the intensity of the activity. In this particular case, the rate of licking (within bursts) may provide an adequate measure of T. The consummatory force of the molar activity (that is, licking) depends on the consummatory value of each lick (c) times the number of licks per unit of time (for example, per second), determined by T. The product of the two gives us C, the magnitude of tendency-reduction per unit of time, for that kind and intensity of activity.

It is obvious, given this conception of the determinants of consummatory force, that the magnitude of consummatory force produced by a certain kind of activity might be different on one occasion and another depending on the strength of the tendency expressed in the activity at the time. Furthermore, the magnitude of the consummatory force of an activity will change as the activity is continued if the strength of tendency changes while the activity is in progress.

The fate of the strength of tendency that supports an activity under the conditions where $F = 0$ and $C = c \cdot T$ (our second case) is given by integrating Equation 1.6, $dT/dt = -C = -c \cdot T$, and by evaluating the constant of integration. Our doing so yields the equation

$$T = T_I \cdot e^{-c \cdot t} \tag{1.9}$$

which describes the exponential decay in the strength of an action tendency that is exposed to the consummatory force of an activity, as shown in Figure 1.4a. The rate of reduction in the strength of an action tendency diminishes as the activity continues because the action tendency itself is becoming weaker with each successive moment. And the strength of that action

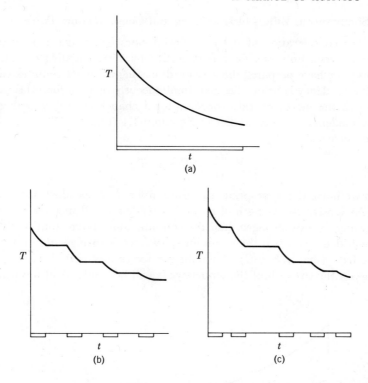

FIGURE 1.4   Examples of the decline in a tendency over a time period t when the tendency is being expressed but not instigated for (*a*) continuous expression, (*b*) regular, interrupted expression, and (*c*) irregular, interrupted expression.

tendency controls the *intensity* of the activity in progress, one of the determinants of the magnitude of the consummatory force.

Figure 1.4 shows three ways in which a tendency might decrease over a fixed time interval depending on whether the activity is occurring continuously, discontinuously at regular intervals for fixed durations, or discontinuously at irregular intervals for fixed durations. If it is appropriate to think of the covert activity of dreaming as one that often occurs in the absence of support by an environmental stimulus so that $F = 0$, Figures 1.4*a*, 1.4*b*, and 1.4*c* represent the decline in the strength of the tendency that has motivated the dream under conditions of uninterrupted and interrupted dreaming. Notice, in the examples of interrupted expression of a tendency, there are additional illustrations of the assumption that a tendency remains unchanged in strength unless influenced by an instigating or consummatory force. This, again, is the assumption of inertia applied to behavioral tendencies.

The Simultaneous Effects of Instigating and Consummatory Forces

In our consideration of the two special cases of change in strength of tendency when only one force is operative (either instigating or consummatory), we have prepared the way for discussing the more complex case in which a tendency is being changed simultaneously by both forces. Here, we deal with the more general expression for a change in the strength of an action tendency as given earlier in Equation 1.4 (that is, $dT/dt = F - C$), which becomes

$$\frac{dT}{dt} = F - c \cdot T \qquad (1.10)$$

when we make the appropriate substitution for C, as specified in Equation 1.8. Obviously, the strength of an action tendency will increase when the instigating force is stronger than the consummatory force (that is, $F > C$) and will decrease when the consummatory force is stronger than the instigating force (that is, $F < C$). When the two forces are equal, there will be no change in the strength of the tendency. It will be stable. And the point at

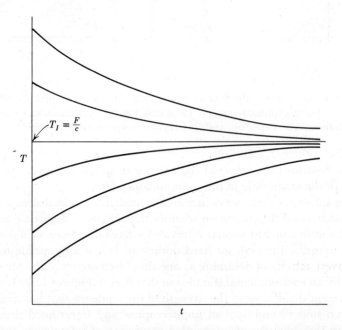

FIGURE 1.5   The fate of the strength of a tendency (T) for different initial values (T_I) when operated on by a fixed instigating force (F) and a consummatory force given by the product of a fixed consummatory value (c) and the intensity of activity (T). Each curve is approaching the same asymptote determined by the ratio, F/c.

which this stability in the strength of the action tendency will occur can be determined from the equation $F = c \cdot T$. The strength of the tendency will become stable when $T = F/c$.

By integrating Equation 1.10, the mathematical statement of the Principle of Change in Strength of Tendency, and by evaluating the constant of integration, we arrive at

$$T = T_I \cdot e^{-c \cdot t} + \frac{F}{c}(1 - e^{-c \cdot t}) \tag{1.11}$$

An examination of some of the properties of this function shows that T, starting out with an initial strength T_I at the beginning of some arbitrary time interval, grows or declines toward an asymptotic value of F/c during the time interval. Whether T grows or declines depends on whether T_I is less than or greater than F/c. Several examples of the fate of T over time for different values of T_I are shown in Figure 1.5. It is assumed that the individual is simultaneously and continuously exposed to a stimulus that produces an instigating force of constant magnitude to undertake an activity and is expressing the tendency in that activity with an intensity determined by the strength of T. Each curve begins at a different initial value for T_I, but all are approaching the same asymptote, F/c.

In Figure 1.6, the strength of T_I is held constant and the magnitudes of F and c are varied. The height of the asymptote (that is, how great the strength of the tendency is when it stabilizes) depends on the relative magnitudes of F and c. The greater the magnitude of F, the higher the asymptotic level of T. The greater the value of c, the consummatory value of the activity, the lower the asymptotic level of T. Figure 1.6 also shows examples of how the rates of growth and decline in the strength of a dominant tendency are influenced by the absolute magnitudes of F and c when their ratio, which defines the level at which stability will occur, is held constant.

Two final points must be noted before we terminate our discussion of the Principle of Change in Strength of Tendency. The first is that, if the instigating force of the environment or the consummatory value of the activity should change within a time interval, as would happen given any change in the nature of the stimulus or the response, the strength of tendency would alter its course and begin to approach a new asymptote defined by the revised F/c ratio. The second point is that the two special cases for the fate of the strength of a tendency resulting from conditions where there is F but not C (Equation 1.7 and Figure 1.3a), and where there is C but not F (Equation 1.9 and Figure 1.4a) may be recovered from the more general statement given in Equation 1.10 by letting $c = 0$ for the first case and $F = 0$ for the second case.

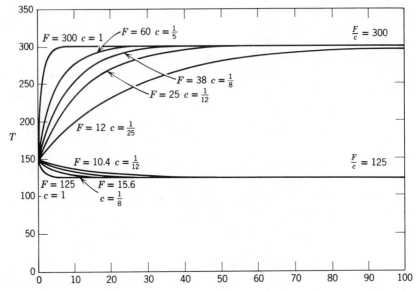

FIGURE 1.6   The fate of the strength of a tendency (T) for the same initial value (T_I) when operated on by different instigating forces (F) and consummatory values (c). Each curve is approaching an asymptote given by the ratio, F/c.

A PRINCIPLE OF CHANGE OF ACTIVITY

A Principle of Change of Activity can be derived from the first two principles. This third principle states that the time required to change from activity A to activity B is given by the time during which the instigating and consummatory forces for T_A and T_B operate to produce a change in the dominance relations of the tendencies from $T_{A_I} > T_{B_I}$ to $T_{B_F} > T_{A_F}$.

As was shown in oversimplified form in Figure 1.1, a change from activity A to activity B depends on a change in the relative strength of the tendencies for the two activities—a change that can occur in any of five ways. We shall consider the first three of these patterns of change now and leave the fourth and fifth until the topics of displacement and substitution have been introduced in Chapter 2.

In Figure 1.7, the first three patterns of change have been redrawn so that the path of T_A, the strength of tendency supporting the initial ongoing activity A, is curvilinear, as called for by Equation 1.11. A change in activity from A to B requires that T_A (supporting the ongoing activity A) be dominated by T_B, a tendency being instigated but not then expressed. From the Principle of Action we know that $T_{A_I} > T_{B_I}$ (that is, the initial strength

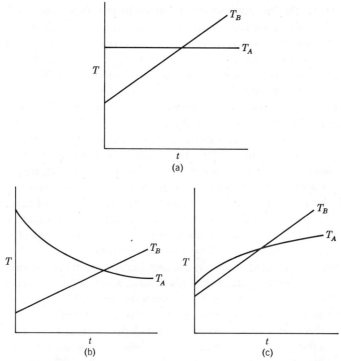

FIGURE 1.7   Three patterns of change in strength of tendencies for activity A and B that result in a change in activity from A to B where T_B is being instigated but not expressed and T_A is being both instigated and expressed.

of T_A is greater than the initial strength of T_B) and that $T_{B_F} > T_{A_F}$ (that is, the final strength of T_B at the point in time that activity B takes over from activity A is greater than the final strength of T_A). For simplicity we shall assume specifically that activity will change from A to B as soon as the tendency for B equals the tendency for A.[4] This enables us to write $T_{B_F} = T_{A_F}$. Because T_B is being instigated but not expressed, it is growing linearly so that $T_{B_F} = T_{B_I} + F_B \cdot t_{B/A}$, as described by Equation 1.7. Notice that $t_{B/A}$ stands for the time interval from the initial point ($t = 0$) until the point in time when activity A gives way to activity B ($t = t_{B/A}$). By substituting the above expression for T_{B_F} in the equation $T_{B_F} = T_{A_F}$, we obtain $T_{B_I} + F_B \cdot t_{B/A} = T_{A_F}$, which may be solved for $t_{B/A}$ to yield

$$t_{B/A} = \frac{T_{A_F} - T_{B_I}}{F_B} \qquad (1.12)$$

[4] See footnote on page 12.

Equation 1.12 is the mathematical statement of a Principle of Change of Activity and should be read as follows: the time $(t_{B/A})$ taken from some arbitrary initial point when activity A is occurring $(t = 0)$ until the final point when activity B replaces activity A $(t = t_{B/A})$ is directly proportionate to the difference between the strength of the tendency sustaining activity A at this final point in time (T_{A_F}) and the initial strength of the tendency to undertake activity B (T_{B_I}) and is inversely proportionate to the magnitude of the instigating force for activity B (F_B).

The form of Equation 1.12 will be recognized as identical to that of Equation 1.2. In fact, the only difference between the two equations is in the notation, with F_B taking the place of the β of Equation 1.2. Since we are referring to an instance in which the nature of the environment and the activity in progress are assumed constant during the interval of observation, the magnitude of the instigating force influencing T_B is assumed constant over the interval $t_{B/A}$. And this magnitude of F_B is exactly equal to β, the average rate of change in T_B during the time interval.

Equation 1.12 is stated generally enough to cover all three patterns shown in Figure 1.7 in that all that needs to be known about T_A is its final strength (T_{A_F}) at the point in time when T_B becomes dominant. However, according to the Principle of Change in Strength of Tendency, the path describing the strength of the tendency for activity A during the interval $t = 0$ to $t = t_{B/A}$ is determined by the mathematical expression given in Equation 1.11. When it is written for the three cases shown in Figure 1.7, this expression becomes

$$T_{A_F} = T_{A_I} \cdot e^{-c_A \cdot t_{B/A}} + \frac{F_A}{c_A} (1 - e^{-c_A \cdot t_{B/A}})$$

The three different cases shown in Figure 1.7 differ in the assumptions made about T_A over the interval of observation. In Figure 1.7a, T_A is assumed constant. This would be the case if T_A had already stabilized at its asymptotic level defined by F_A/c_A at $t = 0$. In Figures 1.7b and 1.7c, T_A is not assumed to be asymptotic at $t = 0$ and, thus, its strength is changing according to Equation 1.11. The difference between the cases shown in the two graphs is only that in Figure 1.7b, $T_{A_I} > F_A/c_A$, so that T_A is decreasing toward asymptote; but in Figure 1.7c, $T_{A_I} < F_A/c_A$, so that T_A is increasing toward asymptote.

When $T_{A_F} = F_A/c_A$, The Principle of Change of Activity remains simple in its mathematical expression. We merely substitute F_A/c_A for T_{A_F} in Equation 1.12 and obtain

$$t_{B/A} = \frac{F_A/c_A - T_{B_I}}{F_B} \tag{1.13}$$

When $T_{A_F} \neq F_A/c_A$, however, the resulting equation is more complex and cannot be solved for $t_{B/A}$.

Equation 1.13 identifies some important empirical determinants of a simple change of activity. It indicates that the time taken to change from an initial ongoing activity to some other activity will depend on the relative magnitudes of instigating force for the two activities (F_A and F_B), the consummatory value of the activity in progress (c_A), and the initial strength of the tendency to undertake the alternative activity (T_{B_I}). It leads us to further questions about the historical antecedents of the instigating force of a stimulus situation, the antecedents of the level of the inertial tendencies for various activities, and to new questions about the factors that are responsible for the consummatory value of an activity. These issues and further complications of the Principle of a Change of Activity are discussed in the subsequent chapters.

SUMMARY

A change in the activity of an individual, from some initial activity that is already in progress when the interval of observation begins to another activity later, defines the fundamental problem for a psychology of motivation. This problem is to explain the change in the dominance relations among behavioral tendencies that is inherent in a change of activity. We shift the focus of conceptual analysis of molar behavior from the traditional dissection of a simple goal-directed episode into its beginning (in a state of motivation), its middle (the period of instrumental striving), and its end (either consummation in a goal activity or frustration), to the joint or juncture between activities—to the instant of change in activity that simultaneously marks the cessation of one and the initiation of another. The two classic problems of motivation, persistence of an activity and initiation of an activity, are two sides of the same behavioral coin—a change in activity.

The traditional focus of interest was an outgrowth of an implicit assumption that the individual is at rest until stimulated to undertake an activity that then would normally run its course. Our shift in the focus of theoretical interest is grounded in a different and more tenable premise: the individual is constantly active, always already doing something when we turn our attention to him for systematic observation of his behavior.

We take the first step toward construction of an explanation of an observed change in activity by viewing the activity in progress as an expression of the then dominant behavioral tendency of the individual. It is a simple principle of action. The change in the dominance relations among tendencies that is then implied by a change in activity requires another principle to account for changes in the strength of an action tendency. The one that is proposed begins with a conservative assumption: tendencies do not change in strength spontaneously. Something must cause the change. Tendencies persist, it is assumed, until changed by the influence of some force.

The assumption of inertia applied to action tendencies is the foundation stone of the conceptual scheme proposed in this and subsequent chapters. In effect, it states that *the behavior of an individual is not completely governed by the immediate stimulus situation.* In stating this, it leaves behind many other implications of the traditional stimulus-response analysis of behavior. The traditional S-O-R paradigm is reconsidered. It was introduced by Woodworth 50 years ago in an early call for conceptual analysis of the *dynamics* of behavior. But his early proposals did not manage to surmount the idea of sensory dominance of behavior, nor did the formal theories of behavior that were soon to follow (see Hebb, 1949, p. 3).

In the present scheme, the functional significance of stimulus (that is, immediate environment) and response (that is, a molar activity) are redefined. *Time is viewed as the duration of a dynamic process* in which the immediate stimulus situation functions to increase, selectively, the strength of tendencies to action; and the activity in progress, which expresses the strongest or dominant tendency, serves to reduce the strength of the tendency motivating it.

The principle of change in the strength of a tendency takes into account the inertial tendency, that is, the strength of a tendency at the beginning of an interval of observation. It identifies the magnitude of the instigating force of a stimulus for some activity with the rate of increase in strength of tendency that the stimulus is capable of producing, and the magnitude of consummatory force with the rate of decrease in strength of tendency that an activity is capable of producing when the tendency is being expressed in that activity. Consummatory force is viewed as jointly determined by the consummatory value of the *kind* of activity in progress and the *intensity* of that activity. The latter is determined by the strength of the tendency then being expressed in the activity.

A principle of change in strength of a tendency is proposed to account for what happens to the strength of T_A, the tendency sustaining the initial activity, and to the strength of T_B, the tendency to undertake an alternative activity, during the interval of observation that ends when the change in activity occurs. The behavioral outcome of the two effects is then summarized in a single principle, *a Principle of Change of Activity:*

$$t_{B/A} = \frac{T_{A_F} - T_{B_I}}{F_B}$$

For the simple case that is considered in this introductory discussion of the concepts, the principle attributes variations in the time taken for a change in activity to come about $(t_{B/A})$ to variations in these basic determinants: (a) the final strength of the tendency that sustains the activity already in progress (T_{A_F}) which, in turn, depends on the magnitude of the instigating force produced by the immediate stimulus situation for that activity (F_A) and the consummatory value of that kind of activity (c_A); (b) the initial strength of the tendency to undertake the alternative activity (T_{B_I}); and (c) the magnitude of the instigating force of the immediate stimulus situation for the alternative activity (F_B).

The simplicity of this principle derives from the fact that time is conceived as the duration of exposure to one or another force, as the duration of a certain rate of change in the strength of a tendency. In other words, time is of central importance in the theoretical account of the dynamics of action because it represents the cumulative effect of continuous or repeated exposure to an instigating or consummatory force.

It is a simple principle, one derived from conceptual analysis of a simple problem. Both will become more elaborate as we begin to consider the complications in the conditions of actual behavior that have been deliberately overlooked in order to present the basic assumptions and concepts of the scheme in a simple form.

PREVIEW

The discussion, thus far, has referred to tendencies to undertake specific activities like solving an arithmetic problem, walking to the coffee room, and eating a hamburger sandwich, etc. How, if at all, are changes in the strength of one particular action tendency related to changes in other action tendencies? Is there any basis for conceiving of families of functionally related tendencies, the various members of which suffer a common fate? We think so, and in Chapter 2 we shall develop an argument for the use of more general descriptive terms like *the tendency to eat, the tendency to achieve, and the tendency to affiliate*, etc., in reference to families of functionally related action tendencies which rise and fall in strength together as a result of displacement and substitution. In Chapter 2 we shall also present a preliminary conception of the relationship between covert perceptual and imaginal activity (thought) and overt activity (action) in further elaboration of the concept of a family of functionally related and correlated tendencies.

Chapter 3 will identify the measurable aspects of the stream of behavior. It will consider both simple ideal conditions of behavior and more complex ideal conditions which yield measures of persistence, latency of response, and preference. It will show how the conceptual scheme can be employed to justify inferences about the magnitude of the instigating force of a stimulus or the strength of a particular tendency from behavioral observations. Chapter 3 will confront the usually neglected problem of the compatibility and incompatibility of various activities and will identify some important effects of various compatibility relations among activities.

Chapter 4 will concentrate on the gap between idealized conditions, in terms of which mathematical models of behavior seem to make a great deal of sense, and the much less than ideal conditions of actual behavior. Our aim is to identify some tenable assumptions that can be made in the use of this conceptual scheme as a guide for the experimental analysis of behavior or in making inferences from behavioral observations. Most interesting and important are the issues that arise when the principle evolved in conceptual analysis of a single change of activity is applied to the sequence of changes in activity that characterize the stream of behavior of an individual. Our treatment will provide a foundation for the theoretical derivation of the operant level of an activity in a constant environment, and the amount of time an individual spends in various activities.

Until Chapter 5, in which we consider the historical determinants of the instigating force of a stimulus, the discussion is focused exclusively on the contemporaneous determinants of behavior, that is, the problem of motivation. Questions and theories about the antecedents of the instigating force of a stimulus are of a different order. The discussion will cover ground that is already familiar in terms of the traditional concepts of conditioning and learning. In Chapter 5, we relate our views concerning the dynamics of action to the classic work of Pavlov and Thorndike. We identify the problem of learning, as traditionally conceived, with change in the instigating force of a stimulus and with the elaboration of behavioral tendencies.

In Chapter 6 we relate our views to the kind of cognitive theory of instigation to action that has evolved primarily in the study of human decision making. Not all psychologists lean on the knowledge of the reinforcement history of an activity for inferences about the power of a stimulus situation to provoke the activity in an individual. The concepts of expectancy, valence (or utility), and motive (from study of individual differences in personality) are examined in relation to this conceptual analysis of the dynamics of action. Our aim is to encourage the integration of study of individual differences in personality and the study of the process of motivation by anchoring the description of personality in a theory about the dynamics of action.

To cover a number of interrelated problems in one relatively uncomplicated sweep (namely, the dynamics of action, the historical determinants of an instigating force, the diagnostic assessment of the strength of an instigating force, and the description of individual differences in personality, etc.), the first six chapters of the book ignore the problems traditionally described as punishment, inhibition, and avoidance behavior. The individual is treated as if he were motivated only by what might be called pleasure-seeking, appetitive-, approach-, or excitatory tendencies. In Chapter 7, a theory of resistance is introduced. It treats the problems of punishment, inhibition, and avoidance in a way that is suggested by cognitive theories of motivation, which imply that the belief that an act will produce a negative consequence and the repulsiveness of that consequence together produce a tendency *not* to undertake the activity, that is, resistance to that activity. This, of course, greatly complicates the picture of the changes in dominance relations among the tendencies that are responsible for a change in activity.

Chapter 8 discusses the historical antecedents and cognitive correlates of the inhibitory force of a stimulus. Then Chapter 9 reconsiders the basic problem of a change in activity as one that implies a change in the dominance relations among *resultant* action tendencies—the outcome of conflict between instigation to action and resistance. The principles advanced in the early chapters and the conclusions reached in the discussion of simpler instances of behavior are covered again in Chapter 9, but by a more general statement of the Principle of Change of Activity that we propose as a guide to the future study of the dynamics of action.

The final chapter considers the central argument of the book from a slightly different perspective, enlarges the discussion of certain topics, and calls attention to some innovations in empirical research that are directly related to the scheme.

MATHEMATICAL NOTES

The Principle of Change in Strength of Tendency states: *the change in the strength of a tendency at any moment in time is equal to the instigating force minus the consummatory force.* In differential equation form this is written

$$\frac{dT}{dt} = F - C \tag{1.4}$$

The consummatory force C is further specified as $C = c \cdot T$ (Equation 1.8) which, when substituted into Equation 1.4, produces

$$\frac{dT}{dt} = F - c \cdot T \tag{1.10}$$

where F, c and T are all ≥ 0. Equation 1.10 is a linear differential equation and, assuming the continuous application of F and C, yields the solution

$$T = T_I \cdot e^{-c \cdot t} + \frac{F}{c}(1 - e^{-c \cdot t}) \tag{1.11}$$

on evaluation of the constant of integration.

It is easily seen from Equation 1.11 that $T = T_I$ for $t = 0$ and $\lim_{t \to \infty} T = F/c$. Furthermore, the first derivative of T with respect to t in Equation 1.11,

$$\frac{dT}{dt} = c\left(\frac{F}{c} - T_I\right)e^{-c \cdot t}$$

shows that T is a monotonic function of t and approaches asymptote with a positive slope for $F/c > T_I$ and with a negative slope for $F/c < T_I$. The second derivative of T with respect to t,

$$\frac{d^2T}{dt^2} = -c^2\left(\frac{F}{c} - T_I\right)e^{-c \cdot t}$$

indicates that T is negatively accelerated in its path from T_I to F/c. Several examples of Equation 1.11 are pictured in Figures 1.5 and 1.6.

Two special cases of Equation 1.11, when $c = 0$ and when $F = 0$, are also of interest. For $c = 0$, Equation 1.11 becomes $T = T_I + F \cdot t$ (Equation 1.7) which is linear with slope of F and intercept equal to T_I. One rather direct way to show the effect of $c = 0$ in Equation 1.11 is to replace $e^{-c \cdot t}$ in the second term by the series $e^{-c \cdot t} = 1 - (c \cdot t) + (c \cdot t)^2/2! - (c \cdot t)^3/3! + \cdots$, prior to setting $c = 0$. When this is done, Equation 1.11 can be written

$$T = T_I \cdot e^{-c \cdot t} + F\left\{\frac{1 - \left[1 - c \cdot t + \dfrac{(c \cdot t)^2}{2!} - \dfrac{(c \cdot t)^3}{3!} + \cdots\right]}{c}\right\}$$

$$= T_I \cdot e^{-c \cdot t} + F\left\{t - \frac{c \cdot t^2}{2!} + \frac{c^2 \cdot t^3}{3!} - \cdots\right\}$$

With Equation 1.11 in this form, setting $c = 0$ yields $T = T_I + F \cdot t$ as specified. In the second case it is apparent that, for $F = 0$, Equation 1.11 becomes $T = T_I \cdot e^{-c \cdot t}$ (Equation 1.9).

CHAPTER 2

THE VICISSITUDES AND FAMILY CHARACTERISTICS OF ACTION TENDENCIES

The title of this chapter is taken in part from an influential essay by Freud (1915) as it is our purpose to deal with two fundamentally important problems that he first illuminated in an analysis of the vicissitudes of instincts (or needs). They are the problems of *displacement* and *substitution*. We shall take into account the possibility that the direct instigation of a particular action tendency and its consummation, when expressed in behavior, may have other, indirect effects. The direct instigation of one activity is likely to spread to influence the strength of tendencies to engage in other related activities. The consummation of a particular action tendency in behavior is likely to produce a comparable reduction in the strength of tendencies to engage in related activities.

The discussion of displacement and substitution will lead us to the conception of a family of functionally related action tendencies that share a common fate. Later in the chapter, we shall elaborate further this concept of a family of highly correlated tendencies to include tendencies to engage in imaginal, perceptual, and verbal activities that are expressed covertly and that run a course which parallels the one of tendencies expressed in overt, motoric behavior. We recognize that we are making contact with an old and difficult problem in our preliminary treatment of the nature of covert activity, or conscious thought, and its relationship to overt action, and we take this step because it seems necessary. The topic is expanded in later chapters.

Our introduction has emphasized that change of activity is the fundamental behavioral problem for a psychology of motivation. In recognizing this, we observe the need for three different kinds of principle. One will refer to observable behavior. It will account for a change of activity. Another will account for the changes in the strength of the tendencies that are expressed in behavior and that govern the timing of changes in activity. A third kind of principle will specify the determinants of the instigating force of a particular stimulus and the consummatory force of a particular activity which, in turn, are responsible for changes in the strength of behavioral tendencies. Except for the specification of the determinants or components of a consummatory force, given in the previous chapter, we shall postpone discussion of this last kind of principle until Chapters 5 and 6. This will permit a thorough treatment of the logically prior problem of the contemporaneous dynamics of action before we consider questions of historical antecedents. The latter are too often given an unwarranted priority in theoretical discussion. We refer to the questions that define the proper focus of interest for the study of learning and the development of differences in personality. Theory about the genesis of the instigating force of a stimulus is related to but not an inherent part of the theory about its function, that is, its motivational significance.

INDIRECT EFFECTS OF A STIMULUS AND AN ACTIVITY

The primitive principle of change in the strength of an action tendency (Chapter 1) restricted our attention to the *direct* instigating force of a stimulus and the *direct* consummatory force of an activity. Now we must consider the *indirect* effects of these forces that define what is meant by displacement and substitution. These are the pertinent questions to ask:

1. Can the strength of a particular action tendency ever be increased if the appropriate stimulus (that is, the one that normally produces direct instigating force for the activity) is not present?[1]

2. Can the strength of a particular action tendency ever be reduced if that tendency is not directly expressed in the activity that normally produces the direct consummatory force?

The first question directs our interest, for example, to a more general effect on appetite of the odor of steak being broiled over charcoal. The second question directs our interest to a more general effect on appetite of one's having consumed a substantial piece of the steak. To answer both questions, we must review the argument concerning the kind of behavioral evidence that is needed to justify the conclusion that a tendency has been strengthened or weakened by an immediately antecedent event.

---

[1] The term "appropriate" will seem less ambiguous after Chapter 6. The concepts of the *unconditioned* and *conditioned* instigating force of a stimulus are then developed. For the present, we shall mean by appropriate a stimulus that innately or as a result of past experience in the presence of similar stimuli can strengthen the tendency to act in a certain way.

The Behavioral Symptoms of a Change in the Strength of a Tendency

Later we shall thoroughly consider the several behavioral tests of the strength of a tendency to engage in a particular activity. Now we merely need to be reminded that willingness to initiate an activity and persistence, once it has been initiated, provide appropriate grounds for inference about the strength of an action tendency. Given the primitive principle of a change of activity, $t_{B/A} = (T_{A_F} - T_{B_I})/F_B$, we can observe that a longer exposure to the instigating force (F_B) is required to bring about an initiation of an activity when the inertial tendency to undertake that activity (T_{B_I}) is weak than when it is strong. If that tendency has been strengthened by an immediately antecedent occurrence, there should be apparent a greater willingness to undertake the activity—what traditionally is called a shorter latency of response to a stimulus for the activity. On the other hand, if the tendency in question (T_{B_I}) has been weakened by an immediately antecedent occurrence, there should be less apparent willingness to initiate the activity, that is, a longer latency of response to an appropriate stimulus. Hence we are able to discover empirically that exposure to the delightful aroma of a steak broiling over charcoal has whetted the appetite and has increased willingness to initiate the activity of eating when a call to supper finally comes. Conversely, we are able to discover empirically that having eaten something beforehand has satisfied (that is, reduced) the tendency to eat and, hence, has diminished the individual's willingness to initiate this activity at the call to supper. This is a phenomenon frequently observed by the parents of small boys who have free access to a cookie jar. Thus the very same behavioral tests can be employed to discover whether the strength of a tendency can be changed *indirectly*, that is, without direct exposure to an instigating force to undertake *that* particular activity produced by a stimulus that either innately or as a result of exposure to it during past training has acquired this property, and without the direct influence of the consummatory force produced by actually engaging in the particular activity.

Displacement

Displacement refers to occasions on which the strength of the inertial tendency to undertake one activity (for example, activity X) is increased by instigation of some other activity (for example, activity Y). This would occur if T_X increased not as the result of a direct instigating force $_{S_1}F_{XX}$, normally produced by an appropriate stimulus S_1, but as an indirect result of the influence of a direct instigating force to engage in some other activity $_{S_2}F_{YY}$, produced by its appropriate stimulus S_2. For example, the effect of exposure to the aroma of the steak being broiled over charcoal will normally increase the strength of the tendency to initiate the activity of eating a steak. If this stimulus, S_2, also has the effect of increasing an individual's willingness to respond more rapidly when presented with some potato chips S_1, it is an instance of the displacement of the instigating force to eat a steak $_{S_2}F_{YY}$ to the tendency to eat potato chips T_X. The strength of T_X has increased without direct exposure to S_1. Therefore, we must speak of an indirect or displaced instigating force to undertake activity X, $_{S_2}F_{YX}$, which is attributable to a relationship that exists between the two activities Y and X.

We suppose that normally the indirect or displaced force F_{YX} will be weaker than the direct force F_{YY}, from which it is derived. That is, we assume that $F_{YX} < F_{YY}$. *The magnitude of the displaced force F_{YX} should depend on the magnitude of the direct force F_{YY}, from which it is derived, and the degree of relationship between the two activities, δ_{YX}.* That is

$$F_{YX} = \delta_{YX} \cdot F_{YY} \tag{2.1}$$

The closeness of the relationship between activities Y and X, whether it depends on an accident in the associative history of an individual or the symbolic equivalence of the two activities (both proposed by Freud) or their functional equivalence as alternative means to the same end, is represented theoretically by δ_{YX}. This symbol defines the extent to which the direct instigation of T_Y by F_{YY} will simultaneously produce indirect instigation of T_X by F_{YX} because there exists some degree of functional equivalence between the two activities Y and X. It is expected that $0 \leq \delta_{YX} \leq 1$, where $\delta_{YX} = 0$ means that activity X is functionally independent of activity Y so that no displaced instigating force for T_X results from a direct instigating force for T_Y, and $\delta_{YX} = 1$ means complete displacement (or spread) of the instigating force for T_Y to T_X. Thus, for $\delta_{YX} > 0$, the stimulus S_2 produces both a direct instigating force $_{S_2}F_{YY}$ on T_Y and an indirect instigating force $_{S_2}F_{YX}$ on T_X.

We must now generalize the concept of displacement to cover the more realistic situation in which a given stimulus complex provides direct instigating forces for a number of different activities. Let us begin with the case in which the environment contains only S_1, the stimulus producing a direct instigating force on T_X (that is, $_{S_1}F_{XX}$) and S_2, the stimulus producing a direct instigating force on T_Y (that is, $_{S_2}F_{YY}$). Since displacement may occur between the two activities in both directions, from X to Y as well as from Y to X, we must allow for two indirect instigating forces, $_{S_1}F_{XY}$ and $_{S_2}F_{YX}$, in addition to the two direct instigating forces. Let us define the *effective instigating forces* on T_X and T_Y, arriving from the stimulus complex S as $_SF_X$ and $_SF_Y$. We may then write $_SF_X = {}_{S_1}F_{XX} + {}_{S_2}F_{YX}$ and $_SF_Y = {}_{S_2}F_{YY} + {}_{S_1}F_{XY}$, since the direct and indirect instigating forces for any activity are additive. These two equations may be rewritten as $_SF_X = {}_{S_1}F_{XX} + \delta_{YX} \cdot {}_{S_2}F_{YY}$ and $_SF_Y = {}_{S_2}F_{YY} + \delta_{XY} \cdot {}_{S_1}F_{XX}$ simply by substituting appropriately for $_{S_2}F_{YX}$ and $_{S_1}F_{XY}$.

Although δ_{YX} may be equal to δ_{XY}, there appears to be no *a priori* reason why this must necessarily be true for all pairs of activities. Therefore, different symbols have been preserved for the two relationships. If δ_{YX} is unequal to δ_{XY}, it means that there is an asymmetry in the relationship between activities X and Y. For example, we might normally expect to find that the aroma of barbecued steak has a greater *direct* instigating force on the tendency to eat steak than the sight of potato chips has on the tendency to eat potato chips. If there is some asymmetry in the relationship between the two activities, we might also find that the *proportion* of the direct instigating force to eat steak that is displaced to the tendency to eat potato chips is greater (or less) than the *proportion* of the direct instigating force to eat potato chips that is displaced to the tendency to eat steak. In the terms of the present hypothesis, the success of an appetizer depends on its δ value for the main course, and we know from general past experience that appetizers and entrees are not interchangeable in their roles.

We are now ready to make our most general statement about the displacement that occurs in a complex environment. Consider a given stimulus situation S in which the tendencies T_A, T_B, T_C, ..., must be taken into account. Assume that S may be analyzed into its elements or components S_1, S_2, S_3, ..., so that S_1 is the stimulus producing direct instigating force on T_A, S_2 is the stimulus producing direct instigating force on T_B, etc. The total instigation produced by S for the activities is then described as follows:

$$_SF_A = {}_{S_1}F_{AA} + {}_{S_2}F_{BA} + {}_{S_3}F_{CA} + \cdots$$
$$_SF_B = {}_{S_1}F_{AB} + {}_{S_2}F_{BB} + {}_{S_3}F_{CB} + \cdots \tag{2.2}$$
$$\text{etc.}$$

These statements are equivalent to

$$_SF_A = {}_{S_1}F_{AA} + \delta_{BA} \cdot {}_{S_2}F_{BB} + \delta_{CA} \cdot {}_{S_3}F_{CC} + \cdots$$
$$_SF_B = \delta_{AB} \cdot {}_{S_1}F_{AA} + {}_{S_2}F_{BB} + \delta_{CB} \cdot {}_{S_3}F_{CC} + \cdots \tag{2.3}$$
$$\text{etc.}$$

An examination of these expressions shows that if a stimulus situation remains constant, even though it is complex, the effective instigating force for each tendency is fixed, so the equations presented in Chapter 1 need not be revised in the light of the phenomenon of displacement. Later in this chapter, after the concept of substitution has been introduced and discussed, we shall again present the key equations from Chapter 1 with displacement and substitution taken into account.

The Concept of a Family of Related Tendencies

In broadening our treatment of the effect of instigating forces to include displacement, we have asserted that, at any particular time, the hierarchy of inertial tendencies to engage in various activities, which describes the motivational state of the individual at that time, may be changed by indirect as well as direct influences. This means that a stimulus that defines an instigating force to engage in a particular activity will often function to produce a family of interrelated forces that increase the strength of a whole family of interrelated action tendencies. Since the family of tendencies is often (but not necessarily always) defined by a common kind of anticipated consequence (what is traditionally called a goal activity), it may simplify discourse somewhat to use a class term like *tendency to eat*, which embraces the numerous members of the family, rather than to list exhaustively all of the specific action tendencies that comprise that class for a particular individual. Although only an approximation, since it lacks the degree of specification needed for precision in the prediction of behavior, this kind of shorthand which refers to classes of functionally related or functionally equivalent activities, is much more feasible and useful for a general description of the momentary motivational state of an individual than an exhaustive listing would be. It is to be understood, however, that to say that the *tendency to eat* has been increased or decreased is only an approximate shorthand description of the nature of the change that has occurred in an individual. This terminology will be employed only for convenience when it does not lead to any false conclusions.

Substitution

The substitute value of one activity for another is greater than zero if the inertial tendency to undertake one activity is reduced by the occurrence of the other. As in the case of displacement, one can discover by the observation of an individual's willingness to initiate a particular activity following the occurrence of some other activity whether the latter has reduced the strength of the tendency to engage in the former. As stated in Chapter 1, the consummatory force of a particular activity depends on the consummatory value of that kind of activity (c), that is, its capacity to reduce a particular tendency, and the intensity of the activity. Since intensity of activity depends on the strength of the tendency that is expressed in it, $C = c \cdot T$.

If the consummatory force of one activity does substitute for another, this is equivalent to providing an indirect consummatory force for the second activity. Specifically, in the situation where activity A is occurring and activity B is not, the substitution from A to B means that there occurs both C_A as the *direct* consummatory force operating on T_A and C_{AB} as the *indirect* consummatory force on T_B. *The magnitude of the indirect, or substitute force C_{AB}, depends on the magnitude of the direct consummatory force C_A and the degree of relationship, γ_{AB}, between the two activities where $0 \leq \gamma_{AB} \leq 1$.* That is

$$C_{AB} = \gamma_{AB} \cdot C_A \tag{2.4}$$

Furthermore, the *substitute consummatory value* of one activity for another, in this case of activity A for activity B, is given by the expression

$$c_{AB} = \gamma_{AB} \cdot c_A \qquad (2.5)$$

This is read: The indirect or substitute consummatory value of activity A for activity B depends on the degree of relationship between the two activities γ_{AB} and the consummatory value of activity A. If $\gamma_{AB} = 0$, activity A does not substitute for activity B at all. If $\gamma_{AB} = 1$, the substitution is complete. Values of γ_{AB} between 0 and 1 reflect the intermediate degrees of substitution of A for B that are possible.

The generalization of the concept of substitution to more than two activities is straightforward as long as we restrict ourselves to the set of incompatible activities. Under this restriction, only one activity can occur at any given time: the activity that expresses the dominant tendency. Therefore, only one direct consummatory force can occur, although it can have substitute consummatory value for many other activities. If we once again let activity A be ongoing and activities $B, C, \ldots$, be nonoccurring alternatives, there is a direct but not an indirect consummatory force on T_A and an indirect but not direct consummatory force on T_B, T_C, ... These latter forces are written

$$\begin{aligned} C_{AB} &= \gamma_{AB} \cdot C_A = \gamma_{AB} \cdot c_A \cdot T_A \\ C_{AC} &= \gamma_{AC} \cdot C_A = \gamma_{AC} \cdot c_A \cdot T_A \end{aligned} \qquad (2.6)$$

etc.

The extent of substitution of activity A for the other activities depends on the values of γ that reflect the degree of relationship between activity A and the other activities.

It is certainly evident that eating one of the meals described on the menu of a restaurant substitutes almost completely for eating one of the other meals, given our behavioral test of subsequent willingness to initiate eating another meal. Similarly, it is sometimes observed that succeeding at one activity may compensate for failure in some other activity, that displaced aggression toward a scapegoat may reduce the tendency to behave aggressively towards the original target of hostility, etc. We offer no new idea as to *why* certain activities are functionally related to others but assert that if they are, we can discover through observation of effects on initiation of activities *that* one tendency is to some degree functionally equivalent to another. In this analysis, we have followed and elaborated an earlier discussion of substitution by Lewin (1938, p. 163). His distinction between substitute *valence* and substitute *value* is preserved in the distinction between displacement and substitution and the possibility that the degree of relationship between particular activities represented by δ for displacement and γ for substitution may be different.

The Common Fate of Tendencies in the Same Family. Thus broadened also to account for substitution, our conception of consummatory force suggests that the hierarchy of inertial tendencies (or unsatisfied needs) that characterizes an individual at a particular time may be changed not only by a reduction in the strength of the particular tendency that is directly expressed in an ongoing activity but also by the indirect, substitutive effect of this activity for other functionally related tendencies in the hierarchy. When an individual is eating a particular food, it makes sense to summarize what is happening by stating that he is reducing his general tendency to eat if this is taken to mean that he is reducing a whole family of inertial tendencies that have in common the particular kind of commerce with the environment called eating. We should be able to discover through observation that another activity, roughly described as being fed intravenously, which has no behavioral communality with eating, belongs in the same family. Freud argued that this is true of sexual activity. Many specific activities having very little in common at the level of a phenotypic descriptive taxonomy of behavior, that is, appearances, were viewed as functionally equivalent in the sense discussed here. The determinants and limits of substitution, explored somewhat by the early Lewinians (Lewin, 1936) and very little with a few exceptions (for example, Feshbach, 1955) thereafter, can be discovered by observation of behavior. It is perhaps the most important neglected problem in the psychology of motivation.

RECONSIDERATION OF THE BASIC PRINCIPLES IN LIGHT OF DISPLACEMENT AND SUBSTITUTION

The Principle of Change in Strength of Tendency stated for activity A is $dT_A/dt = F_A - c_A \cdot T_A$. When integrated to obtain the fate of a tendency over time, this expression yields $T_A = T_{A_I} \cdot e^{-c_A \cdot t} + (F_A/c_A)(1 - e^{-c_A \cdot t})$ as the general statement for the conditions in which T_A is being both instigated and consumed. The effect of including displacement in this expression is very minor because the only result is to permit the breaking down of F_A into its direct and indirect components. This is because all of the elements of the expression are constants and can be grouped arbitrarily. Thus, no change has to be made in the equations to accommodate displacement, but the more detailed expressions for F_A (Equations 2.2 and 2.3) can be used if desired.

The effect of substitution on the strength of a tendency is more complex. If we once again consider only the case of a single ongoing activity A and an alternative activity B that is incompatible with A and, therefore, not occurring, we need make no change in our previous expression for T_A because activity B is not occurring and no question of substitution from B to A arises.[2] The Principle of Change in Strength of Tendency as applied to activity B, however, becomes

$$\frac{dT_B}{dt} = F_B - C_{AB}$$

$$= F_B - \gamma_{AB} \cdot C_A$$

$$= F_B - \gamma_{AB} \cdot c_A \cdot T_A \qquad (2.7)$$

Notice that T_B is acted on by a consummatory force, but an indirect one coming from the expression of T_A, not the direct force provided by occurrence of activity B. Since T_A is changing over time according to Equation 1.11, we need to modify the above expression to read

$$\frac{dT_B}{dt} = F_B - \gamma_{AB} \cdot c_A \left[T_{A_I} \cdot e^{-c_A \cdot t} + \frac{F_A}{c_A} (1 - e^{-c_A \cdot t}) \right] \qquad (2.8)$$

Integrating this and evaluating the constant of integration yields

$$T_B = T_{B_I} + \left[(F_B - \gamma_{AB} \cdot F_A) \cdot t \right] + \left[\gamma_{AB} \left(\frac{F_A}{c_A} - T_{A_I} \right) (1 - e^{-c_A \cdot t}) \right] \qquad (2.9)$$

This expression is one that can produce several, quite different paths for T_B, depending on the relative sizes of certain parameters. In general, however, all functions begin at $T_B = T_{B_I}$ with a slope of $F_B - \gamma_{AB} \cdot c_A \cdot T_{A_I}$ for $t = 0$ and end up in linear form with a slope of $F_B - \gamma_{AB} \cdot F_A$ as $t \to \infty$. The paths in between are illustrated in Figure 2.1.

Let us consider the several set of curves in Figure 2.1.[3] If activity A does not substitute at all for activity B (that is, if γ_{AB} is 0), then the slope defining the trend of T_B will be positive and linear from the very outset, as shown in the broken line of Figure 2.1a. The growth of T_B is most rapid when there is no substitution, the condition we had assumed in Chapter 1.

All the other curves in Figure 2.1a end up in linear form but with a slope

[2] The case of substitution for compatible activities is interesting and important, but we will not develop it here. Our initial investigations into this problem are shown in the notes at the end of this chapter. For now, it will suffice to indicate that for two compatible ongoing activities either the action tendencies for both approach asymptotes less than what they would have approached had there not been substitution or one of the two action tendencies reaches zero and stays there allowing the other to approach its "no substitution" asymptote.

[3] Detailed consideration of the various paths for T_B as derivable from Equation 2.9, the way in which they depend on T_A, and how they enter into changes in activity, can be found in the notes at the end of the chapter.

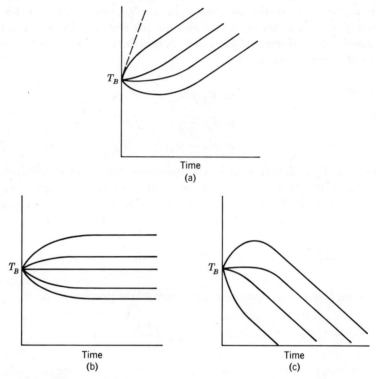

FIGURE 2.1   The types of paths for T_B when T_B is being instigated by F_B and consumed indirectly by C_{AB}.

that is less than the one defined by F_B because there is an indirect consummatory force (C_{AB}) operating to reduce T_B. It is derived from the ongoing activity A. The tendency sustaining activity A (T_A) approaches a level defined by F_A/c_A. As this happens, the indirect consummatory force on T_B, which has an effect opposite to that of F_B, approaches a constant value. Its magnitude will depend on the degree of relationship between the two activities (γ_{AB}) and the intensity of ongoing activity A that can be attributed to F_A.

The fact that all the curves in Figure 2.1a end up with a positive slope means that sooner or later, if the environment remains constant, activity B will be initiated. This will come about under different sets of conditions: (1) whenever F_B is stronger than F_A even though there may be substantial substitution effects (as when γ_{AB} is near 1.00); and (2) when F_A is stronger than F_B but there is little substitution (as when γ_{AB} is near 0).

The first case, when there is substantial substitution, typically occurs in the change from one to another instrumental activity in the sequence of different activities that constitute approach to the same goal, or the change from the final "instrumental activity" to the "goal activity" itself. Here the tendencies that motivate the several activities all belong to the same family. Each activity has some, perhaps considerable, substitute value for the others. Yet the earlier acts in the sequence leading to a goal give way to the later acts because it can be shown that $F_B > F_A$ in each instance of change from one to another activity *of the same family* as the individual approaches the goal.[4]

Another instance of this kind of change from one activity to another *within the same family* is the change from what might be called a less adequate to a more adequate means to an end. If, for example, an individual is driving along a two-lane country road that is a roundabout route to his destination and he comes to an intersection that provides an opportunity to turn on to a superhighway that leads to the same destination, he will normally do so. The example assumes that the so-called "more adequate means" is the one for which there is normally a stronger instigating force.

The second case, in which activity B is initiated even though $F_A > F_B$ because there is very little substitution, is explained by the fact that in a constant environment T_A will sooner or later stabilize at a level defined by F_A/c_A. So the continued growth of T_B implies that sooner or later $T_B > T_A$. The key words in this case are "very little substitution." This means that we are talking about instances that approximate the change from one *kind* of activity to another *kind* of activity (for example, from eating to playing the piano). A little later we shall say more about the general implication for variability in behavior that is contained in the principle of change of activity.

In Figure 2.1b, all the curves depict what might happen when the occurrence of activity A produces an indirect substitute consummatory force on T_B that equals F_B so that the overall slope ends up equal to 0. This means that $F_B - \gamma_{AB} \cdot F_A = 0$, and $\gamma_{AB} = F_B/F_A$. In other words, the instigating force to undertake an alternative activity (F_B) is weaker than the one acting to sustain the ongoing activity (F_A), and the proportionate relationship of the two instigating forces is exactly compensated by the degree of relationship between the two activities (γ_{AB}) which defines the proportional substitute value of the one for the other. This stabilization of the subordinate tendency (T_B) presumes stabilization of the dominant tendency (T_A). It is a unique set of circumstances.

Much more likely are the conditions already discussed that account for Figure 2.1a and the ones that produce the set of linear decreases in the strength of T_B shown in Figure 2.1c. In these latter instances, there arises the possibility that the strength of T_B will be reduced to 0. Again, we expect

[4] In Chapter 5 we shall present an explanation of why stimuli nearer to the goal event produce stronger instigating force.

the slope of T_B to become linear when the indirect consummatory force has stabilized because T_A, one of the determinants of that force, has stabilized. The negative slope can occur only if $\gamma_{AB} \cdot F_A > F_B$. And since the maximum value of γ_{AB} is 1.00 (implying complete substitution of A for B), F_A must always be stronger than F_B for this to happen. Typically, T_B should be weakened when F_A is much stronger than F_B and there is also substantial substitution of A for B.[5]

We now seem to be describing conditions that pertain to the fate of the tendency to undertake an earlier instrumental act in a sequence that leads to a goal after a later instrumental activity has been initiated. For example, after a rat has initiated a left turn (leading to food) in a maze, the tendency to engage in the activity that had immediately preceded the left turn, which is now the subordinate T_B, should fade towards 0 as shown in Figure 2.1c. Similarly, this should happen to the strength of tendencies to undertake activities that are less adequate means to an end once a more adequate means has been initiated and in progress for a time. In our earlier example, the driver who has turned from the circuitous two-lane country road on to the superhighway should lose *all* of his inclination to resume the old route even though the opportunity may arise again along the way. And the individual who is finally engaged in the so-called goal activity of eating, after a sequence of different instrumental activities which got him to the food, should lose his inclination (his inertial tendency) for each of these various instrumental activities as he continues to eat. The tendency sustaining his eating (T_A) approaches asymptote and eating will continue until the tendency to engage in some *other kind* of activity becomes dominant. Meanwhile, the tendencies to undertake various activities that constitute food-seeking behavior, that is, instrumental striving for food, are becoming weaker and weaker until finally, if eating continues long enough, they are reduced to 0. If all the available food in the immediate environment of the individual were to, be consumed before the tendency to undertake some *other kind* of activity became dominant, the individual might be left with some inertial tendency to eat, but certainly very little if any inclination to get up and look for more food.

Summary. The role of substitution in a change of activity is most evident when the change involves activities of the same class and action tendencies which belong to the same family. They are the various instrumental activities that constitute what is called striving for the goal and the various goal

---

[5] It is even conceivable that the continuation of conditions that define $C_{AB} > F_B$ after T_B has dropped to 0 may constitute the conditions for the phenomenon of *oversatiation*. This could be represented by assigning a negative strength to T_B with the implication that a disproportionately long exposure to F_B would be needed on some later occasion to bring T_B back into contention with a dominant T_A.

activities that differ from the former and each other in the magnitude of their consummatory value. Less complicated are the changes from one *kind* of activity to another *kind* of activity, that is, changes that do not involve displacement or substitution.

Our analysis has shown how activities that are instigated by the stronger instigating force are particularly favored when there is substitution. This helps to explain why one activity gives way to another in the instrumental approach to a goal and how the inclination to undertake an earlier act in a sequence is lost once the later act has been initiated. The analysis of the role of substitution also shows how the more adequate means to a goal (that is, the one for which there is stronger instigating force) is likely to gain and to maintain its dominance over less adequate means. Finally, we have observed how a sustained goal activity of a particular kind (that is, an activity having substantial consummatory value) can greatly reduce the strength of the various tendencies that constitute the family of goal-directed activities and, thus, postpone for a time any renewal of the pursuit of that kind of goal activity.

SOME APPLICATIONS TO FAMILIAR MOTIVATIONAL PHENOMENA

An Interpretation of the Phenomena Traditionally Called Drive

Historically, the concept of drive evolved to explain certain behavioral observations: most notably, that the tendency to eat increases as a function of the number of hours the individual has been deprived of the opportunity to eat. Much of the behavioral evidence concerning an increase in the strength of the tendency to eat as a function of the time of deprivation has to do with an increased willingness to initiate eating and other activities that in the past have culminated in eating, which therefore are called food-seeking activities.

Let us consider the traditional operational definition of hunger drive from the viewpoint of the present scheme. The experimenter provides no opportunity for the animal to eat for a given length of time. This is the extent of rigid experimental control. Thus, we know that one thing cannot happen during the time interval of deprivation: the one activity capable of producing the greatest consummatory force on the tendency to eat does not occur. Traditionally, the procedure for making animals hungry has not involved any particular control of the environmental stimulation to which the animal is exposed during the time of deprivation. Therefore, we may assume without contradiction that typically some of the stimuli that impinge on the individual during the time of deprivation must produce instigating forces to eat or to engage in activities that have previously culminated in eating.

These stimuli must produce direct increases in the strength of particular tendencies to eat and, according to our discussion of displacement, they must also produce indirect or displaced forces to engage in other functionally-related activities. Depending on the nature and duration of these instigating forces to which the individual is fortuitously exposed, there will be a gradual increase in the strength of the interrelated tendencies of the family that is subsumed by the shorthand label, *tendency to eat*. Each time an increase in the tendency to eat is produced, it should (according to our assumption of inertia applied to behavioral tendencies) persist unchanged until the next application of either a direct or displaced instigating force or a direct consummatory or substitute consummatory force (see again Figure 1.3c). Some of the activities that occur during the time of deprivation are no doubt motivated by the tendency to eat. But none of them has the high consummatory value of eating itself. Hence, although some consummatory forces may be at work during this period, we must remember the special measures that have been taken to prevent the occurrence of the one kind of activity that has substantial consummatory value for the tendency to eat, namely, eating itself. Since no similar precautions are taken to eliminate instigating forces to eat (even strong ones like the odor of food, which should produce considerable instigation to eat), it seems reasonable to conclude that during the time of deprivation the magnitude and duration of the instigating force to eat far exceeds that of the consummatory force of eating. Hence, there should be a gradual increase in the strength of inertial tendency to eat. This heightened tendency to eat, produced by the same dynamic process that accounts for an increase in the strength of a tendency during the short time period that is traditionally called the latency of response to a stimulus, is expressed in the obvious increased willingness to initiate food-seeking activities and eating. If the tendency to eat is very strong, then the tendency to engage in any other kind of activity must be even stronger if that activity is to occur at all. This would account for the fact that any other kind of activity engaged in by a hungry individual is likely to be engaged in more vigorously than by a less hungry individual. Only activities supported by very strong tendencies can compete successfully with the tendency to eat after food privation. Thus we might explain, in another way, the kind of nonspecific energizing effect posited for drive in S-R behavior theory and might encompass the influence of so-called irrelevant drives.[6] The present scheme leaves room for the influence on tendency to eat of instigating forces that originate in the metabolic process of the organism if some behavioral phenomena should unambiguously require that we posit these forces (for example, the effect of the drive stimulus).

[6] We informally refer to this interesting conjecture suggested to us by Dr. Kent Marquis as The Marquis Theorem. See Chapter 4, p. 120, for another possibility concerning the effect of food deprivation on vigor of performance.

The effect of external inducements to eat on the strength of the tendency to eat during the deprivation period should be paralleled by similar effects when, either by design or fortuitously, an individual is prevented from engaging in other kinds of activity that would effectively consummate other kinds of tendency. Just so long as he is exposed to inducements or temptations to undertake that activity, there should be a gradual increase in the strength of the behavioral tendency. Thus an individual who is deprived of an opportunity to affiliate with others, either because of his geographic isolation or because of their consistent rejection of him for some reason, but consistently exposed to the instigating force of stimuli to engage in affiliative activities, should suffer a gradual heightening of his inertial tendency to engage in activities that involve friendly commerce with other people. We mean to generalize the basic idea that prevention of activity that produces a strong consummatory force on some tendency but not of exposure to stimuli that produce instigating force should, as a function time (duration of exposure), produce a heightening of the tendency to engage in that kind of activity. This we believe is the appropriate explanation of many of the motivational effects produced traditionally by the experimental operation called *deprivation*.

Effect of Experimentally Induced Motivation on Imaginative Behavior

The results of experiments on the expression of experimentally induced motivation in thematic apperception (McClelland et al., 1953; Atkinson, 1958) can be organized in terms of the concepts already introduced. In the first of them, individuals were systematically deprived of food for 1, 4, and 16 hours. The expression of the tendency to eat in the imaginative content of stories then written by them increased as a function of the time of deprivation. Here, paralleling the usual result for instrumental food-seeking in animals, is evidence of a heightened inertial tendency to eat. The initiation of a story concerned with food-seeking activity instead of some other kind of activity, when doubtless there were many other activities suggested by the picture stimuli used to prompt stories, corresponds to the increased readiness to initiate relevant instrumental action when hunger increases. It soon became apparent that there was little reason to think otherwise than that imaginative behavior is governed by the same principles that govern instrumental striving (Atkinson and McClelland, 1948).

The procedures and results of subsequent studies that sought to demonstrate the existence of so-called "psychogenic" needs that might function in a manner parallel to the so-called "biogenic" needs of animal research deserve scrutiny in light of the present conceptualization. Let us consider, as illustrative, some results of the early experiments on the effects of the experimental arousal of *the need for achievement* (*n* Achievement). Among other conditions, college students wrote four imaginative stories in response to four different pictures: (1) in a *neutral* classroom when nothing was done either to heighten or reduce their normal concern with achieving; (2) immediately following a period of explicit *achievement-oriented* performance on several intelligence-type tests which had been presented with instructions that emphasized the importance of doing well and before any knowledge of results; and (3) immediately following the feedback concerning such test performance which was systematically controlled so as to assure either feelings of *success* or feelings of *failure*. The underlying premise in the design of the study was that the state of motivation induced immediately before imaginative stories were written would persist long enough to influence the content of the stories as did the differences in hunger produced by food deprivation.

The average n Achievement scores for these several conditions, a measure of the frequency of achievement-related responses in the stories, were as follows: Neutral, 7.33; Achievement-oriented, 8.77; Success, 7.92; Failure, 10.10 (McClelland, Atkinson, Clark, and Lowell, 1953, p. 184). Consider them in light of the present scheme. In three of the conditions (viz., Achievement-oriented, Success, and Failure), a strong instigating force to achieve had been introduced in the form of an instruction for an intelligence test and the confrontation with such a test. The exposure to this instigating force should have increased the strength of tendency to achieve in these three conditions relative to the Neutral group, which had not been given any specific inducement to achieve over and beyond what is inherent in the classroom situation. According to the assumptions regarding displacement, the indirect or displaced effects of the instigating force to achieve on the intelligence test would amount to a simultaneous increase in the strength of many other specific tendencies to achieve. The activity of merely working at the intelligence test might have had a consummatory value for all groups. By assuming that the intensity of activity was equal in all groups, the consummatory force of working at the task is a constant among the three achievement-oriented groups. In the Success condition, however, each subject was given an opportunity to engage in the additional activity of comparing his scores on the various intelligence tests with norms that were deliberately distorted so that he would experience success. Presumably, this would produce greater consummatory force than the additional activity of examining one's performance in relation to norms deliberately distorted to convey the impression of failure. In these two conditions, the experience of success and failure was systematically controlled in all the subjects. In the achievement-oriented condition, no explicit knowledge of results had been provided and, hence, no systematic control was exerted over possible covert reactions of the subjects when the tests were collected. Some individuals might have felt that they had succeeded, others that they had failed. Consequently, the achievement-oriented condition might be expected to fall between the success group, in which average consummatory force was strongest, and the failure group, in which it was weakest. The results correspond to theoretical expectations that can be derived from the present scheme concerning systematic differences in the strength of inertial tendency to achieve at the time the thematic apperception test was administered. It is of particular interest that the average n Achievement score following success was almost as low as in the neutral condition. This implies that the presumed increase in tendency to achieve, attributable to the instigating force of achievement-orientation, was practically matched by the presumed decrease attributable to the consummatory force of success at the initial task. Even larger differences were obtained among groups in which the prior motivating conditions were more extreme (McClelland et al., 1953, p. 184).

Other results of this experiment, which are typical of the ones obtained with different pictures in thematic apperception, illustrate the idea of a family of interrelated tendencies that share a common fate. The average n Achievement score obtained only from the stories that were written in response to a picture of two mechanics working at some kind of machine was higher than the average n Achievement score obtained when the picture contained just the heads of two men. This implies that the stronger instigating force to achieve is produced by the distinctive cues associated with work and the prior evaluations of performance in the lives of most men. The picture that contained only the heads of two men had cues that were less similar than those of the work scene to cues of specific achievement training experiences. The picture of the heads alone suggests many other kinds of activity or, in the language of the theory, defines instigating forces for many different kinds of activity.

The achievement-related activities described in stories to these particular pictures were rarely if ever instances of an individual taking an intelligence test. Yet the average n Achievement score in response to each picture was increased a comparable amount by the prior experimental induction of motivation by the stimulus of an intelligence test. The evidence of heightened tendency to achieve in many different kinds of activity following inducement to achieve at an intelligence test must be considered an instance of displacement. The instigating force to perform well at the intelligence test that was given prior to the thematic apperception task produced an increase in the strength of other tendencies that share, with the intelligence test, the anticipated consequence of successful performance in relation to a standard of excellence. This, in fact, defines the common goal of the family of tendencies that are more simply described as tendency to achieve or n Achievement. A comparison of the amount of increase in n Achievement in the two sets of stories following achievement-orientation suggests that the degree of displacement (δ) between the intelligence test-taking activity and the imaginative activity suggested by a picture of men working in a shop (usually a theme about inventors) is comparable in magnitude to the degree of displacement from the test-taking activity to the kind of activity described in response to the other picture (usually, a theme about career planning).

The traditional experimental operation for the control of hunger drive and the technique evolved in the studies of "ego-involving" human activities to heighten motivation by failure experience have much in common. In each case, there is experimental intervention to prevent the occurrence of a so-called goal activity that would produce a substantial consummatory force to reduce the strength of tendency. In the case of food deprivation, an exposure to the instigating force of external stimuli is a fortuitous matter. The conceptual schemes of the past do not suggest that time defines the duration of a dynamic process as conceived here, in which stimuli function as instigating forces that increase the strength of tendencies that then persist in their present state until acted on by other subsequent forces. Hence, until now, there has never been any explicit theoretical reason for the paying of strict attention to the nature of the stimulation to which an animal is subjected during the period in which he is deprived of the opportunity to engage in the so-called consummatory activity.

In the case of the experimental induction of achievement motivation, the explicit instruction given to an individual, which emphasizes the importance of doing well because his performance will be evaluated in terms of a standard of excellence, explicitly introduces a strong instigating force to achieve at the task before him. A similar effect might be accomplished in a study of the tendency to eat by systematically exposing animals in the home cage to the odor of food or some other stimulus previously conditioned to eating responses (see Chapter 5), that is, one capable of producing a strong instigating force to eat during the deprivation period. Experimental procedures of this kind have already been tried in several studies (Birch, 1968; Valle, 1968) and have yielded results that are consonant with the theory. They will be considered in the final chapter.

Throughout this book, we shall frequently seek illustrations and applications of the concepts under discussion in references to food-seeking and shock-avoidance as typical of appetitive and aversive behaviors in lower animals. And we shall consider examples of parallel issues about success-seeking and failure-avoidant activities that are characteristic of human achievement-related behavior, as we have begun to do here in order to illustrate the behavioral implications of inertial tendency, displacement, substitution, and the concept of a family of functionally-related activities that provides theoretical justification for descriptive class terms like tendency to eat and tendency to achieve (or *n* Achievement). In other words, we shall continue to apply the concepts and shall seek our concrete illustrations in reference to the empirical domains with which we are most familiar and in terms of which our conceptual analysis has evolved.

Spontaneous Variation in Behavior

Thus far, we have emphasized the effects of preventing an individual from engaging in a consummatory activity. It has been shown that this almost certainly will guarantee a gradual increase in the strength of the tendency to engage in that kind of activity unless equally stringent measures are taken to prevent exposure to the instigating force of stimuli. It is important to note that something very similar happens when an individual is continually engaged in a particular activity for a period of time, one that is not an adequate substitute for certain other activities. Because he is engaging in one kind of activity, he is not doing something else. This, in effect, is a self-imposed time of deprivation for the other kinds of activity. If the environment is rich in possibilities, the instigating forces encountered while engaged in the dominant activity will function to increase the strength of tendencies to engage in other kinds of activity. Figure 1.5 shows that continual expression of a particular tendency in one activity leads toward *stabilization* in the strength of the dominant tendency sustaining that activity. It follows that sooner or later the strength of some other tendency will catch up with and finally exceed that of the initially dominant tendency. Then there will be a "spontaneous" interruption of the initial activity and the initiation of the new one. The theory, as formulated, accounts for this kind of "spontaneous variation" in behavior. It specifically implies that there should be continual changes of activity, the so-called flux of activity that characterizes the behavioral life of an individual, when the environment is relatively rich in possibilities. One might conceive of a veritable behavioral chatter arising in the life of particular individuals, who may be constantly surrounded by the instigating force for too many different kinds of activity. This, according to the present scheme, would be the cost of having too rich a behavioral training and environment, that is, too many competing interests. It is the sort of thing that can be controlled, and it is in everyday life, by exerting control over one's own environment. This is exactly what people do when they do not want to be interrupted while engaging in some activity. They reduce the probability of intrusive stimuli which might produce instigating forces to engage in other activities. Phones are taken off the hook, or secretaries are instructed to postpone intrusions when there is work demanding continual attention. Shades are drawn, doors are closed, and radios are turned off in preparation for an afternoon's nap. Certainly no scholar in his right mind would attempt to write a book under an umbrella at a popular beach in July. No parent expects his little boys to complete their dinner if the neighborhood gang is allowed to start a twilight doubleheader outside the dining-room window.

Motivation is controlled by the manipulation and control of the environmental inducements, which produce instigating forces to activity, and the environmental supports that are needed to allow the consummatory force of certain activities. For example, it is much easier to break the smoking habit if there are no cigarettes immediately available.

Some Other Effects of Heightened Inertial Tendency

There are many other instances of the effects of heightened inertial tendency to engage in some particular activity. Freud emphasized that unfulfilled wishes are expressed in the content of dreams—in the simple undisguised expression of the tendency among children, and in more distorted and displaced forms among adults who suffer conflict regarding the expression of certain tendencies. The classic experiments by Zeigarnik (1927) and Ovsiankina (1928), students of Lewin, that show greater spontaneous recall and resumption of interrupted than of completed activities provided the earliest experimental paradigm for the study of what is here called the effect of an inertial tendency. More recently, a very similar procedure has been introduced by Amsel (1958) for the study of the motivational significance of frustration. Hungry rats are trained to run to a first goal box for food and then in an extended runway to a second goal box for more food. On a test trial, there is no food in the initial goal box and the level of performance in the second alley is then observed to be more vigorous than during trials when there is food in the first goal box. According to the present scheme, this again is an instance of the effect of a heightened inertial tendency. The animals are exposed to the instigating force of the stimuli in the initial alley and goal box, but the experimental procedure on test trials consists of preventing the consummatory force of eating. (This is what occurs on any so-called nonreinforced trial in the animal learning paradigm.) When immediately thereafter the animal is exposed to the instigating force to run and eat in the second alley, the inertial tendency is stronger than if the animal had just been exposed to the consummatory force of eating. Behavior in the second alley expresses the heightened inertial tendency, as does the content of imaginative behavior in the previously cited studies of the effects of failure on achievement motivation. Bower (1962) has suggested that the Amsel effect might be attributed to the perseveration of the anticipatory goal reaction that functions to activate performance, an interpretation that is consistent with the present view and one which suggests a plausible physical mechanism for what is here conceived in aphysiological terms as a kind of motivational momentum called inertial tendency. Kara-benick (1967) has extended the methods of Amsel and Bower and discusses the findings in this area in terms of classical stimulus response theory and the present theory of action.

Alternation of Behavior and Probability Matching

Certain puzzling phenomena are illuminated when viewed in terms of the set of assumptions about forces and inertial tendency that have been intro-duced. In them, one can find the foundation for a systematic explanation of the phenomena of alternation (Montgomery, 1951) and of probability matching (Humphrey, 1939).

Let us consider what happens at the critical choice point. We shall assume that the previous reward training of an animal has been comparable for the left and right turns in a T-maze. The instigating forces to engage in these mutually incompatible activities are thus equal in strength. On a particular occasion, the animal is exposed to both instigating forces at the choice point. As a result, there is an increase in the strength of each of the behavioral tendencies. Whichever one of them attains dominance is expressed in behavior. The key question is: *What is the fate of the tendency that is expressed in the choice as compared to the fate of the tendency that is not expressed in the choice?* By turning left and then eating, the animal has produced the consummatory force of turning left and the consummatory force of eating. Immediately afterward, the specific behavioral tendency to turn left and eat must be substantially weaker than it would have been if these activities had not occurred. But what of the specific tendency to turn right and eat? It has not been directly satisfied or, at best, only partly satisfied. If the substitute consummatory value of a left turning response for a right turning response is very small, there could be a greater inertial tendency to turn right and eat than to turn left and eat immediately after the trial. When the animal again confronts the stimuli of the choice point which define equal instigating forces to turn left and right, there then might be an imbalance in the inertial tendencies that favor the occurrence of the response that was not made on the previous occasion. Such an imbalance in inertial tendencies would be sufficient to provide the foundation for a systematic explanation of alter-nation. The possibility of its occurrence rests on the assumption that the direct expression of a tendency will normally produce a greater reduction than is produced indirectly by substitution.

The conceptual analysis of the phenomena called probability matching can be conceived in similar terms. When an individual who wants to be correct in his choices has learned that a light, which he is asked to predict, comes on 75 percent of the time on the left and 25 percent of the time on the right side of the panel before him, he does not predict left every time and thus, maximize the number of correct choices. Typically, what is observed is probability matching. The individual calls left approximately 75 percent of the time and right 25 percent of the time. If the frequency of being correct has an effect on the instigating force to say left and the instigating force to say right in this experiment (as we are led to propose in Chapter 5), after substantial training the individual is always confronted with a stronger force to say left than to say right. Why does he not always do so?

By applying the same kind of argument already summarized concerning alternation when the two forces are equal, we should expect him more frequently to express the tendency to say left *but with some variability in the response*. Every time he is confronted with the instigating forces to undertake the two mutually incompatible actions and only one is directly expressed in behavior, there could be a greater increment in the inertial tendency to undertake the activity that was not directly expressed in behavior on that occasion. Because the inertial tendency persists, it will gradually increase in strength on repeated occasions in which the instigating force is presented but the relevant activity does not occur. What happens is not unlike what is presumed to happen to the rat deprived of the opportunity to eat but not deprived of the periodic inducements to eat during an interval of time. In time, there should occur an occasion when the inertial tendency to say "right" will be so much stronger than the inertial tendency to say "left" at the beginning of a trial that the tendency to say "right" will attain dominance even though the instigating force to say left is stronger than the instigating force to say right. Particularly intriguing is the possibility that the ratio of the strengths of the instigating forces may correspond to the ratio of the probabilities of being correct and that this ratio defines the average number of unexpressed trials needed for the weaker alternative to catch up with and exceed the more frequently dominant alternative at the time of decision. The problem will be given serious consideration in Chapter 4.

Effect of Delay

When examined very closely, all of the behavioral phenomena attributed to heightened inertial tendency in the preceding pages are instances of *delay* in the expression of the tendency whose strength has been increased by exposure to an instigating force. In some cases, as with the traditional operations employed to control hunger, the delay is a matter of experimental intervention. In other cases, for example, probability matching or alternation behavior, the delay comes about because some other tendency happens to be stronger and the weaker tendency is suppressed, although not itself weakened. And, hence, we should expect to find that the behavioral consequences of introducing a delay, while the individual is exposed to the instigating force to undertake an activity, would normally be consistent with the assumption that what happens during the period is an increase in the strength of the action tendency. This phenomenon, experienced by anyone who has waited for a slow-moving elevator, does fit the theoretical expectation. There is a heightening of the impulse to act which is often experienced as irritation.

These several applications of the conceptual scheme to familiar motivational phenomena may allow a preliminary appraisal of its promise when it is broadened to include displacement, substitution, and the concept of a family of functionally related action tendencies that suffer a common fate. Now we must examine another set of tendencies that belong to the family, the ones responsible for the covert imaginal, perceptual, conceptual, and verbal activities of an individual that often (but not always) run a course parallel to that of overt action.

THE NATURE OF COVERT ACTIVITY

From the perspective of an external observer, conscious thought is to be viewed as covert activity. A covert activity a, in progress, implies $T_a > T_b, T_c, \ldots$ where $T_b, T_c, \ldots$ refer to tendencies to engage in other covert activities (for example, imaginal or perceptual activities) that are incompatible with activity a. There is, in other words, continual competition among tendencies for conscious attention. The dominant tendency and others compatible with it and each other are expressed.

The content of imaginal and perceptual activities is derived from sensory experience. A physical stimulus, quite aside from the instigating force it may produce to undertake a particular motoric activity, will always produce an unconditioned instigating force to engage in a particular perceptual or imaginal activity. This will increase the strength of that imaginal or perceptual tendency. If the tendency becomes dominant, it will be expressed in the covert perceptual activity we refer to as hearing the click of a metronome, seeing the rainbow, feeling the warmth of the sun, etc.

Since overt activity of the individual, an R, immediately produces a certain distinctive sensory consequence, an S, every overt response, via this sensory feedback, will produce an instigating force for the particular perceptual activity that constitutes conscious awareness of making that response. Thus, when there is no serious conflict for conscious attention, the sequence of behavioral events that are recorded by an external observer as S_1-R_1-S_2-R_2-S_G-R_G (perhaps, the familiar rat running from start box to goal box in a maze) may be supposed to have a subjective counterpart in the behaving individual. This is the sequence of covert, perceptual activities produced by and corresponding to $S_1 \cdots R_G$. They are to be considered expressions of perceptual tendencies that are produced by the instigating force of physical stimuli. We might describe the sequence of covert activities as $r_{s_1}\text{-}r_{r_1}\text{-}r_{s_2}\text{-}r_{r_2}\text{-}$ $r_{s_g}\text{-}r_{r_g}$ to indicate that we view this as a stream of covert activity. But having made this point, we can probably communicate more clearly by the notation, $s_1\text{-}r_1\text{-}s_2\text{-}r_2\text{-}s_g\text{-}r_g$, using s and r to represent the perceptual or imaginal activity corresponding to S and R, the two molar physical events that produce the instigating forces for perceptual activity. Both s and r, then, refer to covert activities that have a sensory basis.

Although we shall not digress to develop the argument fully here, we can point out that in the domain of sensory perception the unconditioned instigating force of the stimulus to engage in the perceptual activity appropriate to that stimulus is proportionate to certain physical properties of the stimulus such as its intensity. Thus, in visual recognition, the time of exposure must be longer when the physical intensity of the stimulus is weak and can be shorter when the physical intensity is strong. And the evidence of the effects of motivation on perceptual sensitivity can be viewed as another case of the influence of inertial tendency on initiation of an activity, in this case, a covert imaginal activity. A tendency to engage in a particular imaginal activity will attain dominance more rapidly when the inertial tendency for that activity is already strong before the exposure to the critical stimulus which produces instigating force for that imaginal activity.

In brief, this is our preliminary view of the nature of covert imaginal and perceptual activities. We view the physical stimulus, S, as a source of instigating force to undertake overt activities. We view the physical stimulus, S, as also a source of instigating force to undertake covert imaginal and perceptual activities. The general implication of this dual instigating function of a stimulus is that the sequence of historical events that explains why S may now produce a conditioned instigating force to run and eat, $_SF_{\text{Run : Eat}}$, in a rat (see Chapter 5) should serve at the same time to account for an $_SF_{\text{run : eat}}$, that is, an instigating force to engage in the imaginal or perceptual activities that parallel the overt action sequence. Normally, the tendency for the covert imaginal activity and the tendency for the overt locomotor activity will both attain dominance, one in the domain of covert activity (thought), the other in the domain of overt activity (action) at about the same time. So the rat (we suppose) initiates the activity of running toward the food while experiencing a correlated "intention" of running to eat the food and an expectation of the food. We do not view the covert activity and the overt activity as expressions of the same action tendency. Instead, we view the two activities as expressions of separate tendencies—the one for covert perceptual and imaginal activity, the other for overt motoric activity.

This dual instigating function of a stimulus is shown in Figure 2.2. We conceive two possibilities: (*a*) that S produces separate instigating forces and, thus, separate tendencies for covert perceptual-imaginal activity and

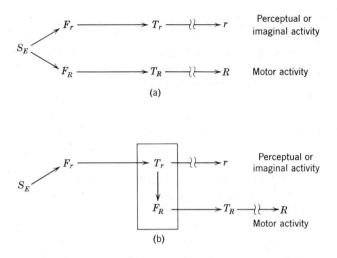

FIGURE 2.2   Two conceptions of the dual instigating function of a stimulus showing the relation between overt and covert activity.

overt motoric activity; or (b) that S produces instigating force to engage in an appropriate perceptual activity and that the strengthened perceptual tendency, whether expressed in consciousness or not, mediates the instigating force for overt action. In the latter case, the one we tend to favor (see Chapter 5), the instigating force to undertake some overt activity that is produced by S is mediated by a perceptual process. But there is no requirement that the perceptual tendency must attain dominance, that. is, must produce the appropriate conscious experience, for it (as the source of instigating force to action) to influence overt activity.

Traditionally, human action has been explained by referring it to the intentions (covert activity) of the individual (Mischel, 1966). We argue that this has come about because there is normally a very high correlation between certain characteristics of the covert activity and certain characteristics of the overt activity. The tendency expressed in the covert activity and the tendency expressed in the overt activity have a common origin in the same stimulus situation and a common natural history. Very frequently, the covert activity antedates the initiation of the overt activity. For example, an individual may begin to think about walking to a restaurant for lunch before he actually begins to walk there. This adds to the traditional belief that the former is the cause of the latter. But, almost as often, an overt activity is initiated, and only later does the corresponding covert activity, which yields the apparent "reasons" for the action, begin. And sometimes there is little if any relationship between the overt activity (for example, driving an automobile to work) and the covert activity (for example, planning a vacation trip). Finally, we must not forget the many instances of overt activity with no corresponding covert activity that Freud identified in developing the concept of unconscious motivation; for instance, the hostile action that is neither preceded nor accompanied by a hostile intention.

We have chosen to speak first of the most primitive form of covert activity, the perceptual-imaginal sequence that parallels an overt action sequence. There are obviously other and more complicated forms of covert activity: that is, conceptual and verbal activities. We tend to view them in the same way that we view activities such as eating dinner or playing the piano. That is, a person deeply engrossed in solving a problem in algebra may be sitting quietly with hands folded and staring out a window. He is likely to be totally oblivious to what is going on outside and to the fact that his hands are folded. An observer would not know that he is engaged in a conceptual activity unless told by the subject. Similarly, the housewife who is quietly deliberating in private conversation with herself about what to include in the shopping list is an enigma to the external observer unless she occasionally mumbles something aloud like, "This time I must remember the flour . . . ," to betray the nature of her covert verbal activity.

The issue presented by covert conceptual and verbal activities, in which an individual may be completely absorbed, is a fundamental methodological problem for psychology: the observer does not always know what the subject is doing. This is particularly true in the case of human behavior. It is as if the observer of a rat that is running in a maze had to confront the problem of a big black screen falling down to block his view every so often. He would not know what the rat was doing when the screen was interposed between them. We accept the fact that much of human behavior is private. The principles of behavior will be uncovered and tested under experimental circumstances designed to minimize this fundamental methodological problem.

The general position taken here is that conscious thought and overt action are not two expressions of the same specific action tendency. Instead, they represent expressions of different tendencies for compatible activities that belong to the same family because these tendencies have a common origin and history. But one can be expressed without the other, depending on the nature and the strength of the competition in the domain of thought and in the domain of action at the time. Normally, however, their mutual occurrence and nonoccurrence is highly correlated.[7] In Chapter 6 we shall learn that the cognitive correlates of overt action provide a source of

---

[7] In this connection, see Ericksen, C. W., 1958. The position taken here was much influenced by his earlier treatment of the general problem. See also Campbell, 1963 and Mischel, 1969.

information from which we can assess the instigating force to undertake particular activities.

SUMMARY

Stimuli that either innately or as a result of prior training can produce direct instigating force to undertake an activity also produce indirect instigating force to undertake other related activities. The extent of displacement, or spread, of instigation depends on the magnitude of the instigating force to undertake a given activity, on which it is based, and the degree of relationship between two different activities. An activity that produces consummatory force and thus reduces the tendency that motivated it can also produce indirect consummatory force which reduces the strength of related tendencies. The extent of substitution depends on the magnitude of the consummatory force, on which it is based, and the degree of relationship between two different activities. Without prior knowledge, one may discover what tendencies belong together in the same family by observing the extent to which instigation of one activity increases the likelihood of initiation of another and the extent to which the occurrence of one can decrease the likelihood of the other. It is often useful to describe the more general instigating effects of a particular stimulus and the more general consummatory effects of a particular activity by referring to the family or class of activities that is affected. Thus, to say that the Tendency to Eat has been strengthened by the instigating force of a particular stimulus or that it has been reduced by the consummatory force of a particular activity is equivalent to saying that all the members of a family of functionally related tendencies to seek foods and eat them have suffered a common fate.

Also belonging to a family of correlated tendencies are the ones that are expressed covertly in imaginal and perceptual activities. Covert imaginal and perceptual activities are highly correlated with overt activities because they originate in the same stimulus situation and share the same natural history. A physical stimulus produces an instigating force to engage in the imaginal or perceptual activity appropriate to that stimulus. The perceptual tendency, whether or not expressed in the domain of conscious experience, may be the proximal physical source of the instigating force for overt activity. Thus, as we view it, the instigating force to overt activity is mediated by a perceptual process, but one which is not always conscious.

The correlation which exists between tendencies that are expressed covertly in thought and the ones that are expressed overtly in action provides a basis for an assessment of the magnitude of instigating force for overt action, a topic that we shall discuss in Chapter 6.

MATHEMATICAL NOTES

Substitution for incompatible activities is quite different from substitution for compatible activities. With incompatible activities only one of the set of activities can be ongoing at any point in time, which means that substitution effects are in only one direction—from an ongoing activity A to alternative activities B, C, ... In working with incompatible activities, we need consider only two activities, since all of the information about substitution effects for this case is contained in the relationship between the two activities.

This is not true when activities are compatible and may be ongoing simultaneously. Here, potentially, we have substitution effects that go all ways. For example, for three compatible activities X, Y, and Z we could have substitution effects from X to Y and Y to X, from X to Z and Z to X, and from Y to Z and Z to Y. Overall, the consequences of substitution for a set of activities depend on the number of compatible activities involved and the pattern of compatibility-incompatibility relationships.

In the following two sections we shall discuss substitution for two incompatible activities and for two compatible activities. In addition, comments about the case of more than two compatible activities will be offered.

Substitution Effects with Two Incompatible Activities

Substitution can only occur from ongoing activity A to alternative activity B in this case. As shown in the text (p. 37) the Principle of Change in Strength of Tendency applied to T_B produces

$$\frac{dT_B}{dt} = F_B - C_{AB} = F_B - \gamma_{AB} \cdot C_A$$

$$= F_B - \gamma_{AB} \cdot c_A \cdot T_A \tag{2.7}$$

which, when the appropriate function for T_A is inserted, becomes

$$\frac{dT_B}{dt} = F_B - \gamma_{AB} \cdot c_A \left[T_{A_I} \cdot e^{-c_A \cdot t} + \frac{F_A}{c_A} (1 - e^{-c_A \cdot t}) \right] \tag{2.8}$$

The expression for T_B is gained by integrating Equation 2.8 and by assessing the constant of integration and is

$$T_B = T_{B_I} + [(F_B - \gamma_{AB} \cdot F_A) \cdot t] + \left[\gamma_{AB} \left(\frac{F_A}{c_A} - T_{A_I} \right) (1 - e^{-c_A \cdot t}) \right] \tag{2.9}$$

It is readily observed from Equation 2.8 that $dT/dt = F_B - \gamma_{AB} \cdot c_A \cdot T_A$ for $t = 0$ and that in the limit $dT_B/dt = F_B - \gamma_{AB} \cdot c_A \cdot (F_A/c_A)$ as $t \to \infty$.

Thus, the initial slope of T_B can be either positive, zero or negative, depending on the relative magnitudes of F_B and $\gamma_{AB} \cdot c_A \cdot T_{A_I}$, as can the final slope depending on the relative magnitudes of F_B and $\gamma_{AB} \cdot c_A \cdot (F_A/c_A)$. Furthermore, by setting $dT_B/dt = 0$ and by solving for t, it can be seen that Equation 2.9 has a single maximum or minimum under certain conditions. The value of t when T_B is maximum (or minimum) is

$$t = \left(\frac{1}{c_A}\right) \ln \left[\frac{\gamma_{AB} \cdot c_A \cdot (F_A/c_A) - \gamma_{AB} \cdot c_A \cdot T_{A_I}}{\gamma_{AB} \cdot c_A \cdot (F_A/c_A) - F_B}\right]$$

A maximum exists for T_B at the specified value of t if the initial slope in Equation 2.9 is positive and the final slope negative, conditions that demand $F_A/c_A > T_{A_I}$, that is, that T_A be rising to asymptote. Conversely, T_B will have a minimum at the specified value of t if the initial slope for T_B is negative and the final slope positive, conditions that require $T_{A_I} > F_A/c_A$, that is, that T_A be falling to asymptote. The complete set of possible paths for T_B over time is pictured in Figure 2.1.

Under certain sets of conditions (that is, certain sets of parameter values) when T_B is subjected to substitution effects from T_A, a change in activity from A to B will take place, under other conditions T_B does not gain sufficient strength relative to T_A to induce a change in activity. We turn now to a specification of these conditions. Since it is apparent that the course of T_B depends on the course of T_A, we shall separate the task into two parts and shall analyze the conditions under which a change in activity will and will not occur, first for a T_A that is rising to asymptote (that is, where $T_{A_I} < F_A/c_A$) and second for a T_A that is falling to asymptote (that is, where $T_{A_I} > F_A/c_A$). We shall organize our investigation further by considering in turn whether the final slope for T_B is positive, zero, or negative in each case. It is, of course, necessary that the initial condition $T_{A_I} > T_{B_I}$ hold true, since A is the ongoing activity at the beginning of the interval of observation.

Case 1. $T_{A_I} < F_A/c_A$ so T_A rises to asymptote. From Equations 1.11 and 2.9 we write

$$T_A = \frac{F_A}{c_A} - \left(\frac{F_A}{c_A} - T_{A_I}\right) \cdot e^{-c_A t}$$

and

$$T_B = T_{B_I} + (F_B - \gamma_{AB} \cdot F_A) \cdot t + \gamma_{AB}\left(\frac{F_A}{c_A} - T_{A_I}\right)(1 - e^{-c_A \cdot t})$$

In addition, we shall find it useful to have

$$\frac{dT_A}{dt} = c_A\left(\frac{F_A}{c_A} - T_{A_I}\right) \cdot e^{-c_A t}$$

and

$$\frac{dT_B}{dt} = (F_B - \gamma_{AB} \cdot F_A) + c_A \cdot \gamma_{AB}\left(\frac{F_A}{c_A} - T_{A_I}\right) \cdot e^{-c_A \cdot t}$$

available.

1. Let $(F_B - \gamma_{AB} \cdot F_A) > 0$, specifying that the final slope for T_B is positive. It is apparent that a change in activity from A to B must occur under these conditions since, as time passes, T_A approaches its asymptote of F_A/c_A and T_B increases linearly. Perhaps, this is most easily seen in the first derivatives of the two functions where $dT_A/dt = 0$ and $dT_B/dt = (F_B - \gamma_{AB} \cdot F_A) > 0$ as $t \to \infty$.

2. Let $(F_B - \gamma_{AB} \cdot F_A) = 0$, specifying that T_B approaches an asymptote as $t \to \infty$. Since both $dT_A/dt = 0$ and $dT_B/dt = 0$ as $t \to \infty$, a change in activity can occur if, and only if, the asymptote for T_A is less than that for T_B. This requires that

$$\frac{F_A}{c_A} < T_{B_I} + \gamma_{AB}\left(\frac{F_A}{c_A} - T_{A_I}\right)$$

but since $T_{B_I} < T_{A_I}$, in addition, the complete statement of the inequality to be satisfied is

$$\frac{F_A}{c_A} < T_{B_I} + \gamma_{AB}\left(\frac{F_A}{c_A} - T_{A_I}\right) < T_{A_I} + \gamma_{AB}\left(\frac{F_A}{c_A} - T_{A_I}\right)$$

This contradicts the specification of Case 1, $T_{A_I} < F_A/c_A$, however, implying that no change in activity can occur under these conditions.

3. Let $(F_B - \gamma_{AB} \cdot F_A) < 0$, specifying a negative final slope for T_B. That no change in activity can take place under these conditions is seen directly by comparing dT_A/dt to dT_B/dt. Such a comparison shows that $dT_A/dt > dT_B/dt$ for all values of t making it impossible for T_B to catch up to T_A.

Case 2. $T_{A_I} > F_A/c_A$ so that T_A falls to asymptote. Again, by using Equations 1.11 and 2.9, we can write

$$T_A = \frac{F_A}{c_A} + \left(T_{A_I} - \frac{F_A}{c_A}\right) \cdot e^{-c_A \cdot t}$$

and

$$T_B = T_{B_I} + (F_B - \gamma_{AB} \cdot F_A) \cdot t - \gamma_{AB}\left(T_{A_I} - \frac{F_A}{c_A}\right)(1 - e^{-c_A \cdot t})$$

Similarly,

$$\frac{dT_A}{dt} = -c_A\left(T_{A_I} - \frac{F_A}{c_A}\right) \cdot e^{-c_A \cdot t}$$

and

$$\frac{dT_B}{dt} = (F_B - \gamma_{AB} \cdot F_A) - c_A \cdot \gamma_{AB}\left(T_{A_I} - \frac{F_A}{c_A}\right) \cdot e^{-c_A \cdot t}$$

1. Let $(F_B - \gamma_{AB} \cdot F_A) > 0$, specifying a positive final slope for T_B. A positive final slope in Case 2 results in a change in activity for the same reasons that it does in Case 1: T_A approaches asymptote whereas T_B continues to increase in strength.

2. Let $(F_B - \gamma_{AB} \cdot F_A) = 0$, specifying that T_B approaches an asymptote as $t \to \infty$. As in Case 1, since $dT_A/dt = 0$ and $dT_B/dt = 0$ as $t \to \infty$, a change in activity can occur only if the asymptote for T_A is less than that for T_B. By taking into account $T_{A_I} > T_{B_I}$, a change in activity will occur if the following inequality is satisfied:

$$\frac{F_A}{c_A} < T_{B_I} - \gamma_{AB}\left(T_{A_I} - \frac{F_A}{c_A}\right) < T_{A_I} - \gamma_{AB}\left(T_{A_I} - \frac{F_A}{c_A}\right)$$

or

$$\frac{F_A}{c_A} + \gamma_{AB}\left(T_{A_I} - \frac{F_A}{c_A}\right) < T_{B_I} < T_{A_I}$$

Since

$$\frac{F_A}{c_A} + \gamma_{AB}\left(T_{A_I} - \frac{F_A}{c_A}\right) < T_{A_I}$$

according to the conditions defining Case 2, $T_{A_I} > F_A/c_A$, values of T_{B_I} exist for which the inequality is true and under these special conditions a change in activity will take place.

3. Let $(F_B - \gamma_{AB} \cdot F_A) < 0$, specifying a final slope for T_B that is negative. Since T_B has a final slope that is negative, a change in activity must occur, if it can occur at all, because T_A declines rapidly enough that it drops below T_B. The question posed is whether, for some value of t,

$$T_{B_I} + (F_B - \gamma_{AB} \cdot F_A) \cdot t - \gamma_{AB}\left(T_{A_I} - \frac{F_A}{c_A}\right)(1 - e^{-c_A \cdot t})$$

$$\geq \frac{F_A}{c_A} + \left(T_{A_I} - \frac{F_A}{c_A}\right) \cdot e^{-c_A \cdot t}$$

given that $T_{A_I} > T_{B_I}$. By putting these two conditions together and by rearranging terms we have

$$\frac{F_A}{c_A} + \left(T_{A_I} - \frac{F_A}{c_A}\right) \cdot e^{-c_A \cdot t}$$

$$- (F_B - \gamma_{AB} \cdot F_A) \cdot t + \gamma_{AB}\left(T_{A_I} - \frac{F_A}{c_A}\right)(1 - e^{-c_A \cdot t}) \leq T_{B_I} < T_{A_I}$$

In order that this basic inequality be satisfied it is necessary that the subordinate inequality

$$\frac{F_A}{c_A} + \left(T_{A_I} - \frac{F_A}{c_A}\right) \cdot e^{-c_A \cdot t}$$
$$- (F_B - \gamma_{AB} \cdot F_A) \cdot t + \gamma_{AB}\left(T_{A_I} - \frac{F_A}{c_A}\right)(1 - e^{-c_A \cdot t}) < T_{A_I}$$

or $(\gamma_{AB} \cdot F_A - F_B) \cdot t < (t_{A_I} - F_A/c_A)(1 - \gamma_{AB})(1 - e^{-c_A \cdot t})$ be satisfied. We see that for each finite $t > 0$ there can be found a value of T_{A_I} sufficiently large that this expression will be true. It is then true that for such values of t and T_{A_I}, values of T_{B_I} can be found so that the basic inequality is satisfied. When these special conditions are realized, a change in activity will occur.

Substitution Effects with Compatible Activities

For two compatible activities X and Y occurring simultaneously, X substitutes for Y at the same time that Y substitutes for X. In differential equation form, we can write this as

$$\frac{dT_X}{dt} = F_X - c_X \cdot T_X - \gamma_{YX} \cdot c_Y \cdot T_Y$$

and

$$\frac{dT_Y}{dt} = F_Y - c_Y \cdot T_Y - \gamma_{XY} \cdot c_X \cdot T_X$$

The solution to these two simultaneous differential equations is

$$T_X = \left[\frac{F_X - \gamma_{YX} \cdot F_Y}{c_X(1 - \gamma_{XY}\gamma_{YX})}\right] + \left(\frac{g_1}{2w}\right) \cdot e^{-(v-w)\cdot t} + (g_2) \cdot e^{-(v+w)\cdot t}$$

and

$$T_Y = \left[\frac{F_Y - \gamma_{XY} \cdot F_X}{c_Y(1 - \gamma_{XY}\gamma_{YX})}\right] + \left(\frac{h_1}{2w}\right) \cdot e^{-(v-w)\cdot t} + (h_2) \cdot e^{-(v+w)\cdot t}$$

where g_1 and g_2 are the constants of integration for the T_X equation and h_1 and h_2 for the T_Y equation. In addition, the notation in the two equations has been simplified by setting

$$v = \frac{c_X + c_Y}{2} \quad \text{and} \quad w = \frac{\sqrt{(c_X + c_Y)^2 - 4c_Xc_Y(1 - \gamma_{XY}\gamma_{YX})}}{2}$$

The constants of integration can be evaluated by imposing the conditions that, for $t = 0$, $T_X = T_{X_I}$, $dT_X/dt = F_X - c_X \cdot T_{X_I} - \gamma_{YX} \cdot c_Y \cdot T_{Y_I}$, $T_Y = T_{Y_I}$, and $dT_Y/dt = F_Y - c_Y \cdot T_{Y_I} - \gamma_{XY} \cdot c_X \cdot T_{X_I}$. The resulting equations are not at all tidy and will not be presented here since they are not needed for our discussion.

It is quickly seen from the equations that T_X and T_Y approach asymptotes of

$$\left[\frac{F_X - \gamma_{YX} \cdot F_Y}{c_X(1 - \gamma_{XY}\gamma_{YX})}\right] \quad \text{and} \quad \left[\frac{F_Y - \gamma_{XY} \cdot F_X}{c_Y(1 - \gamma_{XY}\gamma_{YX})}\right]$$

respectively, as t, the time during which activities X and Y are ongoing, increases. A comparison of these asymptotes with the corresponding asymptotes when there is no substitution is of interest. It is a reasonable conjecture that the asymptotes with substitution operative will be below those without. We can test the conjecture by asking

$$\frac{F_X - \gamma_{YX} \cdot F_Y}{c_X(1 - \gamma_{XY} \cdot \gamma_{YX})} \overset{?}{<} \frac{F_X}{c_X}$$

We notice immediately that this is an interesting question only for $F_X - \gamma_{YX} \cdot F_Y > 0$ (that is, when the asymptote with substitution operative is positive) since it obviously is true for $F_X - \gamma_{YX} \cdot F_Y \leq 0$. It is readily shown that the above inequality is true if $F_Y - \gamma_{XY} \cdot F_X > 0$. Therefore, our conjecture that the asymptotic value for T_X with substitution from activity Y is less than it is without substitution is correct if T_Y also has an asymptotic value that is positive when substitution from activity X is operative.

If either T_X or T_Y with substitution is headed toward a negative asymptote, it will reach zero at some point, assuming no change in activity occurs in the meantime, and will then stay at zero. With the strength of tendency equal to zero, no activity and therefore no substitution can occur, implying that the other tendency T_Y or T_X will begin to approach its asymptote of F_Y/c_Y or F_X/c_X as the case may be.

Since either $F_X > F_Y$ or $F_Y > F_X$ and since $0 \leq \gamma_{XY}, \gamma_{YX} \leq 1$, T_X and T_Y cannot both approach negative asymptotes because this would require that $F_X/F_Y < \gamma_{YX}$ and $F_Y/F_X < \gamma_{XY}$ be satisfied simultaneously, and this is not possible under the stated conditions.

Extending the theory to handle substitution effects among more than two compatible activities is straightforward, but it runs into one particularly awkward problem. For example, for compatible activities X, Y, and Z we can write

$$\frac{dT_X}{dt} = F_X - c_X \cdot T_X - \gamma_{YX} \cdot c_Y \cdot T_Y - \gamma_{ZX} \cdot c_Z \cdot T_Z$$

$$\frac{dT_Y}{dt} = F_Y - c_Y \cdot T_Y - \gamma_{XY} \cdot c_X \cdot T_X - \gamma_{ZY} \cdot c_Z \cdot T_Z$$

and

$$\frac{dT_Z}{dt} = F_Z - c_Z \cdot T_Z - \gamma_{XZ} \cdot c_X \cdot T_X - \gamma_{YZ} \cdot c_Y \cdot T_Y$$

The problem arises in that the solution of these three simultaneous differential equations requires the factoring of a third degree equation, analogous to the necessity that a second degree equation be factored in the course of the derivation of the equations for the two activities, X and Y, just presented. In general, the degree of the equation to be factored is the same as the number of compatible activities being dealt with and, clearly, unless different analytic methods are found, we shall be compelled to proceed in the absence of any very general solutions to the problem of substitution among compatible activities.

CHAPTER 3

MEASURABLE ASPECTS OF THE STREAM OF BEHAVIOR

In the preceding chapter, we began to illustrate how the principles that account for change in the strength of an action tendency and for change of activity can be employed to deduce that certain antecedent events will produce either an increase or decrease in the strength of inertial tendency to undertake a particular activity. The basic assumptions concerning the instigating force of stimuli, the consummatory force of activities, and the inertia of behavioral tendencies provide a conceptual framework from which the behavioral consequences of differences in the strength of instigating force and consummatory value of an activity can also be derived.

Traditionally, the very same behavioral measures have been employed when the observer's intention is to assess how individuals differ in their disposition to behave in a certain stimulus situation, as in the study of personality, and when the observer's intention is to assess a change in a particular individual's disposition to behave in a certain stimulus situation resulting from training and practice, as in the study of learning. From our present perspective, both observers are interested in the behavior-inducing properties of the particular stimulus situation for a particular individual— what is here called the instigating force of a stimulus—that can be attributed to heredity, maturation, and the parameters of prior experience. The study of learning is concerned with the changes in the instigating force of a stimulus that can be attributed to parameters of prior experience. The study of personality is concerned with the individual differences in the strength of the instigating force for an activity produced by the very same stimulus situation. In one case, the successive reactions of an individual to the same stimulus situation are compared. In the other case, the reactions of different individuals to the same stimulus situation are compared.

A very important question has a definite logical priority in the discussion of the determinants of the strength of an instigating force that is produced by a particular stimulus: What behavioral measures (and under what

conditions) will unambiguously identify a difference in the strength of instigating force to undertake some particular activity? Our purpose in the
present chapter is to direct attention to this question. We shall continue, as
in the previous chapters, to consider only what has traditionally been
called approach- or appetitive behavior in our initial effort to identify the
measurable aspects of the stream of behavior that constitute the several diagnostic tests of tendencies and forces. These diagnostic tests make it possible
to discover, empirically, the historical determinants or components of an
instigating force.

Plan of This and the Next Chapter

The first step will be to identify a number of simple and ideal conditions
to show how the logic of the theoretical scheme applies to some of the
traditional behavioral measures. Often they will be imaginary conditions,
since they rarely occur naturally. Even though an experimenter might seek
to achieve these simple, idealized conditions in controlled research, it is
unlikely that he would be able to do so.

Next, we shall begin to consider more complex, but still ideal conditions,
introducing complications that bring the analysis much closer to the actual
conditions of natural behavior and to the ones that are likely to exist when a
psychologist attempts to obtain one of the several possible measures of
tendency or force in experimentation. Most important will be the treatment
of the spurious effects attributable to various compatibility relations among
activities that are often completely ignored.

Our aim in this chapter is to begin to spell out the kinds of inference that
could be made from behavioral observations under ideal conditions and to
develop a clear conception of what is meant by *ideal conditions*. This provides
a foundation for the work of Chapter 4. We appraise the discrepancies that
exist between these theoretical ideal conditions, in terms of which a mathematical model makes good sense, and the much less than ideal circumstances
of the actual empirical events that are studied, even in well controlled
experiments. In Chapter 4, we shall examine the kinds of assumptions that
must be introduced to bridge the gap, to take the place of the accurate
knowledge of the conditions that may prevail, and the behavioral implications of these assumptions. When we have done so, we shall be in a position
to appreciate the theoretical implications of the kinds of behavioral data that
are normally obtained in psychological experiments.

Our general aim in these two chapters is to call attention to some of the
limitations in the observation and description of behavior and some unavoidable limitations in the experimental control of the variables that influence
behavior. Our discussion will elaborate some of the important implications
of the present scheme when it is applied to the diagnostic methods that are

usually employed in the studies of learning and personality and will begin to consider new and potentially more adequate methods of study that are suggested by the present scheme. All of this will provide a foundation for the later consideration of the empirical determinants of the instigating force of a stimulus and for the discussion of the use of this conceptual scheme in the study of learning.

It is perhaps already apparent that the direction of our theoretical approach is diametrically opposite to that of the dominant trend in American psychology as typified by the gradual evolution of S-R Behavior Theory from the time of Thorndike's and Pavlov's early work to the theoretical elaborations of Hull, Spence, and others in this tradition. Historically, the matter of initial, central interest was learning, that is, the changes in observed behavior that could be attributed to parameters of training. Only gradually, over the years, was the need for a clarification of the contemporaneous determinants of behavior recognized as a fundamental problem in its own right. Our view, more like that of Lewin in its point of departure, is fundamentally different. We view the problem of the conceptual analysis of the change of activity as the fundamental and logically-prior theoretical problem and mean to work out from it to recover the empirical problem of learning and to the specification of the conditions which justify the inference that learning, conceived as a change in the instigating force of a stimulus or in the consummatory value of a response for an individual, has occurred.

The Potential Diagnostic Tests of the Strength of Tendency and Force.   What are the measurable aspects of the stream of behavior which provide the potential diagnostic tests of the strength of a behavioral tendency or of an instigating force? Perhaps the first that comes to mind, because it is so frequently employed in both the study of personality and of learning, is choice or preference. When an individual is confronted with the possibility of engaging in two or more alternative actions, which one does he undertake or prefer? Does the subject prefer the option for which the stimulus card states that there is one chance in 10 of winning 9 cents or the option for which the stimulus card states that there are 7 chances in 10 of winning 3 cents? Does the rat at the critical choice point in a T-maze decide to turn left, the response which in the past has been followed by food reward, or right, the response which in the past has been followed by an empty goal box? Does the child prefer a small reward that will be given to him immediately, or a much greater reward that he is promised next week? Here is the method that is exploited in many written tests. The subject is invited to state which of two or more activities he likes best, or in which he would normally prefer to engage (for example, Strong, 1927).

Although it comes to mind first, this method of choice is somewhat more complicated than others when viewed in terms of the present conceptual scheme and, hence, we shall postpone its discussion until we have established a foundation for dealing with it in reference to two other measures that we have already introduced: (1) the initiation of a response to a stimulus (that is, latency), and (2) the persistence of activity in progress. All of these measurable characteristics of the stream of behavior—initiation, persistence, choice—are aspects of a single problem: a change in activity.

A fourth possible measure, the magnitude or intensity of response, which we have assumed to depend only on the strength of the tendency that is expressed in an activity, carries its own set of special problems. Consequently, we shall treat it separately at the end of the next chapter.

THE SIMPLEST IDEAL CONDITIONS

Our introductory discussion in Chapters 1 and 2 has assumed the simplest, ideal conditions in presenting the basic concepts and principles that apply to a change of activity. Now it is time to identify these conditions and to introduce the terms that will be used to distinguish simple conditions from the more complex conditions of behavior.

The term, *activity in progress*, has been used in reference to what the subject is doing during *an interval of observation*. We have referred to the activity in progress when observation begins as activity *A* and the activity which replaces it when the change of activity that terminates the interval of observation occurs as activity *B*.

Up to this point we have been concerned with what we shall now call a *unitary activity*: the subject is doing only one thing, engaging in a single activity, at the time of observation. In other words, we have treated activity *A* as exclusive. Henceforth, we shall contrast the simple case of *unitary activity* with the more complex case of *multiple activity* in which the subject is doing more than one thing. In the latter case, he is *simultaneously* expressing tendencies to engage in two or more different activities that are compatible at the time of observation. Examples of multiple activity are as follows: watching television and drinking beer, taking a warm bath and reading a book, writing a book and smoking a cigarette, walking to work and talking to a friend, etc. These are sets of different activities that can be engaged in at the same time because the activities are compatible. Examples of incompatible activities are: listening to a symphony and arguing politics with a friend, solving mathematical problems and reading a novel, typing a letter and playing a clarinet, etc. As stated earlier, it is assumed that an individual would simultaneously express all of his action tendencies if it were not for the fact that some activities are incompatible either because the same muscles would need to be involved or because the environmental supports with which the individual has commerce in each activity are located in different places.

The terms *unitary* and *multiple* describe the activity in progress at a particular instant. But this activity, whether unitary or multiple, may continue without change throughout the interval of observation, in which case we refer to the activity during the interval as *homogeneous*, or there may be a succession of different activities before a particular activity of interest to an observer (activity *B*) occurs, in which case the term *heterogeneous* is descriptive of the activity in progress. When the activity is *homogeneous*, the same tendency or tendencies are expressed throughout the interval of observation. When the activity is *heterogeneous*, a more complex case, different tendencies are expressed at different times within the interval of observation.

Let us now move from the discussion of terms descriptive of the activity in progress during an interval of observation to the consideration of the action tendency supporting a particular activity. It may be an *elemental action tendency*, in which case the strength of the tendency to engage in that particular activity is attributable to the strength of a single action tendency. This is the simplest case. Or it may be a *compound action tendency*, in which case the strength of the tendency to engage in a particular activity is attributable to the summation of the strengths of several elemental action tendencies because each refers to the very same activity, or activities which are indiscriminable from the viewpoint of the observer. A case in point would be an animal running a maze in which it had always obtained both food and water as reward. Here, the strength of the tendency to run represents the summation of a tendency to run and eat ($T_{\text{Run}:\text{Eat}}$) and a tendency to run and drink ($T_{\text{Run}:\text{Drink}}$). By the use of two subscripts on an elemental action tendency, we mean to represent both the immediate act (or response) the subject is motivated to undertake (the first subscript) and the anticipated consequence (or goal) of that activity (the second subscript). In everyday terms, one might say that the rat in question is running "for the sake of" eating and drinking. At times, however, the observed activity would be described in everyday language as "an end in itself," for example, eating. In this case, the tendency that motivates the activity has only a single subscript: T_{Eat}. Koch (1956) has referred to the latter as *intrinsically regulated activity* in distinguishing it from goal-seeking or *instrumental behavior*. In the present scheme, the issue has to do with whether the tendency being expressed in a particular activity is more adequately described by one or two subscripts.

The same conventions will be followed in reference to the instigating forces that produce and strengthen behavioral tendencies. Thus, an animal might simultaneously be exposed to both an instigating force to run and eat ($F_{\text{Run}:\text{Eat}}$) and an instigating force to run and drink ($F_{\text{Run}:\text{Drink}}$). There is no summation of the two instigating forces because they influence different tendencies. Instead, the summation occurs in the determination of the strength of the compound action tendency to run. The two elemental action tendencies produced by these two different instigating forces summate to determine the strength of the compound action tendency to run, that is, $T_{\text{Run}} = T_{\text{Run : Eat}} + T_{\text{Run : Drink}}$.[1] *It is assumed that elemental action tendencies summate to produce a compound action tendency whenever they refer to the very same immediate activity* (that is, when the first subscript is the same). The logic of the subscripts employed to distinguish the particular instigating forces produced by stimuli, and the particular action tendencies in turn produced by those instigating forces will be clarified further in Chapter 5 when we consider the questions of how tendencies are elaborated and how particular instigating forces are acquired and strengthened.

Definition of the Simplest, Ideal Case

Given the distinctions that have been made in the preceding paragraphs, we are now prepared to identify the simplest, ideal case of a change in activity and to consider the behavioral implications of a difference in the strength of the instigating force to undertake some particular activity. In the simplest case, there would be only two mutually incompatible activities, activity A (in progress) and activity B (the activity which replaces A to constitute the change of activity). Activity A is unitary (that is, exclusive) and homogeneous. And the two activities are functionally independent. That is, γ_{AB} equals 0, so there is no substitution. This means that the simplest case of change of activity is a change from one *kind* of activity to another *kind* of activity, a shift between classes of activity, instead of a change from one activity to another activity within the same class. An example of the latter (a more complex change) would be a change from an instrumental activity that constitutes pursuit of food to the so-called goal activity of eating. Furthermore, T_A and T_B, the only two action tendencies that must be considered in the analysis of the change of activity, are elemental.

In order to consider the conditions *ideal*, the magnitudes of F_A, F_B and c_A must remain constant during the interval of observation, and the exposure of the subject to F_A and F_B must be continuous during the interval of observation.

Latency of Response under the Simplest, Ideal Conditions

An observer would notice that activity A is occurring and continues to occur in unmodified form (though not necessarily in unmodified intensity) until it is supplanted by activity B. The time from the beginning of the interval of observation until activity B is initiated corresponds to the traditional measure of the latency of response B. Figure 1.7 has already presented

[1] An alternative way of designating this compound action tendency, which makes the multiple consequence explicit, is $T_{\text{Run : Eat, Drink}}$.

examples of how T_A and T_B would change during the time interval $t_{B/A}$ and would produce the change in activity from A to B under these simple and ideal conditions. The expression $t_{B/A} = (T_{A_F} - T_{B_I})/F_B$ gives the latency of B if T_{A_F}, the final strength of T_A at the moment of the change in activity, is known. If T_{A_F} is not known, it must be calculated from the equation that specifies the change in T_A during the interval $t_{B/A}$, as a function of T_{A_I}, F_A and c_A (see Equation 1.11).

We might try to imagine this simple, ideal case in concrete terms. A rat is engaged in a unitary activity A in the start box of a maze as the door to the alley (S) is raised which begins the interval of observation and a timing mechanism. At the instant the animal initiates the activity of running the maze (activity B), its body breaks an electronic beam and stops the timing mechanism, yielding the measure of latency of response B. It is obvious from the principle of change of activity that if T_{A_I}, F_A, c_A and T_{B_I} (all the other variables that might influence the latency of response B in this simple ideal case) were constant in a series of observations of different rats, or of the same rat on repeated occasions, we should find that *the latency of response* $(t_{B/A})$ *is inversely proportionate to the magnitude of the instigating force* (F_B). A corollary of this is that under ideal conditions *the ratio of latencies is the reciprocal of the ratio of the magnitudes of instigating forces*, that is, $(t_{B/A})_1/(t_{B/A})_2 = (F_B)_2/(F_B)_1$.

If such simple and ideal conditions were to prevail in a typical study of reward training, and if the effect of this training were to strengthen F_B, the incremental growth of F_B on successive trials would be accompanied by a proportionate decrement in latency of response on successive trials. Moreover, comparisons of the latencies on various trials would justify the following kind of assertion: the instigating force to undertake activity B is now twice as strong as it was on the initial trial, etc.

Probability of Response in a Fixed Time Interval under the Simplest, Ideal Conditions

One step removed from the actual measurement of the latency of response to a stimulus is the mere recording of whether or not a particular response occurs during a particular interval of time that is arbitrarily fixed by an observer. We know from the principle of change in activity that the time $t_{B/A}$ required to produce the change from activity A to activity B is equal to $(T_{A_F} - T_{B_I})/F_B$. Under the simplest, ideal conditions, if a fixed time interval t_k is imposed for observation of whether or not activity B occurs (that is, whether or not activity A is supplanted by activity B), an instance of B will always be recorded when $t_k \geq (T_{A_F} - T_{B_I})/F_B$ and will never be recorded when $t_k < (T_{A_F} - T_{B_I})/F_B$. The minimum force required to instigate the response in a fixed time interval (t_k) is given by the equation, min. $F_B = (T_{A_F} - T_{B_I})/t_k$. In a series of comparisons in which T_{A_F} and

T_{B_I} remain constant, the probability of response will be 100 percent whenever $F_B \geq (T_{A_F} - T_{B_I})/t_k$ and 0 percent whenever $F_B < (T_{A_F} - T_{B_I})/t_k$. It is equally obvious from the above that the magnitude of force that is required to instigate activity B in a fixed time period t_k will depend on the magnitude of the parameters T_{A_F} and T_{B_I}. Only a very strong instigating force (F_B) will instigate the response when the tendency that sustains the activity in progress (T_A) is very strong relative to the inertial tendency to undertake that activity (T_{B_I}). But when T_{B_I} is very strong relative to T_A (although T_A is initially dominant), only a very weak instigating force (F_B) will fail to produce activity B in the fixed time interval.

Our discussion focuses on the use of latency of response and the probability of response in a fixed time interval as measures of the magnitude of a particular instigating force F_B. But it should be apparent from the discussion that if the magnitude of F_B were held constant in a series of comparisons, the same behavioral measure could be employed to assess the strength of any one of the several other variables that influence the magnitude of T_{A_F} (namely, T_{A_I}, F_A, c_A) or T_{B_I} as long as all remaining variables except the one to be measured were held constant in a series of tests.

Persistence, under the Simplest, Ideal Conditions. Another potential diagnostic test of tendency and force focuses on a different aspect of the change of activity: the temporal duration or persistence of the initial activity. When persistence of an activity is to be measured, the observer is prepared to record the cessation of the activity in progress but not necessarily what activity replaces it. An important relationship that follows directly from the consideration of the simplest, ideal conditions is that the measure called the persistence of activity A is identical to the measure called the latency of activity B. Since the defining criterion is the same for the two measures, namely, that activity B supplant activity A, the clock readings, $t_{B/A}$ and $t_{not\ A/A}$ are the same and the expression $t_{not\ A/A} = t_{B/A} = (T_{A_F} - T_{B_I})/F_B$ is appropriate for both.

We merely have to rephrase the assertion already made concerning the general relationship between the latency of activity $(t_{B/A})$ and the instigating force (F_B) to describe how persistence of an activity in progress provides a measure of the magnitude of the instigating force to undertake an alternative activity in the simplest, ideal case: *the persistence of the activity in progress $(t_{not\ A/A})$ is inversely proportionate to the magnitude of the instigating force to undertake the alternative activity (F_B).*

If the time interval of observation is arbitrarily fixed at t_k, and the observer merely records whether or not the initial activity has persisted throughout the time interval, we expect persistence always to be recorded when $F_B < (T_{A_F} - T_{B_I})/t_k$ and never to be recorded when $F_B \geq (T_{A_F} - T_{B_I})/t_k$. The symmetry between the two measures (latency of response and persistence) is shown most clearly and completely in the simplest, ideal conditions.

The persistence of an activity in progress is more frequently considered a measure of F_A, the magnitude of the instigating force produced by the stimulus situation to engage in that particular activity. Since F_A together with c_A define the asymptote of T_A, we can observe that when all other variables affecting $t_{\text{not } A/A}$ are held constant, including F_B, this measure of the time to change activity will be proportionate to the magnitude of F_A. Hence, we may extend our "law" of persistence for the simplest, ideal conditions: *the persistence of the activity in progress* $(t_{\text{not } A/A})$ *is proportionate to the magnitude of the instigating force to engage in that activity* (F_A) *and inversely proportionate to the magnitude of instigating force to engage in an alternative activity* (F_B). We see again, in other words, how the same diagnostic test can provide a measure of any one of the variables affecting the change of activity under appropriately controlled conditions.

MORE COMPLEX, IDEAL CONDITIONS

Conditions are considered complex when more than two activities and the tendencies that motivate them come under discussion. Instead of attempting to examine the general case, we shall confine the discussion to the minimal number of different activities and tendencies that it is necessary to consider in order to make some essential points about each of several different complexities.

The complex conditions include the ones in which the activity in progress prior to the initiation of an activity of critical interest to an observer is heterogeneous or multiple; or the newly initiated activity is multiple; or the two activities are functionally related, so that $\gamma_{AX} > 0$ and there is some substitution; or an activity is motivated by a compound action tendency. These more complex conditions are considered ideal, as in the earlier discussion, when the magnitudes of the several instigating forces (F_A, F_X, F_Y, etc.) and the consummatory values of the activities (c_A, c_X, c_Y, etc.) remain constant during the interval of observation, and the exposure to the instigating forces is continuous throughout the interval of observation.

This expansion of the analysis of the change of activity to include more than two activities provides the first occasion for a discussion of the nature of compatible and incompatible activities and a survey of special problems that arise when there is a multiple activity or a compound action tendency.

Compatible Activities

Two activities are compatible if the individual can engage in both activities simultaneously, and incompatible if this is impossible. It is important to notice that activities and not tendencies are treated as compatible or incompatible. The individual can be simultaneously motivated to engage in a number of different compatible and incompatible activities, but only those tendencies to engage in activities that are compatible can be expressed in behaviour simultaneously.

The compatibility relationship between any two activities is symmetric. If activity X is compatible with activity Y (XcY), then activity Y must be compatible with activity X (YcX). If activity X is incompatible with activity Y ($X\bar{c}Y$), then activity Y must be incompatible with activity X ($Y\bar{c}X$). But because of the physically complex structure of most activities, transitivity in compatibility relationships among activities should not necessarily be expected. It is entirely possible that an activity A is incompatible with another activity X, $A\bar{c}X$, activity X is incompatible with still another activity Y, $X\bar{c}Y$, but that activity A is compatible with activity Y, AcY. This would occur, for example, if A were playing the piano, X were playing a clarinet, and Y were talking to a friend. The individual might be able to play the piano and talk to a friend simultaneously, AcY, but he could do neither of these activities and at the same time play a clarinet, $A\bar{c}X$ and $X\bar{c}Y$. One can think of other examples in which $A\bar{c}X$, but AcY and XcY. A case in point would be when A is eating, X is singing, and Y is listening to music.

The structure for a complete description of an individual's activity at any moment in time is set by the combination of two basic assumptions that we have already introduced concerning the compatibility relations among the activities the individual is motivated to undertake and the hierarchical order of strength among these different action tendencies. The fundamental assumptions are as follows: (a) *if all activities were compatible, then all tendencies to engage in activity would be simultaneously expressed in behavior;* and (b) *the dominant tendency among a set of tendencies to engage in incompatible activities will be expressed in behavior.* It follows that if T_A is stronger than the tendency to engage in any other activity, activity A will occur and will permit the simultaneous expression of tendencies to engage in other activities that are compatible with A but not the tendencies to engage in other activities that are incompatible with A. It is unlikely that all of the tendencies to engage in activities that are compatible with activity A will be expressed. Which activities occur will depend on the patterns of compatibility and incompatibility that exist among the potential activities in the reduced set of behavioral tendencies and the relative strengths of these subordinate tendencies. The strongest among this restricted set of action tendencies will also be expressed and, depending on the compatibility of this subordinate activity with still other activities that are motivated by even weaker tendencies, there is the possibility that still another tendency (the strongest among the residual set) will also be expressed, and so on. Examples of these effects will be found in the sections that follow, as the various measurable aspects of a change in activity are now reexamined in reference to more complex but ideal conditions.

Preliminary Consideration of Choice under Complex but Ideal Conditions

Even the simplest instance of the traditional choice situation must be considered a complex condition within the framework of the present conceptual scheme because at least three different activities must be considered when the role of the initial, ongoing activity is systematically taken into account. If A is the initial, ongoing activity, X and Y are the alternative activities between which a choice is to be made, and all the activities are incompatible ($A\bar{c}X$, $A\bar{c}Y$, and $X\bar{c}Y$), two conditions must be met for a choice to be made. If activity X is to be selected, both inequalities $T_X > T_A$ and $T_X > T_Y$ must be fulfilled. If activity Y is to be selected, both inequalities $T_Y > T_A$ and $T_Y > T_X$ must be fulfilled. In reference to the critical event in the traditional T-maze of animal research, these statements mean that a rat will not supplant its choice-point behavior (activity A), whatever it is, with a left turn unless the tendency to run to the left dominates both the tendency to run to the right *and* the tendency sustaining the choice-point behavior.

This idealized conception of a simple choice between two alternative activities shows it to be another instance of a change in activity. The theoretical account of the change in activity is the same as the one that is proposed for a change in activity under simple conditions except that now T_A may be dominated by either T_X or T_Y and, hence, activity may shift from A to either X or Y.

Figure 3.1 illustrates the dynamics of two-alternative choices. In this example, activity X is chosen over activity Y since T_X dominates both T_A and T_Y at the point in time designated $t_{X/A}$, the instant of choice. It is worth noting that in this ideal case the choice of X over Y (or the opposite) ultimately depends only on the relation of T_X and T_Y to T_A. The shift in activity occurs as soon as either T_X or T_Y dominates T_A, and *the choice is determined by which of the two tendencies dominates T_A first.* The time measure is traditionally called "decision time." Under these conditions T_X and T_Y are not pitted directly against each other but instead each is pitted against T_A. This further emphasizes our conception of choice as a complex instance of change in activity.

This introductory analysis of the two-alternative choice problem has prepared the way for a reconsideration of the behavioral measures called latency, probability of occurrence, and persistence under more complex, ideal conditions. We shall undertake this analysis first and then return to the question of preference in a choice situation after we have explored the implications of a number of different complications.

Latency of Response under Complex, Ideal Conditions

When concerned with the latency of a response, the observer's interest is focused on the initiation of a particular activity B. It is the occurrence of this particular activity, and only this activity, that the observer is prepared to record. But under complex, ideal conditions, the activity in progress before the initiation of activity B may be either homogeneous (as in the simplest case) or heterogeneous. The interval of observation can be filled with one or a number of different activities. For example if, among three incompatible activities, A is the activity in progress at the beginning of the interval of observation and the latency of activity B is of critical interest to the observer, the existence of a tendency (T_O) to engage in a third activity O implies that activity may change directly from A to B (see Figure 3.2a) or from A to O and then to B (see Figure 3.2b) depending on the relative strengths of T_A, T_B, and T_O. In both cases, the latency of B is the time it takes T_B to dominate the stronger of the two tendencies, T_A or T_O. Thus, $t_{B/A} = (T_{A_F} - T_{B_I})/F_B$ if $T_{A_F} > T_{O_F}$, but $t_{B/O} = (T_{O_F} - T_{B_I})/F_B$ if $T_{O_F} > T_{A_F}$.

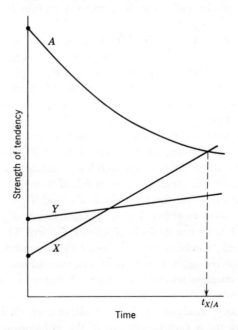

FIGURE 3.1   An example of a shift in activity from A to X in the two-choice situation.

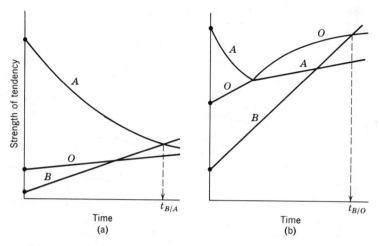

FIGURE 3.2   Examples of the shift to activity B when the interval of observation is (*a*) homogeneous, and (*b*) heterogeneous.

A very similar case occurs when the compatibility relationships among the three activities are $A\bar{c}B$, AcO, and $B\bar{c}O$. The determination of the latency of B is now the same as when all three activities were mutually incompatible though the nature of activity during the interval of observation is different. In this second case, activities A and O can occur simultaneously. Thus the initial activity is a multiple activity, A and O, until T_B dominates whichever is stronger, T_A or T_O. As long as $T_A > T_B$ or $T_O > T_B$, both T_A and T_O will continue to be expressed in behavior since the dominant tendency defines the set of compatible activities that can occur simultaneously. Even when the rank order of the strengths of tendencies is $T_O > T_B > T_A$, both A and O will continue to occur because $T_O > T_B$ means O rather than B will occur and, since A is compatible with O, A will also occur. This follows because incompatibility applies to activities and when T_O dominates T_B, A is free to occur even though $T_B > T_A$ and A and B are incompatible ($A\bar{c}B$). As an example, one might think of A as eating, B as playing the clarinet, and O as talking to a friend. The individual would continue eating and talking to a friend even though the tendency to play the clarinet had become stronger than the tendency to eat under the conditions described.[2]

A third interesting case arises when $A\bar{c}B$, $A\bar{c}O$, and BcO. Again, we shall consider A the initial, ongoing activity at the beginning of the interval of

[2] When one considers the number of different activities with which eating is compatible, and how unlikely it is that the strength of Tendency to Eat is ever reduced to near zero, making food unavailable seems the only promising method of preventing obesity. The same recommendation, and for the same reasons, is suggested for those who seek to break the habit of constantly smoking cigarettes.

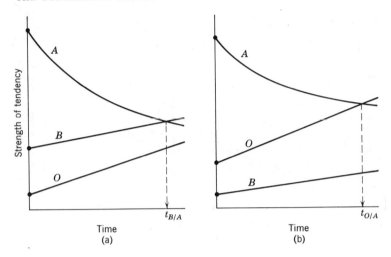

FIGURE 3.3 Examples of shift in activity from A to B under conditions where $A\bar{c}B$, $A\bar{c}O$, and $B\bar{c}O$. In (b) the shift in activity occurs even though $T_B < T_A$.

observation and B the activity of critical interest to the observer and the object of the latency measure. In this case, only activity A occurs prior to the change to activity B. The activity throughout the interval of observation is homogeneous. But the change to B may occur either because $T_B > T_A$ or because $T_O > T_A$. The pattern of incompatibility permits activity O to supplant activity A but, when this happens, activity B can also be initiated no matter what the relative strength of T_B as long as it has a magnitude above zero. Here is an instance where ostensibly, from the observer's viewpoint, there has been a change in activity from A to B but where $T_B < T_A$. The change has occurred because the overall hierarchy of strength of tendencies has shifted from $T_{A_I} > T_{O_I} > T_{B_I}$ or $T_{A_I} > T_{B_I} > T_{O_I}$ to $T_{O_F} > T_{A_F} > T_{B_F}$, which permits the paradoxical occurrence of activity B.

Figure 3.3 shows examples of this kind of change in activity. With the particular pattern of compatibilities among activities that is described, the latency of activity B is given by $t_{B/A} = (T_{A_F} - T_{B_I})/F_B$ when T_B dominates T_A (Figure 3.3a) or by $t_{B/A} = t_{O/A} = (T_{A_F} - T_{O_I})/F_O$ when T_O dominates T_A (Figure 3.3b). A fundamental problem of measurement is presented in this analysis since an observer cannot have complete assurance that a change in activity means that the tendency for the new activity he has observed and recorded is stronger than the one for the initial activity that it has replaced. Only if his observation and description of the change in activity is complete will he have recorded the initiation of the multiple activity B and O when activity A ceases. Then he will be in a position to recognize the possibility of erroneously concluding that T_B necessarily had attained dominance over T_A to produce the change.

A fourth and final case for the measurement of latency under complex, ideal conditions of multiple activity is when $A\bar{c}B$, AcO, and BcO. This reduces to the simple, ideal conditions described initially. Since activity O is compatible with both activity A and activity B, it will occur continuously but will not influence which of the two, A or B, will occur. Thus an individual may change from talking to a friend (A) to whistling a tune (B) while driving his automobile home from work (O). The determination of the change from activity A to B is made as if T_O and activity O were not present at all assuming, as we have throughout this discussion, that the several activities are functionally independent and, therefore, not complicated further by the problem of substitution.

The Effect of Compound Action Tendencies on Latency of Response

The analysis of the four different cases of complex conditions just considered made no mention of whether T_O, the complicating factor, was an elemental or compound action tendency. It can be either, and the implications for measurement of persistence of the initial activity or initiation of some other activity of critical interest to an observer are the same. But a case of special interest arises when T_O is a compound action tendency deriving its strength from two elemental action tendencies, one belonging to the same family as T_A and the other belonging to the same family as T_B. It will be recalled, from the discussion of displacement in Chapter 2, that an instigating force to undertake some specific activity (for example, F_A or F_B), may, in addition to increasing the strength of the tendency to engage in that particular activity (for example, T_A or T_B), have the effect of indirectly (by displacement) strengthening the tendency to engage in some other activity, for example, T_O. This may occur when there is some functional relationship between the several activities as, for example, when the indirectly strengthened tendency refers to some specific activity that is an alternative or substitute means to the same anticipated consequence or goal. It was then assumed that direct instigation to undertake an activity leading to an anticipated goal would normally function to increase, indirectly, the strength of a whole family of functionally related tendencies. Now we are able to see that the simple change of activity involving only two activities, the initial activity A and the one of interest B, which eventually replaces it, will often be complicated by the indirect instigation of a third activity O, which really represents simultaneous expression of the tendencies that are functionally related to both activity A and activity B. Under these circumstances, T_O could be nondominant within each of the two families of action tendencies and instigated only by the indirect or displaced forces derived from the direct instigating forces to undertake activity A and activity B (F_A and F_B). Yet the compound tendency (for example, $T_O = T_{O:A,B} = T_{O:A} + T_{O:B}$), which represents the summation or combined strength of two relatively weak elemental action tendencies that can be expressed in the very same activity O, could dominate either or both T_A and T_B because of the compounding. Thus activity O may approximate what in the Freudian psychology is often referred to as an overdetermined "compromise" between two otherwise incompatible activities. For example, a student wants to study alone in his room to achieve but also wants to go with friends for a beer. Instead of doing either one, he may go to the library and study in the company of others.[3] Sometimes, from the viewpoint of an external observer, an individual engaged in this kind of activity O, who is doing neither A nor B (as the observer has defined these activities), may be engaged in an activity that the observer would ordinarily call "making up his mind" or, perhaps more adequately, "deciding."

Persistence of an Activity under Complex, Ideal Conditions

The symmetry between latency of activity B and the persistence of activity A is lost as we move from the simplest, ideal conditions to more complex conditions. When there is a third activity to be taken into account, the cessation of activity A ($t_{\text{not } A/A}$) no longer necessarily corresponds to the initiation of activity B ($t_{B/A}$). Nor does the initiation of activity B necessarily signify that activity A has just terminated. If $A\bar{c}B$, $A\bar{c}O$, and $B\bar{c}O$, or if $A\bar{c}B$, $A\bar{c}O$, and BcO, then activity A may be supplanted by either B or O, and both must be considered in deriving an expression for the time interval that corresponds to the persistence of activity A.

The persistence of A is the same as the latency of B [that is, $t_{\text{not } A/A} = t_{B/A} = (T_{A_F} - T_{B_I})/F_B$] if B supplants A, and persistence of A is the same as the latency of O [that is, $t_{\text{not } A/A} = t_{O/A} = (T_{A_F} - T_{O_I})/F_O$ if O supplants A.

On the other hand, when the conditions are such that $A\bar{c}B$, AcO, and BcO, activity A will persist until B is initiated. In this case, $t_{\text{not } A/A} = t_{B/A} = (T_{A_F} - T_{B_I})/F_B$.

Under still other conditions, when $A\bar{c}B$, AcO, and $B\bar{c}O$, activity A will continue until activity B is initiated. But for this to occur, T_B must dominate both T_A and T_O. Thus, the time spent engaging in activity A is given by $t_{\text{not } A/A \text{ and } O} = t_{B/A \text{ and } O} = (T_{A_F} - T_{B_I})/F_B$ if $T_A > T_O$ but is given by $t_{\text{not } A/A \text{ and } O} = t_{\text{not } O/A \text{ and } O} = t_{B/A \text{ and } O} = (T_{O_F} - T_{B_I})/F_B$ if $T_O > T_A$.

---

[3] This conception of a "compromise" may embrace instances of so-called novel or creative response which are infrequent because they are definitely subordinate in each of several different families of tendency and so only occur under unique conditions of conflict.

In the latter case, it is worth noting that the persistence of activity A can be prolonged by a dominant T_O even though $T_B > T_A$ because activity A but not activity B is compatible with activity O.

Further Consideration of Choice under More Complex Conditions

Our preliminary consideration of the basic two-alternative choice situation involved only three activities, all mutually incompatible. The further analysis now to be undertaken will include these three activities that are inherent in even the simplest instance of choice (activity A, the initial ongoing activity, and activities X and Y, the two critical alternatives) plus a fourth, the other irrelevant activity O.

If activity O is compatible with activities A, X, and Y, it simply occurs continually and the determination of the choice will be whatever it would have been had T_O not been present. If activity O is incompatible with activities A, X, and Y, it may supplant activity A before either X or Y and become the ongoing activity preceding the choice of interest to the observer. As long as the observer is focusing his attention on the choice of X or Y, the addition of an incompatible activity O will not directly affect preference for X or Y under ideal conditions.[4] This conclusion holds true also when activity O is incompatible with X and Y but is compatible with A, and when activity O is incompatible with A but compatible with both X and Y. Under these several circumstances, T_O has no selective influence that would disturb the otherwise predicted occurrence of X or Y.

However, two other patterns of incompatibility do make an important difference. If activity O is incompatible with the initial activity A and incompatible with only one of the alternatives, Y, considered in the choice (for example, $A\bar{c}O$, $Y\bar{c}O$, but XcO), a choice of X will occur either because $T_X > T_A$ and $T_X > T_Y$, or because $T_O > T_A$ and $T_O > T_Y$ even though $T_X < T_Y$. The latter condition will yield the choice of X because the dominant activity O is initiated, eliminating the possibility of the incompatible activity Y but permitting the compatible activity X.

Finally, if activity O is compatible with activity A and with either activity X or Y but not both, the choice will also be affected. Let us assume the following conditions: AcO, XcO, $Y\bar{c}O$. In this case, X will be chosen as soon as $T_X > T_A$ and either $T_X > T_Y$ or $T_O > T_Y$. But Y will be chosen only when $T_Y > T_A$, $T_Y > T_X$, and $T_Y > T_O$. The opposite bias in choice

---

[4] This would not be true if there were some asymmetry in the functional relatedness of O to X and Y (that is, differential substitution). Also, the irrelevant initial activity O may have some indirect influence on the choice because $T_O > T_A$ implies greater gaps between the tendency sustaining activity in progress and the inertial tendencies for alternatives X and Y. Generally, this kind of change tends to favor choice of the alternative instigated by the strongest force (see pp. 108, 109).

results when activity O is compatible with A and Y but is incompatible with O.

BEHAVIORAL EFFECTS IN EXPERIMENTAL APPROXIMATIONS OF THE SIMPLE, IDEAL CASE

As a first step toward bridging the gap between this conceptual analysis of the determinants of latency, persistence, and choice and the behavioral measures that would actually be employed to appraise the strength of instigating forces, let us consider the kind of experimental error that could be attributed to the uncontrolled effects of some irrelevant activity O even when an investigator has taken great pains to produce conditions that approximate the simplest ideal case of change of activity. We must assume that he has achieved adequate control over T_A and T_{X_I} and can hold these variables constant in a number of diagnostic tests of individual differences in reaction to the same stimulus situation or successive reactions of the same individual (as in the study of learning). His investigation yields measures of latency of activity X, or measures of persistence of activity A, or measures of preference for alternative X versus alternative Y in a simple instance of two-alternative choice. His intention is to infer the strength of the instigating force to engage in activity X from a number of behavioral observations under constant conditions.

How might the obtained results be influenced by an uncontrolled, irrelevant activity O? How will the results depart from the theoretical expectations advanced earlier for the simplest, ideal cases if he were to assume that there were random variations in factors that determine the strength of T_O and that the compatibility relations between an activity O and the other activities inherent in the change of activity paradigm or two-alternative choice paradigm varied over observations?

Tables 3.1 and 3.2 begin to answer these questions. They describe the various compatibility relations between the irrelevant activity O and the other essential activities, and they identify the nature of the departure from theoretical expectation for the simple, ideal case and the specific occasions in which this departure would occur.

The summary presented in Table 3.1 shows that sometimes the uncontrolled effects of the intrusive activity O serve to increase and sometimes to decrease the time measurements that would be expected when the instigating force for activity X (F_X) had a certain magnitude. Thus the simple generalization that the latency of activity X (or persistence of activity A) is inversely proportionate to the strength of instigating force for activity X is sometimes violated. Sometimes, the time measurement overestimates the magnitude of F_X because of this experimental error. Sometimes, the time measurement underestimates the magnitude of F_X because of this experimental error. Can we identify with greater precision the conditions under which these departures from theoretical expectation are most likely to occur?

If our observer has attained a moderately good approximation of the simple and ideal condition, as we have assumed, it is reasonable to assume further that the average strength of T_O is relatively weak. It is not, in other

TABLE 3.1   The Departures from Theoretical Expectation for the Simple, Ideal Case that Are Attributable to Uncontrolled Effects of a Third, Irrelevant Activity O in an Experimental Approximation of the Simple, Ideal Condition for a Change of Activity from A to X

COMPATIBILITY RELATIONS AMONG ACTIVITIES	MEASURE OF LATENCY OF ACTIVITY X	MEASURE OF PERSISTENCE OF ACTIVITY A
Heterogeneous Activity		
1. $A\bar{c}O$ and $X\bar{c}O$	Increased when $T_O > T_A$	Decreased when $T_O > T_X$
Multiple Activity		
2. AcO and XcO	No effect	No effect
3. AcO but $X\bar{c}O$	Increased when $T_O > T_A$	Increased when $T_O > T_A$
4. $A\bar{c}O$ but XcO	Decreased when $T_O > T_X$	Decreased when $T_O > T_X$
Compound action tendency: T_O derived from instigation of A and X	Any of the above	Any of the above

words, an obviously intrusive activity or the experimenter would have noticed activity O and would have taken further steps to minimize its occurrence in his experiment. If T_O is assumed to be relatively weak generally, although varying randomly in magnitude about some average value in a number of instances in which F_X has the same magnitude, we can describe more fully the conditions under which the departure from theoretical expectation is most likely.

Consider first the column concerning the measure of the latency of activity X. The error introduced by activity O for cases 1 and 3 is an increase in the latency of X when $T_O > T_A$. If T_O itself is relatively weak, as here presumed, then T_A must also be weak in these instances. This particular departure from theoretical expectation could be minimized by the construction of procedures for measuring the latency of activity X under conditions in which T_A is quite strong. In other words, if latency of X is to be employed as a measure of the variable F_X, we are led by this analysis to the prescription of a condition in which the initial activity A is sustained by a strong tendency, T_A.

The other error in measurement introduced by irrelevant activity O (case 4) will still occur and, particularly, when T_X is very weak and T_O (though relatively weak) is still able to dominate T_X, that is, $T_O > T_X$. This will

TABLE 3.2   The Departures from Theoretical Expectation for the Simplest, Ideal Case of Two-Alternative Choice Involving an Initial Activity A and Two Alternatives X and Y that Are Attributable to Uncontrolled Effects of a Fourth Irrelevant Activity O in an Experimental Approximation of the Simple Case

COMPATIBILITY RELATIONS AMONG ACTIVITIES	MEASURE OF PREFERENCE
Heterogeneous Activity	
1. $O\bar{c}A$, $O\bar{c}X$, $O\bar{c}Y$	No effect except increased decision time on some occasions
2. OcA, $O\bar{c}X$, $O\bar{c}Y$	No effect except increased decision time on some occasions
Multiple Activity	
3. $O\bar{c}A$, $O\bar{c}Y$, but OcX	Increased preference for X when $T_O > T_Y$
4. $O\bar{c}A$, $O\bar{c}X$, but OcY	Increased preference for Y when $T_O > T_X$
5. $O\bar{c}A$, OcX, OcY	No effect except decreased decision time on some occasions
6. OcA, OcX, $O\bar{c}Y$	Increased preference for X when $T_O > T_Y$
7. OcA, OcY, $O\bar{c}X$	Increased preference for Y when $T_O > T_X$

often occur when F_X is very weak, but even then it would be less likely to happen if T_{X_I} were relatively strong. Hence, we arrive at another prescription for experimental conditions that employ latency as the measure of the variable F_X: a strong inertial tendency to engage in that activity (T_{X_I}).

In summary, we conclude that the simplest, ideal conditions for the use of latency of response to measure the strength of the instigating force to engage in an activity that is produced by the immediate stimulus situation is best approximated (1) when there is a strong tendency sustaining the initial activity (T_A), and (2) when there is also a relatively strong inertial tendency to engage in the critical activity (T_{X_I}).

Now let us consider the column that refers to the measure of persistence remembering that our present intention is to employ time to the cessation of activity A as a measure of the strength of F_X. Again, in cases 1 and 4, we confront departures from the theoretical expectation that are most likely to occur when T_X is very weak (that is, when $T_O > T_X$) which can be minimized by experimental conditions in which T_{X_I} is strong. And another departure from theoretical expectation (case 3) is most likely when T_A is relatively weak. This can be minimized, as already suggested, by experimental conditions in which T_A is strong. Therefore, our earlier prescription for the most adequate conditions for the measurement of the instigating force of a stimulus (F_X) by using latency of X holds true also for the use of persistence of the initial activity as the behavioral measure.

By looking now at Table 3.2 for a summary of the departures from the theoretical expectation for the simplest, ideal case of two-alternative choices that are attributable to uncontrolled effects of an intrusive activity O, we find that sometimes there is an unwarranted preference for X and sometimes an unwarranted preference for Y, that is, a departure from theoretical expectation based on the relative strengths of F_X and F_Y under controlled conditions of T_A, T_{X_I}, and T_{Y_I}. The unwarranted preferences for X in cases 3 and 6 are likely to occur when T_X is very weak and T_O (although itself assumed to be relatively weak) dominates T_X. The unwarranted preferences for Y in cases 4 and 7 are likely to occur when T_Y is very weak and is dominated by the relatively weak T_O.

Once again, we are led to the prescription of strong inertial tendencies $(T_{X_I}$ and $T_{Y_I})$ for the critical activities as an experimental condition most likely to approximate the simple, ideal conditions of choice. And since T_A must initially dominate the tendencies to engage in both alternatives, we are led to the further prescription of a condition in which a strong tendency sustains the initial activity (T_A) when choice is to be employed as the method for measuring the relative strengths of the two instigating forces.

The general recommendations for approximation of the simplest case of change of activity that follow from our analysis depart significantly from the traditional practice of trying to minimize the possibility of what is here called the initial activity in progress, so that it can be ignored. But it would be premature to pursue the matter of appropriate conditions for the measurement of tendencies or forces before taking into account the ways in which the conditions of actual behavioral events depart from the ideal conditions thus far assumed. We have observed that actual conditions are likely to be more complex than the simplest case we have emphasized in introducing the principles. In the next chapter, we must determine what is needed to bridge the gap between these ideal conditions that make theoretical analysis relatively easy and the much less than ideal conditions of actual events. Our aim is constant: to spell out what theoretical inferences can be made from the kinds of observations and measurements it is possible to make.

SUMMARY

The simplest case of change of activity is one in which the initial activity is unitary (rather than multiple) and homogeneous (rather than heterogeneous). The activity that supplants it is also unitary and functionally independent of the initial activity. And both of these activities are motivated by elemental (rather than compound) action tendencies. By multiple activity is meant simultaneously engaging in two or more compatible activities. By heterogeneous activity is meant an interval of observation in which there is a change from the activity that was initially in progress to some other irrelevant activity before the initiation of the critical activity that interests the observer. By compound tendency is meant one that represents the summation of separate elemental action tendencies all of which have in common the immediate next step in activity. By functionally independent is meant that the tendencies motivating the two activities belong to different families so that there is no substitution.

The conditions of the simplest case are considered *ideal* theoretical conditions when it can be assumed that F_A, F_B, and c_A remain constant during the interval of observation; and the exposure of the individual to F_A and F_B is continuous during the interval of observation. The analysis of the simplest, ideal case shows that the time taken to change from one activity to another stands as a measure of the persistence of the activity in progress as well as of the latency of the alternative response. The two classic problems in the psychology of motivation—initiation of an activity and persistence of an activity—are seen to be the two sides of the single problem of a change in activity. Several simple "laws" can be derived: for example, the latency of response is inversely proportionate to the magnitude of the instigating force; the ratio of the latencies for two activities is equal to the reciprocal of the ratio of the magnitudes of the instigating forces for the two activities. These laws provide models of the kind of generalization we shall seek as we move ahead and confront the theoretical complexities of actual behavioral events.

The first complexity of theoretical interest is the intrusion of an irrelevant activity in the simple change from one to another activity or in the choice between two new alternatives. The issue of importance becomes the compatibility of this irrelevant activity with the initial activity in progress and the alternative activity or activities (in choice). The dominance of the tendency for this irrelevant activity can (given certain compatibility relations among the several tendencies) produce a change from activity A to activity X even when $T_A > T_X$, or a choice of alternative Y even when $T_X > T_Y$. Thus, it is essential to identify the conditions under which this might lead to erroneous inferences from behavioral observations about the magnitudes of instigating forces or action tendencies. The analysis is pursued to the point of showing that the conceptual analysis of the dynamics of action may produce some new specifications for optimal conditions of measurement of the behavior-inducing properties of the immediate stimulus situation.

The chapter as a whole is an exercise in the use of concepts and assumptions already advanced in reference to the question of what theoretical inferences can be made from the measures of the latency of response, the persistence in an activity, and the preference among alternatives. It serves to introduce another fundamental problem which we now consider: the conditions of actual behavioral events are not the ideal conditions that have been assumed in the analysis to this point. In the next chapter, we shall try to bridge the gap between the unreal world of ideal theoretical conditions and the real world of behavior for which there must be nearly as much theory about the nature of the conditions as there is about the underlying dynamics of the motivational process.

CHAPTER 4

FROM THE IDEAL CASE TO ACTUAL BEHAVIOR

In two previous chapters we began to confront some of the complexities in a change of activity and to observe how the basic principles of change in strength of tendency and change of activity apply under various complex but still ideal conditions. This analysis began to define the extent of the discrepancy between the simplest ideal cases, in terms of which mathematical models make obvious sense, and actual empirical instances of behavioral change that yield the traditional measures of latency of response, persistence, and choice. The logic of our scheme, when applied to simple and ideal conditions, leads to some simple generalizations—for example, the reciprocal relationship between the strength of the instigating force and the latency of response. Yet observations of actual behavior rarely seem to justify anything that simple and neat. Our aim in this chapter—and we should not lose sight of it—is to appreciate why these simple relationships may not be any more apparent in actual behavioral events than the theoretical expectation of an equal acceleration of heavy and light objects in a free fall is apparent when one watches a feather and a bowling ball dropped from a window. An intrusive activity X, or some other complexity, or a departure from ideal conditions can function to mask what is expected in a simple change of activity just as the resistance of air pressure functions to mask an equivalence implied by a basic principle of physics for the simple and ideal condition.

It is but a step from a description of some of the possible complexities in conditions (for example, substitution, compatibility-relations, etc.) to an acknowledgement of how often the observer is not able to state, with the precision required, the conditions that actually exist for the subject he studies in a given behavioral event. We have observed how the measure of latency (or persistence) will be systematically influenced by functional relationships among the several activities. And sometimes these measures will be longer or shorter than is expected for an instigating force of given magnitude when the logic of the simple idealized case is applied but there is an uncontrolled tendency to engage in an irrelevant activity.

If we were to imagine a number of replications of change of activity with experimentally defined and fixed magnitudes of T_A, T_{B_l}, and F_B that are complicated by an uncontrolled, intrusive activity O, whose compatibility relations with the other essential activities are assumed to vary, and in which T_O is assumed to vary randomly in magnitude from one instance to the next, we could also imagine what the distribution of *obtained* measures of $t_{B/A}$ would be like. Instead of N different time measurements that are exactly equivalent, there would be a distribution of latencies, including those instances identified earlier in Table 3.1 that are longer or shorter than the theoretical expectation. If the magnitude of F_B were then to be fixed at some greater magnitude for another sample of N replications, there would be another distribution of obtained measures of $t_{B/A}$, but this time the average $t_{B/A}$ would be smaller than before. Now suppose that the very same experiment had been performed but that the observer had no prior knowledge about the relative strengths of $(F_B)_1$ and $(F_B)_2$. What theoretical inference could be made from the observation that the average $(t_{B/A})_1 >$ the average $(t_{B/A})_2$? Obviously, it is that $(F_B)_2 > (F_B)_1$. This is a very weak form of measurement of the relative strength of the instigating force produced by two stimuli. Nevertheless, even this is enough to provide a foundation for discovering, through empirical research, the various factors that influence the strength of an instigating force. The basic principles together with more specific assumptions about the nature of conditions will allow a more adequate specification of the expected behavioral consequence. Our aim is to arrive at such a set of tenable operating assumptions.

To do this, we must enlarge our conception of the discrepancy between the simplest ideal conditions and the complex, nonideal conditions of actual behavioral events. In the last two chapters we were concerned only with the effects of slight differences in the complexity of otherwise ideal conditions. Now, we must look hard at the extent to which the conditions of actual behavioral events, whether relatively simple or more complex in terms of the number of different variables to be considered, depart from the requirements of an ideal case. Can it be assumed that F_A, F_B, and c_A have fixed magnitudes during the interval of observation? Can it be assumed that the subject of study is continuously exposed to F_A, F_B, and any other F_X during the interval of observation, and to C_A when, and only when, activity A is said to be in progress? These specifications were the several stated ones for theoretically ideal conditions.

The Fallibility of the Observer

In the description of any concrete instance of a change of activity, the observer defines the stimulus situation to which the subject is exposed during an interval of observation. For example, a rat is placed in the start box of a maze. This constitutes what the observer defines as S. This immediate environment, and the various discriminative stimuli that comprise it, constitute the source of the instigating forces. To assume that F_A and F_B (and F_X in a complex instance) have fixed magnitudes during an interval of observation is to assume that S is constant and that there is no learning, that is, no change in the magnitude of the instigating force produced by any particular discriminative stimulus during this interval. To assume that c_A (one determinant of C_A) has a fixed magnitude is to assume that another possible kind of learning, namely, a change in the consummatory value of the activity, has not occurred during the interval of observation. They appear to be tenable assumptions. But what about the additional assumptions that pertain to the exposure of the individual to the instigating forces of the stimulus situation and the consummatory force of the activity in progress?

The principles advanced in Chapter 1 are formulated from the perspective of an external observer. He defines when an individual is exposed to S and when he is engaging in activity A. And this, in turn, is taken as the duration of exposure to F_A, F_B, and C_A. We must evaluate his ability to do this job of accurately defining the duration of the exposure to the several forces. Essentially, it is a problem in the validity of his coding of what is happening.

We can appreciate immediately the possibility of oversimplification in the assumption that the duration of S defines the duration of F_B by pointing out the error an observer might make in supposing that an individual with a cold or nasal allergy had been tempted to eat (F_B) by the aroma from a steak being broiled over charcoal (S) in his immediate vicinity. Not much different is the case of an individual who, not once during the interval of observation, has attended to a particular visual stimulus that is part of the complex called S by an observer. The problem, in brief, is that an observer reads his clock in reference to the beginning and the end of S and activity A as defined by himself, but that the principles advanced have to do with the duration of an individual's exposure to F_A, F_B and to C_A.

Until now, it appears that we have implicitly assumed a species of individuals who are infinitely sensitive to all potential energy changes at their receptors that are contained within an observer's definition of S. We have treated the subject as if he had eyes in the back as well as the front of his head and had no limit in his channel capacity for processing sensory information. This description fits neither the man nor the animal we have in mind in our examples. It is interesting to speculate about the possibility that it may fit certain species more than others. Our assumption of ideal conditions (or perhaps of an ideal organism) has excluded the whole problem of selective attention.

Change in Activity: A Transition Not an Abrupt Shift

On the response side, our presumption that the duration of the consummatory force corresponds to the duration of an activity as defined by an observer probably overestimates the degree to which he can determine definitively, instead of only approximately, what is going on. In light of our conception of families of functionally related tendencies and the compatibility of various overt and covert tendencies in the same family, it perhaps presumes too much to believe that, when an observer sets a criterion for coding the initiation and the cessation of a particular activity, he has defined exactly the duration of the consummatory force of that activity. A change in activity is more likely to be a transition from the involvement in one activity to the involvement in another instead of the abrupt shift that we have thus far pictured. When, for example, there is a change in the activity of a professor from working at his desk to walking into the coffee room, there are molecular aspects of the gross change in activity that suggest a transition from one to the other comparable to what is even more evident in the transition that occurs when the professor changes jobs. Months before he actually accepts an offer for a new position, he may be thinking about the possibility. And even after the decision to accept is made, he continues to meet his present responsibilities and to complete ongoing tasks even as he begins to lay plans for new endeavors and the move to a new place. At what particular point would an external observer say that the professor had changed from one job to the other? The concept of a family of functionally related action tendencies, coupled with the idea that the tendencies for activities that are compatible with the dominant one will also be expressed, suggests that in slow motion and under a microscope the gross change in overt activity that is noted by an observer would appear as *a transition that involves a change in the dominance relationship of two different families of tendencies and a changing pattern of compatibility relationships.* Thus the professor at work at his desk may begin to think about going to the coffee room even as he finishes writing a paragraph. And, as he stands and begins to leave his desk, he may continue to read what he has just written and to think about the next topic even as he walks "absent-mindedly" out of his office and across the hall to join his colleagues for coffee.

We can bring the problems that arise in our initial specification of ideal conditions into better focus, and can determine the steps to be taken toward a more tenable set of operating assumptions for actual behavior, by applying the principles thus far discussed only in reference to a single change of activity to the more general problem of a sequence of changes of activity in a constant environment. How do the assumptions about ideal conditions stand up in reference to the continuous stream of behavior? What new issues arise that we did not have to confront in the analysis of a simple change of activity?

THE PROBLEM OF BEHAVIORAL CHATTER

Let us look carefully at what the principle of change in the strength of a tendency has to say about the fate of tendencies in the time interval that envelopes the simplest change in activity. At any point in time prior to the change in activity, the tendency for the ongoing activity (T_X), which is both instigated and expressed, is moving toward its asymptotic strength as defined by F_X/c_X (see Equation 1.11 and Figure 1.5). The tendency for the alternative activity (T_Y), being instigated but not expressed, is increasing in strength linearly (see Equation 1.7 and Figure 1.3). As soon as a change in activity occurs, the tendency for the *new* ongoing activity Y will immediately begin to move toward its asymptotic level while the tendency for the *new* alternative activity X will immediately begin to grow linearly. This will result in T_X regaining dominance over T_Y, implying a change in activity back to X, at which point T_Y will grow linearly and T_X will resume its path to asymptote until T_Y once again becomes dominant. It is easy to see that the alternating dominance, first $T_X > T_Y$ then $T_Y > T_X$ then $T_X > T_Y$ again, will continue indefinitely. At the same time, however, after one or, at most, two changes in activity, the reversals in dominance between T_X and T_Y will take place in an infinitely short interval of time, implying infinitely fast alternations between the two activities and suggesting a kind of behavioral chatter.[1] Since the theory about the dynamics of action together with the assumptions that define ideal conditions predicts a phenomenon that does not typically occur when an individual is behaving in a constant environment, we are forced to undertake a critical examination of how adequately these assumptions depict the conditions of actual behavioral events.

We now can appreciate that the infinitely sensitive organism we have implicitly assumed must have long since become extinct if our principles concerning the dynamics of action are sound. He would have suffered the consequence of a chronic inability to concentrate long enough in the activities essential for his survival. And we can imagine that another organism, at

---

[1] The implication from the theory that the two tendencies will reverse in dominance at an infinite rate arises because at the point in time when one tendency catches up to the other the rate of growth of the tendency for the ongoing activity must be less than the one for the alternative activity; otherwise, the subdominant tendency could never gain the level of the dominant tendency. Mathematical details concerning this problem can be found in the notes at the end of this chapter.

the opposite pole, must also have become extinct. This organism is one cap-able of receiving and of processing the stimulation for only one activity at a time—the activity already in progress. This organism would have perished from overconcentration, the single-minded and uninterrupted pursuit of his initial interest in life, whatever it was.

We begin, then, with a realization that the behavior we seek to explain is emitted by an organism whose sensitivity and channel capacity falls between these extremes. The question of differences among species is a particularly interesting one suggested for later analysis. The problem of paramount interest for our present purpose is selective attention.

Selective Attention

The first assumption to come into question is that the stimuli to which an individual is exposed, and therefore the instigating forces F_A and F_B, are constant and continuous throughout the interval in which a change of activity occurs. How likely is this?

Under many, if not most instances of behavior, there should be a continu-ous exposure to the instigating force (F_A) that supports the activity in progress because an integral aspect of an activity in progress is orientation toward relevant features of the environment with which the individual is having commerce and the constant attention to stimuli which produce the instigating force for that activity. But as a result of this, attention is selective. Because an individual is already engaged in one activity and not some other, he is oriented toward the manipulanda and discriminanda that produce the instigating force for that activity and, as a result, may be oriented away from exposure to the stimuli that produce the instigating force to engage in some other activity. An individual who is eating, for example, is continually exposed to the instigating force to eat produced by the sight, smell, and taste of food. And one engaged in an achievement-oriented activity normally has the work to be done immediately before him. Another individual engaged in affiliative activity is in constant and continuous contact with a friend, and so on. Because of this selective orientation and selective attention, *which is itself an inherent aspect of engaging in an activity and often the first behavioral symptom of an activity*, there will generally tend to be a less than systematic and continuous exposure to the instigating forces that are produced by other discriminative stimuli in the immediate environment that is described as constant by the observer. An exposure to these other instigating forces, therefore, is more likely to be aperiodic and incidental during the interval of observation (see Figure 1.3) except, perhaps, when special measures are taken, such as the use of an auditory stimulus instead of a visual stimulus, to produce F_B. The issue here is the general question of the motivational significance of differences between the various senses of an organism, and the differences between species in the extent to which the selective orientation of receptors is essential for an effective contact with the environment. Some receptors require more selective orientation (for example, the eyes), others less (for example, the ears).

At this particular point in our analysis of an empirical instance of a change of activity we confront, head on, some of the fundamental problems in perception. For the concept of an instigating force to overt action, which we have treated as the functional significance of a stimulus for action, is *post* perceptual. It presumes that some feature of what Lewin referred to as the *geographic* environment, that is, the environment as defined by an observer, is being perceived by the subject and, therefore, is included in his immediate *psychological* environment. The concept of the instigating force to action refers to the behavioral implications of this perceptual process, as shown schematically in Figure 2.2*b*, but without necessarily implying conscious awareness. The instigating force to action is mediated by a perceptual process, but the covert expression of the perceptual tendency (that is, the conscious perception of the stimulus) is considered a correlated event but not an essential one (see Ericksen, 1958).

To bridge the gap between ideal conditions, which presumes a continuous exposure to the several different instigating forces produced by discriminable features of the immediate environment (for example, S_1 and F_A for activity A and S_2 and F_B for activity B), and the actual conditions of empirical events, we offer the following operating assumption. *Exposure to the instigating force that sustains the dominant tendency being expressed in the activity in progress is normally more systematic and continuous than the exposure to the instigating forces that influence subordinate tendencies.* The latter is normally more incidental or aperiodic except, of course, when special steps are taken to overcome the bias produced by the selective attention of the subject. This implies that a change in activity is always characterized by a systematic shift in attention from stimuli that are inherently related to the initial activity to stimuli that are inherently related to the activity which supplants it. And, as already suggested, the shift in attention will most often be the harbinger of the more gross change in activity.

The assumption that selectivity in attention is an inherent aspect of engaging in a particular activity tends to give an additional advantage to the dominant behavioral tendency. It serves as an additional conservative factor on the side of resistance to a change of activity. The assumption serves to expand our understanding of what it means to say that an individual is "involved" in a particular activity.

The assumption that the exposure to instigating forces that influence subordinate tendencies is normally more incidental and periodic than the exposure to instigating force for the dominant tendency means that, during

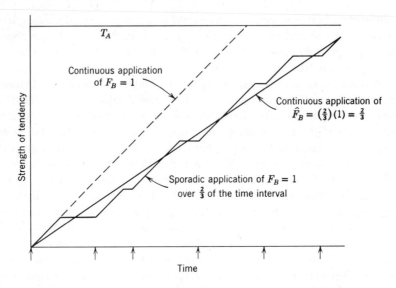

FIGURE 4.1   The actual effect of incidental exposure to an instigating force of a given magnitude, F_B, is equivalent to continuous exposure to a proportionately weaker instigating force $\hat{F}_B$.

the interval of observation, the actual effect of an F_B is equivalent to the one expected from a continuous exposure to a *weaker* instigating force. This is shown in Figure 4.1. The growth in T_B during an interval of observation in which there is only incidental, sporadic exposure to S_2 and, therefore, to F_B is shown to be equivalent to that produced by continuous exposure to a proportionately weaker instigating force for activity B. In order to proceed with our theorizing in terms of continuous exposure to the several instigating forces produced by S, the constant environment as described by an observer, we must assume that the *actual* magnitude of instigating force for an activity that is produced by a given stimulus is systematically stronger when the tendency for that activity is dominant than when it is subordinate. To make this distinction, we introduce the symbol $\hat{F}$ as the term for the magnitude of an instigating force for an activity whose tendency is nondominant while retaining F for the magnitude of an instigating force for an activity whose tendency is dominant. Thus, generally, $F > \hat{F}$.

In effect, we are assuming that even under so-called constant environmental conditions, a change in activity produces a change in instigation like—*but less dramatic than*—the one produced when the new activity actually removes the individual from geographic proximity to the stimuli for the original activity. The professor who leaves the desk at which he has been working when he initiates the activity of going to the coffee room has, as a direct consequence of this change of activity, changed the nature of S as it would be defined by an observer. The coffee room is certainly not the professor's office. He is now systematically exposed to stimuli that produce the instigating force for the affiliative activity of the coffee room, and he is physically removed from stimuli that produce the strongest instigating force to resume writing. At the same time, his tendency to work can reasonably be expected to persist as an inertial tendency, and, perhaps there will be sporadic instigation of it by "reminders" of work (for example, an open book on a table) as he chats. As the tendency to engage in affiliative discourse approaches its limit as defined by F/c (assuming there is substantial consummatory value), the professor may then "spontaneously" resume (that is, initiate again) the activity that had been interrupted. First, he will resume thought about his work, and then attention to the door, and then the steps back to his office. On the other hand, once his writing has been interrupted and he is no longer selectively attending to cues that produce the instigating force to engage in that activity, or is no longer in proximity to these relevant stimuli, he may incidentally be exposed to other stimuli that produce the instigating force to engage in still some third activity like taking a walk around the campus. This may reduce even more the probability of even incidental exposure to stimuli to resume work.[2]

A systematic change in the nature of the environment often occurs as a direct consequence of a change of activity. It is most obvious to an observer when the new activity involves locomotion from one place to another in the geographic environment. This kind of change in the nature of S, as defined by the observer, means that there is a systematic change in the nature and the strength of various instigating forces to which the individual is exposed. Our discussion of selective attention, when S is constant from the viewpoint of an observer, posits a "potential" set of instigating forces of fixed magnitude to which the individual may be either more systematically and continuously exposed or may be only incidentally and sporadically exposed depending on his orientation, as defined by the activity in progress, and other factors such

---

[2] One reader of an early draft was moved to comment: This absent-minded man is wandering around campus unlikely to go back to work. Perhaps, a traveling circus will come by, or a gypsy caravan, and he will run away and be forever removed from the dreary reminders of his former life!

We do not mean to suggest that this wandering away from an interrupted activity will always happen or even that it will happen most of the time. But it will happen some of the time and, we think, for the reason stated. Our reader was concerned with how the *planning* and *scheduling* of activities, which distinguishes human from animal behavior, is to be taken into account. And so are we. At this writing, we consider planning a covert conceptual activity of considerable motivational significance, although we have not, as yet, encompassed the topic in any systematic way.

as whether or not the exposure to a particular instigating force depends on orientation (for example, visual cues) or not (for example, auditory cues). It is quite obvious from everyday observation that one may gain the attention of a friend whose back is turned by calling his name but not by a wave of the hand.   Selectivity of attention works against the onset of behavioral chatter but neither eliminates it nor ameliorates it. Selective attention is one, but not the only nor even the most important factor operating against the difficulty implicit in the idealized case. The second factor is a time lag in the operation of the consummatory force of an activity.

Consummatory Lag

A second assumption that was made in reference to a simple change of activity now seems questionable when it is considered in the context of a sequence of the changes in activity in a constant environment. This is the presumption that in the simplest case (that is, when there is no substitution) the tendency supporting the ongoing activity is influenced by a consummatory force throughout the interval of observation, but the subordinate tendency is untouched by any consummatory effect. Consummatory force, as conceived, is dependent on the expression of a tendency in behavior. This is why no consummatory force was applied to the subordinate tendency in our initial analysis of the simplest change of activity. The earlier presumption now seems questionable for the reason stated somewhat earlier: the change in activity as observed and sharply defined by an observer is probably more accurately conceived as a transition that involves a change in the dominance relationship of two families of functionally-related tendencies. Therefore, it seems quite likely that there will often be a discrepancy between the time when an observer codes the initiation of a particular activity and the time when the full consummatory effect of that activity begins. The observer ordinarily will notice the appearance of some peripheral aspect of an activity—perhaps the orienting reactions that mark the shift of attention from one to another set of stimuli. In any case, it is likely to be an event that precedes the advent of a strong consummatory force. Consider, for example, the initiation of the activity of eating. An observer will begin to code the activity in progress as eating when the subject begins to have contact with the food. But this initial phase of the activity is essentially one of tasting. The consummatory value of eating does not become maximal until some time after that. A similar discrepancy will occur in the case of other kinds of activity. Consider the individual who begins to solve an arithmetic problem. An observer will code the initiation of this problem-solving activity when the individual begins the preliminary acts that define working on the problem, but the full consummatory value of the activity follows in the wake of these initial acts.

We shall assume now that such a delay between the initiation of an activity *as defined by an observer* and the onset of the consummatory process is a general phenomenon. We shall refer to it as a consummatory lag. Specifically, we assume that there is a period of time immediately following the initiation of any activity, as defined by an observer, during which the consummatory value of the activity is zero (that is, $c = 0$). This means, very simply, that there is no consummatory force during some interval immediately after the initiation of an activity. The duration of the consummatory lag at the initiation of an activity will be different for different activities. It will depend on the particular characteristics of the activity.

Also, there should be a consummatory lag at the cessation of an activity *as defined by an external observer*. Since the observer will code the initiation of one activity (and thus the termination of the other) in terms of peripheral symptoms, there is likely to be a similar discrepancy in time between this observer-defined cessation of the activity and the actual cessation of the consummatory force of the activity. The latter will continue for a time after the coded termination of the activity. It will be assumed that the consummatory force operating to reduce the tendency that had been sustaining the activity is not immediately reduced to zero when the change in activity is noticed by the observer but is extended into the interval in which the new activity is occurring.

The duration of the consummatory lag at the cessation of an activity can also be expected to vary among different activities. The tendency to eat continues to be affected by a consummatory force for quite some time following the cessation of the activity of eating, as an observer would define it, because the consummatory process continues well beyond the time when any more food is ingested. On the other hand, the success in solving an arithmetic problem probably has a much shorter consummatory lag. Although, even in this case, an appreciable period of time may be involved if the individual "basks" covertly in his success, that is, relives it in imagination, while overtly beginning to do something else. This possibility is taken account of theoretically by conceiving of the change in activity as a transition that involves a change in the set of compatible activities that occur simultaneously.

In summary, the assumptions of consummatory lag seem justified by the following important considerations:

Molar activities are really constellations of more molecular activities, and it is the pattern of compatibility-incompatibility relations among the latter that determines which tendencies will get expressed. For example, the professor's going to the coffee room involves the overt activity of getting up from his desk and walking across the hall but also certain covert activities that belong to the same family. Specific tendencies from more than one family will be expressed at the same time if they are compatible. This can cause a discrepancy between the observer's description of the initiation and the cessation of an activity and the actual initiation and cessation of the full consummatory force of that activity. For example, the professor may get up from his desk and begin to walk across the hall but may continue to think about what he has been writing until he reaches the coffee room. By coding the initiation and cessation of activities in terms of a limited set of symptoms or criteria that are easily noted, an observer does not take fully into account other molecular activities (particularly the ones that are covert) which may not be initiated and terminated at exactly the same time as the activities that are more easily seen. Sometimes, as in the case of both eating and drinking, a substantial part of the consummatory process that is responsible for the consummatory value of an activity may come after the termination of the activity as coded.

Having acknowledged that any assumption we now advance to correct the oversimplification of our initial view is itself no more than a first approximation, we shall proceed by making the simplest assumptions among the alternatives that suggest themselves. *The consummatory lag at the initiation of an activity is a period of time, t_i, immediately following the initiation of an activity as coded by an observer, during which the consummatory value of the activity is zero (that is, $c = 0$). The consummatory lag at the cessation of an activity is a period of time, t_c, immediately following the cessation of an activity as coded by an observer, during which the consummatory value of the activity continues to have an effect.*

Let us examine the implications of these assumptions about consummatory lag in reference to the problem of behavior chatter, while reserving the details of the algebraic manipulations for the notes at the end of the chapter. In Figure 4.2 the new assumptions about consummatory lag are combined with the new assumptions about selective attention. Consider first what happens to the strength of a tendency at the instant it becomes dominant. Such a tendency, T_X in Figure 4.2, has just begun to be expressed in activity X as defined by an observer. This means that a stronger force F_X is now operative than an instant before when the tendency was subordinate and influenced by $\hat{F}_X$. And there is a consummatory lag at the initiation of activity X, that is, $c_X = 0$ during the interval $(t_i)_X$. At the point of the change in activity, which we shall take as the beginning of our interval of observation, the tendency for the new activity X equals that of the earlier activity Y (that is, $T_{X_I} = T_{Y_I}$). This initial strength of T_X increases linearly during $(t_i)_X$ because there is no consummatory force and (it should be noticed) at a faster rate than it had increased prior to the shift in activity. At the end of the interval of the consummatory lag, $T_X = T_{X_I} + F_X \cdot (t_i)_X$. In the time period subsequent to $(t_i)_X$, T_X is affected by both F_X and $C_X = c_X \cdot T_X$, and, hence, moves steadily toward its asymptote of F_X/c_X according

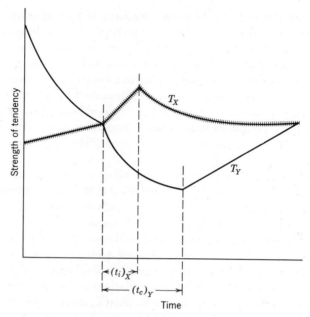

FIGURE 4.2   The change in strength of tendencies following a change in activity, taking into account the effects of selectivity in attention (that is, $\hat{F}_X$ to F_X and F_Y to $\hat{F}_Y$) and of consummatory lag at the initiation $(t_i)_X$ and cessation $(t_c)_Y$ of an activity.

to the now familiar function defined by Equation 1.11.[3] This segment of the path of T_X is also pictured in Figure 4.2 and extends until T_Y catches up to T_X at which point another shift in activity takes place and the interval of observation for a single change in activity ends.

In considering the fate of T_Y, the first thing to recognize is that this tendency was being both instigated and consumed as the dominant tendency just prior to the change in activity. The initial segment of its path in Figure 4.2 is also defined by Equation 1.11. Subsequent to the change from activity Y to activity X, and the assumed change in attention, T_Y is acted on by the weaker instigating force $\hat{F}_Y$ and, given our assumption of a consummatory lag at the cessation of an activity, the consummatory force $C_Y = c_Y \cdot T_Y$ continues to operate during the interval of the lag $(t_c)_Y$. Thus, for this interval $(t_c)_Y$, the trend of T_Y is toward a new and lower asymptote defined

[3] Specifically this equation becomes

$$T_X = [T_{X_I} + F_X \cdot (t_i)_X] \cdot e^{-c_X[t-(t_i)_X]} + \frac{F_X}{c_X}\{1 - e^{-c_X[t-(t_i)_X]}\}$$

where time t is measured from the beginning of the interval of observation (that is, from the point of shift in activity) and $(t_i)_X$ is the duration of the initiation consummatory lag.

by the ratio of the now weaker instigating force and the continued consummatory effect, that is, $\hat{F}_Y/c_Y$. The mathematical function that describes the path of the now subordinate T_Y remains Equation 1.11,[4] and an example of such a path is shown in Figure 4.2 for the interval $(t_c)_Y$. At the end of the interval of the consummatory lag, T_Y turns from its approach to asymptote and begins a linear growth in the manner described by Equation 1.7[5] until the next change in activity. During this interval of linear growth in T_Y, the magnitude of $\hat{F}_Y$ continues to be weaker than when T_Y is dominant (that is, $\hat{F}_Y < F_Y$). The next change in activity occurs when T_Y catches up to T_X and the pattern is repeated.

The introduction of these assumptions about consummatory lags makes the theory more complicated but more tenable in any confrontation with observations (or data) that concern a sequence of changes in activity in a constant environment. The problem of behavioral chatter is dealt with effectively. The two consummatory lags function to drive apart the tendencies for the two activities immediately following a change in activity, thereby, giving an increased advantage to the new ongoing activity and preventing an immediate reversal in the dominance relations of the two tendencies. The assumption concerning selective attention (that is, more continuous exposure and, therefore, a stronger force when a tendency becomes dominant) accentuates the separation of the tendencies immediately following the change in activity. The slope of the growth of the newly dominant tendency is greater than it had been an instant before the change, and the decline of the tendency that has just become subordinate is accentuated by the sudden decrease in the actual magnitude of the instigating force sustaining it. In brief, *the intervals of consummatory lag at the initiation and the cessation of an activity are characterized by sudden changes in the magnitude of the instigating forces and slow changes in the magnitude of the consummatory forces which, together, favor the activity in progress and prevent behavioral chatter.*

[4] For the cessation consummatory lag period $(t_c)_Y$, immediately following the shift in activity,

$$T_Y = T_{Y_I} \cdot e^{-c_Y \cdot (t_c)_Y} + \frac{\hat{F}_Y}{c_Y}[1 - e^{-c_Y \cdot (t_c)_Y}] \qquad (4.2)$$

where T_{Y_I} is the strength of the tendency for activity Y at the point of shift in activity $(T_{Y_I} = T_{X_I})$.

[5] Since our interval of observation begins with the point of shift in activity, T_{Y_I} must refer to the strength of tendency for activity Y at that point. Thus, the course of T_Y subsequent to the cessation consummatory lag interval is properly written

$$T_Y = \left\{ T_{Y_I} \cdot e^{-c_Y \cdot (t_c)_Y} + \frac{\hat{F}_Y}{c_Y}[1 - e^{-c_Y \cdot (t_c)_Y}] \right\} + \hat{F}_Y[t - (t_c)_Y] \qquad (4.3)$$

Given these new assumptions that concern the exposure to the instigating force of stimuli and the consummatory force of an activity, the
individual is no longer locked into almost instantaneous alternations between
the activities when S is constant. We can observe in Figure 4.2 that there will
now be a substantial interval between successive changes in activity depending, in part, on the duration of the consummatory lags and, in part, on the
several familiar variables that systematically control the time it takes to
change from one activity to another, namely, the relative magnitudes of the
instigating forces and the consummatory values of the different activities.

The analysis of a simple change in activity, introduced in Chapter 1,
must be qualified only slightly in light of the assumed effects of a lag in the
operation of the consummatory force of an activity. In a simple change of
activity, the interval of observation begins with activity A in progress and
ends when activity B supplants A. The strengths of the tendencies at the
beginning of the interval of observation are designated T_{A_I} and T_{B_I},
respectively, with $T_{A_I} > T_{B_I}$. If, by the time the interval of observation
begins, T_A and T_B have proceeded beyond their respective consummatory
lags, no modifications are required in the earlier theoretical analysis. If one
or another of the consummatory lags is contained within the observer's
interval of observation for a simple change of activity, and it is not taken into
account, the errors of interpretation could be large or small, serious or not,
depending on the size of parameter values, the purposes of the experiment,
and the magnitude of the effects to be expected. Fortunately, it should not
be difficult, in most cases, to arrange for simple shifts in activity so as to
minimize the perturbations introduced by consummatory lags. All that is
required is that the ongoing activity be in progress for an appreciable
period of time before the introduction of the instigating force for an alternative activity (a condition that would probably be met automatically by an
experimenter's procedures for establishing a well-defined ongoing activity)
and that the subject not have engaged in the alternative activity in the recent
past. By meeting the first requirement we are assured that the period of
initiation consummatory lag has passed. By meeting the second requirement
we are assured that cessation consummatory lag is past.

THE OPERANT LEVEL OF AN ACTIVITY

Our interest in a sequence of changes of activity in a constant environment
leads quite easily into the conceptual analysis of the dynamics of the rate of
an activity (or response) in a given situation that is conventionally employed
as a measure of the operant level of an activity. We can observe the rudimentary form of a derivation of the rate of response by considering the
special case in which the constant S contains S_1 and S_2 that produce the

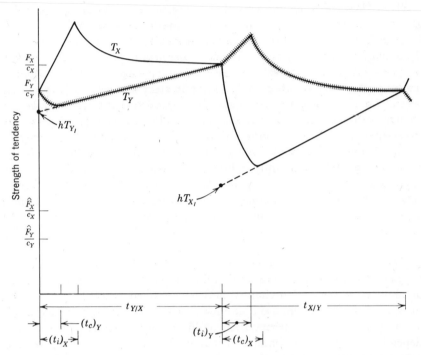

FIGURE 4.3   The details of the changes in strength of action tendencies in a free operant situation.

instigating force for activity X and activity Y, respectively. A sequence of changes from activity X to activity Y to activity X again is shown in Figure 4.3.

In addition to the usual assumptions concerning the constant magnitude of F_X, F_Y, c_X, and c_Y, and the new assumptions that concern selective attention and consummatory lag, we shall assume that there is no substitution and certain initial conditions. As shown in Figure 4.3, activity X has just been initiated as the interval of observation begins. At the time of this initial change of activity, T_Y sustaining activity Y has already approached close to F_Y/c_Y. And the assumed order of the magnitudes of the several instigating forces in the analysis is $F_X > F_Y > \hat{F}_X > \hat{F}_Y$ where $\hat{F}_X$ and $\hat{F}_Y$ represent the weaker magnitudes of the instigating force of S_1 and S_2 that are assumed when T_X and T_Y are not dominant.

At the point of the initial shift in activity, $T_X = T_Y = F_Y/c_Y$. First, let us follow the trend of T_X. During the interval of the *initiation* consummatory lag $(t_i)_X$, T_X grows linearly, $T_X = F_Y/c_Y + F_X \cdot (t_i)_X$. Thereafter, and until the next change of activity, T_X is exposed to the consummatory force of activity X and, hence, heads toward its asymptote F_X/c_X. At the end of the initiation consummatory lag $(t_i)_X$, the magnitude of T_X equals $F_Y/c_Y + F_X \cdot (t_i)_X$. Thus, according to Equation 4.1, the subsequent change in T_X is given by

$$T_X = \left[\frac{F_Y}{c_Y} + F_X \cdot (t_i)_X\right] \cdot e^{-cx[t_Y/x-(t_i)x]} + \frac{F_X}{c_X}\{1 - e^{-cx[t_Y/x-(t_i)x]}\} \quad (4.4)$$

This brings T_X to the point of the change from activity X to activity Y at $t_{Y/X}$ in Figure 4.3. We shall assume that the level of T_X is then approximately F_X/c_X.

Now let us return to the initial change from activity Y to activity X and trace the course of T_Y, which has just become the subordinate tendency. During the interval of the *cessation* consummatory lag, $(t_c)_Y$, T_Y continues to be exposed to the consummatory force of activity Y and there is the assumed loss in attention to S_2, treated by providing for the continuous exposure to the weaker force $\hat{F}_Y$. Beginning at the level F_Y/c_Y, at which it had already become stable, T_Y begins to decline toward the lower asymptote now defined by $\hat{F}_Y/c_Y$ according to Equation 4.2:

$$T_Y = \left(\frac{F_Y}{c_Y}\right) \cdot e^{-c_Y \cdot (t_c)_Y} + \frac{\hat{F}_Y}{c_Y}[1 - e^{-c_Y \cdot (t_c)_Y}] \quad (4.5)$$

Then, after the cessation consummatory lag when it is no longer exposed to any consummatory force, T_Y begins its linear growth defined by $\hat{F}_Y$. This continues until T_Y intersects T_X and the next change of activity occurs at $t_{Y/X}$. The magnitude of T_Y at the end of $(t_c)_Y$ is given by the equation above, and this becomes the initial level from which the subsequent linear growth is plotted according to Equation 4.3:

$$T_Y = \left\{\left(\frac{F_Y}{c_Y}\right)e^{-c_Y \cdot (t_c)_Y} + \frac{\hat{F}_Y}{c_Y}[1 - e^{-c_Y \cdot (t_c)_Y}]\right\} + \hat{F}_Y[t_{Y/X} - (t_c)_Y] \quad (4.6)$$

This brings us to the point of a change from activity X to activity Y at $t_{Y/X}$.

The first component of the above equation identifies the strength of T_Y at the end of the cessation consummatory lag $(t_c)_Y$. The second component tells us that T_Y will (because of $\hat{F}_Y$) grow linearly during the interval of time between the first and second changes of activity, $t_{Y/X}$, *except* during the interval of the cessation consummatory lag, $(t_c)_Y$, already taken into account by the first component. Hence, this early segment of the time interval is subtracted, $t_{Y/X} - (t_c)_Y$, to get the residual of the interval during which exposure to $\hat{F}_Y$ produces the linear growth.

It should be apparent that the above equation, which tells us the strength of T_Y at $(t_c)_Y$, is a stepping-stone back to a much more familiar one. We can extrapolate backward to the strength of a hypothetical $_hT_{Y_I}$, at the beginning of our interval of observation when we started our clock. We can do this by subtracting the quantity $\hat{F}_Y \cdot (t_c)_Y$ from the level of T_Y at $(t_c)_Y$. This recovers the hypothetical $_hT_{Y_I}$ as shown by the hatched line in Figure 4.3. Having done this, we can observe that a familiar expression about the growth of T_Y from this hypothetical point yields a result that is equivalent to the one shown in the equation above: $T_Y = {_hT_{Y_I}} + \hat{F}_Y \cdot t_{Y/X}$. Given this familiar expression for the change in strength of a subordinate tendency from the beginning of an interval of observation to the time of the change of activity, together with the assumption that the strength of the dominant tendency T_X has approached its limit F_X/c_X by the time $t_{Y/X}$ of the next change in activity, we may write

$$t_{Y/X} = \frac{T_{X_F} - {_hT_{Y_I}}}{\hat{F}_Y} = \frac{(F_X/c_X - {_hT_{Y_I}})}{\hat{F}_Y}$$

the familiar expression for a change of activity.[6]

As the change from activity X to activity Y occurs, we end the first time segment $t_{Y/X}$ and begin the new one $t_{X/Y}$ which ends with a later resumption of activity X as shown in Figure 4.3. We can repeat the analysis outlined above, first following the trend of the now dominant T_Y from a level defined by F_X/c_X (where the change occurred) through its linear growth during the initiation consummatory lag $(t_i)_Y$, followed by its decline toward F_Y/c_Y during the remainder of the interval $t_{X/Y}$ once it begins to be influenced by the consummatory force of activity Y. And we can repeat the earlier analysis for the newly subordinate tendency T_X. First, it declines toward a lower asymptote that results from the weaker instigating force $\hat{F}_X$ during the interval of the cessation consummatory lag $(t_c)_X$ during which the consummatory force continues. Then, it grows linearly during the remainder of the interval $t_{X/Y}$ at which time it again becomes the dominant tendency. By following the logic of the argument already advanced, this next change is accounted for by the equation

$$t_{X/Y} = \frac{T_{Y_F} - {_hT_{X_I}}}{\hat{F}_X} = \frac{(F_Y/c_Y) - {_hT_{X_I}}}{\hat{F}_X}$$

[6] An alternate way of writing the equation for $t_{Y/X}$, one that will prove more useful for certain of the comparisons to be made in Chapter 9, is as follows:

$$t_{Y/X} = \frac{T_{X_F} - (T_Y)_c}{\hat{F}_Y} + (t_c)_Y \tag{4.7}$$

This equation is arrived at by using Equation 4.6 and by letting

$$(T_Y)_c = \left\{ \left(\frac{F_Y}{c_Y}\right) e^{-c_Y \cdot (t_c)_Y} + \frac{\hat{F}_Y}{c_Y}[1 - e^{-c_Y \cdot (t_c)_Y}] \right\}$$

The sequence of changes in T_X and T_Y repeats itself indefinitely as long as S remains constant; hence, we can give our attention to the behavioral measure called the rate of response. The question of the rate of activity X is the question of how often activity X occurs in some total time period (t_{tot}). The time between one initiation of activity X and the next is $(t_{Y/X} + t_{X/Y})$ if we start measuring the interval just after activity X has been initiated as shown in Figure 4.3. Thus, we have measures of the total time period in seconds (t_{tot}) and the time required for one occurrence of activity X $(t_{X/Y} + t_{Y/X})$ from which we can compute the number of times activity X has occurred, that is, $n(X) = t_{tot}/(t_{X/Y} + t_{Y/X})$.

The *Rate of Activity X* equals $n(X)/t_{tot}$. By substituting for $n(X)$, we arrive at the following theoretical conclusion:

$$\text{Rate of Activity } X = r(X) = \frac{t_{tot}/(t_{X/Y} + t_{Y/X})}{t_{tot}} = \frac{1}{t_{X/Y} + t_{Y/X}} \quad (4.8)$$

Thus, we have established a relationship between the Latency of Response $(t_{X/Y})$ and the Rate of Response[7]

$$r(X) = \left(\frac{1}{t_{X/Y} + t_{Y/X}} \right)$$

It shows that the measure called rate of response, even more than the latency of response, is affected by the context in which a given activity is observed. In the present special case, it was assumed that S produced the instigating force for only one *other* activity—activity Y. We find that the rate of activity X depends as much on variables that influence the latency of activity Y as on the variables that influence its own latency. This means, in more general terms, that the rate of a particular activity in a given stimulus situation will be as much influenced by variables that control the strength of tendencies for all the competing activities as by variables that uniquely control the strength of the tendency sustaining it. Of particular interest, since it has been ignored in traditional discussions of factors that influence the rate of response, is the systematic effect of the consummatory values of the various activities. This is shown for the simple case of alternation between two activities by substituting the several determinants of $t_{X/Y}$ and $t_{Y/X}$ for these measurements in the above equation for $r(X)$:

$$r(X) = \frac{1}{t_{X/Y} + t_{Y/X}} = \frac{1}{\dfrac{F_Y/c_Y - {_hT_{X_I}}}{\hat{F}_X} + \dfrac{F_X/c_X - {_hT_{Y_I}}}{\hat{F}_Y}}$$

[7] The additional details of this derivation can be found in the notes at the end of the chapter.

TIME SPENT IN A GIVEN ACTIVITY IN A CONSTANT ENVIRONMENT

Another potentially useful behavioral measure is suggested by this analysis, namely, a measure of the proportion of time an individual spends engaging in one or another activity in a given stimulus situation. Look again at Figure 4.3. The measure of the time taken to initiate activity Y given that the individual has just begun to engage in activity X, namely, $t_{Y/X}$, is also a measure of the persistence of activity X or the time spent in activity X on this single occurrence. Similarly, $t_{X/Y}$ provides a measure of the time spent in activity Y on a single occurrence. The total amount of time that is spent engaging in activity X is $n(X) \cdot t_{Y/X}$. The total time that is spent engaging in activity Y is $n(Y) \cdot t_{X/Y}$. From this, we can obtain measures of the proportion of time spent in each of the two activities, that is,

$$\text{Proportion of time spent in activity } X = m(X) = \frac{n(X) \cdot t_{Y/X}}{t_{\text{tot}}}$$

$$m(X) = \frac{t_{\text{tot}}/(t_{X/Y} + t_{Y/X}) \cdot t_{Y/X}}{t_{\text{tot}}}$$

or

$$m(X) = \frac{t_{/YX}}{(t_{X/Y} + t_{Y/X})} \tag{4.9}$$

And, similarly,

$$m(Y) = \frac{t_{X/Y}}{(t_{X/Y} + t_{Y/X})} \tag{4.10}$$

In the special case of only two activities that we have assumed in order to explore the implications of our theory concerning the dynamics of action in reference to a sequence of activities in the same environment, the rate of the two different activities is equal, although the time spent in the two activities may differ substantially. Of course, it is possible to rewrite Equations 4.8 and 4.9 in terms of the parameters of the theory, as was done for $r(X)$. We shall let the reader to do that for himself.

The relationship between the time spent in each activity and the latency of each activity (given that the other is in progress) is particularly interesting for this special case: the ratio of the proportions of the time spent is the reciprocal of the ratio of the latencies. That is,

$$\frac{m(X)}{m(Y)} = \frac{\dfrac{t_{Y/X}}{t_{X/Y} + t_{Y/X}}}{\dfrac{t_{X/Y}}{t_{X/Y} + t_{Y/X}}}$$

or

$$\frac{m(X)}{m(Y)} = \frac{t_{Y/X}}{t_{X/Y}} \tag{4.11}$$

Although a more complex instance than the special case under discussion here, Allison's (1963) report of a negative correlation between the proportion of time a rat spent eating, when given an equal opportunity for affiliative commerce with another rat or with a piece of wire mesh on which it could climb, and the latency of its *initial* eating response is illustrative of the kind of lawful relationship we are led to expect between the measurements based on a single change of activity and more molar measurements taken from the gross stream of behavior. Allison's study points the way toward the systematic use of measurements of the time distribution among activities.

CHOICE

Having explored the implications of our assumptions that concern the selectivity in attention and the consummatory lag in reference to the spontaneous alternation and the distribution of time among activities in a constant environment, let us reconsider the several measures that can be obtained from a single change of activity or from the accumulation of results from a set of trials in which the strength of instigating forces has been held constant throughout.

There are several different ways in which choice data can be obtained. There can be a single observation of the choice between alternatives by each of a number of different individuals on one occasion. There can be a number of observations of the choice made by a single individual on each of a set of separate and widely spaced occasions. Finally, there can be repeated observations from the same individual on a single occasion with a relatively short interval between trials. We shall observe why these several paradigms are not to be considered theoretically equivalent.

Single Observation from Each of Many Individuals on One Occasion.   Recall the simple choice between two alternatives touched on earlier (see Chapter 3, pp. 73, 74, Figure 3.1). Assume, as before, that there is no tendency for an irrelevant fourth activity whose compatibility relations with the critical activities X and Y complicate the picture. Assume further that the presentation of the critical stimuli to undertake activities X and Y does not occur until after the termination of the cessation consummatory lag that follows the last occurrence of each of the activities. The incident of interest is one in which $F_X > F_Y$ and the magnitudes of the two instigating forces are uniform across all the different individuals whose choices on the one occasion are observed.

Our assumption concerning selectivity in attention, namely, that exposure to instigating forces which influence subordinate tendencies is less continuous during the interval of observation, implies that $\hat{F}_X < F_X$ and $\hat{F}_Y < F_Y$ but that generally $\hat{F}_X/\hat{F}_Y = F_X/F_Y$.[8] For any individual, the choice of X or Y on the single occasion will depend on which of the two activities is initiated first. The critical question becomes: *For which activity would the theoretical latency of response be shorter in a single stimulus presentation?* We shall use $(t_{X/A})'$ and $(t_{Y/A})'$ to represent these theoretical latencies of response.

Activity X will be chosen *except when* $(t_{X/A})' > (t_{Y/A})'$. Given the conditions assumed,

$$(t_{X/A})' = \frac{(F_A/c_A) - T_{XI}}{\hat{F}_X} \quad \text{and} \quad (t_{Y/A})' = \frac{(F_A/c_A) - T_Y}{\hat{F}_Y}$$

Hence, activity X will be initiated except when

$$\frac{(F_A/c_A) - T_{XI}}{\hat{F}_X} > \frac{(F_A/c_A) - T_{YI}}{\hat{F}_Y}$$

that is, except when

$$\frac{(F_A/c_A) - T_{XI}}{(F_A/c_A) - T_{YI}} > \hat{F}_X/\hat{F}_Y$$

To simplify the verbal description of this very simple and very important relationship, we shall introduce a technical term for the difference or gap between the strength of the tendency that sustains the activity in progress and the strength of the inertial tendency to undertake an alternative activity (that is, $T_{A_F} - T_{B_I}$ in the general case). We shall refer to this difference which a subordinate tendency must overcome before it can be expressed in behavior as *the inertial gap*. Hence, in our present example $F_A/c_A - T_{X_I}$ is *the inertial gap for activity* X $(_gX)$, and $F_A/c_A - T_{Y_I}$ is *the inertial gap for activity* Y $(_gY)$.

Stated in words, our generalization about choice becomes the following. *In a two alternative choice, the activity instigated by the stronger force will be chosen except when the ratio of the magnitude of that force to the magnitude of the weaker*

---

[8] Obviously the assumption of sporadic incidental exposure instead of continuous exposure to F_X and F_Y carries with it the implication of possible random variation in the extent of incidental exposure to F_X and F_Y among individuals or on repeated occasions. This in turn implies a variation in $\hat{F}_X/\hat{F}_Y$ around the assumed value of $\hat{F}_X/\hat{F}_Y = F_X/F_Y$. This is a source of *common experimental error* that is attributable to our inability to control and to describe the conditions with precision. In the text, we are concerned with the way choice is systematically influenced when we assume exact control of $\hat{F}_X/\hat{F}_Y$. The allowance for effects attributable to common experimental error must then be added to the expected systematic effects in making inferences from experimental data.

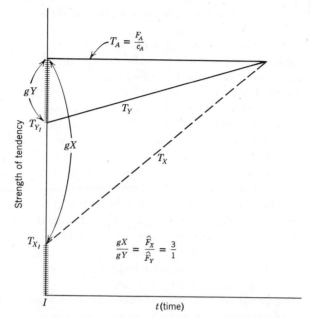

FIGURE 4.4   The relationship between the inertial gaps for activities X and Y $(_gX = T_{A_F} - T_{X_I}$ and $_gY = T_{A_F} - T_{Y_I})$ and the magnitudes of the respective instigating forces in simple choice between two alternatives for the special case in which the theoretical latencies are equal.

instigating force is exceeded by the ratio of their respective inertial gaps. That is, X will be chosen except when $_gX/_gY > F_X/F_Y$. For example, if the ratio of F_X to F_Y is 3 to 1 but the ratio of $_gX$ to $_gY$ is 4 to 1, Y will be chosen.

Figure 4.4 identifies the inertial gaps for tendencies X and Y, and the magnitudes of $\hat{F}_X$ and $\hat{F}_Y$ in the slopes that define the linear growth of T_X and T_Y for the special case in which $(t_{X/A})' = (t_{Y/A})'$. The ratio of the inertial gaps equals the ratio of the instigating forces (that is, $_gX/_gY = F_X/F_Y$) in this case. Given the value of T_{X_I} shown in Figure 4.4, any value of T_{Y_I} greater than the one shown and falling within the plotted $_gY$ would increase the ratio of the inertial gaps and would result in the choice of Y. Given the fixed value of T_{Y_I} shown in the figure, any value of T_{X_I} less than the one shown (and, thus, falling outside the plotted $_gX$) would also increase the ratio of the inertial gaps and would result in the choice of Y. Notice, particularly, that any factor that causes a change in the absolute magnitudes of the instigating forces but does not change the ratio of their magnitudes will have no systematic effect on the choice between the two alternatives. *It is the ratio of the magnitudes of instigating force and not the difference in magnitude which systematically influences choice.* We shall refer to this as *the weak ratio rule for choice.*

When there is a single observation of choice between two alternatives for each of a group of individuals in whom the ratio of the magnitudes of the instigating force is assumed to be the same, there would normally be some variation in the level of F_A/c_A among the individuals and, thus, in the ratio of the inertial gaps. The latter would also depend on uncontrolled factors such as the levels of T_X and T_Y when each was last dominant, the consummatory value of each activity, the duration of the cessation consummatory lag in each case, the substitution during the interval since the last overt expression of each tendency, the length of this "time of deprivation" in each case, and the amount of direct or indirect instigation of each activity during these intervals. The percentage choice of X in such a group of individuals will depend on the distributions of F_A/c_A, T_{X_I}, T_{Y_I} and the derivative distribution of $_gX/_gY$. Whatever the nature of the distribution of the ratio of the inertial gaps among a group of individuals on a single occasion, *the percentage choice of X, the activity instigated by the stronger force, will be greater the higher the ratio of the magnitudes of instigating force.*

From this conceptual analysis of percentage choice of a given alternative among a group of individuals on a single occasion, we may derive behavioral phenomena such as, for example, the increased preference for one of the alternatives as a function of time of deprivation for that alternative. Recall the earlier argument (see Chapter 2) about the incidental exposure to instigating force during the deprivation interval. The longer an animal has gone without food the greater should be the likelihood of its choosing an alternative that constitutes a path to food in preference to one that does not. Why? Because there would have been a systematic increase in the strength of one of the inertial tendencies relative to the other and, consequently, a systematic change in the ratio of the inertial gaps favoring preference of the path to food.

Repeated Observations from a Single Individual on Separate and Widely Spaced Occasions. When a single individual is exposed to the same two instigating forces on a number of different and widely spaced occasions, the conditions are similar to the ones already described for a group of individuals on one occasion. Even though the conditions may justify the assumption that the ratio of the instigating forces is constant across the several occasions, it is likely that there would be some variation in F_A/c_A, T_{X_I}, T_{Y_I} and, thus, in $_gX/_gY$ for the reasons already mentioned. The inferences to be made from the accumulated data that concern percentage choice are the same as the ones already described for single choices of a group of individuals on one occasion.

Repeated Observations from a Single Individual on the Same Occasion. When repeated choices are made by the same individual on a single occasion, the situation becomes more like the one that yields spontaneous alternation and a distribution of time among activities. By virtue of having the subject in a simple and well-regulated environment for a sustained period of time, the experimenter gains more control of the conditions that determine the strength of F_A/c_A, T_{X_I}, T_{Y_I} and $_gX/_gY$ on each trial. Thus, substantially more can be said about how choice will be influenced by the ratio of the magnitudes of the instigating force.

We must make certain simplifying assumptions as we imagine a subject who is repeatedly presented with the stimuli that produce the instigating force to undertake nonsubstitutable activities X and Y. First, we shall assume a constant interval between trials and that the stimuli which instigate activities X and Y are not present in the interval between trials. The individual's behavior between trials is to be considered an expression of T_A which is sustained by S_1, the stimulus situation without the critical stimuli for activities X and Y. It will be further assumed that once the individual has chosen alternative X or Y, his attention to stimuli which instigate that activity is complete for the time until he once again resumes the between-trials activity (activity A) of waiting for the next presentation of the critical stimuli. Finally, we shall continue to assume that $F_X > F_Y$ and that $\hat{F}_X/\hat{F}_Y = F_X/F_Y$.

On Trial 1, as shown in Figure 4.5, $F_X/F_Y > _gX/_gY$ and so, according to the preceding analysis of what should happen on the only or first trial, the individual chooses X. Let us follow the sequence of events shown in Figure 4.5 to observe what conclusions we can reach about the frequency of the choice of X and Y in a series of trials.

Trial 1. Since

$$(t_{X/A})'_1 = \frac{(F_A/c_A) - T_{XI}}{\hat{F}_X} \qquad \text{and} \qquad (t_{Y/A})'_1 = \frac{(F_A/c_A) - T_{YI}}{\hat{F}_Y}$$

the initial choice of X (that is, the initiation of activity X instead of activity Y) implies that $(t_{X/A})'_1 \leq (t_{Y/A})'_1$. The actual "decision time" on Trial 1 is $(t_{X/A})_1$. This defines the duration of exposure to each of the instigating forces prior to the initiation of activity X during which there is linear growth of both T_X and T_Y. While activity X is in progress, and until the individual once again resumes the activity of waiting for the next presentation of the critical stimuli, that is, during the interval $(t_{A/X})$ in Figure 4.5, it is assumed that he is exposed only to F_X. Thus, T_Y persists at the level it had attained by linear growth during $(t_{X/A})_1$, and T_A falls toward zero strength during its cessation consummatory lag $(t_c)_A$ because there has been a withdrawal of

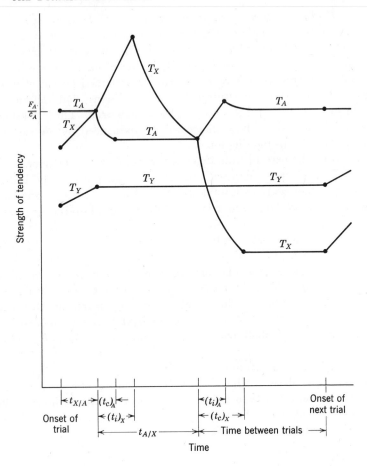

FIGURE 4.5   The details of the changes in the strengths of action tendencies within a trial for a simple idealized two-choice problem.

stimulus support. The T_A then persists at the lower level until activity A is spontaneously resumed at the end of $(t_{A/X})$. When activity X is initiated, and there is the shift in attention represented by the shift from $\hat{F}_X$ to F_X, T_X grows linearly and more rapidly during its initiation consummatory lag, $(t_i)_X$. After that, T_X begins to fall toward the asymptote defined by F_X/c_X and continues on this path throughout the remainder of the interval $(t_{A/X})$ until T_X falls below T_A and the interval between trials begins. During this time, T_A sustains its dominance and approaches close to F_A/c_A as prior to Trial 1.

Trial 2.   We must now identify the new levels of the inertial tendencies for activities X and Y prior to the second presentation of the critical stimuli which will define the beginning of the second trial. It is clear from Figure 4.5 that the interval between trials in this instance is longer than the interval of the cessation consummatory lag $(t_c)_X$. During this lag the strength of T_X has continued to decrease, but now more rapidly than before, because stimulus support of T_X has been withdrawn. Whether Y rather than X will be initiated on Trial 2 depends on the new ratio of the inertial gaps $(_gX/_gY)_2$. And since T_A will again have approached near F_A/c_A before Trial 2 begins, the ratio of the inertial gaps depends entirely on the new levels of the inertial tendencies for X and Y. The new inertial tendency for Y on Trial 2, $(T_{Y_I})_2$ equals $T_{Y_I} + \hat{F}_Y \cdot (t_{X/A})_1$. Its strength is now equivalent to its initial strength (prior to Trial 1) plus the linear growth attributable to exposure to $\hat{F}_Y$ during the first trial when X was chosen.

The new inertial tendency for X, $(T_{X_I})_2$, is uniquely important. Once we have determined what it is, we shall know what the level of T_X will be on any other trial immediately following a choice of X. Why? Because whenever T_X becomes dominant and activity X is chosen, the course of T_X will correspond exactly to the one shown for Trial 1 in Figure 4.5. It will always intersect T_A when its strength is equivalent to F_A/c_A, then rise linearly during the initiation consummatory lag, and then fall as shown in the figure to intersect T_A again, but this time when its strength is equivalent to $(F_A/c_A)[e^{-c_A \cdot (t_c)_A}]$, the level to which the strength of T_A had fallen during its cessation consummatory lag $(t_c)_A$. These two levels of T_A—the one at the initiation and the other at the cessation of activity X—will be the same on every trial that X is chosen. The remaining determinants of the level of inertial tendency for X at the beginning of Trial 2, $(T_{X_I})_2$, are also constant following trials on which X has been chosen. These determinants are c_X and $(t_c)_X$ which define the further decrease in T_X during its cessation consummatory lag.[9]

We shall refer to this new level of T_X following a choice of X as $(T_X)_c$ to distinguish it from T_{X_I}, the inertial tendency on Trial 1. And

$$(T_X)_c = \left(\frac{F_A}{c_A}\right)[e^{-c_A \cdot (t_c)_A}][e^{-c_X \cdot (t_c)_X}] = (T_{X_I})_2$$

Having determined the level of the inertial tendencies for X and Y for Trial 2, we expect X to be chosen again unless $(_gX/_gY)_2 > (\hat{F}_X/\hat{F}_Y)$. We can observe in Figure 4.5 that $(_gX)_2$ is now greater than $(_gY)_2$, so the effect of X having been chosen in preference to Y on Trial 1 is a change in conditions in the direction of increased likelihood of Y. But it may take a number of these changes before the ratio of the inertial gaps exceeds the ratio of the instigating forces. Again, the key issue is whether the theoretical latency of

---

[9] At this point, we assume the kind of choice situation that provides no immediate knowledge of results. Discussion of the differential effects of so-called reinforced and nonreinforced trials is left for Chapter 6.

X or of Y would be shorter in a single stimulus presentation. Now, on Trial 2,

$$(t_{X/A})'_2 = \frac{(F_A/c_A) - (T_X)_c}{\hat{F}_X}$$

This time of exposure required for X to be chosen again is longer than on Trial 1 because, as shown in Figure 4.5, T_X begins its race for dominance from a new and lower inertial level than on Trial 1, namely, $(T_X)_c$. The time of exposure required for Y to be chosen on Trial 2, that is, $(t_{Y/A})_2$, is obviously shorter than on Trial 1 because T_Y grew linearly during the interval $(t_{X/A})_1$ on Trial 1 when X was chosen, and the new level of strength attained as a result of this earlier exposure to $\hat{F}_Y$ has persisted to define $(T_{Y_l})_2$. Thus, we can conclude that $(t_{Y/A})'_2 = (t_{Y/A})'_1 - (t_{X/A})_1$, that is, the theoretical latency of Y on Trial 2 is what it would have been on Trial 1 minus the duration of exposure to $\hat{F}_Y$ that already took place on Trial 1. Let us assume that X is again chosen because $(t_{X/A})'_2 < (t_{Y/A})'_1 - (t_{X/A})_1$.

If we continued the analysis for a third and fourth trial (see notes at the end of the chapter), we would observe that if X were again chosen on trials 3 and 4, $(t_{X/A})_4 = (t_{X/A})_3 = (t_{X/A})_2 = (t_{X/A})_x$. In other words, there is a single value $(t_{X/A})_x$ which represents the latency of X on any trial immediately following a choice of X. And the repeated choice of X can occur only until the cumulative growth of T_Y (attributable to exposure to $\hat{F}_Y$ on each of N trials when X is chosen) has decreased the inertial gap for Y exactly to the point where $(_gX/_gY)_{N+1} > (\hat{F}_X/\hat{F}_Y)_{N+1}$. On each trial, the values of $\hat{F}_X$, $\hat{F}_Y$ and $(_gX)_c$ are the same. [Notice that $(_gX)_c = (F_A/c_A) - (T_X)_c$ during a run in which X is repeatedly chosen.] So *the critical change in the relationship between ratio of inertial gaps to ratio of instigating forces depends solely on the trial by trial growth in the strength of inertial tendency for Y which decreases $_gY$.*

Alternative Y will be chosen for the first time when $(t_{Y/A})'_1 < (t_{X/A})_1 + n_1(X) \cdot (t_{X/A})_x$ where $(t_{X/A})_1$ is the actual time for the first choice of X, $(t_{X/A})_x$ is the time for choice of X on each other occasion, $n_1(X)$ is the number of times X has been chosen in this first run of X's, and $(t_{Y/A})'_1$ is the theoretical latency of Y on the very first trial.

Following the first choice of Y, the conceptual issues parallel the ones already discussed in reference to the first choice of X. There emerges a fixed value $(t_{Y/A})_y$, which represents the latency of Y on any trial immediately following a choice of Y. This corresponds to the $(t_{X/A})_x$ discussed fully above. The interested reader may consult the mathematical notes at the end of the chapter for the step-by-step logic of the argument that leads, finally, to this important conclusion concerning the frequency of the choice of X and the frequency of the choice of Y in an infinitely long series of trials:

$$\frac{n(X)}{n(Y)} = \frac{(t_{Y/A})_y}{(t_{X/A})_x} = \frac{\dfrac{F_A}{c_A} - (T_Y)_c}{\hat{F}_Y} = \frac{(_gY)_c}{\hat{F}_X} = \frac{(_gY)_c}{\hat{F}_X}$$

or

$$\frac{n(X)}{n(Y)} = \left(\frac{\hat{F}_X}{\hat{F}_Y}\right)\left(\frac{(_gY)_c}{(_gX)_c}\right) \tag{4.12}$$

We recover, in the context of repeated choices by the same individual, what earlier we called the weak ratio rule. It is apparent that it is the ratio, and not the absolute difference in magnitude of instigating forces that influences the relative frequency of the choice of X and Y. Whatever the ratio of the inertial gaps, as determined by the differences in the consummatory values of the two activities or the differences in the duration of the consummatory lag at the cessation of the activities, the choice of the activity instigated by the stronger force will be more frequent the greater the ratio of the magnitude of this force to the weaker instigating force.

An even more striking generalization emerges for the special case in which the inertial gaps for X and Y are equal. We might refer to this as *the strong ratio rule of choice*. It would hold true for the repeated choice among two alternatives when the consummatory values of the two activities and the cessation consummatory lags were equal. Perhaps, this condition is achieved when the activities that constitute the choice of X and the choice of Y are very similar (for example, pointing to one or the other alternative) and when there is no differential knowledge of results (for example, success or failure, obtaining a goal or not) to produce differences in the consummatory values. Under these conditions $(_gX)_c = (_gY)_c$ so that $(_gY)_c/(_gX)_c = 1$. Consequently, *the ratio of the frequency of choice of the alternative instigated by the stronger force to the frequency of choice of the alternative instigated by the weaker force is equal to the ratio of the magnitudes of the instigating forces.*

Effect of displacement and substitution.   Thus far our discussion of the spontaneous alternation among activities and choice has presumed that the two critical activities belong to different families. We have assumed, in other words, that δ_{XY} and $\delta_{YX} = 0$ and that γ_{XY} and $\gamma_{YX} = 0$. This means that there is neither displacement nor substitution to change the course of the action tendencies. Now we shall explore some of the effects of displacement and substitution in reference to the problem of repeated choices by an individual on the same occasion. This will provide further elaboration of the implications of the trends presented earlier in Figure 2.1. It is our intention to convey an idea of the increased complexity of the analysis when there is displacement and substitution and to point the way for future work rather than to treat the problem exhaustively.

Let us proceed with the same assumptions about conditions that were made in the previous section concerning repeated choices between activities X and Y with one additional assumption, that is, that there is displacement and substitution because the two activities belong to the same family. This means that we assume δ_{YX} and $\delta_{XY} > 0$ and γ_{YX} and $\gamma_{XY} > 0$ where, as before, activity X is assumed to be the more strongly instigated. We shall refer again to Figure 4.5 to identify the special effects of displacement and substitution, focusing our attention primarily on T_Y, the subordinate tendency.

During the initial interval shown in the figure, $t_{X/A}$, both T_X and T_Y grow linearly until activity X is initiated, but now with steeper slopes than shown because there is displacement from one to the other. During the next interval, $(t_i)_X$, that is, the consummatory lag at the initiation of activity X during which T_X grows linearly because of exposure to F_{XX}, the direct instigating force for activity X, T_Y now also continues to increase as a function of the displaced instigating force $F_{XY} = \delta_{XY} \cdot F_{XX}$. Hence, at the end of the initiation lag, T_Y is stronger by an additional amount equal to $(\delta_{XY} \cdot F_{XX}) \cdot (t_i)_X$ than in the earlier case when there was no displacement.

What happens to T_Y during the remainder of the interval during which activity X is in progress and until activity A is once more resumed? During this time segment, $t_{A/X} - (t_i)_X$, which begins when the consummatory force of activity X takes effect, T_Y is now influenced by both indirect instigation and indirect consummation from activity X. The net indirect effect can be either an increment or a decrement to T_Y depending mainly on two factors, the relative magnitudes of the displacement and substitution parameters and the direction of change in T_X in this interval. The specific equation for the path of T_Y comes from Equation 2.9 and is given in the notes at the end of this chapter.

When activity X ceases and activity A is again initiated, T_X is affected by a cessation consummatory lag that has an indirect effect on T_Y. Equation 2.9 continues to be the appropriate equation for describing T_Y during this interval, with F_{XX} set equal to zero in accord with our earlier assumptions. Again, the details of this equation can be found in the notes, but fortunately an expression for the value of T_Y at the conclusion of the cessation consummatory lag for activity X can be fairly simply written. By letting $(T_Y)_{c_x}$ stand for this value of T_Y we have

$$(T_Y)_{c_x} = [T_{Y_I}] + [\hat{F}_Y(\tilde{t}_{X/A})_x] + \{F_{XX}(\delta_{XY} - \gamma_{XY}) \cdot (\tilde{t}_{A/X})$$

$$- \gamma_{XY}\left(\frac{F_A}{c_A}\right) [1 - (e^{-c_A \cdot (t_c)_A})(e^{-c_X \cdot (t_c)_X})]\}$$

The notation $(\tilde{t}_{X/A})_x$ and $(\tilde{t}_{A/X})$ is used to mark the fact that these latencies are obtained under conditions of displacement and substitution and will, in general, differ from their counterparts $(t_{X/A})_x$ and $(t_{A/X})$ that are obtained in the absence of these two factors. Three components of $(T_Y)_{c_x}$ have been bracketed in the expression and are identifiable as follows: the first, T_{Y_I}, is the initial value of T_Y at the start of the trial; the second, $\hat{F}_Y(\tilde{t}_{X/A})_x$, shows how much T_Y was increased in the interval just prior to the choice of X; and the third gives the increment or decrement in T_Y that is the consequence of the choice of X. Since neither activity X nor activity Y is instigated or consummed in the interval between trials, $(T_Y)_{c_x}$ is the value of T_Y at the beginning of the next trial.

The new value for T_X following a trial on which X is chosen is $(T_X)_c$, the same as it is without displacement or substitution. The analysis of a trial on which alternative Y is chosen produces the expressions for $(T_Y)_c$ and $(T_X)_{c_Y}$ which differ from their counterparts only in the parameters involved.

With these crucial expressions for T_X and T_Y available, it is possible to proceed with the derivation in much the same way as when displacement and substitution were assumed absent. The critical difference is that the third component of $(T_Y)_{c_x}$ and $(T_X)_{c_Y}$ must be taken into account explicitly. We shall jump directly to the obtained equation for $n(X)/n(Y)$ and will give the details of the derivation in the mathematical notes.

When the series of X's and Y's is allowed to become indefinitely long,

$$\frac{n(X)}{n(Y)} = \frac{(\tilde{t}_{Y/A})_y + (\tilde{t}_X)_c}{(\tilde{t}_{X/A})_x + (\tilde{t}_Y)_c} \tag{4.13}$$

or, as is more useful to us at this point, when $(\tilde{t}_{Y/A})_y$, $(\tilde{t}_{X/A})_x$, $(\tilde{t}_X)_c$ and $(\tilde{t}_Y)_c$ are replaced by their equivalents

$$\frac{n(X)}{n(Y)} = \frac{(\hat{F}_X) \cdot (_gY)_c + \hat{F}_Y\left\{F_{YY}(\delta_{YX} - \gamma_{YX}) \cdot (\tilde{t}_{A/Y}) - \gamma_{YX}\left(\frac{F_A}{c_A}\right) \times [1 - (e^{-c_A \cdot (t_c)_A})(e^{-c_Y \cdot (t_c)_Y})]\right\}}{(\hat{F}_Y) \cdot (_gX)_c + \hat{F}_X\left\{F_{XX}(\delta_{XY} - \gamma_{XY}) \cdot (\tilde{t}_{A/X}) - \gamma_{XY}\left(\frac{F_A}{c_A}\right) \times [1 - (e^{-c_A \cdot (t_c)_A})(e^{-c_X \cdot (t_c)_X})]\right\}} \tag{4.14}$$

The effects of displacement and substitution on choice (arrived at by comparing Equation 4.14 with Equation 4.12) are perhaps best summarized in this way. The effects are not simple. A variety of different parameters are important. In general, *displacement tends to decrease the choice of the favored alternative, and substitution tends to increase it.* Displacement operates to favor the denominator of Equation 4.14 more than the numerator both by making $\hat{F}_Y$ more nearly equal to $\hat{F}_X$ and by increasing, differentially, the bracketed terms. Substitution, on the other hand, operates to decrease the bracketed terms and has disproportionately more effect in the denominator than in the numerator of Equation 4.14.

THE MAGNITUDE OR INTENSITY OF THE ACTIVITY IN PROGRESS

Early in our discussion of the measurable aspects of the stream of behavior (Chapter 3), a promise was made to consider the special problems associated with the attempts to measure the magnitude or the intensity of response. Now it is time to fulfill that promise.

The variety of different behavioral measures already treated at length have one thing in common: they are all derivatives of the principle of a change in activity. In contrast, the measures of the magnitude or intensity of ongoing activity are not. We have assumed that the intensity of the ongoing activity, or perhaps what is more adequately described as the degree of involvement of the individual in the ongoing activity, depends only on the strength of the tendency being expressed in the activity. This assumption was introduced in the early discussion of the determinants of the consummatory force of an activity (see Chapter 1). Thus far, that is the use we have made of the concept of the magnitude or the intensity of an activity. Now let us consider the possibility of measuring the intensity of an activity to determine how, according to our conceptual scheme, this measure which depends only on the magnitude of T_A should be related to other measures that always depend on the relative strength of two or more tendencies.

We think first of the vigor of an activity as expressed, for example, in the speed with which a task is performed whether it be running a maze or solving arithmetic problems or getting to the line at the ticket office at the football stadium. Also, we think of the sheer amount of effort expended to overcome a physical obstacle, as in the case of the magnitude of the pull against a source of physical resistance in the classic studies of approach-avoidance conflict (Brown, 1948). And we are reminded of other useful techniques that have been developed to appraise the sheer vigor of a response, such as the pressure exerted in pressing down on a bar (Marzocco, 1951; Birch, 1966) or the pressure exerted on the pencil and, hence, through the paper in writing (see also Brown, 1961). All of them seem to capture what is meant by the intensity or the magnitude of the response. And yet certain problems often arise. For example, Stellar and Hill (1952) and Cotton (1953) have called attention to the fact that the measures of the level of drinking behavior and of speed of running an alley to food are complicated by the fact of interruptions. Sometimes, the animal stops drinking or running to do something else before again initiating the activity of critical interest. And the same kind of thing can happen when the number of arithmetic problems attempted in a fixed amount of time is taken as the measure of intensity. The human subject may have stopped to look out a window or to light a cigarette. Thus what, at first, seems to be a perfectly adequate measure of the intensity of the activity in progress, on further consideration, seems to fit more appropriately the paradigm presented earlier concerning the distribution of time among several different activities.

Sometimes, one cannot conceive of what would constitute an adequate measure of the intensity of an activity as distinct from a measure of persistence. Consider the case of an individual who is thoroughly engrossed in reading a book, or a child who is similarly engrossed in watching television, or a scientist at a microscope on the verge of discovery, or a surgeon transplanting a heart. What aspect of the behavior can be measured in these cases to yield something equivalent to the effort of the rat pulling in its harness against a resistance, or the pressure exerted in hitting a bar? Certainly gross physical exertion, appropriate in the case of the behavior of the linemen in a football game, is not the appropriate measure of the intensity of the behavior of the quarterback to say nothing of its even more obvious inappropriateness as a diagnostic test in the case of the scientist at a microscope or of the surgeon. We must conclude from this relatively brief survey that the technical problems that arise in measuring the intensity of an activity are substantial, and often there will be no really feasible way of measuring the degree of an individual's involvement in an activity other than to measure his persistence.

However, when a measure of the magnitude or intensity of an activity is defensible, as such, it can be added to the set of diagnostic tests of the instigating force, consummatory value, and any other variables that have a systematic influence on the strength of tendency that is expressed in an activity.[10] The intensity of an ongoing activity that has been in progress for some time should stabilize at a level defined by F_A/c_A so, in general, we expect the magnitude or intensity of an activity to be proportionate to the magnitude of the instigating force and inversely proportionate to the consummatory value of the activity. In light of the special assumptions introduced concerning the shift in attention that accompanies the initiation of an

[10] Later (Chapter 8), we shall add the several determinants of resistance that are associated with decrement in the level of ongoing behavior to this list.

activity, coupled with the consummatory lag at the initiation of an activity, we expect the general trend of measures of the magnitude or intensity of an activity to show an initial rapid increase followed by a less rapid and decelerated increase (when there is continued growth in T_A to asymptote), or the kind of decrease discussed in the previous sections (see Figure 4.3) following the interval of the initiation consummatory lag.

Normally, then, we should expect the measures of the intensity of an activity attributable to variations in magnitude of the instigating force to be correlated with other behavioral measures of the same variations in magnitude of an instigating force (for example, latency of response, persistence in the activity, preference, operant level, time spent). But one interesting possibility comes to mind that would operate to diminish, or wash out, the expected correlation between the measure that depends only on the strength of the tendency expressed in the ongoing activity and any of the other behavioral measures that depend on the relative strength of two or more tendencies and, hence, on the principle of change in activity. Certain organic or chemical conditions (for example, caffeine) may have a completely nonspecific effect on the neural excitatory processes that constitute the physical mechanisms of the various aspects of the dynamic process that are described in the principle of change in activity. If so, we should expect much less systematic correlation between the measures of intensity of an activity and the other behavioral measures that are derived from the principle. The technical term for such a nonspecific source of excitation in the traditional S-R behavior theory is *drive*. Let us explore the behavioral implications of drive, that is, nonspecific excitation, according to the present scheme. Consider the implications of this equation:

$$t_{B/A} = \frac{(D)T_{A_F} - (D)T_{B_I}}{(D)\hat{F}_B}$$

It is obvious that the multiplication of the inertial gap for B and the instigating force for B by the same constant D would not change the ratio of the inertial gap to the instigating force and, hence, would have no effect on the latency of activity B, the persistence of activity A, or any of the other derivative measures already discussed which depend on the ratio of inertial gaps and the ratio of instigating forces. But the nonspecific influence would have one notable effect: it would raise the level of T_A and, thus, increase the magnitude or intensity of the performance of activity A. It would affect this behavioral measure of instigating force but not the others and so would serve to reduce the correlation between the one and all the others.

One might also consider the functional significance of any organic or chemical condition that constitutes a nonspecific depressant of neural excitatory processes. Here, we must consider values of D that are less than 1 in the equation above. Again, it is obvious that there would be no change in any of the several measures that depend on the ratio of the inertial gap to the magnitude of instigating force, since that ratio is not changed by a nonspecific depressant as it was not changed by a nonspecific excitant. But the strength of the tendency sustaining the activity in progress would be weakened and, hence, the intensity or magnitude of performance would be weakened. The level of performance would be depressed.

In addition to calling attention to the kinds of technical problems that arise in connection with the measurement of the intensity of an activity, we have suggested the way in which a concept like nonspecific drive can be incorporated into the present scheme should a thorough reexamination of the evidence suggest that our earlier treatment of phenomena traditionally attributed to drive in terms of inertial tendency is inadequate or incomplete. The kind of conceptual scheme we are advancing does not prejudge the need for this kind of extension perhaps also to embrace parameters that define individual differences in "temperament."

SUMMARY

To bridge the gap between theoretically ideal cases and the actual conditions of behavior requires almost as much theory about the nature of conditions as there is theory about the basic process of motivation. This is because the observer of a change in activity is fallible. He is often unable to describe precisely what is happening, hence, there are important discrepancies between his descriptions of the duration of a stimulus or an activity and the actual durations of the exposure of an individual to the instigating and consummatory forces that control the strength of behavioral tendencies. The ideal conditions assumed and exploited in the earlier discussion of a simple change of activity produce behavioral chatter when the dynamic principles are applied to the analysis of a sequence of changes of activity in a constant environment.

Several additional propositions are advanced as tenable operating assumptions about the actual conditions of behavior, given the unavoidable inaccuracies of a fallible observer. They are concerned with the selective attention of the subject (instead of constant exposure to all the potential instigating forces of the immediate environment) and a time lag in the function of consummatory force at the initiation and the cessation of an activity (now considered a transition from involvement in one to involvement in another instead of an abrupt shift). The combined effect of these assumptions is to drive apart the strength of tendencies that are competing for behavioral expression at the instant of a change in activity. This tends to favor the activity in progress and overcomes the behavioral chatter implied in the ideal case.

Armed now with tenable operating assumptions, the change back and forth from one activity to another that characterizes the natural molar stream of behavior was analyzed for the relatively simple case in which only two different activities are instigated by a constant environment. A rudimentary expression for the operant level, or the rate of an activity is shown to be a derivative of the principle of change of activity, as is another potentially useful measure taken the molar stream of behavior: the proportion of time spent engaging in a particular activity. Both are systematically related to the latency of response and both are shown to depend on the immediate context, that is, on the several variables that control the relative strengths of other activities undertaken in the same environment.

The theoretical analysis of choice in terms of the new operating assumptions shows why a single preference from a number of individuals on one occasion is not theoretically equivalent to the repeated preference from one individual on a single occasion. In both cases, however, application of the principle of change of activity in the analysis yields a *weak ratio rule for choice*: preference among alternatives depends on the ratio of the magnitudes of the instigating forces and not on the difference in their magnitudes. And for repeated observations from a single individual on one occasion, we identify particular conditions in which preference should reflect a *strong ratio rule for choice*: the ratio of frequency of choice of one alternative to that of the other is equal to the ratio of the magnitudes of the instigating forces.

The one behavioral measure that is not a derivative of the principle of change of activity is often likely to be very difficult to obtain. That is a measure of the magnitude or the intensity of an activity that we often equate with speed or effort in simple animal behavior but that we are hard put to imagine when the activity is something like a surgeon performing a delicate operation. When it can be obtained, a measure of the level of performance should be correlated with other possible measures of the magnitude of an instigating force because the strength of tendency expressed in an activity, which we assume governs the intensity of the activity, approaches an asymptote defined in part by the magnitude of instigating force (F_A/c_A).

The Principle of Change of Activity, as stated, contains no nonspecific influence on behavior. But should there be certain nonspecific underlying neurochemical parameters that affect the several functions described in the principle (for example, drive in S-R behavior theory), they could be represented as constant multiplicative influences on the several forces and tendencies. This would not change the ratio of the inertial gap to the instigating force for an alternative and, thus, would not influence the several behavioral measures derived from the principle of change of activity. However, a nonspecific multiplicative influence, whether a general excitant or depressant, would affect the strength of the tendency that sustains ongoing activity and so would be systematically reflected in the level or the vigor of performance. Such a nonspecific influence would tend to reduce the expected correlation between the measures of the level of an ongoing activity and the several other behavioral measures, all of which are derivatives of the principle of change of activity (namely, latency, persistence, preference, rate, and time spent).

MATHEMATICAL NOTES

Behavioral chatter, the term used to describe the condition that results when the tendencies for two incompatible activities alternate in dominance at an infinite rate, is implied by the unelaborated theory of action. This property of the theory, which emerges as a problem whenever more than a single change in activity is considered, must be eliminated. Interestingly, the adjustments made to handle this problem simplify and, in a sense, perhaps make possible the derivations from the theory of the operant rate of response, the proportion of time spent in an activity, and the proportion choice of an alternative. These derivations will be discussed in the following sections, but let us begin by showing why the theory as stated in the first three chapters implies behavioral chatter.

The Problem of Behavioral Chatter

Let us consider a situation limited to two incompatible activities, X and Y, so that initially $T_{X_I} > T_{Y_I}$, implying that X is the ongoing activity. We know that T_X is changing in strength according to Equation 1.11,

$$T_X = T_{X_I} \cdot e^{-c_X \cdot t} + \frac{F_X}{c_X}(1 - e^{-c_X \cdot t})$$

and that T_Y is growing linearly, $T_Y = T_{Y_I} + F_Y \cdot t$, so long as T_X maintains its dominance over T_Y. After time $t_{Y/X}$ activity Y supplants activity X because T_Y gains in strength relative to T_X until the criterion for the change in activity, $T_Y = T_X + \Delta$, is attained. It will be recalled (see Footnote 1, Chapter 1) that Δ is a quantity that can be as small as desired.

Since initially $T_{X_I} > T_{Y_I}$ and, subsequently, $T_Y = T_X + \Delta$, we know from the form of the equations for T_X and T_Y that at the point in time when $T_Y = T_X + \Delta$ the condition $dT_Y/dt > dT_X/dt$ must hold true. With $dT_Y/dt = F_Y$ and $dT_X/dt = c_X(F_X/c_X - T_{X_I}) \cdot e^{-c_X \cdot t_{Y/X}}$ this inequality is

$$F_Y > c_X\left(\frac{F_X}{c_X} - T_{X_I}\right) \cdot e^{-c_X \cdot t_{Y/X}}$$

However, the item of major importance is whether the new slope for T_Y

(that is, dT_Y/dt when T_Y is dominant) exceeds the new slope for T_X, which is F_X since T_X is no longer being expressed. Thus, the question becomes: Is

$$c_Y\left[\frac{F_Y}{c_Y} - (T_{Y_I} + F_Y \cdot t_{Y/X})\right] > F_X?$$

First, let us examine what the implications are if this inequality is not satisfied. If the new slope for T_Y is less than the new slope for T_X, there is no way for T_Y to maintain its lead of Δ over T_X, and the discrepance of Δ, which is infinitely small, will immediately be overcome and the opposite condition wherein $T_X = T_Y + \Delta$ will be realized. It is now necessary to ask whether T_X can maintain or can increase its newly acquired lead of Δ over T_Y. This will only happen if the slope for T_X at this point in time

$$\frac{dT_X}{dt} = c_X\left\{\frac{F_X}{c_X} - \left[T_{X_I} \cdot e^{-c_X \cdot t_{Y/X}} + \frac{F_X}{c_X}(1 - e^{-c_X \cdot t_{Y/X}})\right]\right\}$$

is greater than the slope for T_Y, which is F_Y. After simplifying, this inequality is

$$c_X\left[\frac{F_X}{c_X} - T_{X_I}\right] \cdot e^{-c_X \cdot t_{Y/X}} > F_Y$$

which cannot hold true since it is contrary to the condition required for activity to shift from X to Y in the first place. Thus, we reach a situation wherein neither T_X nor T_Y can sustain dominance for any finite interval of time and the system is trapped in a series of infinitely rapid fluctuations between $T_Y = T_X + \Delta$ and $T_X = T_Y + \Delta$, the condition we have termed behavioral chatter.

Next we must pursue the implications of

$$c_Y\left[\frac{F_Y}{c_Y} - (T_{Y_I} + F_Y \cdot t_{Y/X})\right] > F_X$$

which can be rewritten as $F_Y(1 - c_Y \cdot t_{Y/X}) - c_Y \cdot T_{Y_I} > F_X$. The conditions required to satisfy this inequality are $c_Y \cdot t_{Y/X} < 1$ and that F_Y be sufficiently large. Let us assume these conditions so that T_Y will continue to dominate T_X for some new interval of time, $t_{X/Y}$. At the end of this interval when $T_X = T_Y + \Delta$, we know that the slope for T_X must be greater than the slope for T_Y meaning

$$F_X > c_Y\left\{\frac{F_Y}{c_Y} - \left[(T_{Y_I} + F_Y \cdot t_{Y/X}) \cdot e^{-c_Y \cdot t_{X/Y}} + \frac{F_Y}{c_Y}(1 - e^{-c_Y \cdot t_{X/Y}})\right]\right\}$$

or

$$F_X > c_Y\left(\frac{F_Y}{c_Y} - T_{Y_I} - F_Y \cdot t_{Y/X}\right) \cdot e^{-c_Y \cdot t_{X/Y}}$$

Can T_X continue to dominate T_Y for a third finite interval? In order for this to happen, it is necessary that the slope for T_X at this point in time be greater than the slope for T_Y, that is,

$$c_X \left\{ \frac{F_X}{c_X} - \left[T_{X_I} \cdot e^{-c_X \cdot tr/x} + \frac{F_X}{c_X}(1 - e^{-c_X \cdot tr/x}) + F_X \cdot t_{X/Y} \right] \right\} > F_Y$$

or $c_X(F_X/c_X - T_{X_I}) \cdot e^{-c_X \cdot tr/x} - c_X \cdot F_X \cdot t_{X/Y} > F_Y$, but this cannot be since we have seen already that $c_X(F_X/c_X - T_{X_I})e^{-c_X \cdot tr/x} < F_Y$. Nor can T_Y regain dominance and, thereby, make activity Y resume because this would require $c_Y(F_Y/c_Y - T_{Y_I} - F_Y \cdot t_{Y/X}) \cdot e^{-c_Y \cdot tx/y} > F_X$ and, as we have observed above, the opposite must be the case. Therefore, once again the system moves into a never ending series of infinitely rapid fluctuations between $T_Y = T_X + \Delta$ and $T_X = T_Y + \Delta$. This point was reached in two changes in activity instead of one, as previously, because different assumptions about the relative magnitudes of the parameter values were made.

OPERANT RATE OF AN ACTIVITY

Behavioral chatter is a problem in the theory of action as initially stated because there is no way for a newly dominant tendency to maintain its superiority over any finite interval of time. A careful examination of the problem suggests that the difficulty is located in the compatibilities and incompatibilities that must exist between any two families of activities. It seems impossible that all elements of a new activity emerge at the precise moment that the critical characteristics of that activity appear or that all elements of a supplanted activity disappear at this time. Therefore, it is inappropriate to assume that the consummatory forces for the two activities appear and disappear in this way. As a first approximation to what most likely will develop into a complex analysis of this difficulty, we have introduced the concepts of initiation and cessation lags, illustrated in Figure 4.2.

In equation form the initiation consummatory lag for activity X is $(T_X)_i = T_{X_I} + F_X \cdot (t_i)_X$ where $(T_X)_i$ stands for the value of T_X at the end of the initiation consummatory lag interval, T_{X_I} is the value of T_X at the beginning of the lag interval, F_X is the instigating force for activity X with selective attention favoring activity X, and $(t_i)_X$ is the duration of the lag. Similarly, the equation

$$(T_X)_c = T_{X_I} \cdot e^{-c_X \cdot (t_c)x} + \frac{\hat{F}_X}{c_x}(1 - e^{-c_X \cdot (t_c)x})$$

gives $(T_X)_c$, the value of T_X at the end of the cessation consummatory lag interval, $(t_c)_X$, as a function of T_{X_I}, c_X, and $\hat{F}_X$, the instigating force for activity X under the conditions of selective attention that are unfavorable to activity X. The first equation is linear and provides for an increase in T_X on the initiation of activity X because of a delay in the onset of the consummatory force for activity X, whereas the second is adapted from Equation 1.11 and provides for a decrease in T_X on the cessation of activity X because of a delay in the termination of the consummatory force for activity X.

To determine how the assumptions concerning the initiation and cessation consummatory lags solve the problem of behavioral chatter and how they lead to a derivation of the operant rate of an activity when only two activities are involved, let us return to the analysis of the situation that gave rise to behavioral chatter. This is one of a constant stimulus environment in which activity shifts back and forth between X and Y. Since the problem of behavioral chatter originates at the point in time when one activity takes over from the other, we shall pick up our analysis when activity X has just supplanted activity Y, implying $T_{X_I} = T_{Y_I} + \Delta$.

The result of the initiation consummatory lag for activity X and the cessation consummatory lag for activity Y is that T_X grows to $(T_X)_i = T_{X_I} + F_X \cdot (t_i)_X$ and T_Y is altered to $(T_Y)_c = T_{Y_I} \cdot e^{-c_Y \cdot (t_c)_Y} + (\hat{F}_Y/c_Y)[1 - e^{-c_Y \cdot (t_c)_Y}]$, ignoring Δ which can be made infinitely small. If T_{Y_I} is above $\hat{F}_Y/c_Y$, and this can certainly be the case since T_Y was approaching $F_Y/c_Y > \hat{F}_Y/c_Y$ in the interval preceding the point when T_X caught T_Y, the slope for T_Y during its cessation consummatory lag is negative. If T_{Y_I} is below $\hat{F}_Y/c_Y$, the slope for T_Y during its cessation consummatory lag will be positive but less than what it was before T_X caught T_Y, since the asymptote for T_Y has dropped from F_Y/c_Y to $\hat{F}_Y/c_Y$. In either case, since the slope for T_X at the point in time when the change in activity occurs is greater than the slope for T_Y at this point (or T_X could not have caught T_Y) and, since the slope of T_X increases but the slope of T_Y decreases with the shift in activity, there must be a finite interval during which T_X dominates T_Y. A corresponding argument can be made when activity Y supplants activity X, giving a solution to the problem of behavioral chatter.

It is possible that over an extended sequence of alternations $t_{Y/X}$ and $t_{X/Y}$ become constants or, at least, approach asymptotically to constant values. This conjecture is unproved but seems reasonable in that both T_X and T_Y proceed toward their asymptotes each time they are expressed. Perhaps, the stabilizing (if it occurs) will be in the neighborhood of the higher asymptote.

At present, however, we are able to deal only with very special cases, one of which is given in the text. This is the case in which conditions are such that the ongoing tendency can be approximated by its asymptotic value on each change of activity (see Figure 4.3). It is easily seen that for these conditions $t_{Y/X}$ and $t_{X/Y}$ are the same from cycle to cycle and are given by

$$t_{Y/X} = \frac{F_X/c_X - (T_Y)_c}{\hat{F}_Y} + (t_c)_Y \quad \text{and} \quad t_{X/Y} = \frac{F_Y/c_Y - (T_X)_c}{\hat{F}_X} + (t_c)_X$$

Under the special conditions we have assumed, $(T_Y)_c$ and $(T_X)_c$, the values of T_Y and T_X at the end of the cessation consummatory lags for activities Y and X, are the same from cycle to cycle because all their determinants are the same from cycle to cycle.

With $t_{Y/X}$ and $t_{X/Y}$ constant it is only a small step to an expression for the operant rate of response. The definition of the rate of activity X (which equals the rate of activity Y in the two activity case) is the number of times X occurs in an interval of observation divided by the duration of that interval, that is, $r(X) = n(X)/\text{Total Time}$. Also, it is true that the number of occurrences of X equals the total time of observation divided by the average duration of a cycle which, in turn, equals the sum of the average durations for the two activities involved. Thus, $n(X) = \text{Total Time}/\bar{t}_{Y/X} + \bar{t}_{X/Y}$ which produces $r(X) = 1/\bar{t}_{Y/X} + \bar{t}_{X/Y}$.

In our example, $\bar{t}_{Y/X} = t_{Y/X}$ and $\bar{t}_{X/Y} = t_{X/Y}$ and, since $t_{Y/X}$ and $t_{X/Y}$ are known in terms of the parameters of the theory, it is possible to specify the operant rate of response exactly within the theory. That this particular specification will be very useful with data seems doubtful because of the restrictive conditions assumed, but it helps to suggest the kind of relationships among measures to be found within the theory. Much more work is needed to extend the derivation for operant rate to more than two activities and to free it from its too special assumptions.

Choice between Two Alternatives

The derivations for choice to be presented will be confined to the two alternative paradigm in order to avoid the complexities that arise when more than two alternatives are available. Certain assumptions that simplify the algebraic manipulations but do not appear to restrict seriously the generality of the conclusions are made. These assumptions will be introduced as they arise in the derivations. We begin with the choice paradigm in which a single observation is made on a large number of individuals and follow with a paradigm in which repeated observations are made on a single individual by using relatively massed trials, first with assumptions of no displacement or substitution and then with these factors included.

Two-Alternative Choice with a Single Observation from Many Individuals. Let A be the ongoing activity and X and Y the alternatives. The choice of X or Y is determined by which tendency, T_X or T_Y, reaches the level of T_A first. No direct comparison of T_X with T_Y is involved in the choice of X or Y but instead each enters into competition with T_A, as diagrammed in Figure 4.5. Alternative X will be chosen if the time required for T_X to reach T_A is less than the time for T_Y to reach T_A, and alternative Y will be chosen when the opposite is true. More precisely, X will be chosen if and only if $(t_{X/A})' \leq (t_{Y/A})'$ and Y, if and only if $(t_{Y/A})' < (t_{X/A})'$, where the primes are used to denote the theoretical as opposed to the actual latencies. Assume that $F_X > F_Y$ and $\hat{F}_X/\hat{F}_Y = F_X/F_Y$. Since $(t_{X/A})' = (T_{A_F} - T_{X_I})/\hat{F}_X$ and $(t_{Y/A})' = (T_{A_F} - T_{Y_I})/\hat{F}_Y$, these conditions are equivalent to requiring $(T_{A_F} - T_{X_I})/\hat{F}_X \leq (T_{A_F} - T_{Y_I})/\hat{F}_Y$ or, by using the concept of inertial gap, $_gX/\hat{F}_X \leq _gY/\hat{F}_Y$, for a choice of X and $_gY/\hat{F}_Y < _gX/\hat{F}_X$ for a choice of Y. All individuals choosing X satisfy the first inequality; those choosing Y satisfy the second, and the proportion choice of X, $p(X)$, is the proportion of individuals satisfying the first inequality.

The most important characteristic of the derived expressions for the choices of X and Y is that the forces enter as ratios—an outcome labeled the *weak ratio rule* in the text. This property can be seen most easily by rearranging the expressions to state that X will be chosen if and only if $_gX/_gY \leq \hat{F}_X/\hat{F}_Y$ and Y will be chosen if and only if $_gX/_gY > \hat{F}_X/\hat{F}_Y$.

It is apparent that there is no way (without the introduction of a number of additional assumptions) to estimate the magnitude of any of the parameters of the theory by using this choice paradigm. However, it is possible to investigate the effects of experimental manipulations and individual differences on choice at an ordinal level without additional assumptions.

Two-Alternative Choice with Repeated Observations from a Single Individual. As before, let A be the ongoing activity with X and Y as alternatives and with $F_X > F_Y$ and $\hat{F}_X/\hat{F}_Y = F_X/F_Y$. We shall assume further that from one presentation of the choice stimuli to the next the following events occur (see Figure 4.5). Each trial begins with the presentation of the critical stimuli for alternatives X and Y and with activity A (the activity engaged in by the individual between trials) in progress, so that the instigating forces F_A, $\hat{F}_X$, and $\hat{F}_Y$ are operative. Some time later, either T_X or T_Y dominates T_A, assumed to be adequately approximated by F_A/c_A by this time, at which point the new activity (X or Y) commences with the result that the instigating force for that alternative only (F_X or F_Y) is operative. Later, activity X or Y, whichever supplanted activity A, gives way again to activity A, at which point the critical stimuli for X and Y are absent, leaving only F_A operative. This condition continues to hold true until the next presentation of the choice stimuli that defines the next trial. The assumption that $\hat{F}_A$ is absent while alternative activity X or Y is being engaged in is a convenience in that it is not necessary for achieving a derivation: it makes no major alteration in the outcome but it simplifies the derivation. The assumption that activity A, instead of the other alternative activity, supplants the selected alternative activity likewise simplifies the derivation, but it is as yet unproved that the outcome is left unaltered. Finally, we shall assume that the consequence for the individual of choosing either alternative is the same each time that alternative is chosen and that the magnitudes of the instigating forces do not change as a result of the consequences.

The plan for the derivation develops out of the fact that, with only two alternatives, the pattern of choices must be a sequence of runs of X's and Y's. The proportion of choices of $X =$

$$p(X) = \frac{n(X)}{n(X) + n(Y)} = \frac{1}{1 + n(Y)/n(X)}$$

where $n(X)$ and $n(Y)$ stand for the total number of choices of X and Y in a series of choices. In addition, $n(X)$ and $n(Y)$ can be subdivided into $n(X) = n_1(X) + n_2(X) + \cdots + n_j(X)$ and $n(Y) = n_1(Y) + n_2(Y) + \cdots + n_j(Y)$ where $n_1(X)$ is the number of choices of X in the first run of X's, $n_2(X)$ the number in the second run, etc. Therefore, if the expressions in terms of the parameters of the theory can be found for the length of each run of X and Y, $p(X)$ can be written in terms of these parameters and the derivation will be accomplished.

We begin the derivation at the point in time when the individual is engaged in activity A and the critical stimuli for the alternatives X and Y are first presented, that is, with *Trial 1*. Thus, the initial values of T_X and T_Y are T_{X_I} and T_{Y_I}, respectively, and X will be chosen on the first trial if, and only if, $(t_{X/A})'_1 \leq (t_{Y/A})'_1$ where the primes indicate that it is theoretical or calculated latencies that are being compared, that is, values that would be the latencies if the one or the other alternative were chosen. We know further that

$$(t_{X/A})'_1 = \frac{F_A/c_A - T_{X_I}}{\hat{F}_X} = \frac{{}_gX}{\hat{F}_X}$$

and that

$$(t_{Y/A})'_1 = \frac{F_A/c_A - T_{Y_I}}{\hat{F}_Y} = \frac{{}_gY}{\hat{F}_Y}$$

so that X will be chosen if and only if ${}_gX/\hat{F}_X \leq {}_gY/\hat{F}_Y$. Let us assume that X was chosen on Trial 1.

In order to state the conditions for the choice of X on the second trial we need only the new inertial values for T_X and T_Y. For $(t_c)_X$ less than the interval between the trials the new value for T_X is

$$(T_X)_c = \left(\frac{F_A}{c_A}\right)[e^{-c_A \cdot (t_c)A}][e^{-c_X \cdot (t_c)X}]$$

where the symbol $(T_X)_c$ stands for the value of T_X at the end of the cessation consummatory lag interval for activity X. This value of T_X comes about because T_X dominates $T_A = F_A/c_A$, then is dominated by $T_A = (F_A/c_A)[e^{-c_A \cdot (t_0)_A}]$, the value of T_A after its cessation consummatory lag, after which T_X suffers its own cessation consummatory lag specified by $\{(F_A/c_A)[e^{-c_A \cdot (t_0)_A}]\} \cdot e^{-c_X \cdot (t_0)x}$. Recall that both T_A and T_X are falling toward zero according to Equation 1.11 during their cessation consummatory lags because neither activity is instigated at that time. Figure 4.5 helps to make this sequence clear. Not only is $(T_X)_c$ known but it will be the same every time alternative X is chosen. This is readily apparent from the equation for $(T_X)_c$ which shows all of the terms defining $(T_X)_c$ to be independent of trials.

The new value for T_Y is also easily discovered, since T_Y began at T_{Y_I} and was instigated by $\hat{F}_Y$ for time $(t_{X/A})_1 = (t_{X/A})'_1$ where the symbol $(t_{X/A})_1$ without the prime signifies the actual as opposed to the theoretical latency on trial 1. Thus, by Equation 1.7, the new value of T_Y is $T_{Y_I} + \hat{F}_Y(t_{X/A})_1$.

On *Trial 2*, X will be chosen if and only if $(t_{X/A})'_2 \leq (t_{Y/A})'_2$ where

$$(t_{X/A})'_2 = \frac{F_A/c_A - (T_X)_c}{\hat{f}_X} \quad \text{and} \quad (t_{Y/A})'_2 = \frac{F_A/c_A - [T_{Y_I} + \hat{F}_Y \cdot (t_{X/A})_1]}{\hat{F}_Y}$$

It is apparent that each time X is chosen T_X returns to $(T_X)_c$ but T_Y gains an increment in strength. Thus, on some trial, Y will be chosen. We wish to know the length of the run of X's prior to this first choice of Y; that is, we wish to find $n_1(X)$. The derivation can be simplified at this point by noticing that the theoretical latency for X on any trial that follows a choice of X is always the same. This permits the use of the symbol $(t_{X/A})_x$ without a subscript for trials. We can also observe that T_Y, beginning at T_{Y_I} on the first trial, must finally grow to the level of F_A/c_A in order that Y be chosen. The total duration of exposure required to get T_Y from T_{Y_I} to F_A/c_A is the theoretical latency for Y observed on the first trial

$$(t_{Y/A})'_1 = \frac{F_A/c_A - T_{Y_I}}{\hat{f}_Y}$$

This total exposure is achieved over the run of trials in which X is chosen and, if we define $n_1(X)$ as the number of choices of X prior to the first choice of Y, we can write $(t_{Y/A})'_1 = (t_{X/A})_1 + [n_1(X) - 1](t_{X/A})_x + (t_{Y/A})_1$. The latency of the choice of Y, $(t_{Y/A})_1$, must be less than $(t_{X/A})_x$, or Y would not have been chosen on that trial so that we can let $(t_{Y/A})_1 = \phi_1(t_{X/A})_x$ where $0 \lesssim \phi_1 < 1$ and by substitution can obtain

$$(t_{Y/A})'_1 = (t_{X/A})_1 + [n_1(X) - 1](t_{X/A})_x + \phi_1(t_{X/A})_x$$

By solving this for $n_1(X)$, we obtain

$$n_1(X) = \frac{(t_{Y/A})'_1 - (t_{X/A})_1}{(t_{X/A})_x} + (1 - \phi_1)$$

To this point we have $n_1(X)$ choices of X and one choice of Y, which required time $(t_{Y/A})_1 = \phi_1(t_{X/A})_x$. On the next trial, $n_1(X) + 2$, the inertial value of T_X is $(T_X)_c + \hat{F}_X \cdot \phi_1(t_{X/A})_x$, whereas T_Y begins with $(T_Y)_c = (F_A/c_A)[e^{-c_A \cdot (t_c)A}][e^{-c_Y \cdot (t_c)r}]$, the value of T_Y at the conclusion of the cessation consummatory lag for Y. The latency for a choice of Y under these conditions is

$$(t_{Y/A})_v = \frac{F_A/c_A - (T_Y)_c}{\hat{F}_Y}$$

which is the same for each trial following a choice of Y and corresponds to $(t_{X/A})_x$ for activity X.

How long a run of choices of Y can be expected before X is chosen again? By using the same argument as before, the total exposure to $\hat{F}_X$ that is necessary in order to bring T_X up to F_A/c_A is $(t_{X/A})_x = \phi_1(t_{X/A})_x + [n_1(Y) - 1](t_{Y/A})_v + (t_{X/A})_2$ where $(t_{X/A})_2$ is the latency for the next choice of X. Since $(t_{X/A})_2 < (t_{Y/A})_v$, we can write $(t_{X/A})_2 = \psi_2(t_{Y/A})_v$, where $0 < \psi_2 \leq 1$, and $(t_{X/A})_x = \phi_1(t_{X/A})_x + [n_1(Y) - 1](t_{Y/A})_v + \psi_2(t_{Y/A})_v$. Solving this equation for $n_1(Y)$ yields

$$n_1(Y) = \frac{(1 - \phi_1)(t_{X/A})_x}{(t_{Y/A})_v} + (1 - \psi_2)$$

The expressions for $n_2(X)$, $n_2(Y)$, $\ldots$, $n_j(X)$, $n_j(Y)$ can now be projected because T_X requires time $(T_{X/A})_x$ to go from $(T_X)_c$ to F_A/c_A following each choice of X, and T_Y requires time $(t_{Y/A})_v$ to go from $(T_Y)_c$ to F_A/c_A following each choice of Y. Thus

$$n_2(X) = \frac{(1 - \psi_2)(t_{Y/A})_v}{(t_{X/A})_x} + (1 - \phi_2)$$

$$n_2(Y) = \frac{(1 - \phi_2)(t_{X/A})_x}{(t_{Y/A})_v} + (1 - \psi_3)$$

$$\vdots$$

$$n_j(X) = \frac{(1 - \psi_j)(t_{Y/A})_v}{(t_{X/A})_x} + (1 - \phi_j)$$

$$n_j(Y) = \frac{(1 - \phi_j)(t_{X/A})_x}{(t_{Y/A})_v} + (1 - \psi_{j+1})$$

and we can write

$$\frac{n(X)}{n(Y)} = \frac{\dfrac{(t_{Y/A})'_1 - (t_{X/A})_1}{(t_{X/A})_x} + \dfrac{(t_{Y/A})_y}{(t_{X/A})_x}[(1 - \psi_2) + \cdots + (1 - \psi_j)] + [(1 - \phi_1) + \cdots + (1 - \phi_j)]}{\dfrac{(t_{X/A})_x}{(t_{Y/A})_y}[(1 - \phi_1) + \cdots + (1 - \phi_j)] + [(1 - \psi_2) + \cdots + (1 - \psi_{j+1})]}$$

for an interval of observation in which j runs each of X and Y occur.

We can proceed another step in the derivation by noticing that on the average the four bracketed terms involving ϕ's and ψ's should be approximately equal as j becomes larger. The ϕ's and ψ's originate in the latencies for the first choices of X's and Y's in the runs and certainly need not be the same from run to run, nor is there any particular reason for bias between the ϕ's and ψ's. If we set each of the four brackets equal to a constant, call it B_j, we have

$$\frac{n(X)}{n(Y)} = \frac{\dfrac{(t_{Y/A})'_1 - (t_{X/A})_1}{(t_{X/A})_x} + \dfrac{(t_{Y/A})_y}{(t_{X/A})_x} \cdot B_j + B_j}{\dfrac{(t_{X/A})_x}{(t_{Y/A})_y} \cdot B_j + B_j}$$

$$= \frac{\dfrac{1}{B_j}\left[\dfrac{(t_{Y/A})'_1 - (t_{X/A})_1}{(t_{X/A})_x}\right] + \left[\dfrac{(t_{Y/A})_y}{(t_{X/A})_x} + 1\right]}{\left[\dfrac{(t_{X/A})_x}{(t_{Y/A})_y} + 1\right]}$$

Finally, it is to be expected that B_j will increase without limit as $j \to \infty$, in which case in the limit,

$$\frac{n(X)}{n(Y)} = \frac{\dfrac{(t_{Y/A})_y}{(t_{X/A})_x} + 1}{\dfrac{(t_{X/A})_x}{(t_{Y/A})_y} + 1} = \frac{(t_{Y/A})_y}{(t_{X/A})_x}$$

We observe at this point that the extended expression for $n(X)/n(Y)$ will differ slightly for a series in which X is chosen on the very first trial and one in which Y is chosen. This difference becomes less and less important as the length of the series is extended and disappears in the limit.

The specification of choice in terms of the theory of action can be pursued further by substituting

$$(t_{Y/A})_y = \frac{F_A/c_A - (T_Y)_c}{\hat{F}_Y} \qquad \text{and} \qquad (t_{X/A})_x = \frac{F_A/c_A - (T_X)_c}{\hat{F}_X}$$

into the expression for $n(X)/n(Y)$ to obtain

$$\frac{n(X)}{n(Y)} = \left(\frac{\hat{F}_X}{\hat{F}_Y}\right)\left[\frac{F_A/c_A - (T_Y)_c}{F_A/c_A - (T_X)_c}\right] = \left(\frac{\hat{F}_X}{\hat{F}_Y}\right)\left[\frac{(_gY)_c}{(_gX)_c}\right] \qquad (4.12)$$

Once again, choice is shown to obey the weak ratio rule and, perhaps even more interestingly, to obey the strong ratio rule (that is, $n(X)/n(Y) = \hat{F}_X/\hat{F}_Y$) when conditions are such that $(T_Y)_c = (T_X)_c$. The strong ratio rule for the choice between two alternatives (derivable from the theory of action as a special case) is in correspondence with the basic postulate of the Bradley-Terry-Luce theory of scaling (Luce, 1959). Whether the correspondence will continue when more than two alternatives are involved is undetermined as yet.

Two-Alternative Choice with Displacement and Substitution

The behavior from both paradigms of choice (a single observation from many individuals and repeated observations from a single individual) can be expected to be altered when displacement and/or substitution effects are present. Actually, it is difficult to think of activities for which there is either displacement or substitution, but not both, since both depend on the same kind of family relationships. Therefore, we shall introduce the two effects into the derivations for choice at the same time. The condition of special interest is the one in which displacement and substitution operate between the alternatives X and Y but not with respect to the between-trials activity A and either of the alternatives. Thus, under our consideration is the case in which alternatives X and Y come from the same family but one in which activity A does not belong. This case can then be contrasted with the one in which alternatives X and Y come from different families, so that no displacement or substitution is to be expected. We shall continue to assume that $F_{XX} > F_{YY}$ and that $\hat{F}_{XX}/\hat{F}_{YY} = F_{XX}/F_{YY}$.

With displacement present the effective instigating forces for the two alternatives are increased. Specifically, $\hat{F}_X = \hat{F}_{XX} + \delta_{YX} \cdot \hat{F}_{YY}$ and $\hat{F}_Y = \hat{F}_{YY} + \delta_{XY} \cdot \hat{F}_{XX}$ with displacement, whereas $\hat{F}_X = \hat{F}_{XX}$ and $\hat{F}_Y = \hat{F}_{YY}$ without displacement during the interval in which the critical stimuli for alternatives X and Y are presented for choice. The effects of both displacement and substitution enter during the interval in which the one or the other alternative activity is being engaged in.

Two-Alternative Choice for a Single Observation from Many Individuals with Displacement. Under this choice paradigm, substitution is irrelevant because it enters only after the single choice is made. Displacement enters to increase the magnitudes of $\hat{F}_X$ and $\hat{F}_Y$, as already pointed out, but does not alter the derivation given for the no displacement condition.

The conclusion from the derivation presented is that alternative X will be chosen if, and only if, $_gX/_gY \leq \hat{F}_X/\hat{F}_Y$. What is the effect of the presence of displacement on this choice if we assume that $\hat{F}_{XX}$ and $\hat{F}_{YY}$ are the same with and without displacement? The choice of X, the favored alternative, will be greater with displacement than without if

$$\frac{\hat{F}_{XX} + \delta_{YX} \cdot \hat{F}_{YY}}{\hat{F}_{YY} + \delta_{XY} \cdot \hat{F}_{XX}} > \frac{\hat{F}_{XX}}{\hat{F}_{YY}}$$

However, this can be the case only if $\delta_{YX}/\delta_{XY} > (\hat{F}_{XX})^2/(\hat{F}_{YY})^2$; that is, if there is an unusual asymmetry in the displacement parameters that favor alternative X. If δ_{YX} and δ_{XY} are even approximately equal, displacement works against the choice of X, the favored alternative.

Two-Alternative Choice for Repeated Observations from a Single Individual with Displacement and Substitution. It will be helpful to refer to Figure 4.5 as we proceed with this derivation. The basic format of the derivation is the same as for the case of no displacement or substitution: that is, we assess the length of each successive run of X and Y, total them to give the ratio $n(X)/n(Y)$, and finally we evaluate this ratio as the length of the series is allowed to increase without limit. We begin, as previously, with the first trial.

On *Trial 1*, X will be chosen if and only if $(\check{t}_{X/A})'_1 \leq (\check{t}_{Y/A})'_1$ where

$$(\check{t}_{X/A})'_1 = \frac{F_A/c_A - T_{X_I}}{\hat{F}_X} \quad \text{and} \quad (\check{t}_{Y/A})'_1 = \frac{F_A/c_A - T_{Y_I}}{\hat{F}_Y}$$

We shall use the $\check{t}$ notation in the present derivation to denote the fact that these latencies arise under the conditions of displacement and substitution. Assume that alternative X is chosen on the first trial.

On *Trial 2*, X will be chosen again if and only if $(\check{t}_{X/A})'_2 \leq (\check{t}_{Y/A})'_2$, and in order to obtain expressions for these two theoretical latencies it is necessary to discover the values of $(T_{X_I})_2$ and $(T_{Y_I})_2$, the two inertial tendencies at the beginning of the second trial. With the assistance of Figure 4.5 it can be seen that $(T_{X_I})_2 = (T_X)_c = (F_A/c_A)[e^{-c_A \cdot (t_c)_A}][e^{-c_X \cdot (t_c)_X}]$. This value of T_X, which is identical to the one obtained when no displacement or substitution was involved, comes about because T_X first intercepts T_A at F_A/c_A, again at $(F_A/c_A)[e^{-c_A \cdot (t_c)_A}]$, and then undergoes a cessation consummatory lag that is unaffected either by displacement or substitution. Displacement and substitution are not factors because there is no instigating force for activity Y present during this interval nor is activity Y occurring. Thus $(\check{t}_{X/A})'_2 = [F_A/c_A - (T_X)_c]/\hat{F}_X$ which is the same on every trial following a choice of X, permitting the notation $(\check{t}_{X/A})_x$ for this latency.

As might be anticipated, it is T_Y that is affected by displacement and substitution in the course of a trial. Beginning at T_{Y_I}, T_Y grows to $T_{Y_I} + \hat{F}_Y(\check{t}_{X/A})_1$ by the time alternative X is selected and then during X's initiation consummatory lag increases another increment, $\delta_{XY} \cdot F_{XX} \cdot (t_i)_X$. Both displacement and substitution affect T_Y in the next interval of time when X is being expressed and the path of T_Y is given by Equation 2.9. Adapted to the present circumstances, Equation 2.9 is

$$T_Y = [T_{Y_I} + \hat{F}_Y(\tilde{t}_{X/A})_1 + \delta_{XY} \cdot F_{XX} \cdot (t_i)_X]$$
$$+ (\delta_{XY} \cdot F_{XX} - \gamma_{XY} \cdot F_{XX})[(\tilde{t}_{A/X}) - (t_i)_X]$$
$$+ \gamma_{XY}\left\{\frac{F_{XX}}{c_X} - \left[\frac{F_A}{c_A} + F_{XX} \cdot (t_i)_X\right]\right\}\{1 - e^{-c_X[(\tilde{t}_{A/X}) - (t_i)_X]}\}$$

Equation 2.9 also defines the path of T_Y in the next time interval, that of X's cessation consummatory lag, and gives

$$(T_{Y_I})_2 = (T_Y)_{c_x} = [T_{Y_I} + \hat{F}_Y(\tilde{t}_{X/A})_1 + \delta_{XY} \cdot F_{XX} \cdot (t_i)_X]$$
$$+ (\delta_{XY} \cdot F_{XX} - \gamma_{XY} \cdot F_{XX})[(\tilde{t}_{A/X}) - (t_i)_X]$$
$$+ \gamma_{XY}\left\{\frac{F_{XX}}{c_A} - \left[\frac{F_A}{c_A} + F_{XX} \cdot (t_i)_X\right]\right\}$$
$$\times \{1 - e^{-c_X[(\tilde{t}_{A/X}) - (t_i)_X]}\}$$
$$- \gamma_{XY}\left(\frac{F_A}{c_A}\right)[e^{-c_A \cdot (t_c)_A}][1 - e^{-c_X \cdot (t_c)_X}]$$

as the value of T_Y at the beginning of the next trial. By recalling that

$$\left[\frac{F_A}{c_A} + F_{XX} \cdot (t_i)_X\right] \cdot e^{-c_X[(\tilde{t}_{A/X}) - (t_i)_X]} + \frac{F_{XX}}{c_X}\{1 - e^{-c_X[(\tilde{t}_{A/X}) - (t_i)_X]}\}$$
$$= \left(\frac{F_A}{c_A}\right)[e^{-c_A \cdot (t_c)_A}]$$

the expression for $(T_{Y_I})_2$ can be simplified to

$$(T_{Y_I})_2 = [T_{Y_I}] + [\hat{F}_Y(\tilde{t}_{X/A})_1]$$
$$+ \{F_{XX}(\delta_{XY} - \gamma_{XY}) \cdot (\tilde{t}_{A/X}) - \gamma_{XY}\left(\frac{F_A}{c_A}\right)$$
$$\times [1 - (e^{-c_A \cdot (t_c)_A})(e^{-c_X \cdot (t_c)_X})]\}$$

This form of the equation is particularly useful because it isolates three components, the value of T_{Y_I} at the beginning of the first trial, the increment to T_Y in the interval prior to the choice of X, and the result (either an increment or a decrement to T_Y) of the choice of X. Examination of the third component reveals that displacement operates in the direction of an increment to T_Y whereas substitution encourages a decrement but that either an increment or a decrement can occur depending on the parameter values.

This is an opportune time to simplify the derivation by noticing that for all trials on which X is chosen subsequent to a trial on which X was also chosen, the two components, $[\hat{F}_Y(\bar{t}_{X/A})_x]$ and $\{F_{XX}(\delta_{XY} - \gamma_{XY}) \cdot (\bar{t}_{A/X}) - \gamma_{XY}(F_A/c_A)[1 - (e^{-c_A \cdot (t_c)_A})(e^{-c_X \cdot (t_c)_X})]\}$, remain the same. If we divide each component by $\hat{F}_Y$, we obtain the time of exposure to $\hat{F}_Y$, required in order to achieve the change in T_Y indicated. The first term becomes $(\bar{t}_{X/A})_x$, and let us symbolize, the second as $(\bar{t}_Y)_c$ where $(\bar{t}_Y)_c$ is added to $(\bar{t}_{X/A})_x$ if the term on which it is based is positive (because a positive value for this component means that T_Y has been increased as if longer exposure to F_Y had occurred) and subtracted from $(\bar{t}_{X/A})_x$ if that term is negative. Therefore, the net effect on T_Y of any trial on which X is chosen following a trial on which X was also chosen can be written in terms of the duration of exposure to $\hat{F}_Y$ that corresponds to the indicated change in T_Y as $(\bar{t}_{X/A})_x + (\bar{t}_Y)_c$ where

$$(\bar{t}_Y)_c$$
$$= \frac{\{F_{XX}(\delta_{XY} - \gamma_{XY}) \cdot (\bar{t}_{A/X}) - \gamma_{XY}(F_A/c_A)[1 - (e^{-c_A \cdot (t_c)_A})(e^{-c_X \cdot (t_c)_X})]\}}{\hat{F}_Y}$$

Now, the derivation can proceed more simply and quickly because it is possible to break down the total time of exposure to $\hat{F}_Y$ that would be required to bring T_Y from T_{Y_I} to F_A/c_A into parts:

$$(\bar{t}_{Y/A})'_1 = [(\bar{t}_{X/A})_1 + (\bar{t}_Y)_c] + [n_1(X) - 1][(\bar{t}_{X/A})_x + (\bar{t}_Y)_c] + (\bar{t}_{Y/A})_1$$

In words, this equation states that the initial theoretical latency for activity Y, $(\bar{t}_{Y/A})'_1$, is equal to the net exposure to $\hat{F}_Y$ from the first trial on which X was chosen, $[(\bar{t}_{X/A})_1 + (\bar{t}_Y)_c]$, plus the net exposure to $\hat{F}_Y$ from the following $n_1(X) - 1$ trials on which X was chosen, $[n_1(X) - 1][(\bar{t}_{X/A})_x + (\bar{t}_Y)_c]$, plus the exposure to $\hat{F}_Y$ gained on the trial on which Y was chosen. Since $(\bar{t}_{Y/A})_1 < (\bar{t}_{X/A})_x$ or Y could not be chosen, we can write $(\bar{t}_{Y/A})_1 = \sigma_1 \cdot (\bar{t}_{X/A})_x$ where $0 \le \sigma_1 < 1$ and $(\bar{t}_{Y/A})'_1 = (\bar{t}_{X/A})_1 + n_1(X)[(\bar{t}_{X/A})_x + (\bar{t}_Y)_c] - (1 - \sigma_1)(\bar{t}_{X/A})_x$. Solving this last equation for $n_1(X)$ yields $n_1(X) = [(\bar{t}_{Y/A})'_1 - (\bar{t}_{X/A})_1 + (1 - \sigma_1)(\bar{t}_{X/A})_x]/[(\bar{t}_{X/A})_x + (\bar{t}_Y)_c]$.

Similarly, for the subsequent run of Y's,

$$(\bar{t}_{X/A})_x = [\sigma_1 \cdot (\bar{t}_{X/A})_x + (\bar{t}_X)_c]$$
$$+ [n_1(Y) - 1][(\bar{t}_{Y/A})_y + (t_X)_c] + (\bar{t}_{X/A})_{x_{n_1(X)+1}}$$

where $(\bar{t}_{X/A})_{x_{n_1(X)+1}} \le (\bar{t}_{Y/A})_y$ or $(\bar{t}_{X/A})_{x_{n_1(X)+1}} = \theta_1 \cdot (\bar{t}_{Y/A})_y$ for $0 < \theta_1 \le 1$. By making the substitution for $(\bar{t}_{X/A})_{x_{n_1(X)+1}}$ and solving for $n_1(Y)$, we obtain $n_1(Y) = [(1 - \sigma_1)(\bar{t}_{X/A})_x + (1 - \theta_1)(\bar{t}_{Y/A})_y]/[(\bar{t}_{Y/A})_y + (\bar{t}_X)_c]$. Here $(\bar{t}_{Y/A})_y$ and $(\bar{t}_X)_c$ are defined analogously to $(\bar{t}_{X/A})_x$ and $(\bar{t}_Y)_c$. By this point in the series of X's and Y's, T_X and T_Y are no longer affected by their original inertial values, which means that

$$n_2(X) = \frac{(1 - \theta_1)(\tilde{t}_{Y/A})_y + (1 - \sigma_2)(\tilde{t}_{X/A})_x}{(\tilde{t}_{X/A})_x + (\tilde{t}_Y)_c}$$

$$n_2(Y) = \frac{(1 - \sigma_2)(\tilde{t}_{X/A})_x + (1 - \theta_2)(\tilde{t}_{Y/A})_y}{(\tilde{t}_{Y/A})_y + (\tilde{t}_X)_c}$$

$$\vdots$$

$$n_j(X) = \frac{(1 - \theta_{j-1})(\tilde{t}_{Y/A})_y + (1 - \sigma_j)(\tilde{t}_{X/A})_x}{(\tilde{t}_{X/A})_x + (\tilde{t}_Y)_c}$$

$$n_j(Y) = \frac{(1 - \sigma_j)(\tilde{t}_{X/A})_x + (1 - \theta_j)(\tilde{t}_{Y/A})_y}{(\tilde{t}_{Y/A})_y + (\tilde{t}_X)_c}$$

With the length of each run of X's and Y's specified in these terms

$$\frac{n(X)}{n(Y)} =$$

$$\frac{(\tilde{t}_{Y/A})'_1 - (\tilde{t}_{X/A})_1}{(\tilde{t}_{X/A})_x + (\tilde{t}_Y)_c}$$

$$+ \frac{(\tilde{t}_{Y/A})_y[(1 - \theta_1) + \cdots + (1 - \theta_{j-1})] + (\tilde{t}_{X/A})_x[(1 - \sigma_1) + \cdots + (1 - \sigma_j)]}{(\tilde{t}_{X/A})_x + (\tilde{t}_Y)_c}$$

$$\frac{(\tilde{t}_{X/A})_x[(1 - \sigma_1) + \cdots + (1 - \sigma_j)] + (\tilde{t}_{Y/A})_y[(1 - \theta_1) + \cdots + (1 - \theta_j)]}{(\tilde{t}_{Y/A})_y + (\tilde{t}_X)_c}$$

By using the same assumptions as previously, namely, that the bracketed terms involving the σ's and θ's are approximately equal for large j and that each gets indefinitely large as $j \to \infty$, we obtain

$$\frac{n(X)}{n(Y)} = \frac{(\tilde{t}_{Y/A})_y + (\tilde{t}_X)_c}{(\tilde{t}_{X/A})_x + (\tilde{t}_Y)_c} \tag{4.13}$$

as the expression for choice between alternatives X and Y under conditions of displacement and substitution. In this expression

$$(\tilde{t}_{Y/A})_y = \frac{F_A/c_A - (T_Y)_c}{\hat{F}_Y}, \qquad (\tilde{t}_{X/A})_x = \frac{F_A/c_A - (T_X)_c}{\hat{F}_X}$$

and $(\tilde{t}_Y)_c$ and $(\tilde{t}_X)_c$ have the values defined earlier. In addition, $\hat{F}_Y = \hat{F}_{YY} + \delta_{XY} \cdot \hat{F}_{XX}$ and $\hat{F}_X = \hat{F}_{XX} + \delta_{YX} \cdot \hat{F}_{YY}$.

Equation 4.13 can be expanded into

$$\frac{n(X)}{n(Y)} = \frac{(\hat{F}_X) \cdot (_g Y)_c + \hat{F}_Y\{F_{YY}(\delta_{YX} - \gamma_{YX}) \cdot (\bar{t}_{A/Y}) - \gamma_{YX}(F_A/c_A) \times [1 - (e^{-c_A \cdot (t_c)_A})(e^{-c_Y \cdot (t_c)_Y})]\}}{(\hat{F}_Y) \cdot (_g X)_c + \hat{F}_X\{F_{XX}(\delta_{XY} - \gamma_{XY}) \cdot (\bar{t}_{A/X}) - \gamma_{XY}(F_A/c_A) \times [1 - (e^{-c_A \cdot (t_c)_A})(e^{-c_X \cdot (t_c)_X})]\}}$$

(4.14)

A comparison of Equations 4.12 and 4.14 shows that no single statement can be made about the effects of displacement and substitution on choice. It is true that displacement tends to decrease the choice of the favored alternative (X) both by reducing the ratio of $\hat{F}_X/\hat{F}_Y$ from $\hat{F}_{XX}/\hat{F}_{YY}$ to $\hat{F}_{XX} + \delta_{YX} \cdot \hat{F}_{YY}/[\hat{F}_{YY} + \delta_{XY} \cdot \hat{F}_{XX}]$ and by encouraging $(\bar{t}_Y)_c > (\bar{t}_X)_c$ and that substitution tends to increase the choice of the favored alternative by encouraging $(\bar{t}_X)_c > (\bar{t}_Y)_c$. However, it is substitution and displacement in combination in any particular instance that determine the effects on choice, and their interaction can be complex.

CHAPTER 5

GENESIS OF THE INSTIGATING FORCE OF A STIMULUS

Until now, we have treated the instigating force of a stimulus as a constant goad to an activity during the interval of observation in which a change of activity occurs. Our primary interest has been to spell out its functional significance, that is, its role in combination with other variables in the causal sequence that culminates in a change from one activity to another. This is the broad problem of motivation. Now, as we turn to the question of the determinants of the instigating force of a stimulus, we consider the historical problems of conditioning and learning. Later, in Chapter 6, we extend the discussion to include the study of effects of individual differences in personality. Our consideration of the historical determinants of the instigating force of the stimulus provides an occasion for clarifying and justifying the use of two subscripts to describe the nature of the instigating force of stimuli and the behavioral tendencies that are produced by them and expressed in activities (for example, $F_{Run:Eat}$ and $T_{Run:Eat}$). In previous chapters, we have implicitly assumed that tendencies often refer to goal-directed behavior and that the first subscript on both force and tendency should represent the immediate next step in activity along a path to a goal and that the second subscript should represent the anticipated consequence (or goal) of that step. In this chapter and in the next we shall explain more fully why we have taken this view.

Two Perspectives Concerning Instigating Force

At the very outset we must confront the great range of phenomena, traditionally called stimuli, that function as instigating forces. What simple principle concerning the determinants of the instigating force will embrace all the instances—the effect of the metronome on Pavlov's dogs, the effect of the choice point cues in Tolman's rats, the effect on the child of his mother's call to dinner, the effect on the speeding motorist of the road sign which states, "Detroit, next left," the effect of an invitation to play golf with a friend whose ability is known to be nearly equal to your own, etc? None, we think. Hence, we approach these varied phenomena not with a wild hope of discovering one simple assertion about the determinants of the instigating force that will apply to all of them but instead with skepticism about the possibility of this ever being accomplished.

Our orientation is pragmatic. We shall consider the issue of the determinants of instigating force of a stimulus from more than one perspective. The first, in the present chapter, will be that of conditioning and learning in lower animals. This will lead to statements about the historical determinants of instigating force that refer to parameters of the natural history of the individual with similar stimuli. Here, we shall attempt to reconcile the concepts of this theory of action with the traditional concept of reinforcement. We shall be concerned with another kind of theory: one that is closely related but not inherently a part of the theory of action.

A second perspective, discussed in the next chapter, will show a way in which the principle of change of activity might be employed to discover empirically how information about the likelihood and the value of the consequences of an activity is related to the magnitude of the instigating force to undertake the activity. Here, the point of emphasis (as in the domain of human decision making in which language plays an important role) will be to show that the strength of the instigating force to undertake an activity, in fact, does vary with explicit information about the probability and the value of the consequences of activities.

Symptoms of the Strength of Instigating Force

The principle of change of activity and the several tenable operating assumptions advanced as a bridge between simple, idealized conditions and the more complicated and less than ideal conditions of actual empirical events provide the underlying logic for various possible diagnostic tests of the magnitude of the instigating force of a stimulus. Guided by this conceptual scheme, we know what to look for and under what conditions to infer that the instigating force to undertake a particular activity is relatively strong or weak. We can consider any one of the following behavioral measures, when obtained under conditions that adequately control for other systematic influences, as symptoms of the magnitude of the instigating force to undertake a particular activity in a given stimulus situation:

1. The promptness of the initiation of the activity when the stimulus to activity is presented (F_X).

2. The probability of the occurrence of the activity when the interval of observation is arbitrarily limited (F_X).

3. The preference for the activity when appropriate stimuli to undertake

both it and an alternative are presented and the choice is recorded (F_X relative to F_Y).

4. The vigor, magnitude, or involvement in the activity once it has been initiated and in progress for some time, as indicated by an appropriate measure of the level of performance (given $T_{A_F} = F_A/c_A$).

5. The persistence of the activity when it is in progress (given $T_{A_F} = F_A/c_A$).

6. The operant level of an activity and/or the amount of time spent in the activity in a constant environment (see Chapter 4).

Except for the time spent in an activity, there is no novelty in this list of aspects of behavior that are to be considered the potential measures of the power of a stimulus to instigate a response. Latency, probability of occurrence, magnitude, persistence, and the operant level of response have long been considered the relevant behavioral symptoms. The novelty of our argument lies in its identification of additional variables that may influence these same behavioral measures and in its specification of the conditions that must be realized in experimentation to justify the inference that different behavioral results may be unambiguously attributed to differences in the magnitude of the instigating force of the stimulus and not to some other factor. Quite aside from the difficulty of realizing the appropriate conditions in actual experimentation, we at least know what they are (if our basic premises are correct). Hence, we may discover important departures from the appropriate conditions in reviewing the traditional literature on the function of the stimulus, and we may be able to deduce new and more appropriate procedures.

REINFORCEMENT

Since a discussion of the acquisition and the change of the instigating force properties of a stimulus for a particular individual covers ground already familiar to the reader in other terms, it will be helpful to have some concrete behavioral incidents in mind to which the discussion can constantly return for the articulation of similarities and differences between our views and the ones of others. The initiation of food-seeking activity and the analysis of the vigorous and persistent pursuit of food is one of the frequently studied problems in the traditional approach to conditioning and learning in lower animals. And the incident is also a common everyday experience of the reader. Consequently, we use it as a point of reference to clarify the meaning of our concepts of the instigating force of the stimulus, the consummatory value of the response, and behavioral tendency. We can easily show how these concepts are used in reference to this well-known pattern of acquired behavior that in earlier days was discussed in terms of "instinct," "unconditioned and conditioned reflex," "S-R bonds," "expectancy of the goal and demand for the goal," and in modern S-R behavior theory in terms of "primary and secondary reinforcement," "habit," "drive," and "incentive."

Our point of departure for this discussion is the concept of Primary Reinforcement as it was conceived by Hull (1937) about the time that S-R psychology had finally begun to acknowledge that, in fact, there were separate problems of learning and performance (Tolman, 1932) or, as Hull (1935) then put it, the problem of "strengthening of connections or learning" versus the problem of "striving for goals or motivation." Hull then believed that the purposive pursuit of goals (for example, persistent food-seeking activity) was not to be considered innately given, as sometimes seemed to be suggested in the early writings of McDougall on instinct. Instead, he argued, the purposive pursuit of a goal could be derived from principles that would explain the strengthening of connections between stimulus and response (that is, the acquisition of habits).

One should begin, Hull stated, with the assumption that there are certain primary (that is, innate) reinforcing states of affairs. These are the states of affairs that Thorndike (1911) had originally referred to as "satisfying" in the initial statement of the Law of Effect. Thorndike also had pointed out that the satisfying states of affairs could be independently and objectively defined by observing an animal's readiness to approach or to strive for them. These primary reinforcing states of affairs, Hull (1937) also argued in the days before his need-reduction hypothesis, had to be discovered empirically but were, he then assumed—as we also shall assume—always characterized by a particular kind of consummatory commerce (R_G) with a stimulus (S_G).

In the case of interest to us, the reinforcing state of affairs can be described grossly as the event in which food is the stimulus (S_G) and eating is the consummatory activity (R_G). This, we notice, involves an activity that McDougall and others had earlier depicted as instinctive, that is, as an innately-determined compulsion to engage in the activity of eating when presented with food. Here, McDougall had argued, was one of a number of the innately given *ends* of behavior for which adequate means were soon learned. And in reference to the same event, we recall that Pavlov had introduced the technical terms unconditioned stimulus for the food, and unconditioned reflex or reaction for the eating of it. The latter includes the easily measured salivary component. The classic demonstration of conditioning showed that a previously neutral or ineffective stimulus, the sound of a metronome could, if repeatedly followed by the unconditioned stimulus and reaction to it, become a *conditioned* stimulus for a *conditioned* salivary reaction. This reaction would antedate, or anticipate, the occurrence of the initially effective unconditioned stimulus of food in the mouth.

In reference to this kind of event, the kind for which the terms instinctive behavior, unconditioned stimulus and unconditioned reaction, and primary reinforcing state of affairs all seemed appropriate in the context of earlier discussions, we employ the term *unconditioned* instigating force of the stimulus ($_{US}F$) and suggest that the sequence on the first occasion is adequately rendered by $S_{\text{Food}} \rightarrow {}_{US}F_{\text{Eat}} \rightarrow T_{\text{Eat}} \rightarrow R_{\text{Eat}} \rightarrow C_{\text{Eat}} \rightarrow T_{\text{Eat}}$. This sequence is described as follows. The food stimulus functions as unconditioned instigating force to eat. The strengthened tendency to eat is expressed in the activity of eating which, in turn, functions as consummatory force, reducing the tendency to eat.

Unconditioned Instigating Force

We begin by observing that the activity called eating (R_{Eat}) can be provoked unconditionally by a variety of different stimuli and presume that individuals differ quite substantially in the vigor of their unconditioned reaction to this class or family of unconditioned instigating forces. It will be recalled that the instigating force of a stimulus is the capacity of that stimulus to increase the strength of an action tendency in an individual. This implies that properties of both the stimulus and the individual will contribute to the magnitude of an instigating force. The terms *incentive value* and *motive* can be used in reference to these two potential sources of variation (Atkinson, 1964, p. 280). The first term is associated with the nature of the stimulus per se and the second is conceived as a reactive property of the individual (or personality) concerning that class of stimuli or, perhaps more appropriately, concerning the kind of activity produced by that class of stimuli. Specifically, we conceive of the unconditioned instigating force of a stimulus as the product of incentive value and motive in a given instance. Motive refers to individual differences in reactivity to a particular class of stimuli that have in common the property of provoking a particular kind of activity or reaction (in this case eating). Incentive value refers to the systematic differences in reactivity to various stimuli of that class (in this case, the kind of food substance).

In this connection, we call to mind the observation of individual differences in the initial vigor of sucking in human infants, the so-called lead-off response that has often been given considerable emphasis in the discussions of personality development. We suggest that similar differences are to be observed for other "instinctive reactions." Some infants obviously *like* to suck more than others right from the outset. That is, they do it more often and more vigorously than others when given oral stimulation.

It helps, we think, to point out that experiential terms such as "*liking* the activity" or "*attractiveness* of the activity" are often employed in reference to activities such as eating and that these terms can be translated into their behavioral equivalents as Tolman (1923) once did for other terms such as anger, fear, love, and purpose, all of which also seem to have a private-inner, rather than a public-behavioral reference. To like an activity or to find it attractive means, behaviorally, to engage in that activity when given an opportunity. Degrees of liking or attractiveness in the experiential language correspond to variations in the vigor and the persistence of the activity once initiated. One recalls, in this connection, James' instructive conjecture about the private, instinctive reaction of a mother hen to her nest of eggs: "To the broody hen the notion would probably seem monstrous that there should be a creature in the world to whom a nestful of eggs was not the utterly fascinating and precious and never-to-be-too-much-sat-upon object which it is to her" (James, 1890, Vol. 2, p. 387). The same kind of thing could be said of other activities that are *intrinsically regulated*, to use Koch's term (1956), by the immediate stimulus. Initially, an individual does what his nervous system is constructed to do under certain conditions. It seems appropriate for liking, the affective reaction, to be considered the private and covert aspect of the compulsive activity which is the public, observable, and more easily measured aspect of the event.

We can expand the initial behavioral repertoire of the neonate animal by assuming that there are a number of different kinds of instinctive reaction, that is, families of stimuli that provoke essentially the same kind of activity in the animal without prior training. The work of ethologists and developmental psychologists provides a more complete description of the innate potentialities of different species and evidence that often the innate readiness to react in a certain way to certain kinds of stimuli requires a degree of maturation.

With this broadened programmatic picture of the innate behavioral dispositions of the individual, we embrace the concept of innate individual differences in personality. Some individuals will at the outset of life have a stronger motive to engage in activity X than activity Y. In others, the initial dispositional preference may be reversed. Subsequent training may, it will be seen, produce substantial changes.

Conditioned Instigating Force and Elaboration of the Tendency

Let us return now to the question of an individual's learning *to strive for* food, that is, to engage vigorously and persistently in activities that culminate in eating when food is not immediately present to begin with. Thorndike's classic study of trial-and-error learning provides the kind of concrete reference to have in mind, although it will probably simplify our discussion to shift attention to the more frequently employed, standard T-maze in which a rat finds food after turning left but not after turning right at the choice point.

What is the simple, temporal sequence of objective events on the so-called reinforced left-turning trial? At the very molar level it is $S_{\text{Start Box}} \rightarrow R_{\text{Run}} \rightarrow S_{\text{Choice Point}} \rightarrow R_{\text{Turn Left}} \rightarrow S_{\text{Food}} \rightarrow R_{\text{Eat}}$, or more simply $S_1 \rightarrow R_X \rightarrow S_2 \rightarrow R_Y \rightarrow S_G \rightarrow R_G$.

Assuming that we had attained appropriate conditions for use of the Principle of Change of Activity in reference to either the initiation of the run (R_X) from the start box (S_1) or the preference for left turn (R_Y) at the choice point (S_2), we would be forced to conclude from our observations after a series of "rewarded" trials that the instigating force to run out of the start box had become stronger and the instigating force to turn left at the choice point had become relatively stronger than the instigating force to turn right.

We shall describe this traditional evidence of selective strengthening of a response by primary reinforcement as *a change in the instigating force of the stimulus for that individual*. Specifically, we shall say that $_{S_2}F_{\text{Turn Left: Eat}}$, the magnitude of the instigating force to turn left and eat produced by S_2, the choice-point cue, has grown with the repeated rewarded trials as has $_{S_1}F_{\text{Run: Eat}}$,[1] the magnitude of the instigating force to run down the stem of the maze and to eat produced by S_1, the start-box cue. Furthermore, we assume that the conjunction of turning left and eating immediately thereafter has produced another kind of change in the animal which we shall refer to as *an elaboration of the tendency* to eat. We mean to say that the very character of the T-maze activity has been changed in that the tendency to eat has now been elaborated to include turning left. In fact, we can expect further elaboration of the tendency to eat to include running down the stem in addition to turning left (see footnote 1). Thus, as the trials proceed, not only does the magnitude of instigating force of various stimuli of the maze change, the content of the *tendencies* being expressed in the T-maze activity also changes. We suggest that the combination of change in the instigating force of stimuli and elaboration of tendencies is what constitutes what is normally called instrumental learning.

Our view, influenced by the evolution of thought about the Law of Effect within the S-R Behavior theory tradition, is most similar to the Sheffield et al. (1954) drive-induction theory of reinforcement. He has argued, within the general framework of the S-R conceptual scheme, that the cues invariably produced by the occurrence of the "correct" response become more strongly conditioned to the consummatory reaction which soon follows than do the response-produced cues of the "incorrect" response. Consequently, on later occasions, any incipient movement corresponding to the correct response

---

[1] An even more detailed statement is that $_{S_1}F_{\text{Run, Turn Left: Eat}}$, the magnitude of the instigating force to run down the stem of the maze, turn left and eat produced by S_1, the start-box cue, has grown with the repeated rewarded trials.

begins to produce cues that elicit the consummatory reaction, and the excitement of this anticipatory reaction is transmitted to the response in progress, literally giving it a boost in strength as it begins to occur. The cues produced by an incipient incorrect response are not so strongly conditioned to the consummatory reaction. They fail to provide this transfer of anticipatory excitement to the incorrect response. It is this idea of *selective excitation* of responses that in the past have been followed by the goal reaction, whatever the physiological mechanism of it, that we wish to capture in the use of two subscripts to describe the nature of the changes that have occurred because an animal has turned left at a choice point and immediately thereafter has confronted food and eaten it.

To say that the tendency to eat has been elaborated, so that now turning left at the choice point is included, is equivalent to saying that a specific action tendency $T_{\text{Turn Left: Eat}}$ has been added to the already existent set of tendencies all of which share a common goal reaction and, therefore, constitute the family conveniently referred to as "Tendency to Eat" in the dispositional structure of the individual. This means that subsequent exposure to an instigating force that strengthens any one of the specific action tendencies belonging to this family will, according to the principle of displacement, also increase the inertial tendency of this new member of the family. And any consummatory force that subsequently reduces the strength of any one of these specific action tendencies will, according to the principle of substitution, reduce the inertial tendency of this new member.

This concept of elaboration of a tendency suggests that the *dispositional structure* of an individual (his personality), which at the outset of life is probably a relatively simple hierarchical ordering of potentialities for eating, drinking, escape, etc. (the instinctive reactions), comes in time to resemble something more akin to a set of spider webs (to use Tolman's early figure). It soon makes sense to say that the individual begins to express his tendency to eat as he begins to reach for food, or later, as he takes the first step toward a restaurant, and to describe what rats learn in simple T-mazes as "to run and eat," "to turn left and eat," etc. These specific action tendencies are expressed in instrumental striving for the goal, that is, in actions that culminate in the so-called consummatory activity. And, at least in humans, these specific action tendencies are correlated with an individual's cognitive expectations concerning the consequences of particular actions in particular situations. The expectancy (or anticipation) that running will be followed by eating or that running will cause eating to come about is the cognitive correlate of the tendency to run and eat (Chapter 6).

Why Does the So-called Instrumental Act Occur on the First Occasion?   Again looking at the simple T-maze with food at the end of the left alley, we consider the traditional paradox of selective learning: the to-be-correct response must occur the first time for *some reason* if it is to be reinforced. Why does this response, the one that is destined later to be called an instrumental goal-directed activity, occur for the first time? Our answer to this question is a rephrasing of the traditional answer. The response in question, for example, turning left at the choice point, occurs for the first time because the tendency to undertake that activity, however it has been instigated, dominates both the tendency sustaining the preceding choice-point behavior and also the tendency to turn right. This may come about because an unconditioned instigating force to turn left ($_{US}F_{\text{Turn Left}}$) is stronger than the instigating force to turn right or because a generalized, conditioned instigating force to turn left and engage in some other activity X ($_{S}F_{\text{Turn Left}: X}$) is stronger than the instigating force to turn right, or because of a combination of them. The point is that when our intention is to describe the conditions that will produce an elaboration of the tendency to eat and a growth in the instigating force of the choice-point stimulus for the tendency to turn left and eat, we are concerned only with the fact *that* the left-turning response does occur the first time and is followed by eating and not *why* it has occurred.

It is the temporal contiguity, $S_2 \rightarrow R_{\text{Turn Left}} \rightarrow S_{\text{Food}} \rightarrow R_{\text{Eat}}$, that accounts for the two changes that constitute instrumental learning. If S_2, the choice-point cue, initially produces only an $_{S_2}F_{\text{Left Turn}:\text{Explore}}$, which, in turn, produces a $T_{\text{Turn Left}:\text{Explore}}$ that becomes dominant and is expressed in the activity of turning left, and this, in turn, is followed by the unanticipated occurrence of S_{Food}, which functions to produce $_{US}F_{\text{Eat}} \rightarrow T_{\text{Eat}} \rightarrow R_{\text{Eat}}$, there is, in our view, a change in the implications of S_2 for the given individual on a subsequent occasion. This change in the implications of S_2 for him can be described as a change from $_{S_2}F_{\text{Turn Left}:\text{Eat}} = 0$ (on the preceding trial) to $_{S_2}F_{\text{Turn Left}:\text{Eat}} > 0$ (on the subsequent trial). In this case, the initial growth in the instigating force of S_2 for the tendency to turn left and eat corresponds to the event already described as an elaboration of the tendency to eat. If S_2 had produced even a weak $_{S_2}F_{\text{Turn Left}:\text{Eat}}$ on the initial trial, there would already exist a $T_{\text{Turn Left}:\text{Eat}} > 0$ before the occurrence of the so-called reinforcing event on the first trial, and we would speak of increasing the strength of $_{S_2}F_{\text{Turn Left}:\text{Eat}}$ as a result of the first trial instead of elaborating the tendency to eat.

A Principle of Learning.   We propose the following partial and preliminary statement of a Principle of Learning. *A stimulus acquires for its next occurrence a magnitude of instigating force for an activity that is a positive function of the strength of the action tendency expressed in the activity.* This means that if a particular response X occurs as the expression of the elaborated tendency for activity X and G ($T_{X:G}$) in the presence of a given stimulus (S) and is followed by a heightening of $T_{X:G}$ to a level above the one of the just previous occasion when $T_{X:G}$ was expressed in the presence of S, the magnitude of instigating force ${}_S F_{X:G}$ will be increased. This, we presume, is what happens on what is traditionally called a reinforced trial. In our T-maze example, the activity of turning left at the choice point (S_2), which expresses the tendency, $T_{\text{Turn Left:Eat}}$, is immediately followed by the unconditioned instigating force of food, ${}_{US}F_{\text{Eat}}$, which increases the strength of T_{Eat}. It is the height- ened strength of T_{Eat} on which the new ${}_{S_2}F_{\text{Turn Left:Eat}}$ is based.

The principle also applies to the change in instigating force that occurs on a nonreinforced, or extinction trial. If the $T_{\text{Turn Left:Eat}}$ is already being instigated by choice-point cues (S_2), but the stimulus of food does not immediately follow to heighten the tendency to eat after the left turn, there subsequently will be a weaker ${}_{S_2}F_{\text{Turn Left:Eat}}$. Why? Because, according to the principle, the strength of the instigating force of S_2 depends on the strength of the tendency to eat that is expressed in the activity on the previous trial, and this strength is necessarily less without a boost in the tendency that is provided by the unconditioned instigating force of food. This constitutes what is traditionally called an extinction trial. After a series of nonreinforced trials, S_2 would be expected to lose most of its instigating force to turn left and eat.

This preliminary verbal treatment of the relationship of an hypothesis about change in the instigating force of stimulus to the familiar concepts of acquisition and extinction will be supplemented later in the chapter by a more specific and mathematical statement that will help to clarify the details of the hypothesis. But before attempting to increase the precision of what has been said, there are several more general issues to be considered.

The Distinction between Primary and Secondary Reinforcement.   A food stimulus will produce an unconditioned instigating force to eat and a heightening of the tendency to eat. This, in our view, constitutes an instance of primary reinforcement. A nonfood stimulus such as S_2, the choice-point cue of our example, which initially has no effect on the tendency to eat but which, according to our principles of elaboration and learning, acquires instigating force to turn left and eat by being paired with S_{Food} (as described above), can subsequently provide secondary reinforcement. That is, immediately following the occurrence of running from the stimulus situation of the start box (S_1), the conditioned instigating force to turn left and eat of S_2 increases the strength of tendency to eat. This, in turn, accounts for the change in the instigating force of S_1, the start-box cue. Primary reinforcement is provided by *unconditioned* instigating forces. Secondary reinforcement is provided by *conditioned* instigating forces. The two events are alike in that both involve a stimulus-produced increase in the magnitude of a behavioral tendency following the activity of interest. And, in both cases, this can be observed on a subsequent occasion to have increased the strength of instigating force of the immediately preceding stimuli for the tendency supporting that activity.

But alike as primary and secondary reinforcing events are in their implications for learning, they are usually very different in their more immediate motivational effects. The presence of food produces not only a heightening of the tendency to eat but also an occasion for the activity of eating. The consummatory value of eating produces, almost immediately, a decline in the strength of tendency to eat and a stabilization of the tendency at a lower level defined by F/c. The secondary reinforcing stimulus, in contrast, does not itself provide an immediate occasion for the consummatory activity. So normally this event is not immediately followed by reduction in the strength of tendency. During exposure to the conditioned instigating force of a secondary reinforcing stimulus, the behavioral tendency will move toward a level defined by F/c, but this c is substantially less than the c of eating itself. This distinction helps to identify what it is that primary and secondary reinforcing events have in common: a stimulus that functions as a strong instigating force to heighten the strength of a tendency.

The change in instigating force of concurrent or immediately antecedent stimuli is relevant and important for instrumental learning. But we must not ignore the uncommon aspect of primary and secondary reinforcing events— the response side—which, in one case, involves *preparatory activity* and, in the other case, *consummatory activity*. The latter, in our view, does not differ qualitatively from the former but does differ quantitatively in the magnitude of the consummatory value of the activity. And the substantial difference in consummatory value accounts for the grossly different *immediate* motivational consequences of primary and secondary reinforcing behavioral events. In our view, the tendency-reducing aspect of the primary reinforcing event, for example, the reduction of the tendency to eat caused by the eating of food, has nothing whatever to do with reinforcement as is supposed in the drive-reduction principle of reinforcement. Our view of reinforcement corresponds more to the incentive-motivation interpretation of Spence (1956) and to Sheffield's (1954) drive-induction theory of reinforcement, and it stresses the tendency-enhancing property of the primary reinforcing event.

The Separable Aspects of Primary Reinforcing Behavioral Events

Enough has been said of our conception of instrumental learning to warrant a closer look at the kind of behavioral event that has traditionally been called a primary reinforcing state of affairs. Each instance involves an unconditioned reaction to some stimulus, some kind of behavioral commerce (R_G) with a particular kind of stimulus (S_G): for example, eating-food, drinking-water, sexual activity-mate, visual exploration-novel stimulus, etc.

Let us continue to focus on the sequence of food (S_{Food}) and eating (R_{Eat}) as our reference. We can discriminate four potentially independent properties of the behavioral event and, then, can pursue the questions of what, if any, inherent relationships may exist among these properties and what, if any, correlations may now exist among the several properties as a result of the evolutionary history of the species.

The four potentially independent properties, as viewed from the present scheme, are (1) the magnitude of unconditioned instigating force $(_{US}F_{\text{Eat}})$ of the stimulus (S_{Food}), (2) the consummatory value (c_{Eat}) of the activity (R_{Eat}) that is unconditionally provoked by the stimulus (S_{Food}), (3) the reinforcing power of the event, and (4) the adaptive significance of the event.

The first two properties are basic to our theory of action and have been identified with particular parameters of the theory. The latter two properties are not similarly basic, and we shall endeavor to treat them as derivatives of the theory. To do this, let us consider some of the important implications of the basic Principle of Change of Activity in combination with the Principle of Reinforcement outlined in the preceding pages and specifically in reference to the pursuit and the eating of food. We shall search for suppositions that might be advanced about primary reinforcing behavioral events in general.

Of first importance is the fact that the instigating force of the food stimulus (S_{Food}) invariably precedes the activity of eating (R_{Eat}). This means that S_{Food} *will always have its enhancing effect on the behavioral tendency* (T_{Eat}) *before* (R_{Eat}) *can begin to have its consummatory effect on the tendency.* The effect of the natural temporal order is accentuated by initiation consummatory lag. An example of this is shown in Figure 5.1.

General observation tells us that the instigating force of most food stimuli is normally strong but that the consummatory value of eating most foods is also normally quite substantial. Appetite is enhanced by the initial tastes of the meal. But the tendency to eat normally declines as eating and ingestion continues, so that the activity is in time interruptible. The individual, in fact, does change from eating to some other activity before again initiating activities that culminate in eating. We also know that the behavioral event, food-eating, is normally reinforcing and that the activity of eating also has great adaptive significance. It supplies substances that are required for the continued health and vigor of the individual and without which individual survival and survival of the species would be impossible.

Now, given the principle of change of activity as an initial premise, let us consider what would happen if food stimuli had their assumed property of strong instigating force but the activity of eating had very little, if any, consummatory value. Once contact with food had been made and eating had been initiated, the tendency to eat would continue to rise to a very high level defined by $_{S_{\text{Food}}}F_{\text{Eat}}/c_{\text{Eat}}$, and with the exception of the exhaustion of

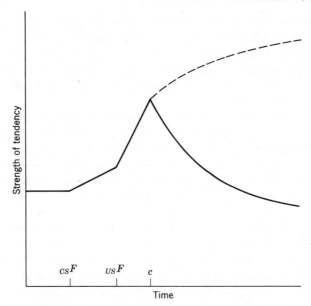

FIGURE 5.1   Growth and decline in the strength of the tendency to eat as a function of different onset times for instigating and consummatory forces.

the supply of available food, the individual would continue eating and would be extremely resistant to change from the activity of eating to some other activity. Notice the broken-line path in Figure 5.1. We might presume that this combination of strong $_{US}F_{Eat}$ from S_{Food} with weak c_{Eat} from R_{Eat} would be a maladaptive combination because (1) it would drastically reduce the probability of engaging in other activities that are requisite for survival of the individual and species; and (2) it would greatly increase the probability that the individual would be intensely involved and literally trapped in a given activity for a great length of time and, therefore, much more subject to attack by predators. We might suppose, then, that the selective process of evolutionary history by now would have worked generally to eliminate the particular combination of strong $_{US}F$ with weak c, thereby, producing a positive correlation between the magnitude of the unconditioned instigating force of stimuli to engage in a particular kind of activity and the consummatory value of that kind of activity.

In contrast, consider another logical possibility: that food stimuli had very weak unconditioned instigating force but that eating had its typically strong consummatory value. According to the Principle of Change of Activity, we would expect that it now would take a substantial duration of exposure to food stimuli to strengthen the tendency to eat—enough so that eating would be initiated and that this would be followed by an immediate decline in the strength of tendency to eat toward a very low level defined by $s_{Food}F_{Eat}/c_{Eat}$. The individual, in other words, would eat less frequently and then would not eat much before being tempted away to engage in some other kind of activity. This is obviously another maladaptive combination, especially if it were typical of the kinds of activities that are required for survival of the individual and the species.

By this line of reasoning, from the principles that have been introduced, we are led to the general conclusion that even though there might be no inherent relationships among the several separate properties of primary reinforcing behavioral events, evolutionary history by now would have produced certain obvious correlations among these separable properties, but ones for which occasional exceptions should still be found in the state of nature.

First, there should have been a relatively rapid extinction of individuals and species for whom the unconditioned instigating force of stimuli to engage in activities that are required for survival was weak and inadequate. They would die off for want of engaging in the requisite activities sufficiently to maintain health and vigor. Second, but for different reasons, a similar fate should have befallen members of a species who, although strongly instigated to engage in certain activities, were deficient in shutoff mechanisms. In the terms of the present theory, they were members of the species for whom the consummatory value of an activity requisite for survival was too low.

Finally, we should expect that individuals and species for whom prevalent stimuli of the environment produce very strong instigating forces to engage in many different activities that have little, if any, particular adaptive significance would also soon tend to become extinct. For even if significant adaptive activities were as strongly instigated, the sheer number and variety of competing activities would mean that something less than an optimal amount of time would be spent in activities requisite to health, vigor, and survival. This suggests that, although exceptions to the rule may still be found in a state of nature, we should expect to find that the average magnitude of instigating force of stimuli to engage in activities that have adaptive significance, generally, will exceed that of stimuli to engage in activities that have little adaptive significance. Yet some of these other behavioral events, not particularly crucial from the viewpoint of survival and evolution, may constitute primary reinforcing events because the instigating force of their stimuli is quite strong. The compelling, enjoyable quality of certain complex patterns of stimulation, which produce an activity often called aesthetic appreciation, may be a case in point.

The conclusion reached from an application of the present conceptual scheme to the analysis of several aspects of the behavioral events that have been identified as primary reinforcements is clear: some earlier hypotheses concerning the nature of reinforcement have mistakenly viewed one or another of the obvious correlations between the reinforcing property and some other property of a behavioral event that are accidents of evolutionary history as an inherent, causal relationship. Thus, for example, the need-reduction principle of reinforcement (Hull, 1943) is suggested by the fact that many reinforcing behavioral events have adaptive significance. It would be expected to cover a large number of instances of primary reinforcement, but not all of them, according to the present argument. And this seems to be the state of the evidence concerning the generality of that principle. According to the present argument, we should expect to find reinforcing events that have little, if any, adaptive significance, particularly if we create experimentally some behavioral possibilities that have not often arisen in the natural habitat of a given species.

The drive-reduction principle of reinforcement (Miller, 1959; Brown, 1961), one step removed from the biological need-reduction hypothesis, focuses more on the property of most primary reinforcing behavioral events to reduce the tendency that motivated the behavior. In the present scheme, this concept is approximated by the concept of the consummatory value of the activity. And again we have argued that even though evolutionary history should have produced by now a correlation between the reinforcing power of an event, which we identify with the magnitude of the unconditioned instigating force of the stimulus to engage in what is commonly called the goal activity, and the consummatory value of the activity (that is, its property of reducing the tendency that caused it), the latter plays no essential role in the process of reinforcement.

The Concept of Reinforcement in Perspective

The Empirical Law of Effect, which states that certain behavioral events enhance and that other behavioral events do not enhance the subsequent probability of the occurrence of the particular activities that have preceded them, has provided the central guide for 70 years of research on learning. In our view, the process that accounts for this enhanced probability of the occurrence of a "reinforced" response under certain conditions, also, accounts for the stability in the probability of the response under other conditions, and the decreased probability of the response under still different conditions.

The change in the instigating force of a stimulus *as a function of its most recent motivational consequences* is ubiquitous. The traditional concept of reinforcement merely identifies one subclass of instances: the ones in which R_X to S_1 is immediately followed by a substantial increase in the magnitude of some behavioral tendency T_G that is caused by the instigating force $_{S_2}F_G$ of the stimulus S_2 that follows R_X. According to the principle of learning that has been introduced, the subsequent magnitude of $_{S_1}F_{X:G}$ produced by S_1 will always be influenced by the magnitude of T_G on the most recent occurrence. So, when the stimulus consequence of R_1 produces strong instigating force, it is likely that subsequently $_{S_1}F_{X:G}$ will be stronger. When the stimulus consequence of R_X produces relatively weak instigating force (as on an extinction trial when the rewarding stimulus is omitted), it is likely that subsequently $_{S_1}F_{X:G}$ will be weaker and, hence, that there will be a decreased probability of occurrence of R_X. There are many other instances in which the stimulus consequence of R_X appears to have very little, if any, effect on the subsequent latency, the probability of occurrence, or the magnitude of R_X. It would appear that in these instances the instigating force $_{S_1}F_{X:G}$, produced by S_1 had not changed in magnitude.

To appreciate how stability as well as change in the motivational implications of environmental stimuli can come about, we must make a more complete and thorough analysis of the details of behavior in the instrumental learning paradigm. Let us do this by considering the instance of a rat running from a starting box, through an alley, to a goal box containing food. A particular trial involves a change from some other activity A to initiation of the run (R_X) in the start box (S_1), continuous exposure to the cue of the alley (S_2) as the run through the alley (R_Y) proceeds until the goal stimulus (S_G) produces the consummatory reaction (R_G) on the so-called reinforced trials. During training, the heightening of T_G by the $_{US}F_G$ of S_G immediately following R_Y to S_2 produces growth in $_{S_2}F_{Y:G}$. This acquired secondary reinforcing property of S_2, in turn, produces a growth in $_{S_1}F_{X.Y:G}$ of S_1. Given ideal conditions, the level of $T_{X.Y:G}$ required to produce the initiation of the run will be the same on successive trials (because T_{A_F} and T_{B_I} are constant), but the time required to produce this level of tendency (the latency of R_X) will decrease because $_{S_1}F_{X.Y:G}$ is increasing in strength. And even though the level of tendency to run and to eat is the same at the initiation of the run on successive trials, it will rise more rapidly during the run and to higher and higher levels on successive trials, each controlled by its ever increasing asymptote, $_{S_2}F_{Y:G}/c_Y$, because $_{S_2}F_{Y:G}$ is also stronger on each successive reinforced trial whereas c_Y does not change. This is why the level of the tendency to eat as the animal enters the goal box just prior to exposure to S_G is higher on successive trials and, consequently, why the maximum level attained by T_G, following the constant boost from the unconditioned instigating force of the food, is greater on each successive trial. This is the condition required for continued growth in the magnitude of instigating forces to undertake the preparatory or instrumental approach activities that constitute *striving for the food*. But as the magnitude of $_{S_2}F_{Y:G}$ grows on successive trials, and the level of tendency produced by it rises, *the animal will run faster, for the magnitude of the tendency is expressed in the vigor of the response*.

The increasing speed of the animal's instrumental approach activity thus will serve to limit the length of exposure to S_2. The faster it runs, the shorter the exposure to S_2. Thus, after a number of trials, the decrease in duration of exposure to S_2 can, on some trial, exactly compensate for the increase in $_{S_2}F_{Y:G}$ attributable to the last rewarded trial. When this happens, the animal will enter the goal box on that trial with the same level of tendency it had on the previous trial. And following the usual boost in T_G, provided by the $_{US}F_G$ of S_G, the maximum level of T_G will be the same as on the preceding trial. When this happens, the magnitude of $_{S_1}F_{X.Y:G}$ and $_{S_2}F_{Y:G}$ will stabilize and, for all intents and purposes, so also will the level of tendencies reflected in the measures on R_X and R_Y in that situation. This stabilization in the food-seeking behavior, often referred to as habitual behavior, comes about *even though the process by which the instigating force of a stimulus on a subsequent trial is determined by the magnitude of tendency following the response on the preceding, or most recent trial, continues to operate on each occasion.*

During a series of reinforced trials, the learning series, the increase in speed of instrumental approach response attributable to the growth of the instigating force of various environmental stimuli limits the duration of that activity. This tends to work against the tendency in its approach to asymptote. The tendency probably does not rise as high as it might if a longer duration of exposure were maintained over trials.

During the extinction series, the influence of vigor of the animal's response on the duration of exposure to the instigating forces has just the opposite effect. As the extinction series begins, S_G (the food reward) is withdrawn and S_3 (an empty goal box) takes its place in the temporal sequence $S_1 - S_2 - S_3$. The stimulus of the empty goal box will initially produce some conditioned instigating force to eat, since it has been repeatedly associated with eating and, thus, should serve as secondary reinforcement. But the boost in the magnitude of the tendency to eat on the first extinction trial will be much less than the one previously produced by the goal box stimuli and the food. As a result, $_{S_2}F_{Y:G}$ and $_{S_1}F_{X.Y:G}$ will be weakened. The latency of initiation of the run (R_X) will increase, and the tendency will move toward a new and lower level defined by $_{S_2}F_{Y:G}/c_Y$ during the run on each consecutive extinction trial. As the tendency during the course of the run becomes weaker over trials, the speed of the instrumental approach response will also decrease. This will serve to increase the duration of exposure to the now weakened instigating force and, thus, enhance the possibility that the magnitude of the tendency will approach its new, and lower limit defined by $_{s_2}F_{Y:G}/c_Y$ on each consecutive trial.

It is apparent that there is an asymmetry in the effect of speed of the instrumental response on the duration of exposure to those stimuli that instigate approach to the goal. When the instigating force of these stimuli is being strengthened during the reinforcement series, the effect of increased speed of response is to reduce or limit the magnitude of the increase in $_{s_2}F_{Y:G}$ that will occur on consecutive trials. When the instigating force of these stimuli is being weakened during the extinction series and when the value of $_{s_2}F_{Y:G}/c_Y$ has fallen below the level of initial strength of $T_{Y:G}$, the effect of the decreased speed of response is to enhance the decrease in magnitude of $_{s_2}F_{Y:G}$ that will occur on each consecutive trial. This asymmetry is eliminated when the duration of exposure is not contingent on the vigor of the instrumental approach response as, for example, in the contrived conditions of classical conditioning when the interval between S_1 and S_G is fully controlled by the experimenter.

We shall now discuss classical conditioning. This provides a good opportunity for the presentation of a mathematical statement of the hypothesis concerning change in the instigating force of a stimulus and for the study of its implications in the simplest instance of learning. Following this, we shall return to some of the complexities in the ordinary instances of behavior.

CLASSICAL CONDITIONING

A classically conditioned response is an expression of a tendency. It is not the complete activity that occurs following a conditioned stimulus but only a part of that activity. In classical conditioning, just as in instrumental learning, the instinctual reaction to the unconditioned stimulus is elaborated over trials. Pavlov (1927) noticed this in regard to salivary conditioning (the domain that we use for reference in our discussion) when he acknowledged that the *CS* produced complex motor adjustments (for example, orienting responses) as well as salivary reaction. He chose to confine his observations to the salivary response but did so knowing that he was leaving out a significant portion of the dog's conditioned activity. We follow him in focusing our attention on the measures of the salivary response, now, however, treating them as measures of the strength of the tendency derived from the unconditioned stimulus of food. We acknowledge that by dealing with only the salivary data we ignore parts of the elaborated tendency to eat, but we do so on the assumption that a quantitative measure of salivating is an accurate index of the strength of the tendency to eat.

In this section, we apply our hypothesis concerning the change in the instigating force of a stimulus to simple salivary conditioning and develop certain aspects of the hypothesis mathematically. The first paradigm to be examined is the one in which the onset of the *CS* precedes that of the *US* and the two stimuli terminate together. Figure 5.2 diagrams this relationship and designates t_1 as the duration of the *CS* before the *US* occurs and t_2 as the duration of the *US*: The overall duration of the *CS* is, thus, $t_1 + t_2$.

Further Development of the Principle of Learning

We now refine the preliminary statement of the Principle of Learning given earlier by adopting a particular working hypothesis. Thus far we have

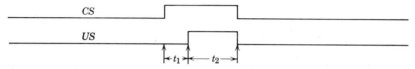

FIGURE 5.2 A simple classical conditioning paradigm in which the *CS* precedes the *US* in onset and the *CS* and *US* terminate together.

said only that the magnitude of the instigating force acquired by a stimulus is a positive function of the strength of the expressed action tendency. We now propose a more complete and quantitative Principle of Learning: *a stimulus acquires for its next occurrence a magnitude of instigating force for an activity that is proportional to the maximum value attained by the product of the strength of the perceptual tendency of the stimulus and the strength of the action tendency expressed during the interval of the activity.*[2] In symbols, this is given by the rule

$$(_sF_R)_{N+1} = \lambda[(T_{s_N})_t \cdot (T_{R_N})_t]_{\text{Max}} \tag{5.1}$$

where (T_s) represents the perceptual tendency, λ is the constant of proportionality, and (T_R) represents the action tendency. This is a *recency hypothesis*. On each occasion when a tendency is expressed in an activity in the presence of a stimulus, the magnitude of instigating force of the stimulus *for that activity* is replaced by a new magnitude of instigating force that depends on the strength of the tendency then expressed. The increase or decrease in the instigating force of a stimulus that occurs on an acquisition or extinction trial, depends directly on the strength of the tendency expressed *on that trial* and only indirectly on previous trials. Let us examine this process in detail by using the simple paradigm of Figure 5.2.

---

[2] The perceptual tendency was introduced in Chapter 2, and is shown in Figure 2.2*b*. The ticking metronome (in Pavlov's experiment) functions as an instigating force for the conscious perception of a ticking metronome. The perceptual tendency, thus produced and strengthened, mediates instigating force for overt reactions. The strength of this perceptual tendency is influenced by the duration of exposure to the instigating force of its stimulus.

To simplify matters, we assume that only the *CS* and *US* have instigating force for the tendency to salivate; that trials are spaced sufficiently apart so that the inertial tendency to salivate is near zero and is negligible when the

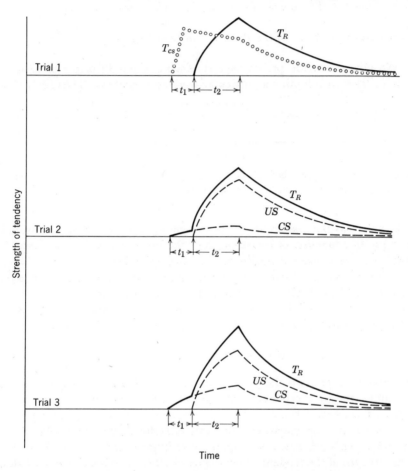

FIGURE 5.3   The theoretical analysis of the first three conditioning trials for the paradigm shown in Figure 5.2. (See the text and the Mathematical Notes for the explanation and mathematical derivation.)

CS is presented; and that no other stronger and incompatible tendencies prevent the immediate expression of any tendency to salivate that is present. We also assume that the *CS* initially produces no instigating force to salivate [that is, $(_{CS}F_{Sal})_1 = 0$] and that the unconditioned instigating force of the *US* remains constant at $_{US}F_{Sal}$. Furthermore, we assume that the initiation consummatory-lag durations for the *CS* and *US* are negligible and can be ignored[3] and that the consummatory value of salivating is relatively small, so that the tendency to salivate rises toward asymptote over the duration of the *CS* and *US*. Finally, we assume that the rate of decline in the perceptual tendency that is instigated by the *CS* (see, again, Chapter 2) is less than the rate of rise in the tendency to salivate, so that the maximum product of the two tendencies is always at the end of the *US* interval. This assumption is reasonable for the paradigm of Figure 5.2 but is probably not reasonable for other paradigms, for example, those of delay, trace, and backward conditioning.

Figure 5.3 illustrates what happens during the first three trials of conditioning according to the theory. On Trial 1 with $_{CS}F_{\text{Sal}} = 0$, only the *US* is effective in strengthening the tendency to salivate (T_{Sal}). Since the duration of the *US* is t_2, the duration of exposure to the instigating force of the *US*, $_{US}F_{\text{Sal}}$, is similarly t_2, and the maximum value of T_{Sal} attained is $[_{US}F_{\text{Sal}}/c_{\text{Sal}}](1 - e^{-c_{\text{Sal}} \cdot t_2})$, according to our basic expression for the growth of a tendency when it is being instigated and consumed (Equation 1.11) and when $(T_{\text{Sal}})_I = 0$.

According to our recency hypothesis, the magnitude of the instigating force of the *CS* is now changed from $(_{CS}F_{\text{Sal}})_1 = 0$ to

$$(_{CS}F_{\text{Sal}})_2 = \lambda' \left[\frac{_{US}F_{\text{Sal}}}{c_{\text{Sal}}} (1 - e^{-c_{\text{Sal}} \cdot t_2}) \right]$$

in which λ' now also includes the constant value of (T_{cs}) from trial to trial.

When the individual is again exposed to *CS* on Trial 2, this instigating force to salivate, newly acquired by *CS*, increases T_{Sal} during t_1, as shown in Figure 5.3, before the onset of the originally effective *US*. During the interval t_1 only $_{CS}F_{\text{Sal}}$ has an effect. But during the interval t_2 both the *CS* and the *US* provide instigating force to salivate. Hence, according to our rule for combination of the strengths of tendencies that refer to the same reaction (see Chapter 3), the total strength of T_{Sal} is now given by the sum of the separate contributions from the *CS* and the *US*. It is apparent in Figure 5.3 that $(T_{\text{Sal}})_2$ reaches its maximum strength at the end of interval t_2 as given by the expression

$$(T_{\text{Sal}})_2 = \frac{(_{CS}F_{\text{Sal}})_2}{C_{\text{Sal}}} [1 - e^{-c_{\text{Sal}} \cdot (t_1 + t_2)}] + \frac{_{US}F_{\text{Sal}}}{c_{\text{Sal}}} (1 - e^{-c_{\text{Sal}} \cdot t_2}) \quad (5.2)$$

Equation 5.2 indicates the general expression for the maximal strength of

---

[3] The derivation for the case, where the initiation consummatory lags for the *CS* and *US* are taken into account explicitly, involves more complex equations, but it does not yield a basically different statement about the conditioning process. The same can be said when the inertial tendency is assumed greater than zero but constant across trials.

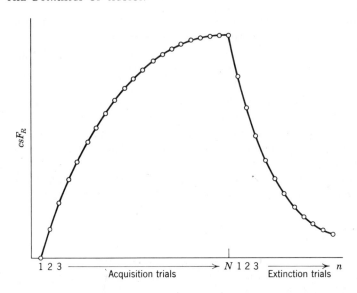

FIGURE 5.4   The acquisition and extinction of $_{CS}F_R$ for the paradigm given in Figure 5.2. See Equations 5.3 and 5.4 for the relevant mathematical functions.

T_{Sal} that holds true for all trials given the paradigm under consideration. To determine the value of T_{Sal} for any specific trial, the magnitude of $_{CS}F_{\text{Sal}}$ must be known for that trial. For Trial 2,

$$(_{CS}F_{\text{Sal}})_2 = \lambda'\left[\frac{_{US}F_{\text{Sal}}}{c_{\text{Sal}}}\left(1 - e^{-c_{\text{Sal}}\cdot t_2}\right)\right]$$

as already shown above. So by substitution of this quantity for $(_{CS}F_{\text{Sal}})_2$ in Equation 5.2 we obtain the strength of $(T_{\text{Sal}})_2$. Now we can proceed to account for $(_{CS}F_{\text{Sal}})_3$ in terms of the strength of $(T_{\text{Sal}})_2$ and so on. In the notes at the end of the chapter we continue the trial-by-trial analysis and arrive at the general expressions for the magnitude of $_{CS}F_{\text{Sal}}$ on any trial and for the limit of conditioning for the conditions under examination.

Figure 5.4 plots the predicted growth of $_{CS}F_{\text{Sal}}$ over trials and shows the negatively accelerated function that represents the acquisition of instigating force for some activity (or reaction) by a stimulus under the temporal conditions given in Figure 5.2. The change in magnitude of $_{CS}F_{\text{Sal}}$ is brought about in training, given the recency hypothesis, because the stronger T_{Sal} produced by a stronger $_{CS}F_{\text{Sal}}$ on each trial is enhanced still further each time by exposure to the constant $_{US}F_{\text{Sal}}$ of the US.

The same principle applies equally well to extinction of $_{CS}F_{\text{Sal}}$ when the US is no longer presented to give the tendency a boost on each trial. Since the principle relies on recency alone, any change, whether upward or downward, in the maximal strength of T_{Sal} that is expressed on a given trial will be reflected in the strength of $_{CS}F_{\text{Sal}}$ on the next trial. On an extinction trial, the *US* is omitted. This means that the maximal strength attained by T_{Sal} is given by the influence of *CS* alone. In the notes, we repeat the analysis to account for the changes in $_{CS}F_{\text{Sal}}$ that occur as a result of the omission of *US* during extinction as shown for three trials in Figure 5.5. The top graph tracks the strength of the tendency to salivate for the last acquisition trial

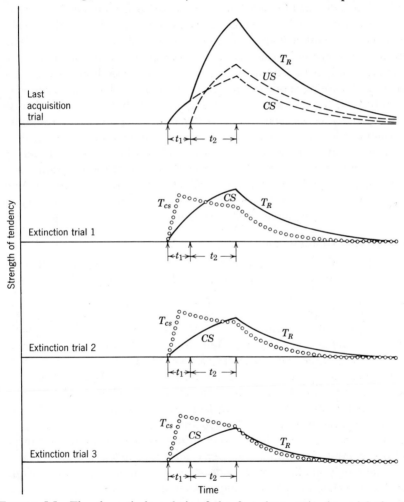

FIGURE 5.5   The theoretical analysis of the first three extinction trials for the paradigm shown in Figure 5.2. Mathematical derivations appear in the text and in the Mathematical Notes.

on which both the CS and US occur. The next three graphs follow T_{Sal} over time within each of the first three extinction trials. It can be seen that the maximal T_{Sal} is less on each succeeding extinction trial. Since the magnitude of $_{CS}F_{Sal}$ is directly dependent on the maximal T_{Sal} on the previous trials, these graphs also show the diminished effect of $_{CS}F_{Sal}$ during the course of extinction. Under the conditions assumed, $_{CS}F_{Sal}$ diminishes from its terminal acquisition level in a negatively accelerated decline to zero as extinction trials are continued. An example of an extinction curve for $_{CS}F_{Sal}$ is included in Figure 5.4 along with the acquisition curve.

The acquisition and extinction functions just derived have the classical negatively accelerated shape traditionally proposed for these curves. Their appearance, however, results from the assumptions made about the conditioning situation, not from the hypothesis about conditioning itself. Our principle of learning is one of strict recency implying that the magnitude of the instigating force of a stimulus changes discretely from one trial to the next and that the new magnitude of the instigating force of a stimulus is determined solely by the strength of tendency expressed most recently in the presence of that stimulus. If the environment provides a series of identical trials for an organism, the acquisition or extinction of the instigating force will be gradual and monotone. If conditions fluctuate from trial to trial, however, the changes in the instigating force of a stimulus will be irregular and can vary in direction as well as in magnitude.

Parameters of Conditioning

The duration of the CS and the US and the time relationships between these two stimuli are known to have effects in classical conditioning. Some of these effects are studied under the headings of delay, trace, and backward conditioning. We plan to discuss certain aspects of these topics in a preliminary way but, before we do so, we wish to explore the implications of another parameter that is especially important from the standpoint of the present theory. This is c, the consummatory value of the activity.

The maximum strength of T_{Sal} attained on any trial during acquisition and extinction is a function of the parameter c_{Sal} (see Equations 5.3 and 5.4 in the Mathematical Notes). With fixed values for the other parameters, large c_{Sal} will result in small $(T_{Sal})_{Max}$ and small c_{Sal} in large $(T_{Sal})_{Max}$. In fact, for very large c_{Sal}, almost no conditioning and very rapid extinction will occur. And interestingly, for very small c_{Sal}, unless λ and $t_1 + t_2$ are correspondingly small, there will not be an asymptote for $_{CS}F_{Sal}$ in acquisition nor a decline in $_{CS}F_{Sal}$ during extinction.

It seems likely that evolution has placed constraints on the magnitudes of c that actually obtain for most activities of organisms living in the world today for reasons similar to the ones presented earlier. For example, it is easy to see that survival is not well served if the instigating force of a stimulus for an activity increases without bound with repeated trials. Under these conditions, the organism would have a greater and greater share of his time taken up by that activity and would be trapped in it eventually. It is an interesting conjecture, however, that some activities for some organisms might have this property but that the world has been so arranged for these organisms that their survival has not yet been threatened.

We now consider briefly how variations in the temporal parameters of the CS and US relate to our hypothesis about learning. Until now, we have confined our discussion of conditioning to the situation in which it could be assumed that the product of the perceptual tendency (T_{cs}) expressed in the perceptual activity for the CS and the tendency to salivate (T_{Sal}) was maximal at the end of the US interval. When this assumption cannot be made, as would be the case in backward conditioning, and as also could be true in delay and trace conditioning, the maximum *product* of the strengths of T_{cs} and T_{Sal}, as specified in Equation 5.1, becomes a critical consideration. The maximum of the products of the strengths of the two tendencies evaluated instant by instant across the time for a trial will not necessarily involve the maximum strength of either tendency taken individually.

In trace conditioning, for example, the CS comes on and goes off before the US comes on. Hence, the $_{CS}F_R$ cannot be expected to gain the full effect of $(T_R)_{Max}$ or of $(T_{cs})_{Max}$. The precise value of the new $_{CS}F_R$ will depend on the maximum value of the product of the two tendencies. Similarly, in the case of backward conditioning, in which the CS is presented subsequent to the offset of the US, the degree of conditioning, if any, will depend on the maximum *product* achieved. The trace and backward conditioning paradigms are illustrated in Figure 5.6 along with the theoretical analyses just outlined. The path of T_{cs} is shown by the dotted curves and that of T_R by the solid curves and, in each case, it will be the maximum value of the product of the two tendencies that gives the new $_{CS}F_R$. We continue to assume that the initiation consummatory lag is negligible for T_R because it makes presentation simpler and does not change in any basic way the conclusions we reach. The details of the path of T_{cs} within the time of a trial, however, are critical to our discussion and we have included the initiation consummatory lag for this perceptual tendency in all three conditioning paradigms. This effect appears as the linear growth in T_{cs} immediately following the onset of the CS after which T_{cs} begins its approach to asymptote. From the three panels of Figure 5.6 it is apparent that there is an optimal timing of the onsets and durations of the CS and the US for best conditioning and that trace, backward, and delay conditioning all deviate from these optimal conditions.

Some data from the studies of classical salivary conditioning suggest that the present hypothesis concerning learning may be pointed in the right

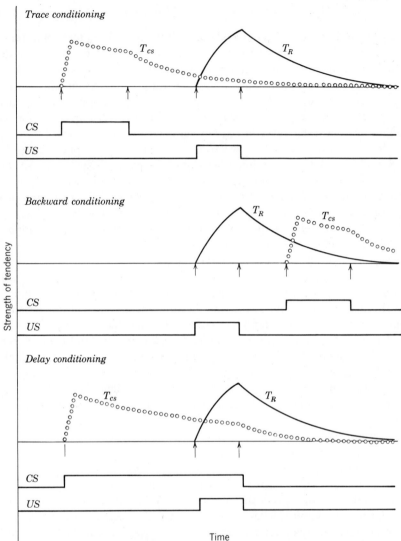

FIGURE 5.6 Trace, backward, and delay conditioning paradigms showing the tendency for the *CS* perceptual activity (T_{cs}) and the action tendency (T_R) on the first trial.

direction. For example, Ellison (1964) reports the results reproduced in Figure 5.7 for delay and trace conditioning. The left-hand set of graphs is for a *CS-US* interval of 8 sec, and the right-hand set for one of 16 sec. From the standpoint of the present theory, the most striking and encouraging aspect of these data is the rising strength of tendency over the effective duration of the *CS*. In fact, the shapes of the curves of Figure 5.7 are not unlike the ones presented for the theory in Figure 5.3. It appears that some of the main features of classical salivary conditioning data, including the ones attributable to delay and trace procedures and to the size of the *CS-US* interval as well as the ones related to the dynamic properties of stimuli operating over time, can be encompassed by the theory of action enriched by a principle of how change in the instigating force of stimuli comes about.

More Complex Changes in the Instigating Force of a Stimulus

Our earlier discussion of how the recency hypothesis of change in insti-gating force can account for the increases, the decreases, and the stability in the strength of instigating forces begins to suggest some possible complexities in the changes of the instigating-force property of a stimulus that tend to be ignored in the traditional account of selective learning. One of the most common of them should occur when the tendency to undertake the activity of interest is a *compound action tendency*, that is, a tendency produced by the summation of separate elemental action tendencies $(T_{X:J} + T_{X:K} + T_{X:L})$, all of which refer to the same next step in activity (X) but to different, nonsubstitutable anticipated consequences $(J, K,$ and $L)$. This situation would be likely to arise when the critical stimulus situation produces a set or *constellation* of different forces to undertake the very same activity, for example, $F_{X:J}, F_{X:K}, F_{X:L}$. These separate instigating forces (each attributable to actual past experience in the same or similar situations or to a displaced derivative of some other direct instigating force produced in the situation) influence the strength of separate tendencies to undertake activity X in that situation. Under these conditions, it is meaningful to speak of *the total force* to undertake a particular activity that is attributable to a *constella-tion of forces* to undertake that activity in the given situation.

It is clear from earlier discussion that on a particular occasion when $T_{X:J} + T_{X:K} + T_{X:L}$ are all being expressed in activity X, motivated by the compound $T_{X:J,K,L}$, the several different outcomes that would normally have the effect of producing a subsequent increase in force, stability of force, and a decrease in force might all occur on a given trial, but each in reference to a different tendency. For example, the immediate consequences of activity X might do all of the following: (1) produce a strong F_J, thus heightening T_J and strengthening $F_{X:J}$, (2) produce just sufficient F_K, given the speed of instrumental approach, to account for the stability of $F_{X:K}$, and (3) fail to include any F_L, thus, producing the state of affairs that weakens $F_{X:L}$. The net result of these several changes in the motivational implications of the critical stimulus might be a higher or lower probability of occurrence of activity X on a later occasion or no change in the probability of occurrence. The change in behavior between Trial 1 and Trial 2 depends entirely on the nature of the several changes in the instigating force property of the stimulus.

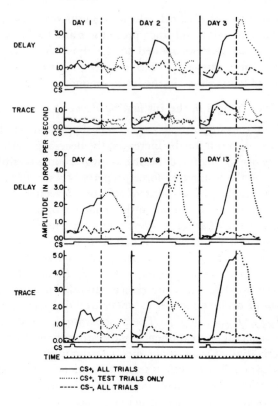

FIGURE 5.7   Data from Ellison (1964) on the conditioned salivary response as a function of delay and trace procedures with 8- and 16-second *CS-US* intervals.

Lawrence and Festinger (1962) have approached this complicated question in their analysis of the effects of intermittent reinforcement by suggesting that, when an animal is not given food reward on every trial during the acquisition phase of training, it has an opportunity to discover some other kind of gratification in the empty goal box on nonreinforced trials. Thus it has an additional basis for later preferring to undertake the activity during the extinction series when food reinforcement no longer occurs. The present analysis highlights the need to distinguish between the *constellation of forces* and *the magnitude of the total force* to undertake a particular activity in a particular situation and suggests that the effect of omitting a particular incentive during extinction will have quite different results when the action tendency expressed is elemental than when it is compound.

To complete our analysis of what happens on the so-called reinforced and nonreinforced learning trial, we must also consider what, if anything,

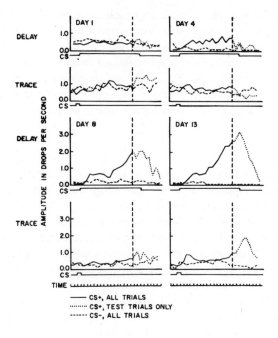

FIGURE 5.7 Continued.

happens to the instigating force of the critical stimulus to engage in some other incompatible activity Y when the tendency to engage in activity Y is not dominant and therefore is not expressed in behavior. The stimulus situation can produce not only a constellation of different forces to undertake a particular activity X, which together constitute the total force for X, but also a *hierarchy* of total forces to undertake mutually incompatible activities X, Y, and Z. We now are asking: What happens to F_Y and F_Z when, in fact, the response to the stimulus is X and neither T_Y nor T_Z are expressed on that occasion?

Our present view is that nothing happens to the instigating force to undertake an activity when the tendency to undertake that activity is not expressed in behavior.[4] On Trial $N + 1$, it will have the same strength as on Trial N. If our presumption is correct, there should be no change in F_Y or F_Z attributable to disuse (that is, nonoccurrence) of the activities Y and Z

---

[4] We assume that a more molecular analysis will show the important role of the sensory feedback from an activity in the learning process. And there is sensory feedback only for activities that do occur.

even over a great number of trials on which the tendency to undertake some other activity was dominant. However great this number of trials may be, our basic assumption concerning the persistence of unexpressed inertial tendencies and its implication of spontaneous variability in behavior implies that sooner or later T_Y and T_Z will attain dominance in the situation and will be expressed in activities Y and Z with consequences that will then serve to modify the strength of F_Y and F_Z according to the principle of learning.

SUMMARY

In this chapter we have attempted to reconcile the concepts introduced to account for contemporary dynamics of action with the traditional concepts of conditioning and selective learning. The latter fields of inquiry have been mainly concerned with the way in which actual experience (training) changes the behavioral implications of particular stimuli for an individual. Learning as traditionally studied constitutes what we refer to as a change in the instigating force of stimuli for a particular individual and the elaboration of his more primitive behavioral tendencies.

Our view of how goal-directed behavior develops in lower animals (not greatly different from the traditional view) begins with the usual assumption of a number of instincts, that is, predispositions to react in certain ways (R_G) to certain stimuli (S_G). These include what are generally called the primary reinforcing states of affairs. They are the given behavioral ends for which animals learn effective means and for which they periodically strive later in life. One may use the term *intrinsically-regulated* behavior (Koch, 1956) in reference to activities, like eating, which are undertaken as ends in themselves because the nervous system is constructed so that exposure to a particular stimulus (S_G) will produce unconditioned instigating force $(_{US}F)$ to undertake the particular activity (R_G). One may also refer to them as intrinsically enjoyable activities. This acknowledges that the inner affective life of an individual bears a systematic and lawful relationship to his overt, behavioral life.

As learning proceeds, many different activities (for example, locomotor activities) that are initially motivated by relatively weak unconditioned instigating forces are undertaken for the sake of their more strongly instigated, and now anticipated, consequences. These activities are ones that in the past have been followed by the so-called primary reinforcing events. The latter, as a result of evolutionary history, tend to be characterized by the strong unconditioned instigating force of the stimulus and by the substantial consummatory value of the response. In contrast to an intrinsically regulated and intrinsically enjoyable activity like eating, an activity undertaken for the sake of what it leads to, for example, running towards food, is traditionally called instrumental activity. In our view, this and all other concrete instances of *striving for the goal* represent elaborations of the original tendency—in this case, the tendency to eat. After learning, the latter can be expressed in a great variety of different situations and in a great variety of different sequences of preparatory, instrumental activities, all of which have previously culminated in the primitive reinforcing event.

The primitive tendency to eat is the family of specific action tendencies that is defined by the set of stimuli that unconditionally provoke the activity of eating. When the tendency is elaborated, the set of functionally equivalent action tendencies that comprise the family will include, for example, the tendency to turn left and eat in this situation, the tendency to run and turn right and eat in that situation, etc. This conception implies that a rat having learned to run, turn left, and eat in a given situation will anticipate eating while running and turning left in that situation. This idea is explicitly expressed in our use of two subscripts to describe the particular instigating forces and the tendencies influenced by them. The first subscript, or first name, refers to the particular next step in the path that has previously led to the goal activity. The second subscript, or family name, refers to the anticipated goal activity that provides the spring or excitement for the instrumental activity. Without attempting to be more specific about the physical mechanisms of instigating force and tendency, we take the position that *the anticipated consequence (or goal) of an activity is another activity* whether it be conceived in more molecular terms as an anticipatory goal reaction or not. This anticipated consequence functions to excite *selectively* those activities that in the past have preceded its actual occurrence.

Our Principle of Learning illustrates how a theory of learning can be phrased to account for changes in variables that are essential for the theoretical account of dynamics of action. A recency hypothesis, advanced to account for the acquisition and the extinction of the instigating force of a stimulus, identifies reinforcement with the boost in an action tendency provided, initially, by the unconditioned instigating force of some other stimulus. Thus, for example, it is the innate or unconditioned instigating force to eat of a food stimulus that constitutes a primary reinforcement. Stimuli that have already acquired substantial conditioned instigating force constitute the class called secondary reinforcement.

The central features in this analysis of learning and extinction are the emphasis given the dynamics of action on the most recent trial in the explanation of changes in the magnitude of an instigating force and, thus, the important role of the fundamental assumption of inertia applied to behavioral tendencies—even in the theory of learning.

With this we conclude our programmatic view of the historical determinants of the instigating force of a stimulus, which refers back to the sequence of stimulus and response and the strength of force and tendency on some earlier occasion. This is the traditional approach in the study of conditioning and learning but is not, as we shall argue in the next chapter, the only valid or useful approach to the question of the determinants of the instigating force of the stimulus given the current state of knowledge.

MATHEMATICAL NOTES

The working hypothesis we have adopted for the conditioning of instigating force to a stimulus is one of recency. It states that "a stimulus acquires for its next occurrence a magnitude of instigating force for an activity that is proportional to the maximum value attained by the product of the strength of the perceptual tendency of the stimulus and the strength of the expressed action tendency during the interval of the activity" (see Chapter 5), which is represented in symbols as

$$(_sF_R)_{N+1} = \lambda[(T_{s_N})_t \cdot (T_{R_N})_t]_{\text{Max}} \tag{5.1}$$

In the text (pp. 157 to 162) we outlined the way in which a CS would acquire instigating force for salivating in a standard conditioning situation made simple by several assumptions (pp. 158 to 159). Only the first three trials, pictured in Figure 5.3, were taken up in detail, however, and we wish to make a more complete derivation in these notes. Again, we shall analyze the conditioning trial by trial and shall then proceed to generalize the result as the emerging pattern becomes apparent.

As is shown in Figure 5.3, the path of $(T_{s_N})_t$, the perceptual tendency of the CS, over the duration of the CS is identical from trial to trial and, for the conditions under examination, the maximum product of $(T_{s_N})_t$ and $(T_{R_N})_t$ always occurs at the end of the US interval. This allows us to rewrite Equation 5.1 as $(_{CS}F_{\text{Sal}})_{N+1} = \lambda'(T_{\text{Sal}})_N$ where λ' is the product of λ, the constant of proportionality, and $(T_{cs_N})_{t_1+t_2}$, the value of T_{cs} at the end of the US interval on each trial, and where $(T_{\text{Sal}})_N = (T_{\text{Sal}_N})_{t_1+t_2}$ in order to simplify the notation.

According to Equation 1.11, describing the path of an action tendency when subject to both instigating and consummatory forces, and the rule for combining the strengths of tendencies that refer to the same activity (see Chapter 3) we are able to write the expression for $(T_{\text{Sal}})_N$, the maximal tendency to salivate on any trial, which occurs at the end of the US interval. This is

$$(T_{\text{Sal}})_N = \frac{(_{CS}F_{\text{Sal}})_N}{c_{\text{Sal}}} [1 - e^{-c_{\text{Sal}} \cdot (t_1+t_2)}] + \frac{(_{US}F_{\text{Sal}})_N}{c_{\text{Sal}}} (1 - e^{-c_{\text{Sal}} \cdot t_2})$$

By using this equation for $(T_{\text{Sal}})_N$ on Trial 1 with $(_{CS}F_{\text{Sal}})_1 = 0$ and

$(T_{Sal})_I = 0$ by assumption, we obtain

$$(T_{Sal})_1 = \frac{_{US}F_{Sal}}{c_{Sal}}\left(1 - e^{-c_{Sal} \cdot t_2}\right)$$

It follows that

$$(_{CS}F_{Sal})_2 = \lambda'\left[\frac{_{US}F_{Sal}}{c_{Sal}}\left(1 - e^{-c_{Sal} \cdot t_2}\right)\right]$$

Proceeding to Trial 2 the equation for $(T_{Sal})_N$ yields

$$(T_{Sal})_2 = \frac{(_{CS}F_{Sal})_2}{c_{Sal}}\left[1 - e^{-c_{Sal} \cdot (t_1+t_2)}\right] + \frac{_{US}F_{Sal}}{c_{Sal}}\left(1 - e^{-c_{Sal} \cdot t_2}\right)$$

By substituting for $(_{CS}F_{Sal})_2$ and rearranging terms, we arrive at the more useful expression,

$$(T_{Sal})_2 = {_{US}F_{Sal}}\left(\frac{1 - e^{-c_{Sal} \cdot t_2}}{c_{Sal}}\right)\left\{1 + \lambda'\left[\frac{1 - e^{-c_{Sal} \cdot (t_1+t_2)}}{c_{Sal}}\right]\right\}$$

This quantity multiplied by λ' is the value for $(_{CS}F_{Sal})_3$ which can be used in the equation for $(T_{Sal})_N$ to obtain

$$(T_{Sal})_3 = {_{US}F_{Sal}}\left(\frac{1 - e^{-c_{Sal} \cdot t_2}}{c_{Sal}}\right)\left\{1 + \lambda'\left[\frac{1 - e^{-c_{Sal} \cdot (t_1+t_2)}}{c_{Sal}}\right]\right.$$
$$\left. + (\lambda')^2\left[\frac{1 - e^{-c_{Sal} \cdot (t_1+t_2)}}{c_{Sal}}\right]^2\right\}$$

It is readily seen from the values derived for the strength of T_{Sal} on Trials 1, 2, and 3 that on the Nth conditioning trial we shall have

$$(T_{Sal})_N = {_{US}F_{Sal}}\left(\frac{1 - e^{-c_{Sal} \cdot t_2}}{c_{Sal}}\right)\left\{1 + \lambda'\left[\frac{1 - e^{-c_{Sal} \cdot (t_1+t_2)}}{c_{Sal}}\right]\right.$$
$$+ (\lambda')^2\left[\frac{1 - e^{-c_{Sal}(t_1+t_2)}}{c_{Sal}}\right]^2 + \cdots + (\lambda')^{N-1}$$
$$\left. \times \left[\frac{1 - e^{-c_{Sal} \cdot (t_1+t_2)}}{c_{Sal}}\right]^{N-1}\right\}$$

Since $_{CS}F_{Sal}$ on Trial $N + 1$ is given by λ' times T_{Sal} for Trial N according to our rewriting of Equation 5.1, this expression for $(T_{Sal})_N$ gives the form of the relationship between the magnitude of $_{CS}F_{Sal}$ and trials as well as between T_{Sal} and trials. The equation for $_{CS}F_{Sal}$ can be written

$$(_{CS}F_{Sal})_{N+1} = \lambda'({_{US}F_{Sal}})\left(\frac{1 - e^{-c_{Sal} \cdot t_2}}{c_{Sal}}\right)\left\{\frac{1 - (\lambda')^N\left[\dfrac{1 - e^{-c_{Sal} \cdot (t_1+t_2)}}{c_{Sal}}\right]^N}{1 - \lambda'\left[\dfrac{1 - e^{-c_{Sal} \cdot (t_1+t_2)}}{c_{Sal}}\right]}\right\}$$

since it is generated by a geometric series.

For

$$0 < \lambda' \left[\frac{1 - e^{-c_{Sal} \cdot (t_1 + t_2)}}{c_{Sal}} \right] < 1$$

the value of $(_{CS}F_{Sal})_{N+1}$ approaches a limit as N, the number of conditioning trials, gets indefinitely large. This asymptotic value is

$$\frac{\lambda'(_{US}F_{Sal})[1 - e^{-c_{Sal} \cdot t_2}]}{c_{Sal} - \lambda'[1 - e^{-c_{Sal} \cdot (t_1 + t_2)}]}$$

and represents the limit of conditioning for the situation under examination.

The learning principle continues to apply during extinction. The only change in procedure instituted in extinction is that the US is no longer given. This means that $_{US}F_{Sal} = 0$ in the determination of T_{Sal}, so that for any trial n during extinction

$$(T_{Sal})_n = \frac{(_{CS}F_{Sal})_{N+1}}{c_{Sal}} [1 - e^{-c_{Sal} \cdot (t_1 + t_2)}]$$

It is straightforward to generate the values of T_{Sal} and $_{CS}F_{Sal}$ for each trial during extinction. On the first extinction trial following N conditioning trials

$$(T_{Sal})_1 = \frac{(_{CS}F_{Sal})_{N+1}}{c_{Sal}} [1 - e^{-c_{Sal} \cdot (t_1 + t_2)}]$$

since $(_{CS}F_{Sal})_{N+1}$ is the conditioned instigating force on this trial. The new value of $_{CS}F_{Sal}$ is $\lambda'(T_{Sal})_1$ allowing us to write

$$(T_{Sal})_2 = \lambda'(_{CS}F_{Sal})_{N+1} \left[\frac{1 - e^{-c_{Sal} \cdot (t_1 + t_2)}}{c_{Sal}} \right]^2$$

for the second extinction trial. Similarly, for the third trial

$$(T_{Sal})_3 = (\lambda')^2(_{CS}F_{Sal})_{N+1} \left[\frac{1 - e^{-c_{Sal} \cdot (t_1 + t_2)}}{c_{Sal}} \right]^3$$

and for the nth extinction trial

$$(T_{Sal})_n = (\lambda')^{n-1}(_{CS}F_{Sal})_{N+1} \left[\frac{1 - e^{-c_{Sal} \cdot (t_1 + t_2)}}{c_{Sal}} \right]^n$$

The last equation translates readily into

$$(_{CS}F_{Sal})_{n+1} = (\lambda')^n \cdot (_{CS}F_{Sal})_{N+1} \cdot \left[\frac{1 - e^{-c_{Sal} \cdot (t_1 + t_2)}}{c_{Sal}} \right]^n$$

The decline in $_{CS}F_{\text{Sal}}$ during extinction as embodied in the equation for $(_{CS}F_{\text{Sal}})_{n+1}$ holds true only if the previous condition that

$$0 < \lambda'\left[\frac{1 - e^{-c_{\text{Sal}}\cdot(t_1+t_2)}}{c_{\text{Sal}}}\right] < 1$$

obtains. Under these conditions $_{CS}F_{\text{Sal}}$ falls from its terminal acquisition level in a negatively accelerated fashion to zero, as extinction trials are continued. An example of an acquisition and extinction curve for $_{CS}F_{\text{Sal}}$ is given in Figure 5.4 for these conditions.

CHAPTER 6

THE COGNITIVE CORRELATES
OF AN INSTIGATING FORCE

In the case of human behavior, where there exists much greater capacity for mediating cognitive processes and language, it is often more useful to describe the instigating force of the immediate stimulus situation in terms of statements and concepts that refer to the cognitive structure of an individual. The essential details of his life history that would account for that cognitive structure are often unknown. We shall consider this an alternative approach to the problem of specifying the strength of instigating forces to undertake particular activities. It is represented in the contemporary study of the determinants of human choice and in one current effort to bring the study and the description of individual differences in personality into coherent contact with the principles of motivation, namely, in the study of achievement motivation.

The Perspective in the Study of Human Decision Making

The kind of theory of behavioral choice that has evolved in economics, in the early work of both Lewin and Tolman, and in the more refined mathematical models of the contemporary research on decision making rests on the premise that the instigation to undertake a particular activity varies with the degree of certainty (expectancy) that it will produce a given consequence and the value, or attractiveness, of that consequence to the individual. Thus Lewin et al. (1944) argued that the *psychological force* on an individual to undertake an instrumental activity in a path leading to a goal activity is related to the subjective probability that the act will lead to the goal activity and the valence, or subjective value of the expected goal activity.

A more general guiding hypothesis concerning the relationship between what we have already referred to as the *total instigating force* to undertake a particular activity and the concepts of expectancy and value is contained in the central premise of contemporary decision theory: $SEU = \psi_1 U_1 + \psi_2 U_2 + \cdots + \psi_n U_n$ (see Edwards, 1954). The subjectively expected utility

175

of a given activity represents a summation of the expected utilities (or to use the Lewinian term, of the *psychological forces*) attributable to all the different expected consequences of the activity. By identifying a single instigating force with a particular product of subjective probability (ψ) and utility of consequence (U)[1] and ignoring the role that consummatory force plays within the theory of action, the summation involved in the calculation of *SEU* can be viewed as equivalent to the summation of the constellation of forces that produces the total instigating force for some activity in a given stimulus situation (see Chapter 5). That is, we may write: total instigating force $= SEU = \psi_1 U_1 + \psi_2 U_2 \cdots + \psi_n U_n$.

This concept obviously allows for the description of the composition of the total instigating force to undertake a particular activity in a given situation in terms of different kinds of immediate expected consequences and also of the more remote, future expected consequences of the activity (Raynor, 1969). It provides a useful basis for the description of the *meaning of an activity* to an individual. Traditionally, it has constituted a mathematical model of the phenomenological aspect of motivation, a refinement of traditional intuitive hedonism.

Having already taken the position that conscious thought (or covert activity) is itself to be viewed as an expression of a dominant tendency (and others that are compatible with it), we must soon subject the concepts of expectancy (or subjective probability) and valence (or utility) to critical examination in order to identify clearly what, from the viewpoint of the present scheme, they refer to. But let us put off the critical examination of these concepts in order first to bring the Principle of Change of Activity into contact with this approach to the problem of determining the instigating force of a stimulus. In the course of our discussion we shall show how the Principle of Change of Activity, as it applies to choice, can be employed to identify various empirical determinants of the instigating force to undertake an activity and to discover the way in which they combine when, as in the case of adult human behavior, there is a substantial capacity for cognitive mediational processes and language.

Let us begin by considering the effect on a speeding motorist of a road sign that states "*Ann Arbor, Next Left.*" This illustrates the powerful control of human behavior exerted by all sorts of signs and signals: for example, Stop, Go, No Parking, Ladies Room, a red light, a green light, a five o'clock whistle, etc. In everyday language we say that the motorist who reads the sign feels certain (that is, he believes) that if he turns left he will be on a road that leads to Ann Arbor. If he is interested in getting there, the sign might seem to an observer to provoke the activity of his turning the automobile to

---

[1] In the various phrasings of the Expectancy x Value theory, the terms subjective value, valence, and utility have the same meaning (Atkinson, 1964).

the left. The road sign obviously provides a stranger to the community with the kind of information about the consequences of turning left at that intersection that he might have received from a policeman in reply to a verbal query. A native to the community might have already acquired this kind of knowledge by having turned left there on one or more occasions in the past and then having experienced the consequence of reaching Ann Arbor even before the road sign was installed. Thus, for the experienced native, the visual cue of a particular gasoline station near that intersection may convey the same information as the road sign to the stranger. When exposed to it, the native, in effect, says to himself: "There is the gasoline station. If I turn left now I will get on to Ann Arbor." This covert reaction to an otherwise neutral environmental cue is functionally equivalent to the reaction to the road sign.

Tolman (1932) took the view that except for the verbal reaction this is also what lower animals learn as they run through mazes, that is, cognitive expectations in which particular environmental cues become signs that certain consequences or significates will soon follow certain actions.

The Cognitive Content and Functional Significance of Learning

We must distinguish between the cognitive content of what an individual learns and the functional or motivational significance of what he has learned. This is an essential point in the traditional distinction between learning and performance. Later we shall want to make a similar distinction between the nature of individual differences in personality and the functional or motivational significance of those differences. The study of both learning and personality requires conceptual schemes that yield adequate descriptions of the subject of interest—in the one case, what an individual has learned and, in the other, how people differ in personality. Given these schemes, we can account for the instigating force of a particular stimulus (that is, its functional significance) by referring to the content of what an individual has learned and, thereby, can go beyond saying merely that the instigating force of the stimulus has changed for him. This is what we do when we entertain the hypothesis that the total instigating force to undertake a particular activity corresponds to the subjectively expected utility of the consequences of that activity. Our hypothesis is that the product of the strength of expectancy that an activity will produce a given consequence and the valence of that consequence can be identified with the magnitude of a particular instigating force. We hypothesize further that the summation of these products across all possible outcomes corresponds, under the conditions observed earlier, to the summation of the separate forces in the constellation which refers to a given activity in a given stimulus situation and which defines the total instigating force for that activity.

One advantage of this approach to the problem of determining the instigating force of a stimulus for a particular individual is that it makes it easy to speak of the effects of learning as some kind of change in the properties of an individual instead of more awkwardly as a change in the functional property of a particular stimulus for him. One can say, for example, that the individual has acquired a stronger belief that turning left at that gasoline station will get him to Ann Arbor or that his expectancy of reaching Ann Arbor by turning left at that gasoline station has been strengthened as a result of having turned left and having reached Ann Arbor. As the expectancy that turning left leads to Ann Arbor becomes stronger, presumably as a function of repeated occurrences, the instigating force to turn left also should be found to become stronger if the value of getting to Ann Arbor does not change for the individual.

The decrease in latency of left turn, or heightened probability of left turn as a result of "rewarded practice," is the behavioral phenomenon summarized by the Empirical Law of Effect. In time, if the person becomes sufficiently certain that turning left will get him to Ann Arbor so that additional confirmations of his belief do not serve to strengthen it further, the latency of the turn and the probability of its occurrence also should be found to have stabilized. If on a later occasion the road no longer leads to Ann Arbor (because, for example, a bridge is washed out so that turning left is no longer followed by getting to Ann Arbor), the expectancy should weaken and so should the magnitude of the instigating force to turn left produced by the sign. This can occur quickly and efficiently if, for example, the road repairmen remember to put up a new sign that states *"Bridge to Ann Arbor Out—Detour"* or if a policeman when asked, "Is that bridge still out?" replies, "Yes."

The Effect of Information About the Consequences of an Activity

In everyday life, it is taken for granted that information about the consequences of activities like turning left at that gasoline station will be related to the likelihood that particular activities will be undertaken or continued. In simple experiments we can discover empirically just how the instigating force to undertake an activity varies with different kinds of information about the consequences of that activity. Consider the following as illustrative (from Atkinson and Birch, 1966).

College students were told that they would be given an opportunity to make a series of choices among different containers. Each container (they were told) held 100 beads among which a given number, 10, 20, . . . 90 were distinctively colored "lucky" beads. If the person, in reaching "blind" into one or another container happened to draw a lucky bead from it, he would be given a certain amount of money. Attached to each container was a small cardboard sign that stated the number of lucky beads in the container (out of 100) and the monetary value of a lucky bead. Thus one sign said, "10 lucky beads—win 9 cents"; another said "50 lucky beads—win 5 cents," and so on. One piece of information defined the objective probability of drawing a lucky bead (without looking); the other piece of information defined the monetary value of drawing a lucky bead. The first piece of information should influence the degree of certainty (expectancy) that reaching into the container will yield a lucky bead; the second, the relative attractiveness (valence) of drawing a lucky bead. The subject was prevented from seeing the bead he had drawn on each trial until the end of the experiment. Thus he had no additional source of information to affect his degree of certainty throughout the experiment.

Given the Principle of Change of Activity applied to the choice between two alternatives when there is a difference in the magnitude of the instigating force, we can look at the results that have to do with the preference among the containers as the basis for inference concerning the way in which the information given subjects influenced the instigating forces to reach into the containers. The results given in Figure 6.1 imply that the instigating force is influenced by both the stated probability of a consequence and the stated value of the consequence. The two kinds of information were simultaneously varied in this experiment according to a rule that the incentive value of a lucky bead should be proportional to 1 minus the probability of winning. According to the strong ratio rule of choice, derivable as a special case of Equation 4.12 in which there is no displacement or substitution and the inertial gap after a choice of an alternative is the same for all alternatives,[2] the obtained data on the total number of times each alternative was chosen should be describable in terms of the relative magnitudes of the instigating forces.[3] Furthermore, under the hypothesis that the instigating force for each alternative is given by the product of the stated probability of winning and the stated value of winning, numerical values for the total number of choices of each alternative can be determined. The results of these calculations are plotted in Figure 6.1, and we can readily observe that they provide an approximation to the data. They seem, at least, to fit the obtained data

---

[2] The conditions of no feedback on each trial as used in this experiment help to make the assumption of equal inertial gaps for the alternatives plausible.

[3] Equation 4.12, adapted to the present experiment in which each of 36 pairs was presented once on a block of trials, yields the following expression for the total number of choices for any of the alternatives, X, for a single subject:

$$n(X) = n(X/Y) + \cdots + n(X/Z) = \left(\frac{F_X}{F_X + F_Y} + \cdots + \frac{F_X}{F_X + F_Z} \right)$$

where $F_X/(F_X + F_Y) + \cdots + F_X/(F_X + F_Z)$ is composed of eight terms one for each of the eight pairs involving alternative X.

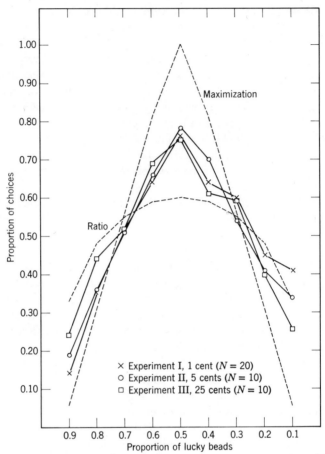

FIGURE 6.1   Choices among containers having different proportions (P) of lucky beads when the dollar value of a lucky bead was equal to $(1 - P)$ times 0.1, 0.5, and 2.5.

as well as the calculations based on the hypothesis of maximization, that is, that the subject will always choose the alternative having the higher expected value. This is also plotted in Figure 6.1. The departures of the obtained preferences for the various containers from the ones based on the principle of maximization can be attributed to the buildup of inertial tendency for the unchosen alternative in each paired-comparison. Sooner or later, as a result of the cumulative inertial tendency, the alternative instigated by the weaker force is chosen. Without the assumption of inertial tendency, the present theory of action would also predict maximization.

The departures from theoretical expectations based on the ratio rule of choice (Equation 4.12) are in the direction of our earlier conclusion (see Chapter 4) that substitution tends to enhance the choice of the normally favored alternative, that is, the one for which the instigating force is stronger. The results imply that the choice of one alternative as a means to the goal of winning some money, to a certain extent, is functionally equivalent to the choice of another alternative as a means to the goal of winning a different amount of money.

The Effect of Multiplying the Forces for Alternatives by a Constant

In the present context, the term *incentive value* is used in reference to the effects on the strength of the instigating force of offering 1 cent and 9 cents. Earlier, in the discussion of conditioning, this same term was used in reference to the effectiveness of different foods in provoking the reaction of eating. Then we also spoke of another variable, *motive*, in reference to individual differences in reactivity to various food stimuli. The same concept can be employed in reference to individual differences in reactivity to monetary incentives. If motive and incentive value combine multiplicatively to determine the valence (that is, attractiveness) of the different amounts of money for an individual, the differences among individuals in the strength of motive for money will not be a factor in the preferences among monetary incentives according to the strong ratio rule. For under this rule, only the *ratio* of forces controls relative preference, and the multiplication of all forces by a constant does not change the ratio in any paired-comparison.

An effect comparable to a difference in motive was produced in the bead experiment by using monetary incentives that were all 5 times the original ones (that is, values ranging from 5 cents to 45 cents) or 25 times the original ones (that is, values ranging from 25 cents to $1.25) with two new sets of subjects. As is shown in Figure 6.1, the multiplication of forces by a constant produced little change in the pattern of preference, in general conformity with the ratio rule.

In this simple experiment, as distinct from many experiments of this type in the field of decision making and in more lifelike choice situations, there is apparently only a single instigating force to win a lucky bead providing instigation for each alternative in the choice. If drawing an unlucky bead had some positive or negative value, or if there were multiple outcomes when a lucky bead was drawn (for example, 5 cents and an orange), we would have to consider the constellation of separate forces to choose one or another alternative and the total instigating force for each alternative.

Since we have postponed a general discussion of inhibitory forces, inhibitory tendencies, and the general topic of resistance until the next chapter, we shall put off until then an analysis of how the expectancy of drawing an unlucky bead and the negative value of loss of money (that is, a punishment) might be related to the pattern of choice. This is an opportune time, however, to examine the concepts of expectancy and value from the standpoint of the theory of action, as promised earlier in the chapter. How are these central concepts of cognitive theories of motivation to be viewed in light of our preliminary treatment of the relationship between covert and overt activities (Chapter 2) and our treatment of the growth and the extinction of instigating force in terms of conditioning and learning (Chapter 5)?

Expectancy and Value Considered Descriptive Properties of Covert Activity

The basic premises of human decision theory are that the subjective expected utility of an alternative is equal to the sum of the products of the subjective probability and utility for all of the consequences of an act and that the alternative having the greatest *SEU* will be chosen from among a set of alternatives. These premises are hypotheses concerning what an external observer must know about his subject in order to make an accurate prediction of his choice behavior. By supposing that the concept of *SEU* can be taken to correspond to the concept of the total instigating force, as here conceived, we bring the theory of decision making and the theory of action into direct contact.

Now, let us consider the meaning of expectancy and value from the perspective of the present theory. To do this, we must acknowledge at the outset that the two concepts refer to phenomenological aspects of motivation. The degree of certainty that an act will produce a given consequence (that is, expectancy or subjective probability) and the attractiveness of the anticipated consequence (that is, the subjective value, valence, or utility) are descriptive properties of covert activity. We must now recall the earlier discussion of the relationship between covert activity (conscious experience or thought) and overt activity (Chapter 2). It was argued that the sequence of covert activities (thought) and overt activities in a typical instance of goal-directed activity were to be viewed as expressions of different but highly correlated tendencies belonging to the same family. This suggests that the degree of certainty one feels concerning the consequence of a particular activity and the degree of attractiveness of that consequence are to be viewed as descriptive characteristics of the covert activity that often (perhaps typically) antedates or accompanies an overt action.

From this perspective, the basic concepts of decision theory, *subjective probability* and *utility*, are viewed here as descriptive dimensions of the covert activity which are highly correlated with choice behavior. This is to say no more about the two variables than often has been said before in describing them as "response-inferred" or "response-defined" variables. The decision theorist must gain knowledge about the various subjective probabilities and utilities of consequences for his subject before he uses his rule to predict the later choice behavior. That is, he must make various measurements of his subject's behavior before the to-be-predicted choice. And this behavior, according to the present view, is the covert activity of the subject when exposed to the same stimulus situation in which overt activity (choice) will subsequently be observed.

The logic of the approach takes the following form. If we let S_1 and S_2 designate two discernable environmental events and ψ and U designate subjective probability and utility, respectively, and if we know from prior observation that $\psi = f(S_1)$, $U = f(S_2)$, and choice $= f(S_1, S_2)$, we can then write: choice $= f(\psi, U)$. The latter equation is an empirical generalization about how three response-defined variables relate to each other. The present theory of action would be an appropriate tool for interpreting the three functions $\psi = f(S_1)$, $U = f(S_2)$, and choice $= f(S_1, S_2)$, since each refers to an instance of activity on the part of the subject of study.

Perhaps the whole point of this discussion can be simplified by suggesting that the Expectancy x Value theory of motivation evolved in the work of Tolman, Lewin, and the contemporary decision theorists is a model of the relationship between the phenomenological (covert) and behavioral (overt) aspects of motivation. It is anchored in observations that show a systematic relationship between the certainty an individual feels about the consequences of an activity and the attractiveness to him of those anticipated consequences, on the one hand, and his willingness to initiate and persist in the activity, on the other hand. Thus one might propose, as a guide in study of overt action, a general hypothesis that the *strength of an instigating force to undertake an overt activity equals the product of the strength of expectancy that the act will produce a certain consequence and the valence of the consequence.*

A Perspective in the Study of Individual Differences in Personality

When an individual confronts the problem of choosing to undertake one task from among a set of tasks that obviously differ in difficulty, he reacts to the environmental cues that define the difficulty of tasks as if each constituted a sign telling him his chance of success and the relative value of success at each task. This is the underlying premise in the current theory of achievement motivation in which the concepts of expectancy and value are used to yield hypotheses about the motivational implications of the difficulty of a task and the effects attributable to individual differences in personality. We shall observe, as we again discuss the studies of achievement-oriented behavior for illustrations related to our scheme, that the concept of strength of motive, introduced to describe relatively general and enduring differences among individuals, can be viewed as a shorthand for statements about how people differ with respect to a whole family of instigating forces.

Let us briefly consider the pattern of behavioral evidence that has helped to define the functional role of individual differences in the strength of achievement motive. Individuals report subjective probabilities of success that are negatively correlated with a physical dimension of task difficulty (Litwin, 1966; Brown, 1963). This is an example of the function $\psi = f(S_1)$, described in the previous section. Their reports of how attractive it would be (or was) to succeed at each of a series of tasks are positively related to the physical dimension of difficulty. This is an example of the function $U = f(S_2)$. The reported attractiveness of success is inversely related to the reported subjective probability of success. In light of this and other consistent evidence, it has been proposed that the incentive value of success is the complement of the subjective probability of success and that the valence of success at a particular task is the product of the incentive value of success at that task and the strength of an individual's motive to achieve success (Atkinson and Feather, 1966, Chapter 20).

Reconsidered in light of what has already been said about viewing the cognitive expectancy and valence as correlates of instigating force, the theory of achievement motivation becomes a theory about instigating forces for achievement-oriented activity in terms of the several components or cognitive correlates. The main implications of assumptions about the components of an instigating force to achieve are shown in Figure 6.2. According to this new interpretation of the theory of achievement motivation, the instigating force to undertake a particular activity in order to achieve success

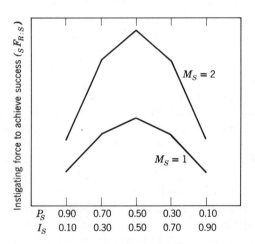

FIGURE 6.2   The main implications of the hypothesis that instigating force equals expectancy times incentive times motive, assuming that expectancy equals probability of success and incentive equals 1 minus probability of success.

should be stronger for tasks of moderate difficulty than for either very easy or very difficult tasks. Those individuals in whom the instigating forces to achieve are generally very strong are said to be strong in achievement motive. Those individuals in whom the instigating forces to achieve are generally very weak are said to be weak in achievement motive. The difference in the magnitude of the instigating force to achieve that is attributed to the general difference in personality is much greater when the task is moderately difficult than when it is either very easy or very difficult.

Figure 6.2 illustrates how the strength of motive to achieve (whatever its historical antecedents) is conceived as having the same enhancing multiplicative effect on the magnitude of all the instigating forces to achieve that influence an individual as he moves about from one life situation to another. Each new opportunity for the exercise of skill, each new test of competence, provides more or less of a challenge to achieve, depending on the subjective probability of success produced by the stimulus of the task. But always the instigation is stronger for the individual described as strong in motive. *Thus, to say that an individual is either strong or weak in motive to achieve is to say an equivalent thing for him about the potential strength of a whole family of instigating forces to achieve. And, in so doing, we define the functional significance, that is, the behavioral implications, of this partial description of his personality.*

It is possible to make a coherent and consistent interpretation of the empirical findings concerning the individual differences in achievement motivation given the logic of the Principle of Change of Activity and the coordination of the term motive with the family of instigating forces, without any assumptions about conditions that have not already been advanced in the earlier interpretations of them.

First, as noted in Chapter 2, we recall that McClelland et al. (1953) developed a method for identifying expressions of the tendency to achieve (n Achievement) in the imaginative content of thematic apperception stories by systematically varying the magnitude of the inertial tendency to achieve in groups of college students immediately before they were given the opportunity to create imaginative stories in response to a series of pictures. The method for content analysis of imaginative stories that was developed in these experiments to yield the thematic apperceptive n Achievement score describes the various ways in which the tendency to achieve is expressed in imaginative content. This frequency measure of individual differences in strength of motive to achieve has provided the integrative link between many subsequent studies concerned with other behavioral effects of inferred individual differences in strength of motive to achieve.

When the Principle of Change of Activity is applied directly to the initiation, magnitude, and persistence of the imaginative activity in which tendency to achieve is expressed, we must begin the interval of observation at the time the subject has just finished reading the instructions for the task and is waiting for the display of the first picture. If the ideal condition for the assessment of differences in motive has been attained (see Atkinson, 1958, Chapter 42), all individuals, at the time, would be equal in the strength of the inertial tendency to achieve. Then, if the tendency that sustains the initial activity of waiting for the first picture is also constant among subjects, we may take the speed of initiating an achievement-related plot instead of some other kind of plot, as one symptom of a relatively strong instigating force to achieve. As the achievement-oriented imaginative activity continues, the strength of the tendency should move toward a level defined by F/c, which is higher if the instigating force is strong than if it is weak. Thus the magnitude, rate, or intensity of achievement-related activity should be stronger as the story is being written for those individuals for whom the instigating force is strong. Furthermore, if the tendency to achieve, now sustaining the imaginative activity in progress is relatively strong, this activity will be more persistent and, thus, more likely to continue without interruption throughout the whole time period allotted for writing the story. All of these predicted symptoms of a strong instigating force to achieve in response to a particular picture—faster initiation of the achievement-related story, greater intensity of activity, greater persistence in the face of possible interference by other kinds of imaginative response—will enhance the likelihood of greater frequency of achievement-related imagery and more complete coverage of all the various aspects of an achievement-oriented plot in a particular story. All this will produce a higher n Achievement score for that story. (See McClelland et al., 1953, pp. 107 to 138; Atkinson, 1958, Chapter 12.)

The concept of motive implies that the person who scores high in response to one kind of picture should also score high in response to another kind of picture. He does (McClelland et al., 1953, p. 190; Atkinson, 1964, pp. 230 to 231). And the person who scores high in response to one set of pictures on one occasion should score high in response to another set of pictures on another occasion. He does. And this should occur even if one test condition is relatively relaxed for all subjects and the other is given under achievement-oriented conditions for all subjects. It does (Lowell in McClelland et al., 1953, pp. 161, 191–194; French, 1955; Haber and Alpert, 1958).

In other words, the evidence that uses only the imaginative response measure of strength of tendency to achieve sustains the view that the differences in n Achievement observed in response to one particular picture in one particular situation refer to something more general—something that is also expressed in response to other pictures and in other situations. Of course, this does not mean that the average response of a group of subjects is the same to all pictures. It varies greatly, as it should, if other determinants of the instigating force to achieve that are more specific to the stimulus itself vary from picture to picture. And it does not mean that the average response of a group of subjects is the same in all situations. The latter should and does vary substantially as a function of the immediate success-failure history of the group and in terms of the strength of the instigating force to achieve in the test situation itself (see, again, Chapter 2, pp. 43 to 47).

What, then, of the relationship of differences in the strength of motive as inferred from the thematic apperceptive n Achievement score to instrumental achievement-oriented activity? According to our principles, and the usual operating assumptions (see Chapter 4) that must be made to get us from the idealized conditions to the actual events that involve samples of subjects who score high and low in n Achievement, the persons who score high in n Achievement, generally, should be more willing to initiate an achievement-oriented activity and, once it is initiated, should perform at a higher level and be more persistent at the activity when they are confronted with an opportunity to engage in some other kind of activity instead. This follows from the assumption that the whole family of instigating forces to achieve is stronger in them.

Illustrative of the evidence that corresponds to each of these particular hypotheses are the following: (1) the persons who volunteer to participate in psychological tests and experiments score higher in n Achievement (Burdick, 1955), (2) the performance level at verbal and arithmetic tasks presented with achievement-oriented instructions is higher among persons who score high in n Achievement (for example, Lowell, 1952; Wendt, 1955; French, 1955), particularly when special measures are taken to exclude the possibility of other incentives that might produce other extrinsic instigating forces and a compound action tendency to undertake the task (Atkinson and Reitman, 1956); (3) the persistence in achievement-oriented performance prior to the knowledge of results, when the alternative is to leave the situation and to engage in some other kind of activity, is greater among persons who score high in n Achievement (French and Thomas, 1958; Atkinson and Litwin, 1960).

Perhaps most critical for this attempt to embrace earlier findings with the conceptual scheme presented in this book are the results obtained on a number of occasions that show a stronger preference for tasks of intermediate difficulty (where the probability of success is near 0.50) among persons who score high in n Achievement than among those who score low in n Achievement (Atkinson and Feather, 1966). According to our analysis of choice (see Chapter 4), preference is controlled by the *ratio* of instigating forces and not the absolute difference between them. And the *ratio* of the strength of force to achieve at a task of intermediate difficulty versus the strength of force to achieve at a very difficult task or a very easy task should not be affected by the strength of the motive if the latter relates to instigating force multiplicatively as proposed in Figure 6.2.

On the face of it, the evidence seems to contradict what our analysis of choice in terms of the principle of change of activity implies, and what seemed clearly demonstrated in the simple choice-of-lottery experiment when the value of monetary incentives was multiplied by 5 or 25 in different conditions of the experiment (Figure 6.1). Is there a plausible explanation of why the ratio of the strengths of instigating forces to undertake a task of intermediate difficulty versus a task that is very easy or very difficult should be greater when the achievement motive is strong, even though the conception of a motive as a multiplicative weighting factor implies that its strength should influence the absolute magnitude of the forces to undertake tasks that differ in difficulty but not their ratio?

One explanation, which does not go beyond assumptions generally made in studies of achievement motivation, considers what happens to the ratio of forces when *compound* tendencies are involved. This can easily be seen by completing the analysis of the determinants of activities called *achievement-oriented* activities. It is usually assumed that other extrinsic (that is, non-achievement-related) tendencies are also expressed in most achievement activities (for example, Feather, 1962). Thus the total strength of tendency to undertake a particular activity is normally considered a compound action tendency. One ubiquitous extrinsic tendency is to gain the approval of the investigator by being cooperative, that is, doing the things that he asks be done. In the familiar ring toss experiment, he asks only that the individual throw the rings. There is no specification by him of which particular level of difficulty to choose. This and other extrinsic tendencies to undertake the various activities are instigated by extrinsic forces having the same magnitude (it has generally been assumed) for each of the several activities. Thus the total instigating force to undertake each of the various activities that correspond to different levels of difficulty in the ring toss game equals $F_{R:\text{Succ}} +$ $F_{R:\text{Ext}}$ in which we assume $F_{R:\text{Ext}}$ is a constant.

What is the effect of adding this constant to each $F_{R:\text{Succ}}$ on the ratio of forces to undertake a moderately difficult versus easy task when the motive for success is strong and weak? Let us suppose that the ratio of forces favoring choice of intermediate difficulty is 9/3 when the motive is strong and 3/1 when it is weak: that is, 9/3 = 3/1. The effect of adding a constant of 1 to each of the forces now produces a ratio of 10/4 when the motive is strong and 4/2 when it is weak and 10/4 > 4/2. The effect of adding the constant is to change the ratio of forces in each case but the change, in the direction of equalizing the forces, is greater the smaller the absolute magnitude of the forces. Given these assumptions, the preference for intermediate levels of difficulty should be more marked among persons in whom the motive to succeed is strong, not because the absolute difference among forces to engage in activities that differ in difficulty is larger, as previously supposed, but because most achievement-oriented activities are overdetermined (that is, the result of compound action tendencies). When the motive is strong, the instigating forces to achieve have proportionately greater influence on differences among the total forces to undertake activities that differ in difficulty than when it is weak. The conclusion we draw from this analysis is that, given a pure case of achievement motivation, one in which the only instigating forces and tendencies were to achieve success, the generally exhibited degree of preference for activities in which the probability of success was near 0.50 would hold true uniformly for all levels of achievement motive.

Before concluding this discussion of the determinants of the instigating force of the stimulus from the perspective of the study of individual differences in personality, it will be profitable to consider two other topics: (a) the effects of success and failure on subsequent strength of force to achieve and tendency to achieve, and (b) some general implications of describing personality in terms of a hierarchy of motives.

THE EFFECTS OF SUCCESS AND FAILURE

The assumption that success strengthens and failure weakens the subsequent expectancy of success at the same and similar activities is supported by evidence that concerns changes in the reported expectations of success following success and failure and by the interpretations of changes in the level of aspiration and persistence in the achievement-oriented activity following success and failure (Atkinson and Feather, 1966). This assumption extends to achievement-oriented activity the more general assumption of cognitive learning theory that expectancy of a goal is strengthened on so-called rewarded trials and weakened on so-called nonrewarded trials (Tolman, 1932). It refers to changes in the cognitive structure that correspond to the reinforcement and extinction of conditioned instigating force as described in the last chapter.

The implications of this assumption, as they apply to the problem of change in level of aspiration following success and failure, are shown in Figure 6.3. The figure shows the changes in the instigating force to achieve that correspond to an increase in the probability of success following success and a decrease following failure. The figure implies that on the first in a series of trials, the individual will select a task of intermediate difficulty (where the probability of success is about 0.50). Then, if he succeeds, the effect will be an increase in his probability of success at the same and similar tasks (Brown, 1963). Since the incentive value is assumed to be the complement of the subjective probability of success, it too should change. Thus

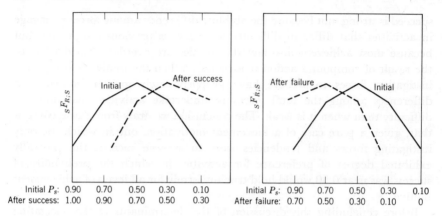

FIGURE 6.3   The effects of success and failure on the subsequent strength of $F_{R:S}$, assuming success increases and failure decreases the subsequent probability of success at the same and similar activities.

there should be a weaker instigating force to undertake the same activity on a subsequent occasion and a stronger instigating force to undertake a more difficult task according to the several assumptions of the theory of achievement motivation. The first task has become too easy and the new task now represents the challenge of intermediate difficulty or risk. An increase in the level of aspiration following success, the most typical result in samples that are unclassified with respect to personality (Lewin et al., 1944), is a striking characteristic of persons who are high in n Achievement (Moulton, 1965). This typical effect of success on the level of aspiration was emphasized by Allport (1943) as one that contradicts the Empirical Law of Effect, according to which the successful activity should show a higher probability of being repeated. From the viewpoint of Expectancy x Value theory, the law of effect should apply only when the strength of expectancy of attaining a goal through some activity and the incentive value of the goal are independent or are positively related, but not when there is an inverse relationship between the expectancy of the goal and the incentive value of the goal, as in achievement-oriented activity (Atkinson, 1964, Chapter 10).

Following failure, there is a decrease in the subjective probability of success at the same and similar tasks which corresponds to the changes in the instigating forces to achieve that are shown in Figure 6.3 for the case of failure. The lowering of aspiration after failure is the most typical result among representative samples of students (Lewin et al., 1944) and particularly among those who are highly motivated to achieve (Moulton, 1965).

Employing this simple assumption of a change in expectancy of success following success and failure, and no additional ones about the effects of success and failure, Feather (1961) predicted and found that persons who were strong in n Achievement would be more persistent in a series of repeated unsuccessful attempts to solve a puzzle when it was initially presented to them as a relatively easy task (one that 70 percent of college students could solve) than when it was presented as a very difficult task (one that only 5 percent of students could solve). His argument was that persons highly motivated to achieve would experience first a rise in instigation to achieve following failure on the initial trials, as subjective probability fell from 0.70 to 0.50, and then a gradual decline of interest following repeated failures until, at some point, the tendency to undertake the task would be weaker than the tendency to undertake another different task. When the initial subjective probability of success was 0.05, the instigation would be relatively weak to begin with and would decline immediately after the initial failures as the probability dropped toward 0. The general paradigm corresponds to the study of extinction after training.

Feather, whose study was undertaken before the influence of inertial tendencies had been proposed (Atkinson and Cartwright, 1964; Atkinson, Chapter 10, 1964), implicitly assumed that the strength of tendency to achieve success at the initiation of each of a series of trials in a failure sequence was determined only by what is here called the instigating force to achieve success. But he recognized the impossibility of deriving an hypothesis about persistence in a given activity without an explicit reference to the strength of tendency to undertake the activity that subsequently replaced it. And this provided an impetus for systematic conceptual analysis of the determinants of change of activity.

Weiner (1965), following the general plan of the Feather experiment, was the first to attempt to isolate the two distinct effects of success and failure implied by the present scheme: (a) the *cognitive learning effect*, described as a change in expectancy of success, which is related to the strength of instigating force of the stimulus to undertake the activity on a subsequent trial; and (b) the *immediate motivational effect*, assuming that success has greater consummatory value than failure, which we refer to as the inertial tendency for a subsequent trial. Following the logic of the theory of achievement motivation (see again Figure 6.2), Weiner assumed that repeated success when initial subjective probability is 0.70 and repeated failure when it is 0.30 should produce comparable successive decreases in the magnitude of the instigating force to achieve. This should produce the same persistence in an achievement-oriented activity among persons strong in n Achievement if there were no differential inertial tendency. But there should be greater persistence following failure if, as is generally assumed, success has greater consummatory value than failure and the assumptions presented here concerning the influence of inertial tendency are essentially correct.

Weiner's subjects confronted the possibility of continuing with another trial on a digit symbol substitution task after repeated success or repeated failure or of initiating, whenever they so desired, a different kind of activity (that is, nonachievement-related) instead. The question of interest was: How long would the subject continue in the achievement-oriented activity before changing to the other kind of activity?

On each trial, the subject confronted a card containing 60 digit symbol substitutions (success condition), or more than 60 (failure condition). The code changed on each card; hence, the subject confronted essentially the same degree of novelty and demand in the task on each trial. Weiner recorded the length of time taken by the subject to complete 60 digit symbol substitutions. This was a measure of speed of performance. In the success condition, the subject always finished the card (success). In the failure condition, the experimenter interrupted the subject after noting his time to complete 60 items but before he had finished the card as required (failure).

The results showed no difference between conditions in time to finish 60 items on the first trial. This evidence of the comparable initial level of performance in the two conditions was consistent with the assumption that points equidistant from the subjective probability of success of 0.50 had been established by the initial instructions so that $_sF_{R:S}$ and $T_{R:S}$ were initially equal in the two conditions. But, on the subsequent trial, the speed of performance was greater following failure than following success, and the number of trials before the shift to the other activity was also greater following failure. Both results are implied by the assumption of greater inertial tendency following failure than following success.

The general pattern of these results is consistent with the assumptions made concerning the components of instigating force to achieve, the effect of success and failure on this instigating force, and the separate effect of success and failure on the strength of the inertial tendency to achieve. In the light of these results, one may reinterpret the earlier results of Feather as probably attributable to both change in the instigating force and in the differential inertial tendency.

The two experiments illustrate how the traditional question of instrumental learning has been identified with change in cognitive expectations, specifically, the expectations of success and failure in particular activities, in the study of achievement motivation. The motivational implications of a change in the expectancy of success derive from the assumption that the expectancy of success is a determinant of the incentive value of success, and both, together with the motive to achieve success, are conceived as related to the strength of the instigating force to achieve success that is produced by a stimulus that defines the opportunity and the occasion for a particular activity. The experiments show an evolution in the method of study designed

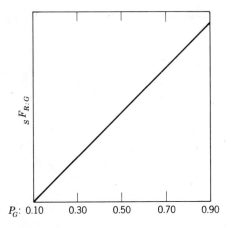

P_G: 0.10   0.30   0.50   0.70   0.90

FIGURE 6.4   The theoretical effect of increasing the strength of expectancy of attaining a goal when the incentive value of the goal is constant (derivation of the Law of Effect).

to separate the two different consequences of success and failure that are so often confounded.

Consider again the analogous problem in the context of a typical study of animal learning in a T-maze in which the food reward always appears in the left goal box. The learning that occurs, described now in Tolman's terms, is a growth in expectancy that turning left will lead to food and to eating. As a consequence of repeated reward (attainment of the goal), there is a correlated growth in the magnitude of the instigating force to run, turn left and eat ($_SF_{Run, \text{ Turn Left:Eat}}$) produced by the stimulus of the start box and to turn left and eat ($_SF_{\text{Turn Left:Eat}}$) produced by the stimulus of the choice point. This correlated growth in expectancy of the reward and $_SF_{R:G}$ is shown in Figure 6.4. In this case, as distinct from the case of the instigating force to achieve success among humans, there is a continual growth in the magnitude of the instigating force as the expectancy of the goal is strengthened by repeated reward according to our hypothesis that the magnitude of the instigating force equals the product of the subjective probability and valence because the incentive value of the goal activity, eating a food pellet, is *constant*. It does not change as the expectancy of attaining it changes. As suggested earlier, the empirical law of effect is recovered for this case. When the instigating forces to run, turn left and eat and to turn left and eat become stronger, as the expectancy of the goal is being strengthened on consecutive trials, the respective tendencies are more likely to attain dominance and to be expressed in behavior. This is what produces the typically observed increased probability of the rewarded response.

Now reconsider the two separate effects of so-called reinforced and non-reinforced trials. When the food is present, the expectancy of attaining it is confirmed and strengthened and there is an increase in the magnitude of the instigating force of the pertinent stimuli. But, since the activity of eating the food has substantial consummatory value, the consummatory force of the goal activity will function to reduce the strength of the tendency to eat and, thus, to decrease the immediate likelihood of the same response. When the food is not present in a nonreinforced trial in the extinction series, the expectancy of the goal is weakened. The corresponding decrease in the subsequent strength of the instigating force of the stimulus should decrease the probability of the response. But the absence of the food means that the animal has been deprived of the opportunity to engage in the consummatory activity, so that the tendency to eat persists (instead of being reduced) and, thus, enhances the immediate likelihood of repeating the activity or of initiating some other, functionally related activity.

The point, briefly stated is the following. *The behavioral implications of the two distinct effects of a primary reinforced trial and a nonreinforced trial are diametrically opposite.* The effect of the primary reward is to strengthen the instigating force but is to weaken the inertial tendency. The effect of the absence of the expected primary reward is to weaken the instigating force but is to sustain the inertial tendency. We believe that this latter effect probably provides a parsimonious explanation of the observed heightening of the level of performance in animals immediately after a nonreinforced trial, the phenomenon that Amsel (1958) has attributed to a frustration reaction in the animal. And we also believe that the confounding of the *learning effect* and the *immediate motivational effect* is responsible, in part, for some of the obscurities surrounding the phenomena of intermittent reinforcement. The nonoccurrence of a reward should weaken the instigating force that is strengthened when the reward is administered but should sustain the inertial tendency.

The effect of a secondary reinforcing stimulus deserves special attention. From the perspective of Expectancy x Value or cognitive learning theory, it would be considered a subgoal. When a particular activity, for example, turning left in a maze, is followed by the familiar goal box (secondary reward), the expectancy of reaching the goal object is strengthened as is the corresponding instigating force. But if the goal box as stimulus is not followed by the goal activity on that trial, it should lose some of its own instigating force or subgoal character. The latter is what would be called the valence of the goal box in a description of the constituents of the instigating force to run and eat produced by the stimulus of the start box. On any particular trial in which the reinforcing state of affairs is a secondary reward, that is, one that does not provide an immediate opportunity for the consummatory activity, the two effects of the rewarded trial should both be in the direction of heightening the subsequent probability of the "reinforced" response. That is, the instigating force of the stimulus to undertake the activity that preceded the secondary reward is strengthened and, because there is no opportunity for consummation, the inertial tendency is also sustained at a high level.

PERSONALITY CONCEIVED AS A HIERARCHY OF GENERAL MOTIVES

The idea of describing individual differences in personality in terms of general psychogenic needs or motives probably had its origin in McDougall's (1908) conception of the individual as a bundle of instincts, that is, of goal-directed dispositions. Murray (1938), parting with the notion that psychogenic needs were necessarily instinctive, later developed this concept, programmatically arguing that a better understanding of an individual could be attained through description of him in terms of the effects he generally strove to bring about than in terms of his generalized habits or traits (Allport, 1937), which told little of his aims and goals. McClelland (1951) included the concept of psychogenic need or motive among his proposed set of three categories for description of personality, advancing a number of sound hypotheses concerning the way in which relatively universal, nonculture-bound motives might be acquired early in life before the development of language, as a result of socialization practices connected with certain fundamental adjustment problems that arise in all societies the world over, for example, relations with people, mastery of the environment, etc.

The development of a theory of achievement motivation (Atkinson and Feather, 1966) followed the innovation in the method for the diagnosis and the measurement of the strength of human motives. It represents an explicit attempt to begin the specification of the nature of the interaction between personality and immediate environment implied by the Lewinian equation $B = f(P, E)$. The conceptual analysis of the determinants of the change of activity presented in the chapters of this book, and its application to the initiation of activity, performance level, persistence, and choice purports to be an even more precise and comprehensive specification of the behavioral implications of individual differences in the strength of motive when the latter is taken as a shorthand reference to a family of functionally related instigating forces.

With this as historical background, let us briefly focus more specifically on what is implied when the basic structure of personality is conceived, in part at least, as a hierarchy of general motives. We can do this by recognizing that the hierarchy of motives defines the way in which the basic personality structure of an individual will selectively enhance the influence of certain immediate environmental inducements more than others. Given the familiar principle

$$t_{B/A} = \frac{T_{A_F} - T_{B_I}}{F_B} = \frac{F_A/c_A - T_{B_I}}{F_B}$$

we can identify the three major sources of selectivity in behavior, particularly when we distinguish, in our conception of the constituents of the instigating force (F_A and F_B), the relatively more general and enduring differences in personality (that is, motive) from the relatively more specific and transient situational influences that are defined by variables that refer specifically to the immediate stimulus situation (that is, as reflected in expectancy and incentive value).

First, there is the selectivity attributable to the fact that the immediate environment of the individual (the stimulus situation) tends to heighten the strength of certain tendencies to action but not others. Second, there is selectivity attributable to persistence into the present of previously instigated but insufficiently consummated tendencies to action, the inertial tendencies that reflect the balance of past inducements to satisfactions—the effects of relative deprivation in the past. Then, finally, there is the selectivity attributable to basic personality structure, the greater arousability of the individual by environmental inducements to engage in one kind of activity instead of another and the variations in persistence in certain kinds of ongoing activity which we associate with differences in strength of motive.

What does the Principle of Change of Activity tell us in general about the consequences of differences in the strength of a motive, that is, the differences in the magnitude of a whole family of instigating forces? It tells us that when some other kind of activity is in progress and the motive of interest is in the position of F_B to prompt a change of activity, the individual with a strong motive will generally show more prompt initiation of that activity than an individual with a weak motive. And when the motive is in the position of F_A, sustaining the activity in progress, there will be greater persistence by the individual for whom that motive is strong. When the motive of interest is weak relative to others, the individual will be slow to initiate the activity and quick to leave it. This means, in general, that *the hierarchy of motives arranged according to their strength will greatly influence the way an individual distributes his time among different kinds of activity* (see Chapter 4). The person who is stronger in motive to achieve than in motive for affiliation will spend more time at work and less in friendly commerce with others. Given a reversal in this hierarchy of only two motives, there will be a reversal in the time distribution of activities. Given simultaneous opportunity for either of the activities, the choice will vary with the difference in motive. This is nicely illustrated in an experiment by French (1956) in which men who differed in *n* Achievement

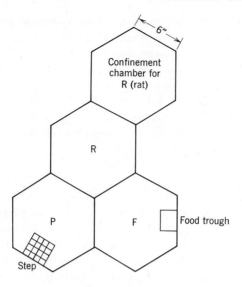

FIGURE 6.5   The hexagon maze in which time spent among different activities is measured (from Allison, 1963, p. 5).

and *n* Affiliation, when asked to choose a work partner for a subsequent test of skill, chose either a friend known to be previously unsuccessful at the kind of task to be undertaken, or a stranger, known to be very successful at this kind of task, in accordance with the stronger motive.

This general issue can and has been studied in lower animals. It requires only some innovation in method. Allison (1964) has studied how animals in a relatively constant environment and under constant conditions of food deprivation distribute their time among three different activities: commerce with food, commerce with another animal, commerce with a wire grid on which they can climb. Let us call these activities eating, affiliation, and play. His method was to present the alternatives in a hexagon maze, Figure 6.5, in paired-comparisons, for intervals of 10 minutes. His measure, sensitive to both differences in willingness to initiate an activity and resistance to change from it, was simply the amount of time spent in one or the other activity. He determined, for each of his animals, the proportion of the total amount of time spent in the activity of eating (that is, in commerce with the food) under 22 hours of food deprivation (see again Chapter 4). These proportions varied considerably, ranging from 0.12 to 0.85. When employed as a measure of individual differences in personality (analogous to the *n* Achievement score in humans) this measure of strength of motive to eat was found to correlate -0.73 ($N = 44$) with latency of the first eating response when placed in the maze and positively with the measures of instrumental performance in a maze having food in the goal box. Allison's measure of the relative amount of time spent in given kinds of activity may provide a model for measuring the more general and molar implications of individual differences in personality that can also be exploited in the study of human behavior. Perhaps this is what thematic apperceptive *n* Achievement and *n* Affiliation scores already represent, that is, indexes of the amount of time spent in imaginative activity of one kind or another in response to ambiguous picture stimuli.

SUMMARY

In this chapter we have been concerned with the approaches to the problem of accounting for the strength of the instigating force of a stimulus that are anchored in the observations of individual differences in reaction to the same stimulus situation. The conceptual analysis of the determinants of human choice is related to the concept of instigating force. We have taken the position that the concepts of expectancy (or subjective probability) and valence (or utility) in theory about human decision making are descriptive dimensions of the covert activity that normally antedates or accompanies overt behavioral preferences. Hence, an equation relating strength of the instigating force to the product of expectancy that an act will produce a given consequence and valence of that consequence describes a correlation between covert activity and overt activity instead of a causal relationship. It provides the foundation for an approach to diagnosis of the strength of the instigating force to undertake a particular activity.

The concept of motive, which is currently employed to describe relatively general and stable differences in personality, is examined from the perspective of the present theory about the dynamics of action. Statements about individual differences in the strength of various motives (*n* Achievement, *n* Affiliation, etc.) are shown to be equivalent to statements about the relative strength of different families of instigating force. Thus, a partial description of the individual differences in personality in terms of a hierarchy of motives may be considered a specification of how an individual prefers to distribute his time among different kinds of activity. Motive is a descriptive dimension of the basic personality structure, one of the three major determinants of selectivity in behavior. The others are the immediate environment and the differential inertial tendencies that are attributable to the previous balance of inducements and consummations or deprivation history of the individual.

The two separate effects of success and failure in achievement-oriented activity, one an influence on the subsequent strength of instigating force and the other on the immediate strength of the inertial tendency to achieve, are distinguished. This analysis provides a model for more general consideration of the two separate effects of any reinforced or nonreinforced trial in the learning paradigm. In each case, the two effects are likely to have diametrically opposite behavioral implications. Thus, the finding of food after a left turn in a maze should strengthen the subsequent instigating force to turn left but should weaken the immediate inertial tendency to undertake this activity. On a nonreinforced trial, the effects would be the opposite. It is suggested that a confounding of these two effects may be responsible for some of the unusual characteristics of intermittent reinforcement on the probability of a response.

The general aim of this chapter is to identify the useful alternative empirical approaches to the problem of accounting for the strength of the instigating force to undertake a particular activity.

CHAPTER 7

RESISTANCE

We began in Chapter 1 with the analysis of the logical implication of an observed change from one activity to another: that a change had occurred in the dominance relations among behavioral tendencies during the interval of observation. We then presented a conception of the dynamic process that causes the change in activity. To simplify our discussion of issues and to easily extend it to the historical question of learning, we confined our attention to appetitive activities. They are behaviors that in the human case, at least, are accompanied by interest, enthusiasm, and the expectation of reward or of some kind of positive consequence. Now, having presented the fundamental structure of our conceptual scheme, we must redress the balance and must complete the analysis by considering aversive behavior, the effects of punishment, and the problems of inhibition and avoidance. To do so, we shall begin again with some further observations concerning the conditions of a change from one activity to another.

Earlier we pointed out that the frequent observation of a change from an ongoing activity A to a particular activity B regularly following the onset of a particular stimulus suggested that the stimulus had produced the instigating force to undertake activity B, thereby bringing about the change in activity. Thus, no matter what the children are doing when mother calls them to dinner, they ultimately come to dinner when they give up the initial activity whatever it is. Likewise, the frequent observation of a change from a particular activity A (for example, eating) to some other activity, when there is no obvious change in the stimulus situation, had suggested that the ongoing activity itself might function to produce a consummatory force that weakens this action tendency relative to others, thus accounting for a shift in activity. In this case, we think of the normal cessation of eating and the change to some other kind of activity following a meal. Thus far, then, we have identified the occurrence or presentation of a stimulus with an increase in the strength of some tendency that is expressed in action and the decrease in the strength of this tendency with the occurrence of the activity itself. Now, we must confront some of the complications that we have sidestepped.

On some occasions we observe that the presentation of a particular stimulus is invariably followed by an apparent weakening or a decrement in the level of the ongoing activity A, whatever it is, and/or a change to some other activity, but this change cannot be adequately described as the initiation of some other particular activity X that is highly correlated with the presence of the stimulus.

When, for example, the children are playing with father's tape recorder without his permission and he is heard to enter the house from work, there is usually a sudden supplanting of this illicit play activity, sometimes by looking at the TV, sometimes by opening a book and apparently studying, and another time by a hasty preoccupation with some legitimate toys on the floor of the playroom. This kind of observation, more adequately described as a cessation of the ongoing activity (the common element), suggests that the tendency sustaining the activity already in progress has somehow been weakened by the force of the new stimulus rather than that some other particular action tendency has been selectively strengthened by the force of that stimulus. When mother calls the children to dinner, the common element is their coming to dinner. When father appears while they are playing with his tape recorder, the common element is the cessation of that ongoing activity.

In days gone by, a similar thing happened when a stern principal appeared on the scene while boys were behaving aggressively in the hallway of the school. There would normally be at least a noticeable decrease in the intensity of the aggressive activity and often a complete cessation of the activity. But the occurrence of the stimulus provided no adequate clue as to what activity would then be initiated by the boys.

There are still other occasions when the presentation of a stimulus while activity A is in progress functions to delay, selectively, the change from A (whatever it is) to some other particular activity Y, even though an appropriate instigating stimulus for activity Y is already present. Here, the onset of the critical stimulus does not produce a general delay in the interruption of activity A by some other activity as would occur if the stimulus had increased the instigating force to undertake activity A. Instead, the new stimulus functions to postpone or eliminate entirely a change from the ongoing activity A to this particular activity Y. This again suggests that the presence of a stimulus may sometimes function to detract from a tendency that would normally be expressed in the initiation of a particular activity. The arrival of the father while children are playing with marbles does not delay the interruption of this kind of play by many activities, although it may completely eliminate the likelihood that the change will take the form of the initiation of playing with his tape recorder which stands nearby. Or, as another example, the appearance of the principal while a group of boys are standing around talking prior to the ringing of the school bell does not increase the persistence of their talking to one another, although it may guarantee that talking does not give way to fighting while he is present. In short, there are many observations that suggest a stimulus may sometimes function to detract, in some way, from a tendency that would normally be expressed in action.

Now consider some other effects of the withdrawal or the removal of a stimulus—effects that might seem paradoxical given our earlier coordination of the instigating force to action with the presence of a stimulus. Sometimes the cessation or the withdrawal of a particular stimulus is followed by an enhancement of the ongoing activity and a decrease in the likelihood of change to any other activity. If there is already in progress a relatively restrained aggressive incident between two boys in the back row of the fifth-grade class, what happens when the teacher is called from the room? The aggressive behavior is intensified. This suggests that the removal of a stimulus has somehow functioned to increase the strength of a tendency that is then being expressed in the ongoing activity.

Sometimes the removal of a particular stimulus while an activity A is in progress has the effect of decreasing the latency of another particular activity Z, as if its removal had the specific effect of strengthening the tendency to undertake that activity. Suppose that the two boys in the back row of the fifth grade are looking at their lessons when the teacher is called from the room. It would not be unusual for her withdrawal to enhance the likelihood of a prompt initiation of aggressive behavior.

What, exactly, is the problem—given our earlier assumptions that the force of a stimulus is responsible for increasing the strength of a tendency and that the force of the response, itself, is responsible for decreasing the strength of the tendency? It is to explain how the removal of a stimulus can have a behavioral effect that appears comparable to the presentation of a stimulus and to explain how the presentation of a stimulus can have a behavioral effect that appears comparable to the occurrence of an activity.

One way to summarize these several effects coherently, and also to be consistent with our earlier presumption that the functional significance of a stimulus is to produce force that increases the strength of some tendency, is to conceive of a dynamic process that is parallel to the sequence defined by the concepts of instigating force, action tendency, and action but which has to do with the suppression and the inhibition of activity. Such a conception of opposition to action, or *resistance*, is already outlined in the general logic of decision theories that account for choice in terms of the expected conse-quences of activities. When the expected consequence of an activity is negative (a noxious or punishing event), the product of strength of expec-tancy times the *negative* value of the anticipated outcome is negative. In our present language, the implication of a negative expected consequence is an *inhibitory* or *negaction tendency* which is expressed in opposition to the action tendency, that is, in resistance to engaging in that activity (Atkinson, 1964, pp. 285 to 292).

In the following discussion we explore the implications of this general idea within the conceptual framework already developed to account for the instigation of action. Our discussion includes the behavioral effects of punishment and the topics of inhibition and avoidance behavior. We first consider an analysis of the resistance or the opposition to an action tendency in which the key concepts, paralleling the ones of instigating force (F) and action tendency (T), are *inhibitory force* (I) and *negaction tendency* (N). We develop the view that, generally, there is conflict between the tendencies to engage in particular activities and the tendencies not to engage in those activities, that it is the *resultant action tendency* which ultimately gets expressed in activity, and that the changes in the dominance relations among *resultant* tendencies to engage in different activities account for the observed changes from one activity to another.

To begin, we investigate the dynamics of negaction tendencies and the consequent effects on both the resultant action tendency and the action tendency. This discussion parallels and extends the treatment of action tendency given in Chapter 1. Then, following the outline of our earlier treatment of historical questions about the growth and the extinction of instigating force to undertake a particular activity and the elaboration of an action tendency (that is, Chapter 5), we consider the growth and the extinction of the force *not* to undertake a particular activity and the elaboration of the negaction tendency that opposes, resists, and dampens the effect of an action tendency. Finally, armed with a reformulation of the Principle of Change of Activity in terms of the relative strengths of *resultant* tendencies to engage in one or another activity (that is, action tendency minus negaction tendency), we discuss the general implications of the scheme in reference to the empirical generalizations about punishment, avoidance behavior, and coordinate behavioral phenomena. And we determine how, if at all, any of the conclusions reached in the earlier chapters are affected by this particular theory of resistance.

THE CONCEPT OF A NEGACTION TENDENCY

Every individual has consciously experienced a tendency not to engage in a particular activity. Perhaps, the urge not to burst out laughing in a church, the urge not to say something sharp to an individual who has provoked anger, or the urge not to hiccough are among the common experiences of this kind. These tendencies not to engage in particular activities will be referred to as negaction tendencies. As conceived, they share many of the properties already attributed to action tendencies. They are impulsive in character, but they block, resist, or negate particular activities rather than compel them. Negaction tendencies are strengthened by the inhibitory force of stimuli in the immediate environment of the individual, for example, the threatening glance of an angry parent to the child about to giggle in church. Like action tendencies, they persist until they have been expressed and, when expressed, they decrease in strength. But unlike action tendencies, which are expressed in the initiation of an activity that can be noticed by an external observer, *a negaction tendency is expressed and is reduced in its opposition to an action tendency, that is, in resistance*. When there is both a tendency to engage in an activity (T) and a tendency not to engage in that activity (N), it is presumed that the two tendencies combine additively the same way two or more action tendencies that refer to the same activity combine in the case of a compound action tendency (see Chapter 3), with the result that the opposition or the resistance to engaging in the activity is represented by subtraction. The *resultant action tendency* ($\bar{T}$) is defined as the difference between the strength of the action tendency and the strength of the negaction tendency: $\bar{T} = T - N$.

In earlier chapters, which dealt explicitly with instances of appetitive or approach behavior that were uncomplicated by inhibition or resistance, the change from one activity to another and the intensity or vigor of ongoing activity were attributed to action tendencies. In these incompletely analyzed and, perhaps, oversimplified instances, $\bar{T} = T$. Now, having extended the conceptual analysis to include resistance, it is apparent that the intensity of ongoing activity and that the changes from one activity to another should more generally be attributed to the magnitude of the *resultant* action tendencies. This means that the implications of the Principle of Change of Activity presented earlier must be viewed as appropriate only for the special and simpler cases in which there is no resistance. It is our task now to reconsider the whole problem of change of activity to see what, if anything, is different in the more general treatment that encompasses competition among resultant action tendencies.

Resistance Distinguished from Consummation and Competition

Before examining the dynamics of negaction tendencies it will be well to have the concept of resistance clearly in mind. It must be distinguished from two other effects that also work against the expression of an action tendency.

Consider first the difference between the effect produced by the consummatory force of an activity that is occurring and the resistance produced by a negaction tendency. When the tendency to undertake a particular activity becomes dominant and is expressed in behavior, the consummatory force of the activity *reduces* the strength of that action tendency. Eating reduces the tendency to eat.

The resistance produced by a negation tendency, in contrast, has no direct influence on the strength of the action tendency it opposes. The negation tendency merely prevents all or some part of the action tendency from being expressed in behavior. The residual or resultant action tendency, $\bar{T} = T - N$, is the amount by which the strength of the action tendency exceeds the strength of the negation tendency. This represents the resultant strength of the action tendency that is free to be expressed in the competition for dominance with other resultant action tendencies and that is to be expressed in behavior. A negation tendency has a suppressive effect on some activity, but it has that effect without removing or weakening the component tendency to engage in the activity. A child, trained to wait until a prayer has been said before eating, may only hesitatingly and gingerly taste what is on his plate under the threat of chastisement but then will spring to the business of lusty eating once grace has been said.

Resistance is set apart from other effects in the theory that work against the expression of an action tendency in a second way—namely, in the form of its relationship to action tendencies. Both resistance and competition refer to interaction among tendencies, but the nature of the interaction is quite different in the two cases. A negation tendency has a graded dampening effect on an action tendency, and always, by its opposition, reduces the magnitude of the residual or resultant tendency that is available for competition with other tendencies for expression in behavior. The resolution of competition among two or more resultant action tendencies, when the activities are incompatible, is all or none. It hinges only on the question of which among the several competing resultant tendencies is strongest. When X and Y are incompatible activities, either activity X or activity Y will occur depending on which of the resultant tendencies, $\bar{T}_X$ or $\bar{T}_Y$, is dominant. The intensity of the activity that is initiated will depend on the strength of the resultant tendency that is expressed in the activity. When a change in the dominance relations occurs, the activity will change discretely and, again, the full strength of the supporting tendency will be expressed in the new activity. This is not what happens when N_X resists T_X to produce $\bar{T}_X$. Since it is $\bar{T}_X$ that is expressed in an activity, the blocking of T_X attributable to N_X has a direct influence on the vigor or the intensity of activity X when it occurs.

A more complete picture of the difference between competition and resistance now can be achieved by combining the two concepts in the paradigm for a change of activity. Consider the set of incompatible activities for which there are action tendencies T_A, T_B, T_C, ... Consider now that, for each of the activities, there may also exist an inhibitory or negation tendency N_A, N_B, N_C, ... These sets combine to yield the set of resultant action tendencies $\bar{T}_A = T_A - N_A$, $\bar{T}_B = T_B - N_B$, $\bar{T}_C = T_C - N_C$, ... The strongest from among this set of resultant action tendencies will be expressed in behavior. Activity A in progress implies that $\bar{T}_A > \bar{T}_B$, $\bar{T}_C$, . . . and, when activity A is supplanted by activity B, $\bar{T}_B > \bar{T}_A$, $\bar{T}_C$, ...

DYNAMICS OF NEGACTION TENDENCIES

The fundamental questions to be answered about negaction tendencies are ones already treated at length in reference to action tendencies (Chapter 1). How do they arise? How do they function? How are they reduced? In brief, the answers are as follows. Negaction tendencies arise from the inhibitory force of stimuli; they oppose or resist the initiation or continuation of particular activities; they are reduced when expressed in resistance. These are the primary issues that must be studied in detail so that we can determine the behavioral implications of negaction tendencies. In presenting this conception, we assume ideal conditions. Later, we shall consider the effects of selective attention and consummatory lags.

We begin again with the conservative assumption that a tendency does not change in strength spontaneously. Something must cause the change in the strength of a negaction tendency. We assume that the strength of a negaction tendency will change over time as a function of the operation of forces that enhance the tendency or that diminish it. A negaction tendency is aroused and is strengthened by the influence of the inhibitory force of a stimulus to which the individual is exposed and is reduced in strength by the force produced in its resistance to an action tendency. Should this latter force be called a consummatory force? A dissipating force? Or, more simply, the force of resistance?

We think that the latter designation, *the force of resistance*, symbolized R, conveys most clearly our notion that resistance is to a negaction tendency what action is to an action tendency: the expression of the tendency that accounts for its reduction. For assistance in overcoming the problems posed by terminology, we have placed in correspondence the parallel concepts for the instigation and the resistance to action in Table 7.1.

TABLE 7.1   Analogous Concepts in the Treatment of Instigation of Action and Resistance to Action

INSTIGATION OF ACTION	RESISTANCE TO ACTION
Instigating force, F	Inhibitory force, I
Action tendency, T	Negaction tendency, N
Action	Resistance
Consummatory force, C	Force of resistance, R

Change in Strength of a Negation Tendency

A change in the strength of a negation tendency depends on the magnitude of the inhibitory force, the magnitude of the force of resistance, and the duration of the exposure to these forces. The differential equation that describes the change in the strength of a tendency not to undertake a particular activity is

$$\frac{dN}{dt} = I - R \tag{7.1}$$

The differential equation is identical in form to the one introduced in Chapter 1 to describe changes in the strength of an action tendency (see Equation 1.4). It says that the rate of change in the strength of the tendency not to engage in an activity is given by the net force, that is, by the inhibitory force of the stimulus minus the force of resistance produced by its expression in active opposition to the tendency to undertake the activity.

The inhibitory force of a stimulus (for example, the impact on the child of the parent's threatening glance in church) is its capacity to increase the strength of the tendency not to engage in an activity and is assumed to be of constant magnitude throughout the interval of observation. The magnitude of an inhibitory force of a stimulus like the magnitude of an instigating force depends on the prior history of the individual, particularly his previous experience with punishment.

The magnitude of the force of resistance (R) defines the extent to which N is reduced per unit time as a consequence of its resistance to T. It is conceivable that two factors determine the magnitude of R: the kind of activity that is being blocked or resisted, and the strength of N that is expressed in resistance to T. We shall use r to represent the extent to which a negation tendency is reduced per unit of time in resisting an activity, allowing for the possibility that this parameter *might* vary as a function of the nature of the activity being suppressed. In dealing with the second factor affecting R, the strength of N that is actually being expressed in resistance to T, we must take into account two different cases that arise as a result of the special nature of negation tendencies.

The resistance of a negation tendency to an action tendency depends on the strength of the action tendency. If the action tendency is stronger than the negation tendency (that is, $T > N$), the full strength of the negation tendency will be expressed in resistance to the action tendency. If, on the other hand, the negation tendency is stronger than the action tendency (that is, $N > T$), then presumably only the strength of the negation tendency required to nullify the action tendency is expressed against it. In this case, an amount of N equal to the strength of T is sufficient to block the expression of T completely. The resultant tendency $\bar{T}$ is reduced to 0 when

$N = T$. The two conditions $T > N$ and $N > T$ define the two different cases. We consider them in order.

Case 1 ($T > N$). On the assumption that the force of resistance (R) is a multiplicative function of r and the N actually expressed in resistance (an assumption which is comparable to the one made earlier concerning determinants of the consummatory force of an activity), we may substitute $R = r \cdot N$ into Equation 7.1. When we do this, we obtain

$$\frac{dN}{dt} = I - r \cdot N \tag{7.2}$$

Equation 7.2 is of the same form as Equation 1.10 presented in Chapter 1 to describe the combined effect of the instigating and consummatory forces on an action tendency. It says, in effect, that the strength of the negation tendency N will increase as long as the inhibitory force is stronger than the force of resistance (that is, when $I > r \cdot N$), that N will decrease when the force of resistance is greater than the inhibitory force (that is, when $r \cdot N > I$), and that N will not change when $I = r \cdot N$. This means that the negation tendency N, like an action tendency that is being continually instigated and expressed, will approach an asymptote and, again, analogous to an action tendency, the asymptotic level for N is given by I/r.

Integrating Equation 7.2 produces

$$N = N_I \cdot e^{-r \cdot t} + \frac{I}{r}(1 - e^{-r \cdot t}) \tag{7.3}$$

Equation 7.3 generates the same family of curves for a negation tendency that Equation 1.11 generates for an action tendency. The initial strength of N is given by the inertial tendency N_I, and the asymptote by I/r.

Figure 7.1 pictures two examples from the family: (1) if the negation tendency is initially above its asymptote ($N_I > I/r$), it will decline to that level; and (2), if it is initially below that level ($N_I < I/r$), it will rise to that level. Although it is not included in Figure 7.1, notice that, even when environmental stimulation is constant, T will not necessarily continue to be stronger than N during an interval of observation. An important implication of the assumptions we have made about action and negation tendencies is that the dominance relationship between them is unstable. We shall examine some of the theoretical and behavioral consequences of this instability, that is, the shift from $T > N$ to $N > T$ to $T > N$ under constant environmental conditions, in a later section dealing with the resultant action tendency. A change from the condition $T > N$ to that of $N > T$ defines a change from Case 1 to Case 2.

Case 2 ($N > T$). When the tendency not to undertake an activity is

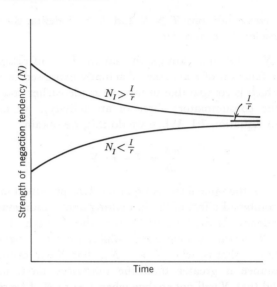

FIGURE 7.1   Examples of the possible changes in strength of negaction tendency (N) as a function of time (t) under the conditions of Case 1 when $T > N$ (see Equation 7.2).

stronger than the tendency to undertake the activity, the action tendency is completely nullified, that is, the resultant action tendency is 0. This means that the individual would not engage in that activity under any circumstances, even if there were no other tendencies competing for expression.

The combination of the condition $N > T$, and the assumption that a negaction tendency is expressed (and reduced) only in resisting an action tendency, produces a dependence of N on T in Case 2. If, for example, T were 0, then none of N could be expressed in resistance, since there would be no action tendency to resist. When T is greater than 0 but less than N, only that strength of N required to nullify T can be expressed in opposition to T. Let us symbolize by $\bar{N}$ the amount of N actually involved in resistance to T on any particular occasion, so that in Case 2 only $\bar{N} = T$ is a determinant of the force of resistance. This means that $R = r \cdot \bar{N} = r \cdot T$ when $N > T$. In other words, there is an excess of negaction tendency—more than enough needed to prevent the expression of T *at that time.*

The basic equation describing a change in the strength of negaction tendency as a function of inhibitory force and the force of resistance is the same as in Case 1 (see Equation 7.1), but when the determinants of the force of resistance are substituted for Case 2, the equation becomes

$$\frac{dN}{dt} = I - r \cdot T \qquad (7.4)$$

This means that as the strength of T changes, the strength of N that is actively involved in resistance will also change. Hence, before integrating this equation to determine the course of N over time, it is first necessary to specify the fate of T over time. This we can do easily, since, with $N > T$, it is impossible for T to be expressed in activity. It is completely blocked. Under these conditions, T grows linearly over time as a function of the influence of instigating force as described in Equation 1.7 of Chapter 1, that is, $T = T_I + F \cdot t$. By making this substitution for T in Equation 7.4, we obtain

$$\frac{dN}{dt} = I - r(T_I + F \cdot t) \tag{7.5}$$

When this equation is integrated and the constant of integration evaluated, we have

$$N = N_I + (I - r \cdot T_I) \cdot t - \left(\frac{r \cdot F}{2}\right) \cdot t^2 \tag{7.6}$$

Equation 7.6 yields the family of curves for the course of N in Case 2 of which three (a, b and c) are shown in Figure 7.2. The linear growth of T, which cannot be expressed because it is nullified by N, is shown for the condition of a constant environment as assumed. Sooner or later—but always—the constantly increasing action tendency (T) becomes equivalent to and then exceeds the negaction tendency (N).[1] This is a prime example of the instability of the dominance relation between an action tendency and a negaction tendency. Case 2, the condition in which $N > T$, is shown to be inherently unstable under the assumed conditions of a constant environment and no displacement or substitution. In time, there is always a change to Case 1, in which T exceeds N.

Which of the three paths shown in Figure 7.2 will be followed by N? This depends on the strengths of the instigating force (F) and the inhibitory force (I) relative to the strength of the other parameters. If the inhibitory force is very strong, N can increase in strength throughout the interval, although the rate of increase will diminish (as in curve a) because the constant growth in T results in a constantly increasing force of resistance throughout the interval. If the inhibitory force is moderately strong relative to the instigating force, there will occur an initial increase in the strength of N, but the constantly rising T increases the force of resistance that operates to reduce N. As shown in curve b, the faster growing force of resistance can overcome the effect of the inhibitory force, and N will begin to decline. Finally, if the

---

[1] T equals N when

$$t = \frac{-(F - I + r \cdot T_I) + \sqrt{(F - I + r \cdot T_I)^2 + 2(r \cdot F)(N_I - T_I)}}{r \cdot F}$$

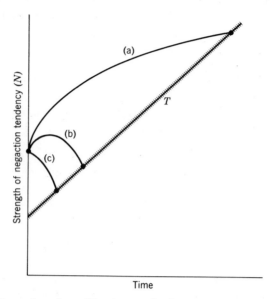

FIGURE 7.2 Examples of possible changes in the strength of negaction tendency (N) as a function of time (t) under the conditions of Case 2 when $N > T$ (see Equation 7.6).

inhibitory force is fairly weak and is unable to sustain N at its initial level, the constantly increasing force of resistance attributable to the growth in T will result in an immediate and ever more precipitous decline in N (as shown in curve c). Clearly, *the action tendency is nullified by the negaction tendency for a longer period of time the stronger the inhibitory force of the stimulus.* Yet, eventually, under the specified conditions, the impulse to action returns and, when T finally exceeds N, there is the possibility once more that the activity will be initiated.

These two cases, determined by whether $T > N$ (Case 1) or $N > T$ (Case 2), cover the possible changes in the strength of negaction tendencies over time under ideal conditions of constant environmental stimulation in the absence of displacement and substitution. Now let us consider the dynamics of the resultant action tendency under these same conditions. To do so requires the simultaneous tracking of the action tendency and the negaction tendency throughout the same interval of time.

DYNAMICS OF RESULTANT ACTION TENDENCIES

The strength of a resultant action tendency can follow any one of a large number of paths through time, even under constant environmental conditions. The assumptions made concerning the arousal of a negaction tendency, which are comparable to the ones proposed for an action tendency, and the additional assumption that a negaction tendency subtracts from an action tendency to yield the resultant action tendency ($\bar{T} = T - N$) generate a rich variety of effects on the resultant action tendency. These varied effects are particularly interesting because they are derived from the dynamic properties of the theory rather than from an appeal to a change in the stimulus situation. *Complexity can be found by turning the theory inward on the dynamic process within the individual without having to look outward for its explanation to some instability in the individual's immediate environment.*

The two cases identified in the discussion of the dynamics of a negaction tendency, Case 1, in which $T > N$, and Case 2, in which $N > T$, help to organize this section on resultant action tendencies. In Case 2, the resultant action tendency is 0 (or negative), so it can not be dominant and, thereby, expressed in behavior. In Case 1, however, there are two possibilities. The resultant action tendency is greater than 0 but may not be dominant and, if so, some other activity is being expressed in behavior (Case 1*b*). Or, the resultant action tendency may be dominant and expressed in behavior (Case 1*a*). The letters *a* and *b*, which identify these subcases, are consistent with our earlier use of *A* to identify an activity in progress and of *B* to identify a tendency that is not then being expressed in behavior.

We shall discuss the three cases, which correspond to the three possible states of a resultant action tendency in the order 1*b*, 2, and 1*a*. Then we shall illustrate how the dynamic properties of action tendencies and negaction tendencies can send a resultant action tendency through a sequence of states (or cases). Throughout the discussion, we assume that the immediate environment is constant, that is, that there is constant instigating and inhibitory force, that other parameters are constant, and that there is no displacement or substitution.

Case 1b.   We begin with the case in which $T > N$ but $\bar{T}$ is not dominant. Either of two things can happen: the resultant action tendency can in time become dominant (a change to Case 1*a*); or the resultant action tendency can in time be nullified (a change to Case 2). With $T > N$ but $\bar{T}$ not dominant, there is a linear increase in the strength of T because it is being instigated by F but not expressed. The strength of N is moving toward asymptote according to the familiar negatively accelerated function shown earlier in Figure 7.1. This is happening to N because the total available strength of N is continually expressed in resistance to T. Under these conditions, the temporal course of $\bar{T}$ is obtained from the difference between the temporal course of T and that of N. The equation for $\bar{T}$ is obtained by

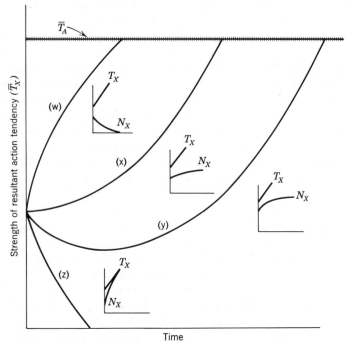

FIGURE 7.3   Four distinguishable paths for $\bar{T}_X$ within Case 1b when $T_X > N_X$ but $\bar{T}_X$ is subordinate to $\bar{T}_A$, the dominant resultant tendency (see Equation 7.7).

substitution from Equation 1.7 for T and Equation 7.3 for N:

$$\bar{T} = T - N = (T_I + F \cdot t) - \left[N_I \cdot e^{-r \cdot t} + \frac{I}{r}(1 - e^{-r \cdot t}) \right] \quad (7.7)$$

The four distinguishable paths for $\bar{T}_X$, the resultant action tendency for some activity X, in Case 1b are shown in Figure 7.3 as curves w, x, y, and z. Notice that all of the curves begin where $\bar{T}_X = T_X - N_X > 0$ but with $\bar{T}_X < T_A$, the dominant tendency which is being expressed in behavior. Three of the four curves (w, x, and y) approach positive linear growth as N_X stabilizes. The slope of this straight-line function is the same for all three curves and is equal to the magnitude of F_X. These three curves (w, x, and y) all remain in Case 1b until $\bar{T}_X$ reaches the level of $\bar{T}_A$, which is shown constant. When $\bar{T}_X > \bar{T}_A$, activity X is initiated, and we move from Case 1b to Case 1a.

The fourth curve (z) is one in which $\bar{T}_X$ decreases in strength until its value is 0 (or negative). This takes us out of Case 1b and into Case 2 where $N_X > T_X$.

Each of the four curves for $\bar{T}_X$ in Figure 7.3 is accompanied by a miniature representation of the relationship between T_X and N_X that must hold true throughout the interval to produce the given path for $\bar{T}_X$. The strength of $\bar{T}_X$ will be likely to decline initially, as in curves y and z, when the negaction tendency is relatively weak at the outset and rises to its asymptote (that is, $N_{X_I} < I_X/r_X$) and the instigating force to undertake activity X is also relatively weak [that is, $F_X < r_X(I_X/r_X - N_{X_I})$]. Whether or not T_X will be nullified (that is, $\bar{T}_X$ drops to 0) as in curve z or will reach a minimum while $\bar{T}_X$ is still positive (as in curve y) depends primarily on the magnitudes of I_X and N_{X_I}. The larger these inhibitory parameters are relative to F_X, the instigating force, the more likely it is that T_X will be nullified.

The two upper curves in Figure 7.3, namely, w and x, have initial slopes that are positive, that is, $\bar{T}_X$ increases in strength from the outset. This will always occur when the initial strength of the negaction tendency is above the asymptotic level defined by the inhibitory force of the immediate stimulus situation (that is, $N_{X_I} > I_X/r_X$) so that N_X will decline at the outset. And it may also occur if the instigating force F_X is strong enough, even though N_X may be increasing at the outset of the temporal interval.[2] The negative acceleration of curve w results from the first condition: the initial decline of N_X to a lower asymptote. The initial positive slope of curve x (in contrast to curve y) results from the second condition: an instigating force, F_X, with sufficient relative strength to overcome the effect of the rise in N_X.

The interpretation of these several conditions is simplified when it is kept in mind that $N_{X_I} > I_X/r_X$ means that N_X will decline to asymptote, and $N_{X_I} < I_X/r_X$ means that N_X will rise to asymptote. In the latter case, the other critical question concerns the magnitude of F_X. Is there sufficient instigating force for activity X to produce an increase in the resultant tendency $\bar{T}_X$ right from the outset and in the face of an initial increase in the negaction tendency N_X? This may be the most generally important question, since it follows from the assumptions that have been advanced that the initial (or inertial) strength of negaction tendencies should normally tend to be quite low. Why? Because negaction tendencies continue to be expressed and, thereby, to be reduced by resistance to action tendencies, even when the individual is no longer exposed to the inhibitory force of a stimulus, just as long as there is some action tendency to resist. For example, an individual whose tendency to engage in an aggressive act has been held in check by a negaction tendency should lose his resistance some time after he leaves the critical situation and should be left with an even stronger unexpressed resultant tendency to aggressive behavior.

[2] The initial slope of $\bar{T}_X$ will be positive under the special condition that $F_X > r_X(I_X/r_X - N_{X_I})$ even if $N_{X_I} < I_X/r_X$.

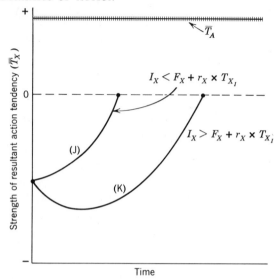

FIGURE 7.4   The possible paths for $\bar{T}_X$ within Case 2, when $N_X > T_X$ so that $\bar{T}_{X_I} \leq 0$. The activity in progress is sustained by $\bar{T}_A$, the dominant resultant tendency.

At this point let us consider what happens when the conditions are such that there is the typical initial rise in N_X, but F_X, the instigating force to undertake activity X, is too weak to prevent the nullification of T_X. This is shown in curve z of Figure 7.3. It constitutes a change from Case $1b$ to Case 2.

Case 2.   We have already reviewed the temporal course of N and T for Case 2 in Figure 7.2. When $N > T$, T is nullified. We can continue to conceive of a resultant action tendency but, now, its magnitude is a negative value: that is, $\bar{T} = T - N < 0$. The negative value of $\bar{T}$ specifies the extent to which N exceeds T. This is the amount of increase in $\bar{T}$ that is required to return to Case $1b$, in which $\bar{T}$ would again be eligible to participate in competition with other resultant action tendencies for dominance. A return to Case $1b$ can come about as a result of changes in either or both T and N. These are the changes that have already been plotted in Figure 7.2.

The temporal course of $\bar{T}_X$ in Case 2 is shown in Figure 7.4. It is obtained by plotting the difference between the curves for N_X and T_X already shown in Figure 7.2. In Case 2, $\bar{T}_X$ begins with a negative value given by $T_X - N_X$, and then it either rises directly with positive acceleration to 0 (curve j), or it declines temporarily to a minimum and then rises with positive acceleration to 0 (curve k). The slope of $\bar{T}_X$ in Case 2 will initially be negative (a declining trend) if the inhibitory force is sufficiently strong to counteract the combined effects of the instigating force and the initial force of resistance (that is, $I_X > F_X + r_X \cdot T_{X_I}$). Under these conditions, the constant rate of increase in N_X, produced by the inhibitory force, is initially greater than the combined rate of decrease in N_X, produced by the force of resistance, plus the constant rate of increase in T_X, produced by F_X. But as T_X grows, the force of resistance ($R_X = r_X \cdot T_X$) also grows. Hence, the initial advantage of the inhibitory force is lost, and the trend of $\bar{T}_X$ is reversed. The declining trend of $\bar{T}_X$ will continue for a longer time when the inhibitory force is very strong relative to the other parameters. *Although in principle it is generally expected that $\bar{T}_X$ will always become positive again, in actuality there may be instances in which the inhibitory force is so strong and ubiquitous that nullification could be a long-time fate of T_X.*

When the inhibitory force is weaker than the combination of instigating force and the initial force of resistance (that is, $I_X < F_X + r_X \cdot T_{X_I}$), $\bar{T}_X$ will begin to rise toward 0 immediately as in curve j of Figure 7.4. These trends of $\bar{T}_X$ in Case 2 are more easily discussed in reference to Figures 7.2 and 7.4 than in reference to Equation 7.8,[3] which is obtained by substitution from Equation 1.7 for T and Equation 7.6 for N in Case 2. Equation 7.8 is discussed in the mathematical notes at the end of the chapter.

Once there is a change from the state in which $N_X > T_X$ to $T_X > N_X$, that is from Case 2 to Case 1b, under the conditions of a constant environment that have been assumed throughout this discussion, the growth of $\bar{T}_X$ continues to be the positive accelerated growth toward linearity shown in curve x of Figure 7.3. This guarantees that the strength of $\bar{T}_X$ will increase to intercept the dominant tendency $\bar{T}_A$ and finally will bring about the initiation of activity X.

From this discussion of inhibitory force, negaction tendency, and resistance when the resultant action tendency is not dominant, we may draw an important conclusion about the behavioral implications: *the imposition of resistance on a tendency not being expressed delays the expression of that tendency.* It increases the latency of response and/or temporarily lowers the probability that that activity will be initiated. *The effect of introducing an inhibitory force is a temporary suppression of the response.* When the activity in question is finally initiated in the face of resistance, we move from Case 1b to Case 1a, to which we now give our attention.

Case 1a. In Case 1a, not only is $T > N$, but $\bar{T}$ is dominant. To trace the temporal course of $\bar{T}$ when it has become dominant, we must again be able to trace the separate courses of T and N from which the course of $\bar{T}$ is derived.

[3]
$$\bar{T} = (T_I - N_I) + (F - I + r \cdot T_I) \cdot t + \left(\frac{r \cdot F}{2}\right) \cdot t^2 \qquad (7.8)$$

Fate of the Negaction Tendency in Case 1a. The temporal course of N will be the same as in Case 1b, already shown in Figure 7.1, since the essential condition $T > N$ still prevails. In light of the preceding analysis of Case 1b when $\bar{T} > 0$ but not dominant, we can reasonably expect that typically, if there is no change in the stimulus situation, either N will already have risen and be near its asymptote I/r, or that it will be on the rise and will be approaching that level when $\bar{T}$ becomes the dominant tendency. But the fact that $\bar{T}$ is now being expressed in behavior introduces a determinant of the temporal course of T and $\bar{T}$ not already considered in our discussion of Case 1b, namely, C, the consummatory force of the activity.

Fate of the Action Tendency in Case 1a. We must reconsider the fate of an action tendency that is being expressed in behavior (Chapter 1), remembering that, until this chapter, we have been dealing with the problem of change of activity only when there is no resistance. Now we shall attempt to recover the conclusions reached for that special case, in which $N = 0$, from a more general statement.

We can most easily observe the effect of resistance on the temporal course of both the action tendency T and the dominant resultant action tendency $\bar{T}$ by looking first at the conditions that prevail when there is stability in the strength of $\bar{T}$ and the level of the activity motivated by it. Then, with an intuitive grasp of how resistance functions in relation to the ongoing activity and the tendencies sustaining it, we can move to a consideration of some of the more interesting but complex changes in a dominant $\bar{T}$ that are derivable from a few simple principles stated in equation form. Most of the formal derivations, however, will be appended in the mathematical notes.

The resultant action tendency $\bar{T}$ will become stable when both T and N, from which it is derived, have become stable. Given that $T > N$, N will approach stability as the inhibitory force and the force of resistance approach equality, that is, as $I = R = r \cdot N$. This is the same as N approaching the level I/r, as pointed out in the discussion of Case 1b.

The action tendency T approaches stability as the instigating force of the stimulus situation and the consummatory force of the activity become equal, that is, as $F = C$. We are reminded that the consummatory force of an activity (as conceived) depends on the kind of activity in progress and on the intensity of that activity, or on the degree of involvement of the individual in that activity. *We now assume that the intensity of an activity, or the degree of involvement in it, is determined by the strength of the resultant action tendency $\bar{T}$.*

In Chapter 1, where we made the effort to keep our explanation simple until the main structure of the conceptual scheme had been exposed, the consummatory force of the response was attributed to a multiplicative function of the consummatory value of the activity and the strength of action tendency that accounts for the intensity of activity, or the degree of involvement of the individual in that activity, that is, $C = c \cdot T$. This equation was presented for the special case in which there was no resistance, that is, $\bar{T} = T - N = T - 0 = T$. Now, having developed the concept of a negaction tendency that opposes or dampens the action tendency and that reduces the strength of the resultant tendency that is available for expression in behavior, we must employ the more general conception of the determinants of a consummatory force:

$$C = c \cdot \bar{T}$$

or

$$C = c(T - N) \tag{7.9}$$

It follows that T approaches stability as F and C approach equality. According to Equation 7.9, this will occur when $F = c(T - N)$ or when $T = F/c + N$. And since the level at which N becomes stable is given by I/r, we may complete the specification of the level at which T becomes stable: T will become stable when $T = F/c + I/r$.

It is clear, thus far, that with no inhibition, T approaches stability at a level defined by F/c. This was the specification advanced in Chapter 1 for that special case. But, when there is resistance to its expression, T does not stabilize until it has become even stronger by an amount equivalent to the level of the negaction tendency ($N = I/r$) which opposes it.

Finally, what of the dominant resultant action tendency $\bar{T}$? At what level does its strength stabilize? Since the stability of $\bar{T}$ depends on the stability of T and N from which it is derived (that is, $\bar{T} = T - N$), we obtain by substitution the following specification for the level at which the strength of $\bar{T}$ will stabilize:

$$\bar{T} = \left(\frac{F}{c} + \frac{I}{r}\right) - \frac{I}{r}$$

or

$$\bar{T} = \frac{F}{c}$$

From all of this, we conclude that, in general, *it is the resultant action tendency being expressed in behavior that will move toward, and become stable at a level defined by the ratio of the instigating force of the stimulus and the consummatory value of the response, F/c.* In the special case in which there is no resistance, so that the resultant action tendency and action tendency are equivalent, the latter also will stabilize at this level. But more generally when $N > 0$, the action tendency T will stabilize at a level defined by the level attained by the resultant action tendency ($\bar{T}$) plus an amount equivalent to the level attained by the inhibitory tendency (N) which opposes it, that is, $F/c + I/r$.

This means, in general, that over a period of time during which an individual is continuously exposed to stimuli that produce a constant instigating force to undertake an activity and a constant inhibitory force to negate the activity, and the activity is in progress in the face of resistance, *the action tendency will rise to a higher level than could be attained if there were no resistance to its expression.* It is apparent that a negation tendency, as conceived, certainly does not reduce the strength of the action tendency that it opposes. In fact, it has just the opposite and the paradoxical effect of allowing the action tendency to gain even more strength than it would if there were no resistance to its expression in behavior.

The higher asymptotic level attained by T, when there is resistance, comes about because only a magnitude of tendency equivalent to the difference between T and N, the resultant $(\bar{T})$, is expressed in the activity. As a consequence, the consummatory force $(C = c \cdot \bar{T})$, corresponding to any given magnitude of T, is less than it would be if no N were present. With a smaller consummatory force functioning to reduce T while F is instigating and strengthening it, T must attain a higher level before C can become equivalent to F, the condition required to stabilize the strength of the tendency.

This implication of the conceptual scheme is an obvious source of hypotheses about the consequences of punishment. Inherent in the scheme is a property of bottling up the action tendency to create the potential for a sudden but temporary surge in the intensity of an activity if the inhibitory force of the stimulus situation were to be suddenly removed. Since T is at a higher level than $\bar{T}$, which controls the intensity of the ongoing activity, something must happen when the inhibitory force sustaining N is suddenly withdrawn. The negation tendency should be rapidly reduced through continued resistance to the strong T. As this happens, $\bar{T}$ can increase and can produce a surge in the intensity of the activity. But this will increase the consummatory force of the activity, thus, bringing about a reduction of T and a return to the level at which $\bar{T} = T = F/c$.

We shall consider this and some related hypotheses in a later section which deals with several aspects of the problem of punishment. Now, however, we must discuss the temporal course of T and $\bar{T}$ for Case 1a in terms of this conception of how resistance functions in reference to the dominant tendency that is being expressed in the ongoing activity. We know already that the level at which $\bar{T}$ can ultimately become stable under constant environmental stimulation is the same, namely, F/c, no matter how strong the resistance.

Our task will be simplified by first considering what happens when an activity is initiated with no change in the environmental stimulus situation as $\bar{T}$ passes through condition 1b to 1a. Earlier we concluded that, since imposing resistance functions to delay the initiation of an activity, the negation tendency may very likely be near its asymptote at the time the

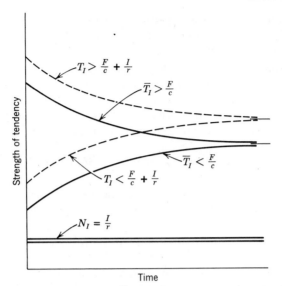

$$-T_I > \frac{F}{c} + \frac{I}{r}$$

$$-\bar{T}_I > \frac{F}{c}$$

$$-\bar{T}_I < \frac{F}{c}$$

$$-T_I < \frac{F}{c} + \frac{I}{r}$$

$$-N_I = \frac{I}{r}$$

Time

FIGURE 7.5   The parallel course of $\bar{T}$ and T when an activity is initiated (Case $1a$) after N has become stable at I/r. Depending on its initial strength, T rises or falls to its asymptote, F/c.

activity is finally initiated. Hence, let us first assume that N has already become stable. What, then, is the course of T and $\bar{T}$ once the activity is initiated, assuming the same constant environmental condition as previously?

The basic general postulate for change in the strength of an action tendency under constant conditions is

$$\frac{dT}{dt} = F - C$$

$$= F - c \cdot \bar{T}$$

or

$$\frac{dT}{dt} = F - c(T - N) \tag{7.10}$$

If N is already stable, and therefore constant, the paths of both T and $\bar{T}$ to their respective asymptotes are described by the familiar negatively accelerated growth if T_I and $\bar{T}_I$ are below asymptote, or by the equally familiar negatively accelerated decline if they are initially above asymptote. These parallel trends, shown in Figure 7.5, correspond to the ones derived earlier in Figure 1.5 for the special case in which $\bar{T} = T$.

What happens to T when N is not already asymptotic? The appropriate function describing the strength of negation tendency over time (Equation

7.3) can be substituted for N in Equation 7.10 above. Then this equation can be integrated to yield a function that describes the path of T over time under the constant conditions that have been assumed.[4] The variety of paths that T can follow depends on the several parameters of the resulting equation (Equation 7.11). Figure 7.6 contains four panels that illustrate the various possibilities. We are again reminded that the various changes in strength of T, as shown in Figure 7.6, are derived from the theory about the dynamics of the process and not by an appeal to some change in the immediate stimulus situation. Consult the mathematical notes at the end of the chapter for a more detailed specification of the conditions under which each of these trends might be expected to occur.

The point of immediate interest is to see how T is affected by changes in N when $\bar{T}$ is dominant (that is, under Case 1a). We find a new variety of possible paths for the strength of T in addition to the ones suggested in Chapter 1 when no consideration was given to resistance. In describing these possible paths, we pick up T at the point in time when the initiation consummatory lag interval is ended instead of at the point of shift in activity in order to focus on that portion of Case 1a that is most interesting.

We recall from Chapter 4 that we have assumed a consummatory lag interval at the initiation of an activity just after an action tendency becomes dominant. During this interval, the now stronger instigating force appropriate to an ongoing activity is operative, but the consummatory force is absent. It develops that the initiation consummatory lag plays no part in determining the way in which T is affected by N because N is not influenced by an initiation consummatory lag. This is true for two reasons. First, the concept of initiation consummatory lag does not apply directly to N (that is, one would not speak of a lag in the onset of resistance by N) because N always and continuously resists T. Second, even though T is affected by the initiation consummatory lag, N remains unaffected because in the case under discussion (Case 1a) $T > N$. This means that all of N is already in use against T, and the path of N is toward asymptote I/r, independent of the course taken by T.

The initiation consummatory lag does affect T directly by helping to boost its strength over the level present at the time of the change in activity. This occurs because there is no consummatory force to reduce the action tendency during the interval of the consummatory lag at the initiation of an activity, thus, the tendency grows in strength linearly during that interval.

---

[4] The resulting equation is

$$T = T_I \cdot e^{-c \cdot t} + \left(\frac{c}{c-r}\right)\left(N_I - \frac{I}{r}\right)(e^{-r \cdot t} - e^{-c \cdot t}) + \left(\frac{F}{c} + \frac{I}{r}\right)(1 - e^{-c \cdot t}) \quad (7.11)$$

For additional details, see the notes at the end of the chapter.

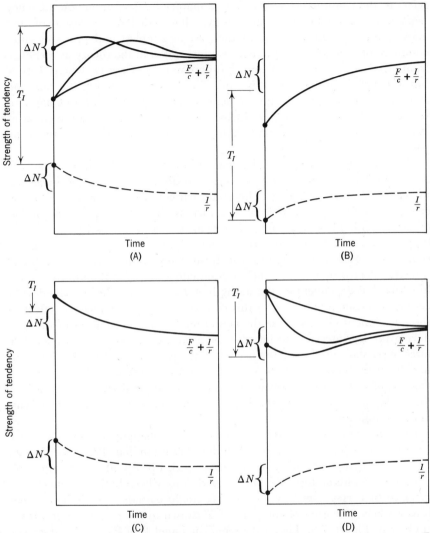

FIGURE 7.6   Examples of the paths available to T in Case $1a$, when $T > N$ and $\bar{T}$ is the dominant tendency (see pp. 224, 225 for the discussion of conditions A, B, C, D).

Since N is unaffected by initiation consummatory lag and T is only affected by being provided an interval for a constant increment in strength, we may begin following the path of T, under Case $1a$, at the end of the initiation consummatory lag.

This is an opportune place to look also at the implications of the cessation consummatory lag in relation to resistance. Cessation consummatory lag refers to the continuance of the consummatory force of an action tendency beyond the point at which an observer has coded the cessation of that activity and the initiation of another. In its simplest and probably most common form, a change in activity is represented in the theory as a change from Case 1a, where $T > N$ and $\bar{T}$ is dominant, to Case 1b, where $T > N$ but $\bar{T}$ is not dominant. For this kind of a change in activity, the cessation consummatory lag presents no problem not already dealt with in Chapter 4 because under Case 1b, $T > N$ during the interval of the cessation consummatory lag, and this means that changes in N proceed independently of the path of T.

However, the conditions of the change in activity could be such that the dominant $\bar{T}$ (Case 1a) not only became subordinate (Case 1b) but proceeded to become nullified (Case 2). This could happen if the main reason for the change in activity was a very sudden increase in the strength of negaction tendency arising from a strong punishment. Under such conditions, it would be possible for N to become greater than T before the termination of the cessation consummatory lag interval. If this happens, in addition to T being directly affected by the cessation consummatory lag, N is also affected, since its strength is dependent on the strength of T in Case 2. The overall effect of cessation consummatory lag in this case would be to enhance the effect of the punishment both because the action tendency T is reduced in strength during the lag interval and because the weakened T provides for a smaller force of resistance reducing the negaction tendency N. Neither the initiation nor the cessation consummatory lag produces any special difficulties for our analysis of resistance. However, they do make an analysis of the details of the dynamics of the time interval immediately following a change in activity more complicated.

In returning to our discussion of the effects of changes in N on T in Case 1a, it will be helpful to focus on something that is familiar. Panel B in Figure 7.6 shows what might be expected if we pick up T and N just after the initiation consummatory lag under conditions where both tendencies are rising to their respective asymptotes. We might consider the curve in Panel B as a likely extension of the path of T drawn in the miniature graph for curve x in Figure 7.3. The curve for T in Panel B of Figure 7.6 does not require the assumption that N, shown in the lower hatched curve of Panel B, has already reached its asymptote.

Panel D shows what might happen to T if the consummatory value of the activity is very substantial. The strength of T would begin to decrease toward its asymptote as soon as the consummatory force came into play. The possibility that T might decline to a minimum and then rise to its asymptote is shown in Panel D.

Panels A and C might be considered illustrative of possible extensions of the conditions described for curve w of Figure 7.3. If an activity is initiated before a declining N has stabilized, and if T is rising to an asymptote defined by a relatively strong F, the several curves for T_X shown in Panel A are possibilities. If T_I is above its asymptote and N is also decreasing, the several curves shown in Panel C are possibilities.

Of course, we do not have to assume that the environment remains constant as a tendency passes through Case 1b to stability in Case 1a. We have done that merely to get some idea about what trends would be most likely after an activity is initiated. The four panels in Figure 7.6 are more generally descriptive of the temporal course of the several tendencies when $\bar{T}$ is dominant following some change in the stimulus situation, which redefines the strength of instigating and inhibitory forces, or some change in the nature of the activity being undertaken, which redefines the magnitude of c (and possibly r). It is then assumed that these new parameters remain constant throughout the time period shown. Thus, for example, Panel B shows what might happen following a change in the stimulus situation that increases the magnitude of both F and I or a change in the stimulus situation that produces an increase in I paired with a change in the nature of the response which decreases c.

Panel D shows the effect of a change in the stimulus situation that increases I while decreasing F, or the effect of an increase in I coupled with a change in activity that increases the magnitude of c.

Panel A portrays the changes immediately following a withdrawal or weakening of the inhibitory force of the stimulus situation coupled with an increase in F or a decrease in c.

Panel C shows the trends that would typically follow a decrease in the magnitude of both F and I, or a decrease in I coupled with an increase in c.

We must remember that once a particular $\bar{T}$ becomes dominant as, for example, when the pursuit of food is initiated, the stimulus situation and the particular kind of activity in progress (what tradition calls instrumental or consummatory response) changes from moment to moment. Each change redefines the limits toward which the strength of T and N will move and the shape of the curve describing the trends of T and N. In the natural course of activity, the stimulus situation and/or the nature of the response will often change before the strengths of the several tendencies have stabilized for that particular set of conditions.

The Fate of the Resultant Action Tendency in Case 1a.   We are now ready to consider the temporal course of the resultant action tendency for Case 1a in which it is the dominant tendency. The illustrations of the possible temporal paths of $\bar{T}_X$ under the constant conditions of F_X, I_X, c_X and r_X are shown in Figure 7.7. The trend of $\bar{T}_X$ is derived from the trends of T and N already shown, since $\bar{T} = T - N$.

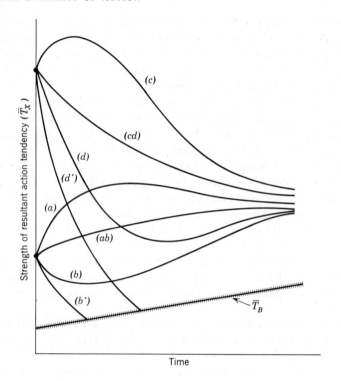

FIGURE 7.7   Possible paths for $\bar{T}_X$ within Case 1a when $T_X > N_X$ and $\bar{T}_X$ is the dominant tendency being expressed in activity. (Identifying letters refer to panels in Figure 7.6. Growth of subordinate tendency, $\bar{T}_B$, is shown.)

Each curve in Figure 7.7 is labeled a, b, c, d in reference to the four panels in Figure 7.6 which describe conditions from which a particular trend in $\bar{T}_X$ may result. The equation[5] describing the change in a dominant $\bar{T}$ is discussed in the mathematical notes at the end of the chapter. It combines the equations already given for change in T and N when $\bar{T}$ is dominant.

Let us consider the possibilities in Figure 7.7. If $\bar{T}_X$ is below its asymptote at the beginning of the interval, that is, $\bar{T}_{X_I} < F_X/c_X$, any one of the four paths a, ab, b, or b' may result. All four are derived from the conditions shown in Panels A and B of Figure 7.6, which require an initial positive slope (that is, growth) for T. For the conditions described earlier in Panel A, $\bar{T}_X$ may either rise above asymptote and then fall to it (curve a) or may rise monotonically with negative acceleration to the asymptote (curve ab).

5   $\bar{T} = \left(N_I - \dfrac{I}{r}\right)\left(\dfrac{r}{c-r}\right)(e^{-r \cdot t} - e^{-c \cdot t}) + \left[(T_I - N_I) - \dfrac{F}{c}\right]e^{-c \cdot t} + \dfrac{F}{c}$ (7.12)

The former (curve a) can occur only when N_X falls to asymptote as in Panel A. But the latter (curve ab) can result from conditions described in Figure 7.6 by either Panel A, where N is falling, or Panel B where N is rising. Only when N_X rises to asymptote as in Panel B will $\bar{T}_X$ decline and then rise to asymptote (curve b) or decline below the level of $\bar{T}_B$, the criterion for return to Case $1b$ (curve b').

Following our earlier discussion of what is most likely to be the trend if the stimulus situation has remained constant as $\bar{T}$ moves from subordinate (Case $1b$) to dominant status (Case $1a$), we focus on curve ab, which presumes that N_X is near its asymptote at the time activity X is initiated. If N_X is declining rapidly at that moment, we expect curve a; if it is rising more rapidly than T_X, we expect curves b or b'.

If $\bar{T}_X$ is above its asymptote at the beginning of the interval, that is, $\bar{T}_{X_I} > F_X/c_X$, it can rise to a maximum (curve c), simply follow a negatively accelerated decline (curve cd), or decline below and then rise back to asymptote (curve d), or decline to such an extent that it falls below $\bar{T}_B$, the criterion for a return to Case $1b$ (curve d'). The conditions shown in Panels C and D of Figure 7.6, which prescribe an initial slope that is negative for T, permit $\bar{T}$ to show a simple decline to asymptote. In Panel C, N falls to asymptote; in Panel D it rises to asymptote. Only the condition shown in Panel D will permit $\bar{T}_X$ to decline below its asymptote and to increase the possibility that it will fall below $\bar{T}_B$ as in curve d'. In addition, the conditions of Panel C permit $\bar{T}_X$ to rise initially and then fall to asymptote.

Generally speaking, the most apparent feature of the fate of $\bar{T}$, when it is the dominant tendency, is that it is headed to an asymptote given by F/c and will eventually attain this level under constant conditions except when I/r is sufficiently great that $\bar{T}$ becomes nondominant before this can happen. The terminal stability of $\bar{T}$ in Case $1a$, when it is dominant, contrasts with the terminal linear growth (except if nullified) in Case $1b$, when it is not the dominant tendency. The trends of $\bar{T}_X$ in Figure 7.7 should be compared with the ones in Figure 7.3 to emphasize this essential difference in the fate of the resultant action tendency. The figures imply that *imposing an inhibitory force will delay the initiation of an activity, but not indefinitely* (Figure 7.3), *and may suppress the level of performance of an activity after it is initiated, but not indefinitely* (Figure 7.7), *under constant conditions.* The suppressive effect of resistance, in other words, is temporary.

CHANGE OF ACTIVITY RECONSIDERED

Our theoretical account of a change from one activity to another posits a changing hierarchy of behavioral tendencies. The dominant tendency is expressed in behavior. When there is a change in the dominance relations among the tendencies, there is a change of activity.

None of the conclusions reached in earlier chapters concerning the determinants of a change of activity are violated by including resistance. But these earlier conclusions are now explicitly recognized as limited in scope to very special conditions in which there is neither resistance to the activity in progress nor to the alternatives being instigated by cues in the immediate environment of the individual.

The Principle of Change of Activity set forth in Chapter 1 (Equation 1.12) is unchanged except that now, in a more general statement, it will be made to refer to resultant action tendencies instead of action tendencies. The restatement will acknowledge that the time required to change from activity A (in progress) to activity B is an interval in which inhibitory force and the force of resistance as well as the instigating force and the consummatory force operate to bring about the change from $\bar{T}_{A_I} > \bar{T}_{B_I}$ to $\bar{T}_{B_F} > \bar{T}_{A_F}$.

The five ways in which a change of activity might come about that were presented graphically in Figure 1.1 are still valid as the representations of the average changes in the strengths of *resultant* tendencies, but they grossly oversimplify the details of these changes. The addition of inhibitory force, negation tendency, and resistance to the list of determinants of a change of activity permits $\bar{T}_A$ and $\bar{T}_B$ to follow a much greater variety of paths during the interval. The set of paths for $\bar{T}_A$ and $\bar{T}_B$ that will yield a change from activity A to activity B can be achieved by combining any one of the curves shown in Figure 7.7, the admissible paths for the resultant tendency sustaining an activity in progress, with any one of the curves shown in Figure 7.3, the admissible paths for the resultant tendency to undertake an alternative activity. The variety of combinations of paths for $\bar{T}_A$ and $\bar{T}_B$ is considerable. It includes all pairs except the ones in which the strength of $\bar{T}_B$ decreases to zero (that is, is nullified) at a rate which prevents a declining $\bar{T}_A$ from intersecting it. Figure 7.8 presents three combinations drawn from the earlier figures to illustrate the many possibilities.

Before confronting the formidable task of restating the Principle of Change of Activity in more general terms, which we will do in Chapter 9, it will be instructive to follow the temporal course of the strength of the tendencies involved in a change of activity through the several states (Cases 1a, 1b, 2) discussed at length in the preceding sections. This will provide a descriptive summary of the role of resistance in a change of activity.

From the standpoint of $\bar{T}_A$, a change from activity A to B constitutes a shift from Case 1a to Case 1b. From the standpoint of $\bar{T}_B$, the same change of activity constitutes a shift from Case 1b to Case 1a. Shifts from Case 1b to 2 and from Case 2 to 1b may also occur.

Under constant conditions, the interplay among the effects produced by

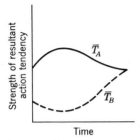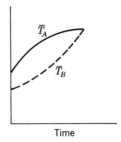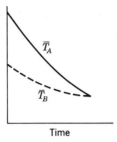

FIGURE 7.8   Three of the possible patterns of change in the strength of resultant tendencies for activity $A(\bar{T}_A = T_A - N_A)$ and for activity $B(\bar{T}_B = T_B - N_B)$ which culminate in a change of activity. (See Figures 7.3 and 7.7 from which these patterns were derived.)

the instigating force, the inhibitory force, the consummatory force, and the force of resistance guarantees a single minimum strength for any resultant action tendency followed by the growth and the ultimate possibility of expression in activity. Thus a tendency beginning in Case 2 will sooner or later rise, and a tendency beginning in Case 1*b*, although it may initially decline into Case 2, will also sooner or later rise and will not decline again unless the conditions change.

An external observer cannot easily distinguish a resultant action tendency in Case 1*b* from one in Case 2 by any simple and direct means. Obviously, neither one is the dominant tendency controlling the activity in progress. But the difference between the two cases matters in a more subtle way. An action tendency that is completely blocked or nullified (that is, Case 2) is removed from the set of tendencies that might be expressed if the activity were compatible with the dominant ongoing activity. And it is removed from the set of tendencies that define further compatibility relations (see Chapter 3). Thus, whether a tendency is in Case 1*b* or Case 2 can have an influence on what other activity might supplant the ongoing activity when a change does occur.

Figure 7.9 is designed to illustrate the movement of a resultant action tendency through a sequence of states (the various cases). At the outset, activity X is in progress and is supported by a $\bar{T}_X$ that is free of resistance (that is, $\bar{T}_X = T_X$ because $N_X = 0$). It is assumed that $\bar{T}_X$ has already become stable at F_X/c_X. While activity X is in progress, cues in the immediate environment also provide instigation for activity Y (that is, F_Y). And $\bar{T}_Y$ is growing linearly because there is no N_Y.

In other words, we shall begin with assumptions for special conditions discussed in earlier chapters, that is, no resistance to the ongoing activity or to the instigation to undertake an alternative activity. We assume this to be the state of affairs in the first segment (t_0 to t_1) of the total interval of time

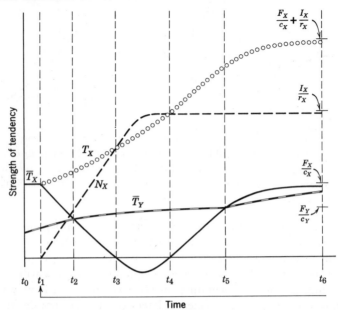

FIGURE 7.9   The temporal course of action, negation, and resultant tendencies, under constant environmental conditions.

to be considered. Each segment of interest is designated by a hatched vertical line through the graph. In order not to complicate Figure 7.9 more than is necessary, we do not represent the details of initiation and cessation consummatory lags, nor do we discuss these effects explicitly in the following paragraphs. As pointed out earlier in this chapter, consummatory lags do not interact with the effects of resistance except under some very special conditions, so that their inclusion would not enhance the present discussion.

Now let us assume that there is only one change in an otherwise constant environment. At t_1, a stimulus which implies that engaging in activity X may be punished is introduced, and it continues as part of the constant stimulus complex throughout the remainder of the time interval shown. One might add flesh and blood to this example by imagining that the subject of study is a child, activity X is playing with a neighbor's lawn mower, one of the child's own toys is the source of F_Y, and that the appearance of the owner of the lawnmower at t_1 is the source of I_X.

During the initial segment, t_0 to t_1, $\bar{T}_X$ in Case 1a is stable at F_X/c_X and $\bar{T}_Y$ grows linearly, since with no resistance $\bar{T}_Y = T_Y = T_{Y_I} + F_Y \cdot t$.

At t_1, an I_X is introduced. The following happen.

1. $\bar{T}_Y$ continues its linear growth.
2. N_X begins growth toward its asymptote (I_X/r_X) because I_X has been

introduced, and N_X is being fully expressed in resistance to T_X because $T_X > N_X$ as in Figure 7.1.

3. $\bar{T}_X = T_X - N_X$ declines as in curve d' in Figure 7.7.

4. T_X begins its growth toward a new asymptote given by $F_X/c_X + I_X/r_X$ as shown in Panel B of Figure 7.6.

During this interval, activity X continues but the vigor and/or the degree of involvement in the activity is progressively weaker. The end of the interval is defined by t_2 at which point $\bar{T}_Y$ intersects $\bar{T}_X$ and a change from activity X to activity Y occurs.

At t_2, $\bar{T}_Y$ is dominant and activity Y is initiated. $\bar{T}_X$ is now the subordinate tendency. We have shifted from Case $1a$ to Case $1b$. The following things happen during this segment.

1. $\bar{T}_Y$ is expressed in activity Y and begins to grow toward its asymptote F_Y/c_Y.

2. N_X continues its growth toward the asymptote I_X/r_X, as in the previous segment, because $T_X > N_X$ as before.

3. T_X, no longer influenced by C_X because activity X has ceased, begins a linear growth according to $T_X = T_{X_I} + F_X \cdot t$.

4. $\bar{T}_X$ continues to decline, but the rate of decline is diminished because T_X is now growing linearly (see curve z in Figure 7.3).

The end of this interval is marked by t_3, where $N_X = T_X$ and, hence, $\bar{T}_X$ is nullified, that is, $\bar{T}_X = 0$. If I_X had not been so relatively strong, T_X would have continued stronger than N_X, and the next segment would be missing.

At t_3, with activity Y still in progress, $\bar{T}_X$ has moved into Case 2. The following things happen.

1. $\bar{T}_Y$, still sustaining the ongoing activity Y, continues to grow to its asymptote F_Y/c_Y.

2. N_X continues its growth but with a slightly different path (see curve a in Figure 7.2) because the force of resistance (R_X) now depends on T_X and not N_X, since $N_X > T_X$.

3. T_X continues the linear growth begun in the last segment.

4. $\bar{T}_X = T_X - N_X$ falls below zero, reaches a minimum, and begins to rise as shown in Figure 7.4.

This segment ends at t_4 when $\bar{T}_X$ again equals 0 as a result of the linear growth in T_X having caught up with N_X (See Figure 7.2).

At t_4, $\bar{T}_X$ has returned from Case 2 to Case $1b$ in which $T_X > N_X$ but $\bar{T}_Y > \bar{T}_X$. The following things happen beginning at t_4.

1. The dominant $\bar{T}_Y$ supporting activity Y is becoming more stable as it continues its growth toward asymptote F_Y/c_Y.

2. N_X resumes its growth toward the asymptote I_X/r_X according to the path defined by the earlier conditions (t_1 to t_3) in which the force of resistance operating to reduce N_X is determined by the level of N_X, that is, $R_X = r_X \cdot N_X$.

3. T_X, still not influenced by C_X because activity X is not occurring, continues its linear growth.

4. $\bar{T}_X$ shows positively accelerated growth following its minimum in the last segment (like curve y of Figure 7.3) as it heads toward linear growth with slope equal to F_X.

This segment ends at t_5 when $\bar{T}_X$ has grown sufficiently to intersect $\bar{T}_Y$ and bring about a change from activity Y to activity X.

At t_5 there is a resumption of activity X as $\bar{T}_X$ moves from Case 1b to Case 1a in which it is again the dominant resultant tendency. The following then occur.

1. N_X, now rather stable, continues growth toward asymptote I_X/r_X.

2. T_X, once again influenced by C_X produced by activity X in progress, grows toward its asymptote $F_X/c_X + I_X/r_X$.

3. $\bar{T}_X$, now being expressed in activity X, begins to approach its asymptote F_X/c_X, the level at which it had stabilized in the initial segment (t_0 to t_1).

We conclude our discussion of Figure 7.9 with activity X again in progress. The child who gave up tinkering with the neighbor's lawn mower in favor of playing with his own toy when the neighbor appeared on the scene, after an interval in which he appeared to regain his courage, has now resumed his tinkering with the lawn mower. But as we look beyond the graph, we anticipate that the child will return again to his own toy and then will fluctuate between the two activities if conditions remain constant (see again Chapter 4). But it is more than likely that the neighbor will caution the child against touching the lawn mower, thereby effectively increasing I_X, the resistance to that activity, and the temporal duration of the next swing of $\bar{T}_X$ through Case 1b to Case 2 to Case 1b to Case 1a. Perhaps before the child is sufficiently motivated to touch the lawn mower again, he will be tempted to engage in some other activity that will take him out of the stimulus situation. If so, he would successfully avoid punishment for touching the mower.

This simple incident shows how the onset of a stimulus that produces an inhibitory force to cause resistance to an activity in progress can produce a change of activity. The temporary suppressive effect of an inhibitory force is illustrated by the subsequent resumption of the initial activity. And then, finally, near the end of the incident when the activity is again occurring and the tendency that sustains it has become fairly stable, while the tendency to undertake an alternative is growing linearly, we return to the kind of conditions for change of activity discussed extensively in previous chapters.

To simplify the presentation of the essential properties of resistance, we have unrealistically assumed that the stimulus situation has remained constant throughout the sequence of changes of activity.

We notice, in conclusion, that $\bar{T}_X$ began and ended at the same level, namely, at the asymptote given by F_X/c_X. This affirms the temporary suppressive effect of an inhibitory force. During the same interval, the negaction tendency N_X has grown to its asymptote and, perhaps most interesting, the tendency to undertake the "threatened" activity T_X has become stronger as a result of the resistance to its expression. Its initial asymptote was F_X/c_X; with resistance, it reached the higher level defined by $F_X/c_X + I_X/r_X$. The resistance, which caused the child in our example temporarily to give up playing with the lawn mower, functioned to produce a self-imposed "time of deprivation" during which there was a constant temptation to undertake the forbidden activity. As a result, the tendency grew in strength, became substantially stronger than earlier, and allowed this activity to be initiated again in the face of resistance. We would expect to observe evidence of this very strong tendency, partly held in check by resistance, if the neighbor in our example were called inside to answer the telephone. Then we might expect a temporary surge in the vigor or the degree of involvement of the child's play with the lawn mower, like that suggested in curve a of Figure 7.7, immediately following the removal of the inhibitory force that sustains the resistance. Also suggested, is the implication that maintaining the suppression of a certain behavior requires that the magnitude of the inhibitory force be increased periodically.

SUMMARY

In this chapter we have begun an analysis of aversive behavior and of some of the effects of punishment in confronting the problem of resistance. We have added the concepts of negaction tendency, resultant action tendency, inhibitory force, and force of resistance to the theory of action. Negaction tendencies oppose action tendencies to define resultant action tendencies (that is, $\bar{T} = T - N$), and changes in the dominance relations among resultant action tendencies account for the observed changes of activity. A negaction tendency N is strengthened by inhibitory force I and is weakened by the force of resistance R. Like the instigating forces for action, inhibitory forces are produced by environmental stimuli. The force of resistance, which originates in the expression of a negaction tendency in its opposition to an action tendency, has its counterpart in the consummatory force that arises from the expression of an action tendency in behavior.

The concept of resistance both complicates and enriches the theory of action. The Principle of Change in Activity, as expressed in Chapter 1 for action tendencies alone, is now restated in terms of *resultant* action tendencies. This means that a shift in activity from A to B is interpreted as a change from $\bar{T}_{A_I} > \bar{T}_{B_I}$ to $\bar{T}_{B_F} > \bar{T}_{A_F}$ (or equivalently $T_{A_I} - N_{A_I} > T_{B_I} - N_{B_I}$ to $T_{B_F} - N_{B_F} > T_{A_F} - N_{A_F}$) instead of a change from $T_{A_I} > T_{B_I}$ to $T_{B_F} > T_{A_F}$. This revision of the Principle of Change in Activity includes explicit recognition that one activity may give way to another for reasons that are negative as well as positive and, since action and negation tendencies are governed by separate processes acting through time, the possible ways in which a change in activity can come about are numerous indeed. We have presented the basic structure for a more general conception of the determinants of a change in activity and have illustrated certain details of the underlying processes.

In developing the dynamics of resultant tendencies, three cases were distinguished and were dealt with separately. The three cases follow from two new assumptions that were introduced concerning resistance. First, it is assumed that the force of resistance functions to its fullest extent as long as the action tendency is stronger than the negation tendency (Case 1a and Case 1b) but that, when the reverse is true (Case 2), the force of resistance will depend on the strength of the action tendency, since only the strength of negation tendency that is sufficient to nullify the action tendency will then be involved in resistance. The second new assumption is that the consummatory force operating to reduce an action tendency that is being expressed in behavior is a function of the strength of the *resultant* action tendency instead of the strength of the action tendency. For the activity in progress (Case 1a), this assumption makes the strength of action tendency itself a function of the negation tendency. When the resultant action tendency is subordinate (Case 1b), the alterations in the strength of action tendency are independent of consummatory force and, therefore, are not influenced by the negation tendency.

The equations describing the course of action, negation, and resultant action tendencies for each of the three cases are given in the chapter. Although these equations are often complex and unwieldy in their details, certain generalizations about the effects of resistance are possible. Most interesting and important, perhaps, are the following.

1. In Case 1a where $\bar{T}$ is dominant, the asymptotic value of T is the sum of the asymptotic values for T and N (that is, $F/c + I/r$). This means that resistance to an ongoing activity does not serve to lessen the fundamental impulse to engage in that activity but instead, paradoxically, serves to increase it.

2. In Case 1b where $\bar{T}$ is greater than zero but nondominant, the suppressive effect of a constant inhibitory force is temporary. The presence of N

detracts from T, but as N approaches its asymptote over time the change in $\bar{T}$ approaches the linear growth that would characterize it if there were no resistance.

3. In Case 2 where $N > T$ and the tendency to engage in the activity is completely nullified, the suppressive effect of a constant inhibitory force is once again temporary. It is only a matter of time before T will catch up to and surpass N so that Case 2 gives way to Case 1b.

The implication common to all three of these generalizations is that *the effect of resistance is transitory*. Resistance only serves to delay the inevitable triumph of the action tendency. It causes an even stronger action tendency than would occur if there were no resistance. An example of a change in activity that displays these phenomena which are attributable to resistance is presented in the final section of the chapter.

MATHEMATICAL NOTES

Mathematical details are called for on three interrelated topics in our study of resistance. These topics are (1) the dynamics of negation tendencies themselves, (2) the dynamics of resultant action tendencies, and (3) the more subtle but yet direct effect of negation tendencies on action tendencies under certain conditions. The format of these notes (including the section headings) will follow that of the text to facilitate the coordination of the two.

Dynamics of Negation Tendencies

The basic differential equation that describes the change in the strength of a negation tendency with respect to time is

$$\frac{dN}{dt} = I - R = I - r \cdot \bar{N}$$

where I is the inhibitory force for negation tendency N, R is the force of resistance resulting from N opposing T, r is a parameter reflecting the degree to which N is reduced per unit of time in resisting T, and $\bar{N}$ is the magnitude of N that is actually expressed in resistance to T.

In *Case 1*, where $T > N$, all of N is engaged in resisting T (that is, $\bar{N} = N$), so that the appropriate differential equation is

$$\frac{dN}{dt} = I - r \cdot N \tag{7.2}$$

This equation, when integrated, yields Equation 7.3:

$$N = N_I \cdot e^{-r \cdot t} + \frac{I}{r} (1 - e^{-r \cdot t})$$

It is apparent that Equations 7.2 and 7.3 are of the same form as Equations 1.10 and 1.11, which describe action tendencies in Chapter 1, so that comments about the earlier equations in the notes to Chapter 1 apply also to these equations, which describe the dynamics of negaction tendencies under Case 1.

Case 2 comes about when $N > T$. This means that only that amount of N necessary to nullify T is in actual use (that is, $\bar{N} = T$), so that $dN/dt = I - r \cdot T$ (Equation 7.4). With $N > T$, it is apparent that T cannot be expressed in activity and, since it is being instigated by F, will grow linearly as stated in Equation 1.7, so that

$$T = T_I + F \cdot t \quad \text{and} \quad \frac{dN}{dt} = I - r(T_I + F \cdot t) \quad (7.5)$$

It is straightforward to solve this equation and to evaluate the constant of integration by using $N = N_I$ at $t = 0$. The result is

$$N = N_I + (I - r \cdot T_I) \cdot t - \left(\frac{r \cdot F}{2}\right) \cdot t^2$$

given as Equation 7.6 in the text.

In considering this equation, we must make sure that we remain within the interval during which Case 2 holds true. Given Case 2 initially, we can determine how long Case 2 will continue in force by setting $T = N$ and by solving the resulting quadratic equation for t. That is, Case 2 gives way to Case 1 when

$$T_I + F \cdot t = N_I + (I - r \cdot T_I) \cdot t - \left(\frac{r \cdot F}{2}\right) \cdot t^2$$

This yields

$$t = - \frac{(F - I + r \cdot T_I) + \sqrt{(F - I + r \cdot T_I)^2 + 2(r \cdot F)(N_I - T_I)}}{r \cdot F}$$

as the duration for Case 2. The possible paths of N in Case 2 are easily discovered by examination of the first derivative of Equation 7.6, $dN/dt = (I - r \cdot T_I) - r \cdot F \cdot t$. Initially (that is, for $t = 0$), N will rise if $(I - r \cdot T_I) > 0$ and will decline if $(I - r \cdot T_I) < 0$, but as t gets larger dN/dt becomes smaller and can change from positive to negative. N can reach a maximum in Case 2 but will do so if and only if $(I - r \cdot T_I) > 0$ and $(I - r \cdot T_I)/r \cdot F$, the value of t for which N is a maximum is less than the value of t that defines the point of change from Case 2 to Case 1, as given above. These conditions will be satisfied if

$$F < \frac{(I - r \cdot T_I)^2}{2(I - r \cdot N_I)}$$

which, in turn, requires that $(I - r \cdot N_I) > 0$. Figure 7.2 illustrates the three types of paths N may take: (a) monotone increasing when $(I - r \cdot T_I) > 0$ and $F \geq (I - r \cdot T_I)^2/2(I - r \cdot N_I)$, (b) increasing to a maximum then decreasing when $(I - r \cdot N_I) > 0$ and $F < (I - r \cdot T_I)^2/2(I - r \cdot N_I)$, and (c) monotone decreasing when $(I - r \cdot T_I) < 0$.

Dynamics of Resultant Action Tendencies

The resultant action tendency is defined as $\bar{T} = T - N$. In dealing with $\bar{T}$ as a function of time it is necessary to divide Case 1 where $T > N$ into Case 1a where $\bar{T}$ is dominant and into Case 1b where $\bar{T}$ is nondominant. Case 2 where $N > T$ remains as before. Following the organization of the text we shall consider the three cases in the order 1b, 2, and 1a.

Case 1b. A resultant tendency can remain in Case 1b only temporarily and must move either into Case 1a or Case 2 with time. In Case 1b $T = T_I + F \cdot t$ and $N = N_I \cdot e^{-r \cdot t} + (I/r)(1 - e^{-r \cdot t})$ making

$$\bar{T} = (T_I + F \cdot t) - \left[N_I \cdot e^{-r \cdot t} + \frac{I}{r}(1 - e^{-r \cdot t}) \right] \qquad (7.7)$$

The first derivative of this expression with respect to t is

$$\frac{d\bar{T}}{dt} = F + r\left(N_I - \frac{I}{r} \right) \cdot e^{-r \cdot t}$$

We observe that $d\bar{T}/dt$ can be either positive or negative depending both on the relative magnitudes of certain parameters and on the size of t. For $t = 0$, $d\bar{T}/dt = F + r(N_I - I/r)$ and in the limit as $t \to \infty$, $d\bar{T}/dt = F$. Thus, although $\bar{T}$ can have an initial slope that is positive, zero, or negative depending on the magnitude of $F + r(N_I - I/r)$, eventually its slope must become positive and equal to F.

Complicating the picture, however, is the possibility that $\bar{T}$, as a consequence of its initially negative slope, may drop below zero and, thereby, may leave Case 1b for Case 2. This will happen according to Equation 7.7 if for some finite value of t, $N_I \cdot e^{-r \cdot t} + (I/r)(1 - e^{-r \cdot t}) > T_I + F \cdot t$, given $T_I > N_I$. An examination of this expression shows that for fixed values of F, r, T_I, and N_I there will always exist values of I large enough that the inequality is satisfied. This path for $\bar{T}$ is depicted in curve (z) of Figure 7.3.

Another way to show that $\bar{T}$ can enter Case 2 and also to discover the conditions under which $\bar{T}$ can begin with a negative slope and can reach a minimum within Case 1b is to observe that if $\bar{T} < 0$ at its minimum, then it must enter Case 2, but that if $\bar{T} \geq 0$ at its minimum it remains in Case 1b. By setting $d\bar{T}/dt = 0$ and by solving for t, it can be determined that $\bar{T}$ has a single minimum at

$$t = \frac{1}{r} \ln \left\{ \frac{r[(I/r) - N_I]}{F} \right\}$$

if and only if $F + r(N_I - I/r) < 0$; that is, if and only if $\bar{T}$ has an initial slope that is negative.

If $\bar{T}$ is to enter Case 2, it is necessary that the inequality $\bar{T} = (T_I + F \cdot t) - [N_I \cdot e^{-r \cdot t} + (I/r)(1 - e^{-r \cdot t})] < 0$ be satisfied for

$$t = \frac{1}{r} \ln \left\{ \frac{r[(I/r) - N_I]}{F} \right\}$$

Substituting this value of t into Equation 7.7 and simplifying produces the inequality

$$T_I + \left(\frac{F}{r}\right) \ln \left\{ \frac{r[(I/r) - N_I]}{F} \right\} - \frac{I}{r} + \frac{F}{r} < 0$$

that must be satisfied. Notice that for fixed values of the other parameters, values of I large enough to satisfy the inequality can be found, since fundamentally it is the ln (I) that is pitted against $-(I)$ in determining the sign of the expression. Thus, it is shown again that large values of I tend to send $\bar{T}$ into Case 2.

It is also possible for $\bar{T}$ to reach a minimum within Case 1b and, therefore, never enter Case 2, as is illustrated in curve (y) of Figure 7.3. This will occur if

$$T_I + \left(\frac{F}{r}\right) \ln \left\{ \frac{r[(I/r) - N_I]}{F} \right\} - \frac{I}{r} + \frac{F}{r} \geq 0$$

That values of I exist which satisfy this inequality when the other parameters are fixed is demonstrated by choosing

$$\frac{r[(I/r) - N_I]}{F} > 1$$

near to 1. This can be done by letting

$$\frac{r[(I/r) - N_I]}{F} = 1 + \mathscr{E}$$

where $\mathscr{E} > 0$. This allows the inequality of concern to be rewritten as $(T_I - N_I) \geq (F/r)[\mathscr{E} - \ln(1 + \mathscr{E})]$ and, since $T_I - N_I > 0$ for Case 1b, it is possible to find values of $\mathscr{E}$ so that the inequality is satisfied. These values must be relatively small, and they imply a relatively modest negative initial slope for $\bar{T}$.

If the initial slope, $F + r(N_I - I/r)$, is greater than or equal to zero, $\bar{T}$

rises monotonically with time. The second derivative,

$$\frac{d^2\bar{T}}{dt^2} = -r^2\left(N_I - \frac{I}{r}\right) \cdot e^{-r \cdot t}$$

shows, however, that $\bar{T}$ may rise with either positive or negative acceleration. For $F > r(I/r - N_I)$ and $I/r > N_I$, $\bar{T}$ will grow with positive acceleration as in curve (x) in Figure 7.3, whereas, for $F > r(I/r - N_I)$ and $N_I > I/r$, $\bar{T}$ will grow with negative acceleration as illustrated in curve (w), Figure 7.3. For all paths of $\bar{T}$, except the ones that carry $\bar{T}$ into Case 2, however, the final positive slope of $\bar{T}$ means a constantly increasing resultant tendency over time and the eventual entry into Case $1a$.

A point of interest about $\bar{T}$ in Case $1b$ is the question of whether the addition of resistance, despite its admittedly transitory nature, always hinders the growth of $\bar{T}$. We can gain an answer to this question by comparing the magnitudes of $\bar{T}$ with resistance ($\bar{T} = T - N$), using Equation 7.7 with $N_I = 0$, to that of $\bar{T}$ without resistance ($\bar{T} = T$), using Equation 7.7 with $N_I = 0$ and $I = 0$. It is easily seen that $(T_I + F \cdot t) - (I/r)(1 - e^{-r \cdot t}) < T_I + F \cdot t$ for $0 < t < \infty$ indicating that, when resistance is imposed on an action tendency, constantly instigated but not expressed, the resultant action tendency is less at each subsequent point in time than it would have been without the imposed resistance.

Case 2.   In this case with $N > T$, so that N is engaged only to a level necessary to nullify T, $N = N_I + (I - r \cdot T_I) \cdot t - [(r \cdot F)/2] \cdot t^2$ (Equation 7.6), and $T = T_I + F \cdot t$. These equations combine to give $\bar{T} = (T_I - N_I) + (F - I + r \cdot T_I) \cdot t + [(r \cdot F)/2] \cdot t^2 < 0$ (Equation 7.8), where $(T_I - N_I) < 0$. The first derivative of $\bar{T}$ with respect to time, $d\bar{T}/dt = (F - I + r \cdot T_I) + (r \cdot F) \cdot t$, displays the most important characteristic of $\bar{T}$ in Case 2: that, when t becomes large enough, the slope on $\bar{T}$ must be positive, implying that $\bar{T}$ must leave Case 2 for Case $1b$.

The initial slope for $\bar{T}$, $d\bar{T}/dt$ for $t = 0$, is $F - I + r \cdot T_I$, which can be either positive or negative depending on the relative magnitudes of the parameters. If and only if its initial slope is negative (that is, $F - I + r \cdot T_I < 0$) will $\bar{T}$ have a minimum in Case 2 and, under these conditions, the minimum will occur at $t = (I - F - r \cdot T_I)/r \cdot F$. Prior to its minimum, $\bar{T}$ decreases with negative acceleration ($d^2\bar{T}/dt^2 = r \cdot F$) and, subsequent to the minimum, $\bar{T}$ increases with positive acceleration. An example of such a path for $\bar{T}$ is curve (k) of Figure 7.4. If $\bar{T}$ begins with positive slope (that is, $F - I + r \cdot T_I > 0$), it will grow with positive acceleration as long as it remains in Case 2, as illustrated in curve (j) of Figure 7.4.

Last, by setting $\bar{T} = 0$ and by solving for t, the time that $\bar{T}$ will remain in

Case 2 is found to be

$$t = \frac{(I - F - r \cdot T_I) + \sqrt{(I - F - r \cdot T_I)^2 + 2(N_I - T_I)(r \cdot F)}}{r \cdot F}$$

When this value of t is substituted into the expression for $d\bar{T}/dt$, the result shows that $\bar{T}$ always leaves Case 2 for Case 1b with positive slope and acceleration.

Case 1a. With $T > N$, the course of N is the familiar

$$N = N_I \cdot e^{-r \cdot t} + \frac{I}{r}(1 - e^{-r \cdot t})$$

but with $\bar{T}$ dominant, so that the activity is occurring, new consideration must be given to T. The original statement of the change in an action tendency per unit time, when no resistance is involved, was given in Chapter 1 as $dT/dt = F - C = F - c \cdot T$ because $C = c \cdot T$. Resistance, however, protects an action tendency from expression. This requires that the consummatory force be rewritten as $C = c \cdot \bar{T} = c(T - N)$. This, in turn, requires that

$$\frac{dT}{dt} = F - c(T - N) \tag{7.10}$$

which is the more general statement for dT/dt.

We can replace N by its equivalent in $dT/dt = F - c(T - N)$, giving

$$\frac{dT}{dt} = F - c \cdot T + c \left[N_I \cdot e^{-r \cdot t} + \frac{I}{r}(1 - e^{-r \cdot t}) \right]$$

as the linear differential equation to be solved. The solution, when the constant of integration is evaluated by setting $T = T_I$ for $t = 0$, is

$$T = T_I \cdot e^{-c \cdot t} + \left(\frac{c}{c - r} \right) \left(N_I - \frac{I}{r} \right)(e^{-r \cdot t} - e^{-c \cdot t}) + \left(\frac{F}{c} + \frac{I}{r} \right)(1 - e^{-c \cdot t}) \tag{7.11}$$

In discussing the characteristics of this expression for T, it will be helpful to know the first derivative

$$\frac{dT}{dt} = c \left(\frac{F}{c} + \frac{I}{r} - T_I \right) \cdot e^{-c \cdot t} + \left(\frac{c}{c - r} \right) \left(N_I - \frac{I}{r} \right)(c \cdot e^{-c \cdot t} - r \cdot e^{-r \cdot t})$$

The initial slope for T is obtained by setting $t = 0$ in this expression to give $dT/dt = c(F/c - T_I + N_I)$. Also, by letting $dT/dt = 0$, solving for t, and by simplifying the result, we obtain

$$t = \left(\frac{1}{c-r}\right) \ln \left[\frac{(c-r)(F/c - T_I + N_I)}{r(N_I - I/r)} + 1\right]$$

which indicates that, for certain values of the parameters, a single maximum or minimum for T exists. For $c - r > 0$ a maximum or minimum exists if

$$\frac{(c-r)(F/c - T_I + N_I)}{r(N_I - I/r)} > 0$$

and for $c - r < 0$ if

$$-1 < \frac{(c-r)(F/c - T_I + N_I)}{r(N_I - I/r)} < 0$$

From Equation 7.11 it is readily observed that T approaches an asymptote of $F/c + I/r$ as $t \to \infty$. Thus, in general, T can begin with an initial slope that is positive or negative and can rise or fall monotonically or with a single maximum or minimum to an asymptote given by $F/c + I/r$. Figure 7.6 illustrates these paths for T in four panels representing the four combinations of initial slopes for T and N.

In Panel A a positive initial slope for T is combined with a negative slope for N. This means that $(F/c - T_I + N_I) > 0$, and that $N_I < T_I < (F/c + I/r) + (N_I - I/r)$, and that $(N_I - I/r) > 0$. According to the inequalities given above, T will always have a maximum if $c - r > 0$ and may have a maximum or may rise monotonically to asymptote if $c - r < 0$, depending on the relative magnitudes of the parameter values.

Panel B combines a positive initial slope for T with a positive slope for N. These conditions, $(F/c - T_I + N_I) > 0$, implying that $N_I < T_I < (F/c + I/r) - (I/r - N_I)$, and $(N_I - I/r) < 0$ when imposed on the inequalities indicate that the resulting T rises monotonically to asymptote both for $c - r > 0$ and for $c - r < 0$.

In Panel C both T and N have negative initial slopes; that is, $(F/c - T_I + N_I) < 0$, implying that $T_I > (F/c + I/r) + (N_I - I/r)$, and that $(N_I - I/r) > 0$. When used in the inequalities to test T for a minimum, these values show that no minimum exists and that T declines monotonically to asymptote when both T and N have negative initial slopes.

Last, Panel D presents the result of combining a negative initial slope for T with a positive slope for N. These conditions require that $(F/c - T_I + N_I) < 0$, or equivalently that $T_I > (F/c + I/r) - (I/r - N_I)$, and $(N_I - I/r) < 0$. According to the inequalities, T will always have a minimum for $c - r > 0$ and may have a minimum or may decline monotonically to asymptote for $c - r < 0$ depending on the relative magnitudes of the various parameters.

We are now prepared to consider the dynamics of the resultant action tendency in Case 1*a* armed with the separate equations for T and N. Since $\bar{T} = T - N$, we can use Equations 7.3 and 7.11 to arrive at

$$\bar{T} = \left(N_I - \frac{I}{r}\right)\left(\frac{r}{c - r}\right)(e^{-r \cdot t} - e^{-c \cdot t}) + \left[(T_I - N_I) - \frac{F}{c}\right] \cdot e^{-c \cdot t} + \frac{F}{c}$$

$$(7.12)$$

According to this equation $\bar{T} = T_I - N_I$ for $t = 0$ and, as $t \to \infty$, $\bar{T}$ approaches an asymptote of F/c.

The first derivative of Equation 7.12 with respect to t gives

$$\frac{d\bar{T}}{dt} = \left(N_I - \frac{I}{r}\right)\left(\frac{r}{c - r}\right)(c \cdot e^{-c \cdot t} - r \cdot e^{-r \cdot t}) - c\left[(T_I - N_I) - \frac{F}{c}\right] \cdot e^{-c \cdot t}$$

which for $t = 0$ shows the initial slope for $\bar{T}$ to be $r(N_I - I/r) - c[(T_I - N_I) - F/c]$. In addition, by setting $d\bar{T}/dt = 0$ and solving for t, we can obtain

$$t = \left(\frac{1}{c - r}\right) \ln \left(\frac{c}{r}\right)\left\{1 - \left[\frac{c(T_I - N_I - F/c)}{r(N_I - I/r)}\right]\left[\frac{c - r}{c}\right]\right\}$$

as the value of t for which $\bar{T}$ is either a maximum or a minimum. It is notable that $\bar{T}$ has at most, a single maximum or minimum. The relationships among parameters that must hold true if $\bar{T}$ is to have a maximum or minimum are as follows. For $c - r > 0$, the inequality

$$\frac{c(T_I - N_I - F/c)}{r(N_I - I/r)} < 1$$

must be satisfied and, for $c - r < 0$, it is necessary that

$$-\left(\frac{c}{r - c}\right) < \frac{c(T_I - N_I - F/c)}{r(N_I - I/r)} < 1$$

obtain.

In examining the possible paths that $\bar{T}$ can take in Case 1*a*, we follow the format of Figure 7.6 with its four panels. Our discussion is organized around three questions to be asked for each panel. What is the sign of the initial slope for $\bar{T}$? Where, with respect to its asymptote, does $\bar{T}$ begin? Can $\bar{T}$ have a maximum or minimum?

In Panel A, T has a positive initial slope, $(F/c - T_I + N_I) > 0$, and N has a negative slope, $(N_I - I/r) > 0$. These conditions combine to yield a positive initial slope for $\bar{T}$. It also follows directly that $\bar{T}$ must start below asymptote since, from the conditions imposed by the positive initial slope for T,

$$\left[\frac{F}{c} - (T_I - N_I)\right] > 0$$

Since $\bar{T}$ has a positive initial slope and starts below its asymptote, it must either rise monotonically or must reach a maximum and decline to asymptote. When tested in the two inequalities, the conditions of Panel A in Figure 7.6 always result in a maximum for $c - r > 0$ and may, or may not, produce a maximum for $c - r < 0$, depending on the relative magnitudes of the parameters. These two paths for $\bar{T}$ are shown in Figure 7.7 as curves (a) and (ab).

In Panel B, T has a positive initial slope, $(F/c - T_I + N_I) > 0$ as does N, $(N_I - I/r) < 0$. The initial slope for $\bar{T}$ may be either positive or negative depending on the parameter magnitudes, but $\bar{T}$ must start below asymptote for the same reason as held in Panel A. Thus, if the initial slope for $\bar{T}$ is negative, $\bar{T}$ must either decline enough so as to leave Case $1a$ and enter Case $1b$ or must reach a minimum followed by a rise to asymptote. These two possibilities are shown in curves (b') and (b) in Figure 7.7. If the initial slope for $\bar{T}$ is positive, neither of the two inequalities that must be satisfied for the existence of a maximum can be satisfied, indicating that $\bar{T}$ must increase monotonically to asymptote as shown in curve (ab) of Figure 7.7.

In Panel C, T has a negative initial slope, $(F/c - T_I + N_I) < 0$ as does N, $(N_I - I/r) > 0$. Again, the initial slope for $\bar{T}$ can be either positive or negative according to the magnitudes of the parameters, but $\bar{T}$ must start above asymptote, since the negative initial slope for T dictates $[F/c - (T_I - N_I)] < 0$. With $\bar{T}$ beginning above asymptote if the initial slope for $\bar{T}$ is positive, it follows that $\bar{T}$ must rise to a maximum and then must decline to asymptote, as illustrated by curve (c) in Figure 7.7. If, however, the initial slope of $\bar{T}$ is negative, neither of the inequalities required for the existence of a minimum are met, implying that $\bar{T}$ declines monotonically to asymptote as in curve (cd) of Figure 7.7.

Last, in Panel D, T has a negative initial slope, $(F/c - T_I + N_I) < 0$ while N has a positive slope, $(N_I - I/r) < 0$. These conditions combine to require that $\bar{T}$ have a negative initial slope and, since $[F/c - (T_I - N_I)] < 0$ as in Panel C, $\bar{T}$ must begin above asymptote. When tested by the two inequalities, $\bar{T}$ is found always to go to a minimum or to enter Case $1b$ for $c - r > 0$ but to do so only with certain parameter values for $c - r < 0$. These three possibilities are also presented in Figure 7.7, labeled as curves (d), (d'), and (cd), the last illustrating the path of $\bar{T}$ when the parameter values yield a monotone decline to asymptote for $\bar{T}$.

A point of interest in Case $1a$ is the demonstration that the addition of resistance to an action tendency that is being expressed always results in a smaller resultant tendency. This is not immediately obvious in that the resultant tendency with resistance present is approaching the same asymptote as the resultant tendency without resistance; namely, F/c, and the asymptote for the action tendency is higher with resistance than it is without resistance.

The comparison of interest can be made by opposing $\bar{T} = T_I \cdot e^{-c \cdot t} + (F/c)(1 - e^{-c \cdot t})$, Equation 1.11, to $\bar{T} = (N_I - I/r)(r/(c - r))(e^{-r \cdot t} - e^{-c \cdot t}) + [(T_I - N_I) - F/c]e^{-c \cdot t} + F/c$, Equation 7.12, if we set $N_I = 0$ so that $\bar{T} = T_I$ for $t = 0$ in both cases. Doing so yields

$$\bar{T} = T_I \cdot e^{-c \cdot t} + \frac{F}{c}(1 - e^{-c \cdot t}) - \frac{I}{r}\left(\frac{r}{c - r}\right)(e^{-r \cdot t} - e^{-c \cdot t})$$

Since $[(e^{-r \cdot t} - e^{-c \cdot t})/(c - r)] \geq 0$ for all c and $r \geq 0$, it is clear that $\bar{T}$ in the second equation, where resistance has been imposed, is less than in the first equation for all $t > 0$. This implies that the addition of resistance to an action tendency produces a decrement to the resultant action tendency, although, it should be noted, the decrement is ever smaller as t becomes larger.

A related point of interest concerns the effect on $\bar{T}$ of removing the inhibitory force I. With Case 1a in force, Equation 7.12 is appropriate and, as previously given,

$$\frac{d\bar{T}}{dt} = \left(N_I - \frac{I}{r}\right)\left(\frac{r}{c - r}\right)(c \cdot e^{-c \cdot t} - r \cdot e^{-r \cdot t}) - c\left[(T_I - N_I) - \frac{F}{c}\right] \cdot e^{-c \cdot t}$$

When I and t are each set equal to zero, we find that $d\bar{T}/dt = N_I \cdot r - c(\bar{T}_I - F/c)$ as the initial slope for $\bar{T}$ immediately on the removal of I. This expression shows that $\bar{T}$ rises when I is withdrawn unless $\bar{T}_I$ is unusually high. If $\bar{T}_I$ is great enough that $c(\bar{T}_I - F/c) > N_I \cdot r$, $\bar{T}$ will decline. This is because the C operating to reduce $\bar{T}$ is sufficient to overcome the input to $\bar{T}$ that arises from the removal of I.

However, if, for example, $\bar{T}$ had approached asymptote prior to the removal of I, so that $\bar{T}_I = F/c$ when $I = 0$, $d\bar{T}/dt = N_I \cdot r$, which is certainly positive. Under these conditions, $\bar{T}$ starts at F/c, rises and returns to approach F/c again and, therefore, must have a maximum. When determined by setting $d\bar{T}/dt = 0$ and solving for t, the maximum is found to occur at $t = (1/(c - r)) \ln (c/r)$, which is always greater than zero.

CHAPTER 8

THE INHIBITORY FORCE
OF A STIMULUS

In this chapter, we consider the source, genesis, and cognitive correlates of inhibitory forces. Paralleling our earlier treatment of instigating force, we discuss this subject from three perspectives: (1) the traditional study of conditioning and learning, (2) the study of human decision making, and (3) the study of individual differences in personality as typified by the current interest in the avoidance of failure.

RESISTANCE FROM THE PERSPECTIVE OF
CONDITIONING AND LEARNING

In the study of conditioning and learning in lower animals, the topics of greatest traditional interest are punishment and avoidance behavior. We shall look at these topics through the conceptual spectacles proposed in the present treatment of resistance but without reference to the long history of the study of these problems and of other schemes of analysis (see Solomon, 1964). Our initial premise is that an individual is so constituted that *some stimuli are inherently aversive*. Prior to any learning experience by the individual, such a stimulus will produce an *unconditioned inhibitory force* $_{US}I$ for him. Thus, for example, the effect of onset of shock to the feet of a rat standing on a grid is conceived as an unconditioned inhibitory force that produces a rapid increase in the tendency *not* to continue standing or walking on the grid. This causes resistance to the ongoing activity and, thereby, increases the probability of a change of activity. It is our intention to view all the various stimuli that have been described as innately noxious or aversive, or as having the capacity to provoke an innate withdrawal reaction (Schneirla, 1959), as sources of unconditioned inhibitory force with the kinds of behavioral implications spelled out in Chapter 7 (see also, Boe and Church, 1968).

By using the Principle of Learning set forth in Chapter 5, we shall show how unconditioned inhibitory forces can give rise to conditioned inhibitory forces. To prepare the ground for this derivation and to make contact as

245

promptly as possible with the most familiar topics in the domain of resistance, we shall begin with an analysis of punishment and avoidance conditioning. The training procedure in which the initiation of some particular activity is followed systematically by a stimulus that produces inhibitory force is called *Punishment*. The training procedure in which every activity is punished except one, the occurrence of which prevents exposure to inhibitory force, is called *Avoidance Conditioning*.

An Analysis of Punishment

Several aspects of a punishing state of affairs need to be distinguished. We, perhaps, can make the general points in reference to the simple example of a child exposed to the heat of the flame into which he has just placed his hand. His immediate reaction is the result of a long evolutionary history. What are some of the logical possibilities that a long process of natural selection has tended to favor or to eliminate?

The flame, a stimulus, could conceivably produce an unconditioned instigating force to continue this particular kind of commerce with the environment. The result would be a strengthening of the already dominant tendency that sustains the activity, a consequence contrary to the best interests and well-being of the individual. That possibility has long since been eliminated for many or most of the potentially destructive stimuli that occur frequently in the natural environment of living organisms.

A second possibility is that the stimulus of the flame burning the skin produces neither instigating nor inhibitory force. This is another possibility guaranteed to weaken the vigor and to shorten the life-span of the individual.

Next is the possibility that the intense heat of the flame produces an unconditioned inhibitory force that strengthens a negaction tendency opposing the tendency to hold the hand in the flame. This certainly would lessen the likelihood that the activity in progress would continue, especially, if the unconditioned inhibitory force were very strong.

Even more adaptive would be an arrangement in which the stimulus of the burning heat of the flame produced both a strong unconditioned inhibitory force, which would immediately weaken the resultant tendency sustaining the activity in progress, and a strong unconditioned instigating force to withdraw the hand. It may be surmised that species that have managed to survive the many potential threats to survival posed by certain stimuli that are prevalent in the natural environment are those for whom the noxious stimulus selectively strengthens a uniquely adaptive action tendency at the same time that it suddenly weakens the resultant tendency expressed in the dangerous activity in progress. Resistance to the ongoing activity, by itself, would provide an occasion for initiation of some other activity that might constitute a withdrawal from the potentially destructive stimulus. But this adaptive result is likely to be much more prompt when the stimulus also provides direct instigation to withdraw or escape.

What about the one remaining possibility? The burning sensation of the flame might provoke only a very strong unconditioned instigating force to withdraw the hand. This would immediately heighten the tendency to withdraw the hand and cause a change from the ongoing activity to withdrawal of the hand. Is not this enough in the way of a motivational property to guarantee the adaptive reaction needed to account for the survival of the individual? We think not. For this characteristic of a stimulus, the production of a strong instigating force to undertake some activity, is the defining characteristic of a reinforcing state of affairs (see Chapter 4). If the flame, like food in the mouth, merely produced a strong unconditioned instigating force to undertake an activity and an immediate surge in the strength of that tendency, we should expect to find organisms engaging in behavior appropriately described as a purposive pursuit of the opportunity to engage in the goal activity of escaping from a self-engulfing conflagration. This fatal dilemma, as far as we know, seems to be one faced only by the moth. Furthermore, if resistance were merely a matter of incompatible activities, it is difficult to understand how one could ever teach an animal to stop licking the sucrose tube by shocking its rear foot.

The idea that the heat of the flame, as unconditioned inhibitory force, produces a sudden increase in the strength of a negation tendency is central to our explanation of why actions leading up to contact with the flame are *less* likely rather than more likely to occur on a later occasion. The distal stimulus, the sight of the flame, having immediately preceded and accompanied the direct tactual contact with the flame and the effect of that contact, will acquire more *conditioned inhibitory force*, than instigating force, and the tendency *not* to touch the flame will be elaborated to include the activity of reaching out toward the flame (that is, *not* to reach out and touch the flame). If the initial sequence of the child's activity has included reaching out and grasping or touching the flame, the effect of the sudden and greater increase in the *inhibitory* tendency instead of the action tendency produced by the first actual contact with the flame will be to endow the sight of the flame with more conditioned inhibitory force. This produces a negation tendency that resists a second inclination by the child to reach out and to touch the flame. As a result, instead of merely having the tendency to withdraw from the pain of the flame elaborated to include the instrumental sequence of approaching, reaching out, and touching it (that is, the kind of activity that we should expect if reaction to contact with a flame was equivalent to the reaction to food in the mouth), there is *an elaboration of a tendency not to reach out and touch the flame that subsequently resists any inclination to repeat the activity.*

If inhibitory force is acquired by a previously neutral stimulus in this way, how is that inhibitory force extinguished? The conditioned inhibitory force of the sight of the flame, acquired as a result of the sudden heightening of a negaction tendency following the act of reaching into the flame, can be lost or extinguished only if the child repeats the activity and the activity is not followed by the onset of the punishing stimulus. Even if it were somehow possible to prevent direct contact with the flame from ever again burning the child, the extinction of the inhibitory force would be unlikely. Why? Because the child never again engages in the activity of reaching out and touching the flame. *A strong conditioned inhibitory force, once acquired, functions to delay (and hence to prevent) the occurrence of the sequence of activities and exposures to the consequences of these activities that is required to bring about any kind of change in the strength of that inhibitory force.* Thus we should generally expect that the inhibitory effects acquired by environmental stimuli will be much less influenced by real changes in the environment than the instigating effects acquired by these stimuli. The instigating force of a stimulus always functions to enhance the likelihood of the occurrence of an activity and of exposure to any changes in the consequences. The inhibitory force of a stimulus works to eliminate this possibility.

The Conditioned Avoidance Response

It is only a small step from this blow-by-blow account of how a child learns to resist undertaking one particular activity to an account of the genesis of a conditioned avoidance response. Let us consider the problem of an animal that has been placed in one side of a box, exposed to a buzzer signal for several seconds, and then shocked as long as it continues to engage in one or another kind of activity on that side of the box. If it crosses a small barrier in the middle of the box and goes to the other side, both the sound of the buzzer and the shock on the grid floor of the box cease.

After several trials in this traditional avoidance training apparatus, the animal initiates the activity of crossing the barrier to the safe side of the box shortly after the onset of the buzzer signal and before the onset of the shock. The animal, in other words, has learned to avoid the shock. This response, once acquired, is quite resistant to extinction. If the shocks have been very intense, the animal may continue indefinitely to initiate the activity that constitutes avoidance of the shock (Solomon, Kamin, and Wynne, 1953; Solomon and Wynne, 1954; Solomon and Brush, 1956).

In this example, and more generally for phenomena referred to as *active avoidance*, a particular stimulus has acquired the property of conditioned inhibitory force for each of the several activities that have occurred and been systematically punished. Only one activity has been allowed to occur without immediate punishment: the one that constitutes leaving the stimulus situation where the shocks are applied. Just as long as the stimulus situation produces some instigating force to undertake the activity of leaving it, or there is some inertial tendency to undertake that activity, the effect of systematically weakening the resultant tendencies to undertake other activities in the place where punishment is applied will sooner or later be that *the resultant tendency to leave the situation should become dominant by default* and be expressed. When this occurs, although other activities are still in the process of being punished, it is called an escape reaction. When it occurs before the shock is applied, it is called an avoidance reaction.

Often, the so-called avoidance response is one that is initially instigated by the shock, itself, as an escape reaction. That is, the onset of the shock produces an unconditioned instigating force to withdraw in addition to the unconditioned inhibitory force that is the source of resistance to the ongoing activity. The former can be the source of a subsequent conditioned instigating force to withdraw.[1] Sometimes, however, the stimulus complex of the box and barrier produce instigating force to climb over to the other side even without the application of shock to the animal's feet. One can discover this by placing the animal in the box and by observing its activities on the very first occasion with no application of shock. Sooner or later, if the tendency to climb over the barrier is among the various activities originally instigated by that stimulus situation, the animal will climb over the barrier. Since this often will happen even without the first application of shock, we may consider the effect of the punishments applied to other activities during training as merely that of shortening the latency of an activity that would have been initiated anyway.

The present conceptual analysis of the problem does not depart from the traditional analysis in asserting that the so-called avoidance response must occur, for whatever reason, on the first occasion if it is to become the solution to this problem. And we should expect the instigating force of the stimulus situation to undertake this particular "avoidance" activity to become stronger or weaker in subsequent trials depending on its immediate consequences. If, for example, the animal confronts food and eats it after climbing over the barrier, the instigating force to undertake this activity should become stronger. But even if the stimulus consequence of the avoidance response is such that the instigating force to undertake this activity is weakened on successive trials, the avoidance response will continue to occur

---

[1] Notice that a conditioned instigating force to withdraw from the situation based on an unconditioned instigating force to escape from shock will no longer be reinforced once the animal begins to avoid the shock by prompt withdrawal. Hence, it should soon extinguish. It is only a temporary measure, one that functions to get the animal away from the threat very early in training.

if resistance to all other activities is very strong. And *just as long as the avoidance response occurs before, and therefore instead of one of the other previously punished activities, there is no basis for extinction of the conditioned inhibitory force of the stimulus that causes and sustains the resistance to each of these other activities.* Even though the experimenter may have decided never again to shock the animal following the onset of the buzzer for doing certain things it used to do in the box, the inhibitory forces that have been acquired will effectively prevent the animal from ever discovering this. *The extinction of an inhibitory force requires that the previously punished activity be performed but without being punished.* The rat, for example, must undertake the activity of grooming on the grid side of the box without this activity being interrupted or immediately being followed by a sudden increase in negaction tendency attributable to the inhibitory force of the shock. Without this boost in the strength of negaction tendency following the activity, the conditioned inhibitory force of the buzzer and other situational cues will diminish. And when this occurs, the strength of resultant action tendency for each of the previously punished responses will gradually regain its initial strength. Each of these tendencies then will again compete effectively with the tendency to leave the situation. In time, the animal will stay on the side of the box where earlier it had been shocked, and it will once again do all the things it did before the shock was introduced. The latency of the so-called avoidance response will increase until, in the traditional language, one says that *it* has extinguished.

We repeat, for emphasis, that all or most of the changes that bring about the so-called avoidance response initially, that account for its stability, and that finally lead to its disappearance are, from the viewpoint of the present conceptual analysis, changes in the strength of the initially effective competing tendencies. We tend to minimize the importance of changes in the strength of instigating force to undertake the so-called avoidance activity. The apparent selective strengthening of this response over repeated trials is attributed to selective nonpunishment of this one among all the competing alternatives. Instead of implying that its strength has increased relative to that of competing tendencies in the hierarchy instigated by situational cues, the traditional view of the matter, the present account implies that the strength of resultant tendencies for competing activities have decreased relative to it.

The Conditioning of Inhibitory Force

We are now ready to consider in some detail the genesis of resistance by undertaking an analysis of the conditioning of an inhibitory force. We shall make use of the Recency Principle of Learning already presented in Chapter 5 to describe the process by which a neutral stimulus gains and loses inhibitory force. This principle, applied to the instigating force, states: a stimulus acquires for its next occurrence a magnitude of instigating force for an activity that is proportional to the maximum value attained by the product of the strength of the perceptual tendency of the stimulus and the strength of the action tendency expressed during the interval of the activity.

Parallel in form to this learning principle for instigating force, *the Principle of Acquisition of Inhibitory Force states: a stimulus acquires for its next occurrence a magnitude of inhibitory force for an activity that is proportional to the maximum value attained by the product of the strength of the perceptual tendency of the stimulus and the strength of the negaction tendency expressed in resistance to an ongoing activity during the interval of that resistance.* This principle is given by the equation,

$$(_SI_R)_{N+1} = \theta[(T_{s_N})_t \cdot (N_{R_N})_i]_{\text{Max}} \tag{8.1}$$

where θ is the constant of proportionality, (T_s) represents the perceptual tendency and (N_R) the negaction tendency. Thus, we apply a recency principle to the acquisition of inhibitory forces as well as to instigating forces. On each occasion when the stimulus is contiguous with resistance *to an ongoing activity*, the magnitude of inhibitory force of the stimulus on that occasion is replaced by a new magnitude that depends on the maximum strength of the negaction tendency at the time.

Two aspects of the proposed principle of learning for inhibitory force deserve emphasis because they highlight the parallel form of the two learning principles. First, *inhibitory force can only be conditioned when there is resistance to an ongoing activity*, that is, when the corresponding action tendency is actually being expressed. It is a fundamental property of negaction tendencies that they *always* oppose action tendencies, whether or not the resultant tendencies are expressed in activity. But according to our principle of acquisition of inhibitory force, conditioning will take place only with respect to activities that are occurring. This is a property or a qualification that holds true also for the conditioning of action tendencies.[2] The second common aspect is our tentative hypothesis that the basic relationship between conditioning and the strength of tendencies, as stated in Equations 5.1 and 8.1, is the same for instigation and inhibition.

Implicit in this Principle of Acquisition of Inhibitory Force is the premise that all such conditioning is based on punishment. This is to say that the growth and the extinction of the inhibitory force of a stimulus depend on the occurrence of a particular activity and the occurrence or absence of another stimulus already capable of producing a strong inhibitory force.

We can distinguish the two types of procedure traditionally used in the conditioning of inhibitory force. In one type, the experimenter selects a

[2] We assume that a more molecular analysis will show the important role of the sensory feedback from an activity in the learning process. And there is sensory feedback only for activities that do occur.

particular activity (for example, bar pressing, running an alley, eating food, etc.), makes sure that this activity is occurring in the presence of some stimulus (the *CS*), and then introduces a noxious stimulus (the *US*) that results in the diminution or cessation of the particular activity. This is a classical method for punishing a particular activity as well as for conditioning an inhibitory force to the *CS*.

In the second type of procedure, the experimenter pays no special attention to what the subject is doing when the *US* is introduced. He simply pairs a *CS* and *US* a number of times in one setting, and then, in another setting, observes the effect on some selected activity (for example, bar pressing, running an alley, eating food, etc.) of presenting the *CS* while that activity is in progress. The initial part of the experiment, in which the *CS* and *US* are paired without regard to the activities of the subject, is not customarily regarded as fitting the punishment paradigm. But from the standpoint of the present theory, with its fundamental premise that living organisms are always doing something, the second procedure should also be considered one of punishment. It differs from the first only in that the experimenter has not attempted to control or to identify the various activities that are being punished beyond being careful to determine that the critical response, later to be observed, is not obviously present in its entirety.

According to our conception, the conditioned inhibitory force of a stimulus acquired by the second procedure will be effective in blocking some particular activity on a later occasion only to the extent that this critical activity includes components of response in common with the set of originally punished activities. When such an overlap in the nature of the response occurs, presentation of the *CS* on a later occasion increases the negaction tendencies for these several common components and results in the resistance that can prevent the occurrence of the critical activity or can so modify its appearance that it would not be coded as occurring by the observer. For certain responses—perhaps, the startle reaction is an example—the *CS* may strengthen negaction tendencies that block potentially interfering responses, so that the observed effect of the presentation of the *CS* is an increment instead of a decrement in the critical response (see, for example, Brown, Kalish, and Farber, 1951).

Thus, we view the second type of procedure used to condition inhibitory forces as not essentially different from the first as to the conditioning process itself. Conditions are more definite and better specified under the first procedure, so we shall refer to it in a detailed analysis of the conditioning of inhibitory force derived from our Principle of Learning. Furthermore, because inhibitory conditioning is highly dependent on time relationships among the presentations of the *CS* and the *US* and on the occurrence of particular activities, we have chosen a special set of conditions for this analysis—one which yields a relatively simple solution. We shall be able to make some general comments about what happens to inhibitory conditioning under certain other conditions after the analysis.

Let us consider the following inhibitory conditioning procedure. A hungry dog is in a chamber where he has been fed many times in the past by means of a mechanism that raises a door to allow him access to a dish of food. Now he will be punished for eating. On the first conditioning trial, he is given a strong electric shock a short time after he begins to eat. The shock remains on for a predetermined time and terminates simultaneously with the lowering of the door which also terminates access to the food. Shock is administered on each trial that the dog eats, but only if it eats, and the shock is of sufficient intensity to make the dog stop eating every time.

Our aim now is to describe the conditioning process that culminates in the dog's failure to initiate eating within a specified interval following the presentation of the food dish. We shall describe the process by which the sight and the smell of the food acquires sufficient inhibitory force to prevent eating.

The following observable sequence occurs on each conditioning trial. The subject is engaged in some initial activity Y when the door is raised, presenting the food (onset of the CS). Shortly thereafter, the subject begins to eat (a change from activity Y to activity X). Then a strong shock is administered (onset of the US). The subject soon ceases eating (a change from activity X back to activity Y). After a predetermined period, measured from its onset, the shock is turned off and the door to the food dish is lowered (termination of US and CS). If the subject does not begin to eat within a certain time on any trial, the shock is not administered and the door is lowered to end the trial.

To simplify our discussion, let us assume that there is no resistance to the initial activity Y and that T_Y has become relatively stable before the CS is introduced on each trial. In the early trials, the instigating force of CS will increase the strength of T_X, the tendency to approach and to eat the food, even as $_{CS}I_X$, the conditioned inhibitory force, is becoming stronger on each successive trial. The resultant tendency to eat $\bar{T}_X$ will come to dominate $\bar{T}_Y$ on each of the early trials and, hence, eating will be initiated on each trial.

On the very first trial, there should be no conditioned inhibitory force $(_{CS}I_X = 0)$. Shortly after eating is initiated, the US (shock) is administered. The tendency to inhibit the ongoing activity X increases in strength as a function of duration of exposure to the unconditioned inhibitory force of the shock $(_{US}I_X)$. This negaction tendency (N_X) is expressed in resistance to T_X sustaining activity X. But activity X, eating, continues as long as $\bar{T}_X > \bar{T}_Y$. And during this interval, $\bar{T}_X$, T_X, and N_X are governed by the conditions of Case 1a (see Chapter 7). On this first trial, and all subsequent trials, the continued exposure of the subject to the constant magnitude of $_{US}I_X$ of the shock in time produces sufficiently strong N_X so that $\bar{T}_X < \bar{T}_Y$. Eating ceases, and $\bar{T}_X$, T_X, and N_X are then governed by the conditions of Case 1*b* (Chapter 7). If the magnitude of $_{US}I_X$ is sufficiently great, N_X can completely nullify T_X in which case $\bar{T}_X$, T_X, and N_X are governed by the conditions of Case 2 (Chapter 7).

According to the recency principle (Equation 8.1), the *CS* present on each trial during which the negation tendency N_X resists the ongoing activity of eating will acquire some inhibitory force for a subsequent occasion. The magnitude of conditioned inhibitory force $_{CS}I_X$ acquired on each trial is proportional to the maximum value of the product of the strength of N_X expressed in resistance to ongoing activity X on that trial and the strength of the perceptual tendency of the *CS*, (T_{cs}). The latter follows the same temporal path on each trial, as shown earlier in Figure 5.3 for the conditioning of instigating force. Its value will be the same from trial to trial for that point in time when the product is maximized (see Mathematical Notes). Thus we concentrate on the increasing strength of N_X from trial to trial and the derivative growth in magnitude of $_{CS}I_X$.

The strength of N_X within each trial can be partitioned into two components. One component is attributable to the *CS*. The other component is attributable to the *US*. Specifically, we may write[3]

$$(N_{X_N})_t = [f(_{CS}I_X)_N]_t + [f(_{US}I_X)_N]_t$$

The component attributable to the *CS* changes from trial to trial; the component attributable to the *US* is constant (see Mathematical Notes). Again, to simplify, let us assume that the level of N_X produced by exposure to the *CS* up to the time at which activity X is initiated on each trial can be approximated by its limit of growth for that trial, $[(_{CS}I_X)_N]/r_X$. This would permit us to rewrite our principle of learning (Equation 8.1) in the form

$$(_{CS}I_X)_{N+1} = \theta'\left[\frac{(_{CS}I_X)_N}{r_X} + f(_{US}I_X)\right]$$

in which θ' now also includes the constant value of (T_{cs}) from trial to trial.

On Trial 1, *CS* produces no conditioned inhibitory force, that is, $[(_{CS}I_X)_N]/r_X = 0$, so that conditioning is based on $N_{X_1} = f(_{US}I_X)$, whatever that strength may be as determined by the parameter values of the situation (for example, intensity and duration of shock). And we are able to account for the magnitude of conditioned inhibitory force acquired for the second trial by writing $(_{CS}I_X)_2 = \theta' \cdot [f(_{US}I_X)]$. It follows that on Trial 2 the level of N_X, on which conditioning is based, will be stronger than on Trial 1. That

---

[3] Figure 5.3, prepared for the conditioning of instigating force, is also instructive for the present discussion, since we again assume that *CS* and *US* terminate together on each trial.

is,

$$N_{X_2} = \frac{(_{CS}I_X)_2}{r_X} + f(_{US}I_X)$$

And, when $(_{CS}I_X)_2$ is replaced by its equivalent, $\theta' \cdot [f(_{US}I_X)]$, we obtain an expression for the magnitude of conditioned inhibitory force on Trial 3:

$$(_{CS}I_X)_3 = \theta'\left\{\theta' \cdot \left[\frac{f(_{US}I_X)}{r_X}\right] + f(_{US}I_X)\right\}$$

If we continue this analytic procedure (as in the Mathematical Notes at the end of the chapter), we can derive a general expression for the magnitude of the inhibitory force on any trial that is similar to the one derived earlier for instigating force.

This conditioning function has the familiar negatively accelerated form commonly ascribed to learning, but there is an important factor we have ignored in our derivation that makes this function inappropriate as a generalization about inhibitory conditioning. The factor ignored is that as inhibitory conditioning to the CS proceeds, the time taken to initiate activity X (the eating activity in our example) becomes longer and longer until it exceeds the time allowed by the experimenter. When this happens, the trial is terminated without the occurrence of either activity X or the US, and no conditioning occurs. Thus, the conditioning function holds true only so long as the activity to be punished continues to occur.

This factor has a bearing on the extinction of inhibitory forces. No extinction of $_{CS}I_X$ is to be expected as long as activity X fails to occur. In order to obtain extinction of the inhibitory force, it is necessary for conditions to change in some way so that activity X will occur and will not be followed by the US.

In this regard, it will be instructive to consider briefly a somewhat different inhibitory conditioning situation in which activity X does occur on each trial. Such a situation might be as follows. A dog confined in a chamber is allowed access to food by the raising of a door. After being well trained to approach and to eat the food under these conditions, an inhibitory conditioning procedure is instituted. As the dog is eating, a buzzer (the CS) is sounded and a fixed interval of time later a strong shock (the US) is administered if the dog is still eating. The buzzer and shock terminate together after predetermined durations. We assume that the situation is one in which the dog will approach and eat the food in the absence of the buzzer, that is, sufficient nonbuzzer-nonshock eating trials are provided to maintain the eating activity.

Our interest is in the inhibitory conditioning of the CS in this situation. Without going into the details of the process, it is quite clear that, since the

N_X basic to the conditioning on each trial is determined by the sum of the effects from the $_{CS}I_X$ and the $_{US}I_X$ on that trial, whether or not the US is presented is crucial. If conditioning proceeds to the point where the buzzer is effective in stopping the eating activity prior to the time when the shock is due, so that no shock is administered, the N_X for conditioning on that trial will be less than on the previous trial and the new $_{CS}I_X$ will be correspondingly smaller. This would constitute an extinction trial. Similarly, if the experimenter simply decided not to give the US on a particular trial whether or not the buzzer stopped the eating, the same result would follow. *The crucial condition that must be met if inhibitory conditioning is to take place on a given occasion is that the activity that is the target of the negaction tendency must occur in the face of resistance. The result of the conditioning may be either an increase in $_{CS}I_X$ (an acquisition trial) or a decrease (an extinction trial), but there can be conditioning at all only if the activity in question occurs.*

The discussion of the acquisition and the change of the inhibitory force of a stimulus has taken us over ground already familiar in the traditional language of conditioning and learning in lower animals. The derivation of avoidance behavior, outlined earlier in the chapter, differs substantially from the explanation evolved within S-R behavior theory in terms of fear as an acquired drive and fear-reduction as reinforcement of the avoidance response (Mowrer, 1939; Miller, 1948; Solomon and Wynne, 1954). The description of the conditioning of inhibitory force emphasizes recency rather than accumulation and requires that an action tendency be expressed in behavior if conditioning or extinction of an inhibitory force is to occur.

RESISTANCE IN THE STUDY OF DECISION MAKING

Just as no single principle will embrace all of the different instances of instigating force of a stimulus, no single principle that we can think of makes equally good sense of the effects of the buzzer that has been paired with shock or the shock, itself, in an avoidance conditioning experiment; the effect on a child of a father's verbal warning to stop giggling in church; the effect on a motorist of the road sign which says "No Left Turn" or "Dangerous Curve Ahead"; etc. All of these instances are ones of inhibitory force. Once again, we take a pragmatic stance and consider the issue of the strength of inhibitory force in other terms.

Within the context of the study of human decision making, an unwillingness to initiate an activity, or to continue it, has been found to correlate with the degree of certainty an individual feels that the act will produce a negative consequence and with the negative value, or repulsiveness, of that consequence to him. In the conceptual scheme evolved by Tolman, Lewin, and modern decision theorists, the product of subjective probability or expectancy that an act will produce a negative consequence and the negative valence, or disutility, of the consequence is itself negative. Thus, when it is added algebraically to compute the subjectively expected utility (*SEU*), or what Lewin called the *Resultant Force*, this component subtracts from the total to imply a weaker tendency to undertake or to choose that alternative. As mentioned earlier, this conception provided the seed for the present treatment of resistance.

Many of our previous points about the relationship between covert activity (thought) and overt activity (action) in reference to instigating force and action tendency in Chapter 6 can and should be extended to include inhibitory force and negation tendency. For example, the very same sequence of historical events that constitutes the sufficient condition for the acquisition of an inhibitory force will also produce an elaboration of the covert, perceptual, and imaginal tendency corresponding to the sequence that we describe as an expectancy of punishment. Thus the simple sequence of events, $S_1 - R_1 - S_Q$ (where S_Q is an aversive stimulus), yields, on a later occasion, both the $_{S_1}I_{R_1:Q}$ that is the source of N_{R_1} in the domain of overt activity, and a separate tendency $T_{r_1:q}$ that constitutes the expectancy and the negative valence of punishment when it is covertly expressed. As previously, we continue to view the concepts of expectancy and valence as descriptive of the covert activity that normally accompanies the occurrence of the overt action sequence, as correlates but not causes of the observable behavioral phenomena.

We argued earlier that the tendency for the perceptual and imaginal activity and the related tendency to undertake an overt locomotor activity normally attain dominance at about the same time. Hence, an individual typically initiates an activity while experiencing the correlated covert expectation of a positive consequence. In the case of negation, the same temporal relationship holds true, but there is one essential difference. Expression of a negation tendency takes the form of resistance to an activity. Consequently, it will be the suppression of an overt activity, that is, the delayed initiation or inhibition of an overt activity, that is correlated with the covertly expressed expectation of a negative consequence. In view of this, our earlier suggestion that the strength of the instigating force of a stimulus might be inferred or diagnosed from evidence about an individual's expectations when confronted with that stimulus (guided by the hypothesis that the instigating force is equal to the product of expectancy and valence for the case of positive outcomes) can be extended to include a similar guiding hypothesis that concerns the inhibitory force for the case of negative outcomes.

It is sometimes difficult to accept the idea that the inhibitory force of a stimulus, engendered by giving an individual information about probable negative consequences of an activity, will have behavioral implications comparable to the ones established by conditioning with an aversive stimulus like shock. The latter seems more physical, more lawfully determined, and therefore more real. We surmount this difficulty by calling to mind the fact that the extreme resistance of many individuals to flying in an airplane is not based on the actual pain of near fatal injury in an earlier crash, but on information or misinformation about that possibility. And the generally depressing effect of the nuclear threat on human behavior, during certain frigid periods of the cold war, is not based on the actual severity of unconditional punishment in the recent history of living persons but on the expectation of catastrophe in the near future no matter what activity might be in progress. Most of the inhibitory forces and, for that matter, many of the instigating forces that play a central determinative role in the affairs of civilized man are engendered by *the exposure to information that controls expectations about the consequences of various activities*. Whether this information is not only sufficient but also necessary to establish instigating and inhibitory forces is one of many unsolved questions left for future study.

An Analogue of Avoidance Training

The gap between the inhibitory force produced by emotional conditioning in animals and inhibitory force in the context of human decision making can be closed to some extent. Let us consider the demonstration of a behavioral effect closely analogous to the one achieved by traumatic avoidance conditioning (Solomon and Wynne, 1954). Students were subjects, and the rewarding and punishing consequences of their several activities were only a varied number of points won or lost.[4] The experiment was designed to follow the paradigm of training for a conditioned avoidance response but in a context of human decision making with the kind of immediate knowledge of results that is known to change an individual's conscious reportable expectations. In this experiment, however, the subjects were not asked what they expected. They were merely given an opportunity to initiate one or another activity in the face of the changing implications of the immediate stimulus situation.

Each subject was tested individually in a small room, seated at a table on which there were five different colored cards (red, white, green, blue, and yellow) arranged within easy reach. He was told that he would be paid an amount of money proportionate to the number of points he accumulated during the period. He was also told that he could place his hand on any one of the colored cards, or on none of them, in each of a series of choices. Every

---

[4] This experiment was part of a more general study of determinants of human choice (Horner, Karabenick, and Atkinson, 1965; Atkinson and Birch, 1966).

four seconds, at the ticking of a timing mechanism, the experimenter consulted a previously arranged schedule of gains and losses for each alternative response and announced the number of points won or lost for the activity then in progress. For example, if the subject had his hand on the red card when the timing mechanism clicked at the end of a four-second interval, the experimenter might say, "Win 20."

During an initial period of 90 choices, the prescheduled outcomes for each alternative varied about a different average number of points won that ranged from 0 for "pass" to 50 for white. The idea was to make it impossible for any subject to learn that he would win exactly 20 points for red, 30 points for green, etc., but to allow the development of an expectation of more points for some alternatives and fewer points for others in order to establish fairly stable behavioral preferences as shown in Figure 8.1.

Then, following the conventional procedure employed to establish that the stimulus which later will be used as the signal of danger (that is, the CS) has no initial systematic effect on response, a bank of lights in front of the subject was turned on for a predetermined number of choices on several separate occasions but without any change in the preschedule of the number of points awarded for each of the alternatives. The relative frequency of choice of the different alternatives was unaffected by the light during this period of habituation.

Finally, avoidance training was begun. The alternative of "hand on the blue card," second weakest in the initial preferential ordering as shown in Figure 8.1, was arbitrarily chosen by the experimenter to be analogous to an avoidance response. During this phase of the experiment, a loss of 1000 points (analogous to the US of extreme shock) was introduced when the subject failed to make the avoidance response within six choices (24 seconds) after the onset of the light signal (CS). The light signal was terminated along with the punishment when the avoidance response was made. After a series of from six to nine choices without the light signal, in which the original schedule of rewarding outcomes was again followed, another avoidance training trial was begun with the onset of the light signal. Avoidance training was continued until the subject reached a criterion of 10 successive avoidances of loss of points by choice of the blue alternative soon after the onset of the signal. Throughout the avoidance training, the consequence of choosing blue continued to be the same low average number of points won that had produced its less preferred status prior to avoidance training.

In other words, when the light came on, the situation was analogous to that of an animal standing on a grid with the buzzer on. The subject had a limited amount of time (the interval between CS and US) to initiate the avoidance response. The animal had to get off the grid to turn off the buzzer and to avoid the shock. The student had to put his hand on the blue card to

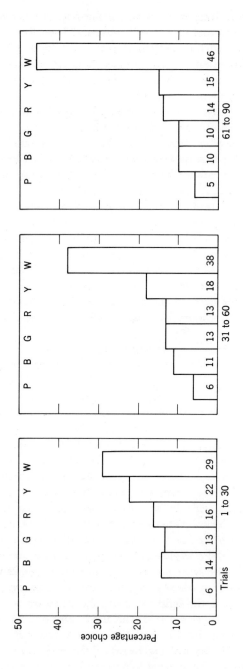

FIGURE 8.1   The percentage choice among six alternatives (P, B, G, R, Y, W) which differed in average incentive value during three blocks of 30 trials for each of 10 male subjects (from Karabenick, Horner, and Atkinson, previously unpublished).

turn off the light and to avoid the "shock" of losing 1000 points. The loss of this number of points was relatively severe in light of the average number of points won for each of the alternatives.

After the avoidance response had been learned to criterion, an extinction series was begun. The new rule guiding the behavior of the experimenter was that the original preschedule of points won would be followed whether the light was on or off. The subject would no longer be "shocked" no matter what he did.

Of 36 subjects run by three different experimenters, only two failed to reach the criterion of avoidance learning between 11 and 85 training trials with the signal light on. The improved competitive position of the blue alternative following systematic punishment of all the alternatives is shown in Figure 8.2, which compares the relative frequency of each alternative just prior to and immediately after the onset of the signal light late in training.

In the extinction series, only 7 of the 36 subjects met the criterion of failing to choose blue within the time prescribed on five consecutive occasions when the CS was presented. Ten showed partial extinction within the two hour period, but 17 showed no evidence of extinction of the avoidance response. These 17 subjects continued to choose blue very soon after the onset of the light without ever again risking a loss of points. The test period was extended substantially for one subject in order to determine how resistant to extinction an avoidance response established under this procedure might be. After 205 trials, each defined by the onset of the signal light, this subject continued to initiate the avoidance response immediately. This resembles, but with no visible symptoms of traumatic anxiety or its reduction during training and extinction, the kind of extremely stable avoidance behavior that we often incorrectly view as falling only within the special province of the study of emotional conditioning.

This simple paradigm for study of a sequence of human choices, a set of cards on which the subject can place a hand or not, provides an exhaustive catalog of the activities (excepting, of course, compatible activities) that are undertaken during the period of observation. It offers the possibility of the systematic study of other classic experimental paradigms that have been evolved first in the study of lower animals.

RESISTANCE FROM THE PERSPECTIVE OF STUDY OF PERSONALITY

The inhibitory force of a stimulus is its capacity to increase the strength of a negation tendency in the individual either innately, as a consequence of earlier conditioning, or as a result of the information it provides concerning

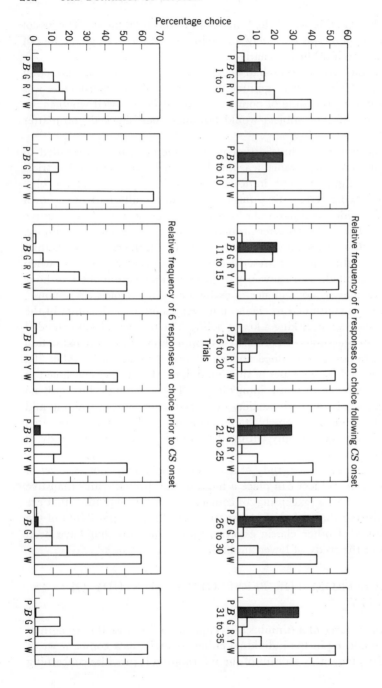

FIGURE 8.2 The percentage choice among six alternatives (P, B, G, R, Y, W) showing the improved competitive position of the only unpunished response (B), as avoidance conditioning proceeded. The onset of a light (cs) was shortly followed by punishment of P, G, R, Y, W.

the probable consequences of a certain activity. As we did earlier in the case of the unconditioned instigating force of a stimulus, we now point out that inhibitory force will be influenced both by properties of the stimulus and of the individual. The terms *incentive value* and *motive* were introduced to refer to the effects attributable to the kind of goal object and to individual differences in the vigor of the initial goal reaction, respectively, in our earlier discussion of the determinants of the unconditioned instigating force of a stimulus. These concepts are equally useful in reference to the unconditioned inhibitory force of a stimulus. Consider, for example, the heat of a flame. Within limits, variations in the temperature of the flame constitute variations in the incentive value, and motive refers to the individual differences in the reactive property of individuals to this class of stimuli.

In the symbol $_{US}I_R$ the response or activity referred to and the class to which it belongs represent having commerce with the particular stimulus (US) or that kind of stimulus. There is a force to negate or to inhibit that particular kind of commerce. This strengthens the tendency to inhibit or to negate that kind of commerce. We can speak of a value of the incentive to negate that kind of commerce and of a motive to inhibit or to negate any and all instances of that kind of commerce with the environment. Although technically correct and parallel to the treatment of incentive and motive in reference to the instigating force, there remains some ambiguity and awkwardness in the naming of inhibitory forces, negation tendencies and their determinants. It is true that both primary reinforcing states of affairs and primary punishing states of affairs are appropriately described in behavioral terms as some kind of commerce of the individual with a stimulus. In the case of the primary reinforcement we call eating, there is the observable sequence $S_G - R_G$. Since we can distinguish the kind of commerce with a stimulus called eating from another kind called drinking or still another called sexual activity, etc., we are able to name the forces, tendencies, and their determinants in terms of the distinguishable kind of commerce or activity that they engender. The description of the activity implies the presence and the supportive role of a stimulus.

In the case of the primary punishment we call being burned by a flame, there is also a behavioral sequence $S_Q - R_Q$, where R_Q is the innately determined negative reaction to the aversive stimulus. From the viewpoint of an observer, there is very little that is obviously different about the topography of inhibitory reactions to various stimuli. They have in common the discontinuance of whatever kind of commerce was occurring. It is not a simple matter and it is of questionable utility to try to name negations without explicit reference to the stimulus. It is much easier to identify and to name the aversive stimulus. Thus we speak of a force not to have commerce with a flame, or a force to negate contact with a flame, or a force to inhibit contact with a flame and, later, of a force to avoid contact with a flame. We use the same language to describe the negation tendency.

Motive, conceived as negative reactivity to a certain class of aversive stimuli, carries an implication of individual differences in predisposition to learn to resist activities that produce that kind of consequence. The concept of motive can also be used in reference to the kinds of consequences which, as a result of earlier learning experience, have *acquired* or *conditioned* inhibitory force. Thus, in the study of achievement-oriented behavior, it is useful to refer to individual differences in the strength of motive to avoid failure without implying that various stimulus situations which constitute failure necessarily produce *unconditioned* inhibitory force. The concept of motive to avoid failure refers to the individual differences in the strength of the family of inhibitory forces that are produced, and the family of negation tendencies that are strengthened, whenever an individual confronts a stimulus situation which defines the possibility of performing poorly in relation to a standard of excellence that will be applied to the evaluation of his performance.

According to the current theory of achievement motivation, the strength of the force to negate an activity that might culminate in failure is inferred from the subjective probability, or expectancy of failure, and the valence of failure in that activity. Further assumptions parallel the ones advanced to account for the instigating force to achieve success. The valence of failure is considered the product of incentive value of failure at a particular task and the strength of motive to avoid failure in the individual. The incentive value of failure is assumed to be the negative value of the complement of the subjective probability of failure. These several assumptions imply that the strength of force to inhibit or to resist achievement-oriented activities, which might also lead to failure, is greatest when the probability of failure is intermediate and the motive to avoid failure is strong.

The behavioral consequences of a strong motive to avoid failure are directly opposite to the ones of a strong motive to achieve success. The resistance to undertaking an activity that might be followed by failure takes the visible form of less willingness to initiate tasks at which performance is evaluated, a decrement in the level of performance of these tasks when they are undertaken, a vulnerability to interruption that produces less persistence, and a weakening of the otherwise expected preference for moderately difficult tasks which, in the extreme, takes the form of actual avoidance of moderately difficult or moderately risky ventures (Atkinson and Feather, 1966).

In the next chapter, we shall discuss more thoroughly the concept of motive in reference to a family of inhibitory forces, but not until we have considered a reformulation of the Principle of Change of Activity that includes resistance.

SUMMARY

In this chapter we considered the determinants of the inhibitory force of a stimulus from three perspectives that paralleled the earlier treatment of instigating force in Chapters 5 and 6. Beginning with the assumption that some stimuli are inherently aversive, that is, capable of producing unconditioned force to negate the activity then in progress, we view the acquisition of conditioned inhibitory force by other stimuli and the elaboration of negaction tendencies to be the consequences of punishment.

Given the premise of a constantly active individual, our treatment of the phenomena of active avoidance emphasizes that in avoidance training all of the various activities that occur in a given stimulus situation are punished except one that constitutes leaving the situation. Hence, the stimulus situation acquires inhibitory force for all these initially effective competing alternatives, and the so-called avoidance response becomes dominant by default. The latter occurs while initiation of the previously punished alternatives is delayed by resistance. And as a result, the inhibitory force affecting these blocked alternatives does not extinguish. Extinction of an inhibitory force requires that a previously punished activity be performed but without being punished, that is, without the boost in strength of negaction tendency provided by the inhibitory force of the punishing stimulus which, according to the recency principle now applied to inhibition, constitutes the "reinforcing" event. Where the traditional view of avoidance conditioning emphasizes the selective strengthening of the so-called avoidance response relative to its competition, we emphasize the weakening by resistance of the resultant tendencies for the competing alternatives relative to it.

The recency principle, applied to the acquisition and the extinction of inhibitory force refers to the parameters of the aversive stimulus (that is, its intensity and duration) following the initiation of an activity as important determinants of the magnitude of conditioned inhibitory force. And it identifies the crucial condition for the extinction of the inhibitory force as the repeated occurrence of the previously punished activity, in the face of resistance, but without punishment.

From the perspective of the study of human decision making, we coordinate the concept of inhibitory force with the product of subjective probability and utility when the value of the consequence of an activity is negative. And, following the argument advanced earlier in reference to instigating force, we consider the expectancy and the valence of punishment as the cognitive correlates instead of the causes of inhibitory force. These covert expressions of the perceptual and imaginal tendencies are correlated with the presence of a negaction tendency that delays or inhibits the initiation of a particular activity.

In a simple human decision-making analogue of avoidance training in animals, the extreme resistance to extinction of an avoidance response, comparable to the one that was obtained with intense emotional conditioning in animals, was produced merely by controlling the information given to subjects about the number of points won or lost following choices among several alternatives in the presence of a signal light.

The concept of an avoidance motive, employed in reference to the individual differences in personality, refers to a family of inhibitory forces. Just as one can observe individual differences in reactivity to foods, as a class of stimuli, one can observe individual differences in the unconditional aversive reaction to noxious stimuli. The terms incentive value, in reference to the effects of differences among the stimuli of a particular class, and motive, in reference to individual differences, can be usefully employed in reference to inhibitory force as well as to instigating force. In the study of achievement motivation, for example, the concept of motive to avoid failure refers to a family of inhibitory forces associated with the expectancy of failure. In situations that involve the evaluation of an individual's performance in relation to some standard of excellence, these inhibitory forces produce negaction tendencies, that is, tendencies to avoid failure, which comprise resistance to achievement-oriented activities. Further implications of individual differences in the strength of avoidance motive will be considered more fully in the next chapter.

MATHEMATICAL NOTES

The paradigm for which the conditioning of inhibition was derived in the text (pp. 253 to 255) is as follows. The subject is engaged in some ongoing activity (activity Y) when a door is raised presenting food (onset of the CS). The subject begins to eat (a change in activity from Y to X) and a strong shock (onset of the US) is then administered. The subject ceases eating (a change in activity from X back to Y), and after a predetermined period of time measured from its onset, the shock is turned off and the door to the food dish is lowered (termination of the CS and US). In this paradigm the time interval between the initiation of activity X and the onset of the US is fixed as is the total duration of the US. Depending on the specific conditions and, particularly, on the intensity of the US, it is possible that, subsequent to the onset of the US, the system of action and negaction tendencies remains in Case 1a throughout the duration of the US, but this need not be true. It is also possible for Cases 1b and 2 to become involved or even that Case 1a is reentered before the US is terminated. The latter would be signified by the reoccurrence of activity X while the US was still on. We confine our attention to the situation in which the US is successful in blocking activity X until it terminates, so that, at most, Cases 1a, 1b, and then 2 are involved. In this respect, it is important to recall that by our Principle of Learning the conditioning of inhibition can only take place in Case 1a because resistance to an ongoing activity is a requisite for the conditioning process.

The rule for conditioning inhibitory force to a stimulus is contained in Equation 8.1. Adapted to the present situation, this equation becomes

$$(_{CS}I_X)_{N+1} = \theta[(T_{cs_N})_t \cdot (N_{X_N})_t]_{\text{Max}}$$

Since the CS is held constant from trial to trial, the perceptual tendency of the CS (T_{cs}) follows the same path point-for-point in time on each trial. Thus, $(T_{cs_N})_t = (T_{cs_{N+1}})_t$ for all t. From this, it follows that if the maximum product, $[(T_{cs_N})_t \cdot (N_{X_N})_t]_{\text{Max}}$, from the equation above occurs at the same point in time on each trial, the value of $(T_{cs_N})_t$ will be the same from trial to trial. That $[(T_{cs_N})_t \cdot (N_{X_N})_t]_{\text{Max}}$ is invariant in time over trials (or, at least, approximately so) can be shown in the following way.

The path of N_{X_N} across the time within a trial can be partitioned into two components, one part attributable to the CS and the other part to the US. Specifically, we may write $(N_{X_N})_t = [f(_{CS}I_X)_N]_t + [f(_{US}I_X)_N]_t$. (Figure 5.3, prepared for the conditioning of instigating force, may be of help in this discussion where, once again, we have assumed that the CS and US terminate together on each conditioning trial.) We shall assume that $(N_{X_N})_t$ can be approximated by $[(_{CS}I_X)_N]/r_X$ at the point in time when activity X is initiated. This means that $[f(_{CS}I_X)_N]_t = [(_{CS}I_X)_N]/r_X$ is constant over the duration of the US on each trial. By this assumption we are, in effect, presuming that on each trial enough time passes between the onset of the CS and the initiation of activity X that N_{X_N} has an opportunity to approach an asymptote of $[(_{CS}I_X)_N]/r_X$. This assumption gains plausibility, perhaps, when it is recalled that the interval between the onset of the CS and the initiation of activity X is a function of the time taken for the shift from the ongoing activity Y to the eating activity X and that this time, depending as it does on the resultant tendency for X, will increase as $_{CS}I_X$ gets larger.

As a consequence of this assumption about $[f(_{CS}I_X)_N]_t$ the path of $(N_{X_N})_t$ subsequent to the onset of the US is dependent solely on the path of $[f(_{US}I_X)_N]_t$ within a trial. The proof that for the conditions of our analysis the path of $[f(_{US}I_X)_N]_t$ across t is identical from trial to trial is given next.

Invariance of the US Contribution in Case 1a. As has been pointed out, it is sufficient to show the invariance of the US contribution in Case 1a because this is the only case in which inhibitory conditioning can take place. We begin the proof at the point in time in the trial when activity X is initiated, which means that Case 1a is in effect, since $T_X > N_X$ and $\bar{T}_X > \bar{T}_Y$. By our assumption $N_{X_N} = [(_{CS}I_X)_N]/r_X$. In Case 1$a$ all of N_X is in use against T_X so that the path of N_X does not depend on the level of T_X, and according to Equation 7.3 we can write

$$N_{X_N} = \frac{(_{CS}I_X)_N}{r_X} \cdot e^{-rx\cdot t} + \frac{(_{CS}I_X)_N}{r_X}(1 - e^{-rx\cdot t}) = \frac{(_{CS}I_X)_N}{r_X}$$

for the time interval t_1 between the initiation of activity X and the onset of the US. In the next time interval t_2 between the onset of the US and the supplanting of activity X by activity Y, which defines the end of Case 1a,

$$N_{X_N} = \frac{(_{CS}I_X)_N}{r_X} \cdot e^{-rx\cdot t} + \frac{(_{CS}I_X)_N + (_{US}I_X)}{r_X}(1 - e^{-rx\cdot t})$$

or

$$N_{X_N} = \frac{(_{CS}I_X)_N}{r_X} + \left(\frac{_{US}I_X}{r_X}\right)(1 - e^{-rx\cdot t})$$

This equation is particularly helpful because it separates the contributions of the CS and US to N_{X_N} and identifies $(_{US}I_X/r_X)(1 - e^{-rx\cdot t})$ as the $[f(_{US}I_X)_N]_t$ of our basic equation for $(N_{X_N})_t$.

It is apparent that $(_{US}I_X/r_X)(1 - e^{-rx\cdot t})$ is the same from one trial to another if the time over which this function is operative remains the same. The time at issue is t_2, the time that the system of action and negaction tendencies stays in Case 1a after the onset of the US. Since the time from the initiation of activity X until the onset of the US, t_1, is the same from one trial to another, it will suffice to prove that the duration of Case 1a, $t_1 + t_2$, is invariant over trials. We shall do this by showing that the paths of $\bar{T}_Y$ and $\bar{T}_X$ from the point at which activity X takes over from activity Y to the point at which activity Y again becomes ongoing remain the same from one trial to the next.

Let us take up the simpler $\bar{T}_Y$ first. At the point where activity X is initiated, $\bar{T}_Y = F_Y/c_Y$ by assumption, following which $\bar{T}_Y$ undergoes its cessation consummatory lag and then begins to grow linearly as a result of the application of the instigating force for activity Y. These conditions remain constant from trial to trial. Consequently, $\bar{T}_Y$ on each trial starts at the same level and follows the same path in the interval bounded by the two shifts in activity.

The path of $\bar{T}_X$ in Case 1a is defined by Equation 7.12. Adapted to trial N and written for the fixed interval between the initiation of activity X and the onset of the US, t_1, this equation is

$$(\bar{T}_X)_N = \left[\frac{(_{CS}I_X)_N}{r_X} - \frac{(_{CS}I_X)_N}{r_X}\right]\left(\frac{r_X}{c_X - r_X}\right)(e^{-rx\cdot t} - e^{-cx\cdot t})$$
$$+ \left(\frac{F_Y}{c_Y} - \frac{_{CS}F_X}{c_X}\right)e^{-cx\cdot t} + \frac{_{CS}F_X}{c_X}$$

which simplifies to

$$(\bar{T}_X)_N = \left(\frac{F_Y}{c_Y} - \frac{cs F_X}{c_X}\right)e^{-c_X \cdot t} + \frac{cs F_X}{c_X}$$

an expression that remains the same across trials. In the next interval t_2, between the onset of the US and the return of activity Y,

$$(\bar{T}_X)_N = \left[\frac{(cs I_X)_N}{r_X} - \frac{(cs I_X)_N + (us I_X)}{r_X}\right]\left(\frac{r_X}{c_X - r_X}\right)(e^{-r_X \cdot t} - e^{-c_X \cdot t})$$

$$+ \left[\left(\frac{F_Y}{c_Y} - \frac{cs F_X}{c_X}\right) \cdot e^{-c_X \cdot t_1} + \frac{cs F_X}{c_X} - \frac{cs F_X}{c_X}\right] \cdot e^{-c_X \cdot t} + \frac{cs F_X}{c_X}$$

Simplifying this expression gives

$$(\bar{T}_X)_N = -\left(\frac{us I_X}{r_X}\right)\left(\frac{r_X}{c_X - r_X}\right)(e^{-r_X \cdot t} - e^{-c_X \cdot t}) + \left(\frac{F_Y}{c_Y} - \frac{cs F_X}{c_X}\right)$$

$$\times e^{-c_X(t_1 + t)} + \frac{cs F_X}{c_X}$$

which does not involve N on the right-hand side, thereby, indicating that the path of $\bar{T}_X$ is the same for all trials in the t_2 interval. Since the path of $\bar{T}_X$ is the same each trial over the t_1 and t_2 intervals separately, it is the same each trial for their sum which defines the duration of Case 1a.

Thus, we have shown that the paths for $\bar{T}_Y$ and $\bar{T}_X$ are repeated each trial for the interval $t_1 + t_2$, beginning when activity X takes over from activity Y and ending when activity Y resumes, which implies that the duration of this interval is the same from trial to trial. Knowing that $t_1 + t_2$ as well as t_1 is the same each trial permits us to conclude that t_2 is also the same each trial. The interval t_2 between the onset of the US and the resumption of activity Y is the time during which $(us I_X / r_X)(1 - e^{-r_X \cdot t})$ is operative. With both the function describing the contribution of the US to N_{X_N} and the time during which that function is applied shown to be independent of trials, it follows that the contribution of the US to N_{X_N} at each point in time in Case 1a is the same from trial to trial and our proof is complete.

Invariance of the US Contribution to N_X in Cases 1b and 2. Even though the magnitudes of N_X in Cases 1b and 2 are not pertinent to the conditioning of inhibition, this is a good opportunity to continue tracking N_{X_N} throughout the duration of the US. We left N_{X_N} at the point where activity Y takes over again from activity X. The equations of Case 1a continue to hold true during the subsequent fixed cessation consummatory lag interval for activity X, meaning that the path of N_X is the same each trial during this interval as well. At the conclusion of the cessation consummatory lag $T_X > N_X$ but $\bar{T}_Y > \bar{T}_X$ and the equations for Case 1b are appropriate. We shall show that the contribution of the US to N_X is the same from trial to trial for Case 1b just as it was for Case 1a.

Under Case 1b, N_X continues to act against T_X with its full strength, since $T_X > N_X$. Again by using Equation 7.3, we can write

$$N_{X_N} = (N_{X_I})_N \cdot e^{-r_X \cdot t} + \frac{(_{CS}I_X)_N + (_{US}I_X)}{r_X}(1 - e^{-r_X \cdot t})$$

where t is the time in Case 1b. However, we know in addition that

$$N_{X_N} = \frac{(_{CS}I_X)_N}{r_X} + \left(\frac{_{US}I_X}{r_X}\right)(1 - e^{-r_X \cdot t_2})$$

where t_2 is the time in Case 1a after the onset of the US, so that $(_{US}I_X/r_X)(1 - e^{-r_X \cdot t_2})$ is the amount of N_X added during that time. It has been shown that t_2 is the same from trial to trial, making $(_{US}I_X/r_X)(1 - e^{-r_X \cdot t_2})$ constant from trial to trial.

By substitution and simplification, we obtain

$$N_{X_N} = \left[\left(\frac{_{US}I_X}{r_X}\right)(1 - e^{-r_X \cdot t_2})\right] \cdot e^{-r_X \cdot t} + \frac{(_{CS}I_X)_N}{r_X} + \left(\frac{_{US}I_X}{r_X}\right)(1 - e^{-r_X \cdot t})$$

from which it is apparent that only $(_{CS}I_X)_N$ can change with trials. The remaining terms (the ones that reflect the effect of the US) are independent of trials, providing the proof we seek.

Case 1b gives way to Case 2 when N_X reaches and exceeds T_X: that is, when $N_X > T_X$. In Case 2, there is more than enough N_X to nullify T_X, so that the force of resistance acting to reduce N_X depends on the level of T_X, not on that of N_X. This state of affairs yields Equation 7.6 which, when adapted to the present circumstances, is

$$N_{X_N} = (N_{X_I})_N + [(_{CS}I_X)_N + _{US}I_X - r_X \cdot (T_{X_I})_N] \cdot t - \left(\frac{r_X \cdot _{CS}F_X}{2}\right) \cdot t^2$$

where $(N_{X_I})_N$ and $(T_{X_I})_N$ refer to the values of N_X and T_X when Case 2 is entered and t to the time that elapses in Case 2. Two relationships, known to be true, assist the derivation. First, $(N_{X_I})_N = (T_{X_I})_N$ because this defines entrance into Case 2 and, second,

$$(N_{X_I})_N = \frac{(_{CS}I_X)_N}{r_X} + \left[\frac{(_{US}I_X)}{r_X}\right][1 - e^{-r_X(t_2+t_3)}]$$

where $t_2 + t_3$ is the total time covered from the onset of the US until the beginning of Case 2, because the same equation defines the path of N_X throughout this time interval. After substituting into the earlier equation for

N_{X_N} and simplifying the result, we obtain

$$N_{X_N} = \frac{(cs I_X)_N}{r_X} + \left(\frac{us I_X}{r_X}\right)[1 - e^{-r_X(t_2+t_3)}] + [(us I_X) \cdot e^{-r_X(t_2+t_3)}] \cdot t$$
$$- \left(\frac{r_X \cdot cs F_X}{2}\right) \cdot t^2$$

Once again, it is only $(cs I_X)_N$ that can change from one trial to the next; the effects of the US are independent of trials. Altogether, then, the change in N_X due to the US is identical from trial to trial for Case 1a, Case 1b, and Case 2 and, therefore, for each point in time that the US is on.

We can now complete the derivation of conditioning for inhibitory force. Put together, the fact that $(T_{cs_N})_t$ and $[f((us I_X)_N)]_t$ do not alter their paths across time within a trial from one trial to the next and the assumption that by the time activity X is initiated $[f((cs I_X)_N)]_t$ can be approximated on each trial by $[(cs I_X)_N]/r_X$, it follows that there is a value of t within each trial subsequent to the onset of the US that is the same for all trials for which $[(T_{cs_N})_t \cdot (N_{X_N})_t]$ is a maximum. Strictly speaking, this is true only if conditions are such that the maximum product is attained after the onset of the US, but this is the most likely arrangement for the paradigm under consideration. For the value of t, at which the product is a maximum, both $(T_{cs_N})_t$ and $[f((us I_X)_N)]_t$ are constants from trial to trial, whereas $[f((cs I_X)_N]_t = [(cs I_X)_N]/r_X$, assumed constant after the US comes on each trial, may change from trial to trial as conditioning proceeds. Thus, to determine the course of inhibitory conditioning to the CS, the sight and smell of the food, we must know two things about each trial: (a) that activity X (eating) occurs, and (b) the value of $[(cs I_X)_N]/r_X$. It is important to remember that *if eating does not occur on a particular trial, no change will occur in the inhibitory force of the CS* since one of the basic requirements for a conditioning trial (resistance to an ongoing activity) has not been met.

According to our Principle of Learning, the conditioning of inhibitory forces depends on the magnitudes of $(T_{cs_N})_t$, $[f((us I_X)_N)]_t$ and $[(cs I_X)_N]/r_X$. For our present purposes, we need not be concerned with the actual values that these terms might have in particular situations. To determine these values could be quite difficult. Our task is to use the Principle of Learning to describe the general course of inhibitory conditioning for the situation we have specified, and we proceed with that now.

In line with the preceding discussion, we can rewrite our Principle of Learning as

$$(cs I_X)_{N+1} = \theta\left\{(T_{cs}) \cdot \left[\frac{(cs I_X)_N}{r_X} + f(us I_X)\right]\right\}$$

where (T_{cs}) and $f(us I_X)$ are constants determined by the value of t that makes the product

$$(T_{cs})_t \cdot \left\{ \frac{(_{CS}I_X)_N}{r_X} + [f(_{US}I_X)]_t \right\}$$

a maximum or as

$$(_{CS}I_X)_{N+1} = \theta' \left[\frac{(_{CS}I_X)_N}{r_X} + f(_{US}I_X) \right]$$

This form takes advantage of the fact that (T_{cs}) is constant from trial to trial, permitting it to be absorbed into the constant θ'. It is reasonable to assume that for the dog of our hypothetical experiment the CS has no conditioned inhibitory force on the first trial, that is, $(_{CS}I_X)_1 = 0$. Thus, on Trial 1 the conditioning is based on $N_{X_I} = f(_{US}I_X)$, whatever that strength may be as determined by the parameter values of the situation, and we are able to write $(_{CS}I_X)_2 = \theta' \cdot [f(_{US}I_X)]$.

It follows that on Trial 2 the value of N_X on which conditioning is based is

$$N_{X_2} = \frac{(_{CS}I_X)_2}{r_X} + f(_{US}I_X)$$

and that, when $(_{CS}I_X)_2$ is replaced by its equivalent $\theta' \cdot [f(_{US}I_X)]$ and the result simplified we obtain

$$(_{CS}I_X)_3 = \theta' \cdot \left\{ f(_{US}I_X) \cdot \left[\left(\frac{\theta'}{r_X} \right) + 1 \right] \right\}$$

As this procedure is continued for a few more trials, it is easily seen and proved that the course of conditioning for inhibitory forces, like the course of conditioning for instigating forces, follows a geometric progression, and we can write

$$(_{CS}I_X)_N = \theta' \cdot [f(_{US}I_X)] \cdot \left[\left(\frac{\theta'}{r_X} \right)^{N-2} + \left(\frac{\theta'}{r_X} \right)^{N-3} + \cdots + 1 \right]$$

This equation simplifies to

$$(_{CS}I_X)_N = \theta'[f(_{US}I_X)] \left[\frac{1 - (\theta'/r_X)^{N-1}}{1 - (\theta'/r_X)} \right]$$

For $0 < (\theta'/r_X) < 1$, $(_{CS}I_X)_N$ approaches an asymptote of

$$\frac{\theta'[f(_{US}I_X)]}{1 - (\theta'/r_X)}$$

as the number of conditioning trials increases indefinitely.

CHAPTER 9
SYSTEMATIC EFFECTS OF INSTIGATION AND RESISTANCE

Now, at last, we are prepared to reconsider the several measurable aspects of the stream of behavior as a function of both instigation and resistance in a final set of theoretical proposals that concern the dynamics of action. We shall build on the foundation of earlier chapters to identify and to summarize the behavioral implications of the Principle of Change of Activity.

We began in Chapter 1 with analysis of a simple change of activity, confining our attention to the change in the dominance relationship between two incompatible action tendencies from different families. This avoided the complexities introduced by displacement, substitution, irrelevant activities, and resistance. By dealing with idealized conditions at the outset, we postponed our confrontation with the difficult questions later discussed in terms of selective attention, consummatory lag, and common experimental error. All of these topics but one, resistance, were considered and included in the theory of action by the end of Chapter 4. At that point, we were able to add some interesting and potentially useful theoretical statements about the determinants of choice, the rate of an activity, and the proportion of time spent in an activity to the earlier statements about the latency, the vigor, and the persistence of an activity. Then we examined the genesis and cognitive correlates of an instigating force (Chapters 5 and 6) in order to complete our coverage of the instigation of action. This done, we followed (in Chapters 7 and 8) with a parallel discussion of the dynamics of resistance and the genesis and cognitive correlates of an inhibitory force. Now, in the present chapter, we bring all the pieces together as we reconsider the general problem of a change of activity and as we explore several implications of the more comprehensive Principle of Change of Activity that our conceptual analysis has produced.

Actually, in Chapter 1, we realized that an algebraic solution to the simultaneous equations required for a general statement of how long it would take an individual to change from one activity to another is not possible. Certain special conditions were shown to yield quite simple solutions. Under other conditions, approximations are necessary or weaker predictions must be made. It should come as no surprise that extension of the theoretical analysis to encompass resistance complicates the problem of tracking the derivations of the theory still further. We acknowledge this. It will require extensive use of a computer to map the interactions among tendencies that lie behind the stream of behavior. Nevertheless, we can formulate a programmatic Principle of Change of Activity that combines the effects of both instigation and resistance, and by again making certain simplifying assumptions, we can use this principle to study the systematic influence of inhibitory force, negaction tendency, and resistance on the initiation, the vigor, and the persistence of an activity, the choice among alternative activities, and the distribution of time among activities.

As we first stated in Chapter 7, activity A in progress implies that $\bar{T}_{A_I} > \bar{T}_{B_I}, \ldots$ An observed change from activity A to activity B, therefore, implies a change in the dominance relations among the *resultant* tendencies described as $\bar{T}_{B_F} > \bar{T}_{A_F}, \ldots$ This change in dominance relations can come about in an awesome variety of ways; some of them are now summarized in Table 9.1. All of these different possibilities are encompassed by the programmatic Principle of Change of Activity that we present in this chapter.

Reconsideration of the Fundamental Problem of a Change of Activity

It will be best to begin again at the beginning and to recall that in Chapter 1 two parameters, α and β, were introduced to represent the average rate of change in T_A and T_B, respectively, over the interval of observation in which a change from activity A to activity B had occurred. By defining

$$\alpha = \frac{T_{A_F} - T_{A_I}}{t_{B/A}} \quad \text{and} \quad \beta = \frac{T_{B_F} - T_{B_I}}{t_{B/A}}$$

it was possible to write $T_{A_F} = T_{A_I} + \alpha \cdot t_{B/A}$ and $T_{B_F} = T_{B_I} + \beta \cdot t_{B/A}$, which yielded the statement $t_{B/A} = (T_{A_I} - T_{B_I})/(\beta - \alpha)$ (Equation 1.1) as the basic empirical equation for a simple change of activity. We soon settled on an alternative form of this equation, $t_{B/A} = (T_{A_F} - T_{B_I})/\beta$ (Equation 1.2), as our chief focus of interest.

We are now ready to expand this initial analysis of the average changes in the strength of tendencies during an interval of observation to include the effects of resistance. Parallel to the definitions of the rate of change in T_A and T_B, the rate of change in $\bar{T}_A$ and $\bar{T}_B$ during the interval of observation

TABLE 9.1   A Variety of Possible Causes of the Change, or a Delay in the Change, from an Initial Activity A to Activity B

Change of Activity Described as:	When the Stimulus Situation is Constant	Following Introduction of a Stimulus	Following Withdrawal of a Stimulus
Cessation of activity A	C_A reduces T_A (consummatory behavior)	I_A increases N_A (punishment of present activity)	Loss of F_A leads to reduction of T_A (removal of incentive or promise of reward for present activity)
Initiation of an activity B		F_B increases T_B (promise of reward for new activity)	Loss of I_B leads to reduction of N_B (removal of threat of punishment for new activity)
Delay in cessation of activity A		F_A strengthens T_A (added incentive or promise of reward for present activity)	Loss of I_A results in a weakened N_A (removal of punishment or threat of punishment for present activity)
Delay in initiation of an activity B		$I_B, I_C \ldots$ strengthen $N_B, N_C \ldots$ (unconditional threat of punishment for any new activity)	Loss of F_B suspends the growth of T_B (withdrawal of promise of reward for new activity)

can be expressed as

$$\frac{\bar{T}_{A_F} - \bar{T}_{A_I}}{t_{B/A}} \quad \text{and} \quad \frac{\bar{T}_{B_F} - \bar{T}_{B_I}}{t_{B/A}}$$

respectively. We can then substitute the components of $\bar{T}_{A_F}$ and $\bar{T}_{A_I}$ for these terms and write

$$\frac{\bar{T}_{A_F} - \bar{T}_{A_I}}{t_{B/A}} = \frac{(T_{A_F} - N_{A_F}) - (T_{A_I} - N_{A_I})}{t_{B/A}}$$

$$= \frac{(T_{A_F} - T_{A_I})}{t_{B/A}} - \frac{(N_{A_F} - N_{A_I})}{t_{B/A}} = (\alpha - \alpha')$$

where

$$\alpha' = \frac{(N_{A_F} - N_{A_I})}{t_{B/A}}$$

is the rate of change in the strength of the negaction tendency N_A during the interval of observation. Similarly,

$$\frac{\bar{T}_{B_F} - \bar{T}_{B_I}}{t_{B/A}} = (\beta - \beta')$$

where

$$\beta' = \frac{(N_{B_F} - N_{B_I})}{t_{B/A}}$$

is the rate of change in the strength of N_B.

These new definitions permit us to write $\bar{T}_{A_F} = \bar{T}_{A_I} + (\alpha - \alpha')t_{B/A}$ and $\bar{T}_{B_F} = \bar{T}_{B_I} + (\beta - \beta')t_{B/A}$, two expressions that yield

$$t_{B/A} = \frac{(T_{A_I} - T_{B_I}) - (N_{A_I} - N_{B_I})}{(\beta - \alpha) - (\beta' - \alpha')} \tag{9.1}$$

when solved for $t_{B/A}$ and simplified.

The new equation (Equation 9.1) corresponds to Equation 1.1, but it attributes the change in activity to changes in resistance as well as the instigation of action. Equation 9.1 states that the time required for a change from activity A to activity B is equal to the difference in the initial strengths of the action tendencies $(T_{A_I} - T_{B_I})$ minus the difference in the initial strengths of the negaction tendencies $(N_{A_I} - N_{B_I})$ divided by the difference in the average rates of change for the two action tendencies $(\beta - \alpha)$ minus the difference in the average rates of change for the two negaction tendencies $(\beta' - \alpha')$ during the interval of observation.

Two additional equations, alternative forms of Equation 9.1 and paralleling Equation 1.2 and Equation 1.3, can be written

$$t_{B/A} = \frac{\bar{T}_{A_F} - \bar{T}_{B_I}}{(\beta - \beta')} = \frac{(T_{A_F} - T_{B_I}) - (N_{A_F} - N_{A_I})}{(\beta - \beta')} \tag{9.2}$$

and

$$t_{B/A} = \frac{\bar{T}_{B_F} - \bar{T}_{A_I}}{(\alpha - \alpha')} = \frac{(T_{B_F} - T_{A_I}) - (N_{B_F} - N_{A_I})}{(\alpha - \alpha')} \tag{9.3}$$

The utility of Equations 9.1, 9.2, and 9.3, all of which are expressed in terms of the average rate of changes in action and negaction tendencies during the interval $t_{B/A}$, lies in the assistance they can give in identifying how environmental events affect the time required for a change in activity. They capture the basic reciprocal form of the relationship between the strengths of tendencies, both action and negaction, and the rates of change in those tendencies in the determination of the persistence of an ongoing activity and/or the latency of the initiation of an alternative activity. Even though an algebraic solution for $t_{B/A}$, the time required for a change in activity, is not generally attainable when the effects of resistance are included, we can go well beyond this preliminary description of the change in the light of our theory concerning instigation and resistance.

A PROGRAMMATIC PRINCIPLE OF CHANGE OF ACTIVITY

The occurrence of a change from activity A to activity B means that initially $\bar{T}_{A_I} > \bar{T}_{B_I}$ and, subsequently, $\bar{T}_{B_F} = \bar{T}_{A_F}$. This latter relation can be written as $T_{B_F} - N_{B_F} = T_{A_F} - N_{A_F}$. According to our theoretical presumptions, each of these four terms can be expressed as a function of its initial value (T_{B_I}, N_{B_I}, T_{A_I}, and N_{A_I}), certain fixed parameter values, and the time $t_{B/A}$ between the beginning of the interval of observation and the initiation of activity B.

We know that initially $\bar{T}_A$ is in Case 1a and that $\bar{T}_B$ is either in Case 1b, where $T_B > N_B$, or in Case 2, where $N_B > T_B$. If $\bar{T}_B$ is in Case 2, it must move into Case 1b before the change in activity can occur. If $\bar{T}_B$ is in Case 1b at the outset, it might move into Case 2 and then back to Case 1b prior to a change in activity, or it might remain in Case 1b throughout the interval of observation depending on the conditions that prevail. If $\bar{T}_B$ begins in Case 2, the total time required for the change in activity will be the time required for $\bar{T}_B$ to move from Case 2 to Case 1b,[1] plus the additional time required for $\bar{T}_B$ to grow to the level of $\bar{T}_{A_F}$ while in Case 1b. If $\bar{T}_B$ begins in Case 1b, moves to Case 2 and then back to Case 1b before gaining dominance over $\bar{T}_A$, a third component is included in the total time required for a change of activity, namely, the time taken by T_B to go from Case 1b to Case 2.[2]

To keep our exposition simple, we shall not pursue the implications of Case 2 for change in activity but will confine our discussion to the situation in which $\bar{T}_B$ gains dominance over $\bar{T}_A$ without passing through Case 2.

The appropriate expressions for T_{B_F} and N_{B_F} under Case 1b and T_{A_F} and N_{A_F} under Case 1a are presented in Equations 1.7, 7.3, 7.11, and 7.3, respectively. By substituting for T_{B_F} from Equation 1.7 and recalling that $\hat{F}_B$ is applicable, the relation $T_{B_F} - N_{B_F} = T_{A_F} - N_{A_F}$ can be rewritten as $(T_{B_I} + \hat{F}_B \cdot t_{B/A}) - N_{B_F} = T_{A_F} - N_{A_F}$. This can be solved for $t_{B/A}$, as follows:

$$t_{B/A} = \frac{(T_{A_F} - N_{A_F}) - (T_{B_I} - N_{B_F})}{\hat{F}_B} \tag{9.4}$$

Although this equation is not practical for the purposes of experimental investigations of the theory except under special conditions, it is useful as a reference for our discussion of change in activity.

[1] This time is given by the value of t in Equation 7.8 that makes $\bar{T}_B = 0$ (see Figure 7.4).

[2] This time is given by the value of t in Equation 7.7 that makes $\bar{T}_B = 0$ (see Figure 7.3).

First, notice from Equation 9.4 that $t_{B/A}$ is greater for larger values of T_{A_F} and smaller values of T_{B_I} and $\hat{F}_B$, just as was true for a change in activity without resistance (see Chapter 1). Furthermore, although the equations describing the course of T_A when there is resistance (Equation 7.11) and when there is not (Equation 1.11) are different, they share the property of yielding greater magnitudes of T_{A_F} for larger values of F_A and T_{A_I}. In fact, Equations 9.4 and 7.11 both reduce to their counterparts, Equations 1.12 and 1.11, when there is no resistance. There are, then, no major alterations in the way in which $t_{B/A}$ is affected by F_A, T_{A_I}, $\hat{F}_B$, and T_{B_I}, as inhibition is taken into account. Let us look at how $t_{B/A}$ is affected by the resistance to an activity in progress and by the resistance to an alternative activity.

The Effect of Resistance to the Activity in Progress

When a stimulus producing force to inhibit the activity in progress is introduced, the suppressive effect is short lived. As a result of resistance, the action tendency T_A will become stronger and will compensate for the dampening effect of N_A on its expression as it approaches the higher asymptotic level defined by $F_A/c_A + I_A/r_A$. The transitory suppression takes the form of a decrement in the degree of an individual's involvement in activity A and is caused by the reduction of $\bar{T}_A$ (see Chapter 7 notes). This means that for a time, at least, the individual acting in the face of resistance is more vulnerable to interruption if $\hat{F}_B$ and/or T_{B_I} is relatively strong. The curves in Figure 7.7 labeled (b), (b'), (d), and (d') provide several examples of the effect of increased resistance on the temporal course of the resultant tendency $\bar{T}_A$, sustaining the activity in progress.

We may conclude that the extent and duration of the temporary suppressive effect of resistance to the activity in progress will be greater the stronger the force of the stimulus situation to negate the activity in progress. The effect will be a decrement in the level of performance of activity A and a more prompt change from activity A to B than without resistance to A when T_{B_I} and/or $\hat{F}_B$ is relatively strong and is capable of producing an interception of $\bar{T}_A$ during the critical period of vulnerability to interruption. This relationship is shown in Figure 9.1 between $\bar{T}_X$ and $\bar{T}_{A_1}$ as contrasted to that between $\bar{T}_Y$ and $\bar{T}_{A_1}$.

The general effect of the introduction of force to inhibit an activity in progress by punishment, or the threat of punishment, is to decrease persistence in that activity and to cause a more prompt initiation of some other activity when, but only when, the inertial tendency and/or the instigating force to undertake an alternative activity is relatively strong. When the combined effect of inertial tendency and instigating force is only a very weak resultant tendency to undertake an alternative activity (for example, $\bar{T}_Y$ in Figure 9.1), only a much more severe punishment or threat of punishment for continuance of the ongoing activity would be likely

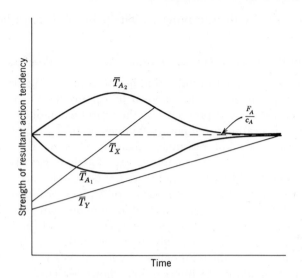

FIGURE 9.1   The transitory periods of increased vulnerability to interruption produced by the introduction of I_A in curve $\bar{T}_{A_1}$ and decreased vulnerability to interruption by the withdrawal of I_A in curve $\bar{T}_{A_2}$. The latency of the relatively strongly instigated alternative $(\bar{T}_X)$ is affected by the temporary effect of the resistance to activity A, but the latency of the weaker alternative $(\bar{T}_Y)$ is not.

to produce sufficient suppression of ongoing activity to allow a more prompt change of activity than would occur had there been no resistance to the initial activity. Once $\bar{T}_A$ has approached the level defined by F_A/c_A, its strength is what it would have been without the introduction of I_A. Thereafter, the continued presence of constant resistance to activity A has no further effect on the persistence of that activity or the latency of any alternative.

The temporary period of increased vulnerability to a change of activity produced by punishment or the threat of punishment for the continuance of the initial activity is of central importance in our explanation of avoidance behavior (see Chapter 8). It follows from what has been said here, and from our earlier discussion, that acquisition of an avoidance response should require less intense and less frequent punishment when instigation for the avoidance activity is already relatively strong (for example, $\bar{T}_X$ in Figure 9.1) but should require very intense or more frequent punishment when the instigation is very weak (for example, $\bar{T}_Y$ in Figure 9.1). We suggested earlier that successful escape from potential threats to survival would be more prompt if noxious stimuli, like the heat of a flame, produced an unconditioned instigating force to withdraw in addition to an unconditioned force to negate the activity then in progress. The point of these earlier remarks is now illustrated in Figure 9.1.

The Effect of Removal of Resistance to the Activity in Progress

The effect of removing a stimulus that has been producing force to inhibit the activity in progress, that is, removal of I_A, produces a result that is just the opposite of the one produced by the introduction of I_A (see Chapter 7 notes). Now, instead of a temporary dampening of $\bar{T}_A$ relative to what it would have been without resistance, there is a temporary surge in the strength of $\bar{T}_A$. This makes a prompt change of activity less likely than had I_A continued and less likely than had there not been resistance to activity A. This can occur because the earlier presence of N_A has permitted the bottling up of T_A which then later becomes available for expression as N_A is reduced. As $\bar{T}_A$ becomes temporarily stronger, the involvement of the individual in activity A becomes correspondingly stronger until $\bar{T}_A$ diminishes and approaches, once again, the level defined by F_A/c_A. As a result of this period of decreased vulnerability to interruption, shown by curve $\bar{T}_{A_2}$ in Figure 9.1, the latency of a strongly instigated alternative like $\bar{T}_X$ in the figure is increased relative to conditions of the continued presence of I_A or the complete absence of I_A but, as previously, there is no effect at all on the latency of the more weakly instigated alternatives. An example of the latter is $\bar{T}_Y$ in Figure 9.1. The parameters determining its strength are such that it would intercept $\bar{T}_A$ only after the temporary surge in strength of $\bar{T}_A$.

Because the effects on latency of both the introduction and the withdrawal of inhibitory force for the activity in progress are temporary, they are likely to be limited to strongly instigated alternative activities or ones for which the inertial tendency is very strong. Resistance to ongoing activity should not always decrease persistence in it nor make a prompt change in activity more likely. It should not do so when the immediate environment together with the inertial hierarchy of the individual fails to provide a strong alternative course of action and the resistance is only moderate. It should, of course, always do so if the resistance to ongoing activity is extreme enough.

Sometimes, as shown in the curve labeled (a) in Figure 7.7, an effect comparable to the withdrawal of inhibitory force will occur, although I_A is maintained. As explained earlier, this can happen when N_{A_I}, for whatever reason, is very strong and diminishes in its resistance to T_A.

The Effects of Resistance to an Alternative Activity

We now discuss the systematic effects on $t_{B/A}$ of variations in the amount of resistance to an alternative activity. Typically, the continued presence of a tendency to resist undertaking activity B, N_B, can be attributed to the inhibitory force, I_B, produced by the same stimulus situation that accounts for F_B. The presence of the negation tendency N_B increases the latency of activity B by subtracting N_{B_F} from T_{B_I} as shown in Equation 9.4. This, in effect, increases the magnitude of the inertial gap $_g\dot{B}$, which $\bar{T}_B$ must overcome if it is to be expressed in behavior. This is one of several ways of representing the effect on $t_{B/A}$ of resistance to the alternative activity. It indicates that N_{B_F}, whatever its strength, must be overcome by T_B before a change in activity can take place. The strength of N_{B_F} is defined by Equation 7.3. It varies directly with the magnitudes of N_{B_I} and I_B. If the stimulus situation remains constant, the strength of N_B approaches its asymptotic level, $\hat{I}_B/r_B$, and the longer the time taken for the change in activity to occur, the more nearly will N_{B_F} approach that level.

It is unlikely that Equation 9.4 will be generally useful in dealing with the details of behavioral data on change of activity because, in it, $t_{B/A}$ is related to the final magnitudes of T_A, N_A, and N_B, that is, their values when the change of activity occurs. The strength of each tendency changes with time and is not under direct experimental control. If, however, it could be assumed that $\bar{T}_A = (T_A - N_A)$ and N_B had already approached the limits of their growth (or decline) and would remain relatively constant thereafter, the strength of each of these variables could be approximated by its asymptotic value. This assumption would be justified in situations where activity A had been in progress for a considerable period of time prior to the change in activity under stimulus conditions that provided constant magnitudes of the instigating forces, F_A and $\hat{F}_B$, and of the inhibitory forces, I_A and $\hat{I}_B$.

By substituting the asymptotic values $(F_A/c_A + I_A/r_A)$, I_A/r_A, and $\hat{I}_B/r_B$ for T_{A_F}, N_{A_F}, and N_{B_F}, respectively, in Equation 9.4, we obtain

$$t_{B/A} = \frac{\left[\left(\dfrac{F_A}{c_A} + \dfrac{I_A}{r_A}\right) - \dfrac{I_A}{r_A}\right] - \left(T_{B_I} - \dfrac{\hat{I}_B}{r_B}\right)}{\hat{F}_B}$$

When simplified, this equation becomes a useful analytical principle of change of activity *for the conditions that have been assumed*:

$$t_{B/A} = \frac{F_A/c_A - (T_{B_I} - \hat{I}_B/r_B)}{\hat{F}_B} \tag{9.5}$$

Notice that Equation 9.5 differs from its counterpart in Chapter 1 (Equation 1.13) where resistance was assumed to be absent only by the term $\hat{I}_B/r_B$. From Equation 9.5 and Figure 9.2 we can observe that $t_{B/A}$ is prolonged by the presence of $\hat{I}_B$.[3] Insofar as its influence on the time to change

---

[3] It will become clear in the later sections on the choice and the rate of an activity that this statement is true only if T_{B_I} is independent of $\hat{I}_B$. This would be the case if the negaction tendency had zero strength up to the beginning of the interval of observation as shown in Figure 9.2.

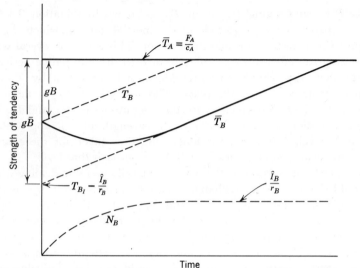

FIGURE 9.2   The effect of resistance to an alternative activity (when it can be assumed that $N_B = \hat{I}_B/r_B$ before the change of activity occurs) is equivalent to beginning the interval of observation with a larger inertial gap and no resistance (see text and the Mathematical Notes).

activity goes, an N_B that has stabilized before the change of activity has an effect equivalent to a weaker inertial tendency for activity B when there is no resistance. Figure 9.2 shows that the growth of $\bar{T}_B$ is linear with a slope defined by $\hat{F}_B$ over that portion of the interval of observation after N_B has become stable. The initial depression of $\bar{T}_B$ and the delay in its linear growth during the time in which N_B is rising to $\hat{I}_B/r_B$ can be equated to a linear growth for $\bar{T}_B$ throughout the interval of observation, but one that begins at a weaker initial level equivalent to $T_{B_I} - \hat{I}_B/r_B$, as shown in Figure 9.2. Under the conditions assumed, then, the presence of resistance to an alternative activity corresponds to an increase in the inertial gap by an amount equal to the asymptotic level of that resistance. That is,

$$_g\dot{B} = \frac{F_A}{c_A} - \left(T_{B_I} - \frac{\hat{I}_B}{r_B}\right) = \left(\frac{F_A}{c_A} - T_{B_I}\right) + \frac{\hat{I}_B}{r_B} = {}_g B + \frac{\hat{I}_B}{r_B}$$

We observe again, comparing Equation 9.5 to Equation 1.13, that $t_{B/A}$ is unaffected by the presence of I_A once the dynamic processes controlling T_A and N_A have brought them close to their asymptotic levels.[4]

[4] However, since both the instigation of action and the resistance to action are, in the last analysis, physical processes that involve the expenditure of energy, it is suggested by Equation 9.4 (the unsimplified version) that *the same level of performance of an activity and of persistence of that activity in competition with other activities must involve a greater expenditure of energy when there*

LATENCY AND PERSISTENCE

Guided by Equation 9.5, yet reminded of the special conditions assumed by this equation, we may formulate several generalizations that concern the relationship of instigating force, inertial tendency, and inhibitory force to latency and persistence.

Instigating Force as a Determinant of Latency of Response.   We must imagine an experiment in which all the variables are constant except the magnitude of instigating force to undertake the alternative activity B. Let $(F_B)_1 > (F_B)_2$, $(\hat{F}_B)_1 > (\hat{F}_B)_2$, and $(\hat{F}_B)_1/(\hat{F}_B)_2 = (F_B)_1/(F_B)_2$. It follows from Equation 9.5 that $(t_{B/A})_1 = {}_g\bar{B}/(\hat{F}_B)_1$ and $(t_{B/A})_2 = {}_g\bar{B}/(\hat{F}_B)_2$. Since ${}_g\bar{B}$ is a constant, we have $(\hat{F}_B)_1 \cdot (t_{B/A})_1 = (\hat{F}_B)_2 \cdot (t_{B/A})_2$, and we recover the generalization advanced in Chapter 3 that the ratio of the latencies of response (under otherwise comparable conditions) is equal to the reciprocal of the ratio of the magnitudes of instigating force, that is,

$$\frac{(t_{B/A})_1}{(t_{B/A})_2} = \frac{(F_B)_2}{(F_B)_1}$$

Inhibitory Force as a Determinant of Latency of Response.   Now we must imagine conditions in which all the variables except the magnitude of force to inhibit activity B are constant. Let r_B also be constant, but let I_B take on several values so that $I_B = 0$ and $(I_B)_1 < (I_B)_2 < (I_B)_3$. When $I_B = 0$, ${}_g\bar{B} = {}_gB$ and $t_{B/A} = {}_g\bar{B}/\hat{F}_B = {}_gB/\hat{F}_B$. However, in the case of $(I_B)_1 > 0$,

$$({}_g\bar{B})_1 = {}_gB + \frac{\hat{I}_B}{r_B} \quad \text{and} \quad (t_{B/A})_1 = \frac{({}_g\bar{B})_1}{\hat{F}_B}$$

When there is a force to inhibit the initiation of activity B, the latency of response is increased, and the magnitude of inhibitory force determines the amount of this increase in latency as shown below:

$$\Delta(t_{B/A})_1 = (t_{B/A})_1 - (t_{B/A}) = \frac{({}_g\bar{B})_1}{\hat{F}_B} - \frac{{}_gB}{\hat{F}_B} = \frac{{}_gB + [(\hat{I}_B)_1]/r_B - {}_gB}{\hat{F}_B}$$

$$= \frac{[(\hat{I}_B)_1]/r_B}{\hat{F}_B} = \left(\frac{1}{r_B}\right)\left(\frac{(\hat{I}_B)_1}{\hat{F}_B}\right)$$

is resistance. The increased effort attributable to resistance might be expected to be proportionate to the strength of the inhibitory force, I_A. This conjecture, which transcends the implications of our theory concerning the dynamics of action, per se, reminds us that we are describing the stream of behavior of an organism for whom physical effort and fatigue are closely related problems. The phenomenology of changes in activity with and without resistance deserves special study in this regard.

From this we may conclude that *the increase in latency of response produced by the resistance to an alternative activity is proportionate to the magnitude of the inhibitory force.*

From this follows a very simple corollary concerning the comparative effects of two inhibitory forces:

$$\Delta(t_{B/A})_2 = (t_{B/A})_2 - (t_{B/A}) = \left(\frac{1}{r_B}\right)\left(\frac{(\hat{I}_B)_2}{\hat{F}_B}\right) \qquad \text{so that} \qquad \frac{\Delta(t_{B/A})_2}{\Delta(t_{B/A})_1} = \frac{(I_B)_2}{(I_B)_1}$$

The ratio of the increases in the latency of response produced by the inhibitory forces under otherwise comparable conditions is equivalent to the ratio of the inhibitory forces.

Here, also, it is instructive to recall the earlier treatment of the acquisition and the extinction of the conditioned avoidance response (Chapter 8). Once the earlier punishment of the various activities in a stimulus situation has established forces to inhibit those activities, the temporary suppression of those activities by resistance is all that is needed to allow the tendency to engage in some other never-punished activity to win consistently in the competition for expression in behavior on the subsequent trials. The resistance to an activity, like a check block in a football game, need do no more than delay temporarily the forward progress of the competing tendencies to guarantee the occurrence of the so-called avoidance response. And this, we recall (Chapter 8), protects the several inhibitory forces from changing strength from one trial to the next.

Inertial Tendency as a Determinant of Latency of Response.   Now we must assume that all the instigating and inhibitory forces are constant and that only T_{B_I}, the strength of the inertial tendency for the alternative activity, is allowed to vary. We are reminded that systematic control of hours food privation, for example, would be expected to produce systematic variation in the strength of the inertial tendency to undertake an activity constituting approach to food. For the conditions we have assumed

$$_g\bar{B} = \frac{F_A}{c_A} - \left(T_{B_I} - \frac{\hat{I}_B}{r_B}\right) = \frac{F_A}{c_A} + \frac{\hat{I}_B}{r_B} - T_{B_I} = \text{constant} - T_{B_I}$$

Let $\hat{F}_B$ also be assumed constant, allowing us to explore the implications of variations in T_{B_I} for $T_{B_I} = 0$ and $(T_{B_I})_2 > (T_{B_I})_1 > T_{B_I}$. According to Equation 9.5,

$$t_{B/A} = \frac{\text{constant}}{\hat{F}_B}, \qquad (t_{B/A})_1 = \frac{\text{constant} - (T_{B_I})_1}{\hat{F}_B},$$

$$(t_{B/A})_2 = \frac{\text{constant} - (T_{B_I})_2}{\hat{F}_B}$$

This shows that the latency of response is reduced by the inertial tendency to undertake activity B. A simple generalization emerges concerning the amount of this reduction:

$$\Delta(t_{B/A})_1 = (t_{B/A}) - (t_{B/A})_1 = \frac{\text{constant}}{\hat{F}_B} - \frac{\text{constant} - (T_{B_I})_1}{\hat{F}_B} = \frac{(T_{B_I})_1}{\hat{F}_B}$$

The decrease in latency of response attributable to the presence of the inertial tendency to undertake an activity not in progress is proportionate to the magnitude of that inertial tendency. And, again, there is a simple corollary concerning the comparative effects of the different magnitudes of inertial tendency under otherwise comparable conditions:

$$\Delta(t_{B/A})_2 = (t_{B/A}) - (t_{B/A})_2 = \frac{(T_{B_I})_2}{\hat{F}_B}, \qquad \text{so that} \qquad \frac{\Delta(t_{B/A})_2}{\Delta(t_{B/A})_1} = \frac{(T_{B_I})_2}{(T_{B_I})_1}$$

That is, *the ratio of the decreases in latency of response produced by inertial tendencies of different magnitudes under otherwise comparable conditions is equal to the ratio of the magnitudes of the inertial tendencies.*

Finally, there is one more set of generalizations to be made about latency and persistence. They clearly identify the nature of the role of the factors that influence the strength of the resultant tendency that is sustaining the activity in progress.

Since $_gB = F_A/c_A - \bar{T}_{B_F}$ under the conditions assumed, both F_A and c_A are important determinants of persistence and latency. Let us assume that the asymptotic level of the resultant tendency sustaining the activity in progress is varied while other variables affecting the change in activity are constant. Let $F_A/c_A < (F_A/c_A)_1 < (F_A/c_A)_2$. We then have

$$(t_{B/A}) = \frac{(F_A/c_A) - \text{constant}}{\hat{F}_B} \qquad \text{and} \qquad (t_{B/A})_1 = \frac{(F_A/c_A)_1 - \text{constant}}{\hat{F}_B}$$

implying that $(t_{B/A})_1 > (t_{B/A})$. *The difference in the persistence of an activity in progress (or the latency of some alternative) that is attributable to a difference in the strength of the resultant tendency sustaining that activity* (that is, *the level of F_A/c_A) is proportionate to the magnitude of the difference in strength of that tendency.* That is,

$$\Delta(t_{B/A})_1 = (t_{B/A})_1 - (t_{B/A}) = \frac{(F_A/c_A)_1 - (F_A/c_A)}{\text{constant}}$$

When the difference in level of $\bar{T}_{A_F}$ is attributable to a difference in the magnitude of F_A where $(F_A)_1 > F_A$, the increase in the persistence of A is proportionate to the magnitude of that difference in instigating force. That is,

$$\Delta(t_{B/A})_1 = \frac{(F_A)_1 - (F_A)}{\text{constant}}$$

These generalizations about the systematic effects of the several determinants of instigation and resistance on $t_{B/A}$, the time to change from one activity to another, describe what should happen when both the strength of the resultant tendency that sustains activity in progress and the resistance to the alternative have become relatively stable before the change in activity occurs. Nevertheless, they constitute a useful description of the general nature of the influence of the several variables on a simple change of activity for conditions that begin to approximate the ones assumed and, of course, give a better description the closer the approximation.

EFFECT OF RESISTANCE ON CHOICE

In Chapter 4, we discovered that the choice between two alternatives depends on the ratio of the magnitudes of the instigating forces, whether the data are obtained from a single observation from many individuals on one occasion or from repeated observations of a single individual's choices on the same occasion. Now, we must determine what are the systematic effects that inhibitory force and resistance have on choice.

Single Observation from Many Individuals on One Occasion. Let us reconsider the choice behavior of a number of individuals in whom the strength of instigating forces is controlled so that $F_X > F_Y$ and $\hat{F}_X/\hat{F}_Y = F_X/F_Y$, but uncontrolled variations among individuals in F_A/c_A, T_{X_I}, and T_{Y_I} produce random variations in $_gX$ and $_gY$ as they confront the choice. Now, we consider what, if any, difference is made by the presence of $\hat{I}_X$ and $\hat{I}_Y$ forces to inhibit expression of each alternative.

We can begin the analysis with our earlier conclusion regarding choice when there is no resistance: in a two alternative choice, the activity instigated by the stronger force will be chosen except when the ratio of the magnitude of that force to that of the weaker instigating force is exceeded by the ratio of the respective inertial gaps. That is, X will be chosen except when $_gX/_gY > \hat{F}_X/\hat{F}_Y$.

As in the discussion of latency, we continue to deal with the situation in which N_X and N_Y at the time of choice can be approximated by their asymptotic values, $\hat{I}_X/r_X$ and $\hat{I}_Y/r_Y$, respectively. Thus we are able to use Equation 9.5 to determine the proportion of choices of X and Y. According to Equation 9.5,

$$(t_{X/A})' = \frac{F_A/c_A - T_{X_I} + \hat{I}_X/r_X}{\hat{F}_X} = \frac{_g\bar{X}}{\hat{F}_X}$$

and

$$(t_{Y/A})' = \frac{F_A/c_A - T_{Y_I} + \hat{I}_Y/r_Y}{\hat{F}_Y} = \frac{_g\bar{Y}}{\hat{F}_Y}$$

where $(t_{X/A})'$ and $(t_{Y/A})'$ are theoretical latencies. Activity X, the alternative instigated by the stronger force, should be chosen except when $(t_{X/A})' > (t_{Y/A})'$, that is, except when $_g\bar{X}/\hat{F}_X > _g\bar{Y}/\hat{F}_Y$ or $_g\bar{X}/_g\bar{Y} > \hat{F}_X/\hat{F}_Y$.

We first identify the conditions under which the presence of an inhibitory force has no systematic influence on choice and, then, we identify the conditions under which it has an effect and describe the nature of that effect. Resistance will have no effect on choice when the expression including resistance, $_g\bar{X}/\hat{F}_X > _g\bar{Y}/\hat{F}_Y$, is equivalent to the earlier expression without resistance, $_gX/\hat{F}_X > _gY/\hat{F}_Y$. Since $_g\bar{X} = _gX + \hat{I}_X/r_X$ and $_g\bar{Y} = _gY + \hat{I}_Y/r_Y$, we seek the condition in which

$$\frac{_gX}{\hat{F}_X} + \frac{\hat{I}_X/r_X}{\hat{F}_X} > \frac{_gY}{\hat{F}_Y} + \frac{\hat{I}_Y/r_Y}{\hat{F}_Y}$$

reduces to $_gX/\hat{F}_X > _gY/\hat{F}_Y$. This condition exists when

$$\frac{\hat{I}_X/r_X}{\hat{F}_X} = \frac{\hat{I}_Y/r_Y}{\hat{F}_Y}$$

which may be rewritten

$$\frac{\hat{I}_X/r_X}{\hat{I}_Y/r_Y} = \frac{\hat{F}_X}{\hat{F}_Y}$$

And, since we normally assume that $r_X = r_Y$, *the condition in which resistance has no effect on choice may be described very simply as one in which the ratio of inhibitory forces equals the ratio of the instigating forces.*

It follows that whenever $\hat{I}_X/\hat{I}_Y > \hat{F}_X/\hat{F}_Y$, the ratio $_g\bar{X}/_g\bar{Y}$ will be increased, favoring the choice of Y among some individuals who without resistance would have chosen X. And whenever $\hat{I}_X/\hat{I}_Y < \hat{F}_X/\hat{F}_Y$, the ratio $_g\bar{X}/_g\bar{Y}$ will be decreased, favoring the choice of X among some individuals who without resistance would have chosen Y.

It also follows that the presence of an inhibitory force for one alternative only will always increase the likelihood that the other will be chosen, and that the presence of equal inhibitory force for the two alternatives will always favor the choice of the alternative instigated by the stronger force because $1 < \hat{F}_X/\hat{F}_Y$. Again we notice that it is the *ratio* of forces, this time of inhibitory forces, and not the magnitude of their difference that has a systematic influence on choice.

An Application to Choice among Achievement Tasks which Differ in Difficulty.   It has frequently been observed that individuals described as strong in motive to avoid failure show less preference for moderately difficult tasks than those described as weak in motive to avoid failure (Atkinson and Feather, 1966). How is this result to be reconciled with the present analysis of the role of resistance in choice?

It was apparent earlier (Chapter 6) that the weak ratio rule of choice implies that under *ideal* conditions of achievement motivation, that is, where responses are motivated *only* by the instigating force to achieve success, persons who differ in the strength of the motive to achieve success would not by expected to differ in the degree of preference for moderately difficult tasks. This conclusion followed from the assumption of current theory that the motive has a multiplicative effect on the whole family of instigating forces to achieve success and, thus, does not change the *ratio* of forces normally favoring choices with probability of success equal to 0.50. It was argued then that the conventional assumption in research that achievement-oriented activities are overdetermined, that is, are motivated by compound action tendencies, implies that the ratio of total instigating forces ($F_{Tot} = F_{Succ} + F_{Ext}$), favoring the choice of the moderate risk alternatives for all individuals, would always be greater for a strong motive than for a weak motive if the extrinsic instigating force to undertake various alternatives is equal for the two motive strengths. This conclusion was drawn because the addition of a constant to each force in the ratio produces less change in the ratio with the larger original magnitudes.

So much for the interpretation of the fact that persons described as strong in the motive to achieve success show the greater preference for moderately difficult tasks. What about the additional fact that individuals described as strong in motive to avoid failure in terms of their scores on anxiety scales display weakened preferences for moderately difficult tasks?

According to the current theory of achievement motivation, the motive to avoid failure has a multiplicative influence on the magnitude of forces to resist actions that might lead to failure. Furthermore, it is a consequence of the assumptions of that theory that the ratio of inhibitory forces stemming from anticipated failure at different tasks equals the ratio of instigating forces to achieve the anticipated success. This means that the ratio of the magnitudes of the inhibitory forces to avoid failure in two activities will always exceed the ratio of the *total* magnitude of the instigating forces for the two activities when each of the latter, as already assumed, is a composite of F_{Succ} plus a constant F_{Ext}. Here, we have an instance of $\hat{I}_X/\hat{I}_Y > \hat{F}_X/\hat{F}_Y$ implying less likelihood of choice of the activity motivated by the stronger instigating force (in this case, a moderately difficult task) among a number of individuals on a single occasion.

Repeated Observations from a Single Individual on the Same Occasion. As we consider the question of choice between two alternatives when the data are obtained by repeated choices of a single individual on one occasion, let us recall the method of analysis and the conclusions reached in Chapter 4 for the case of no resistance. In our derivation we traced the course of the separate tendencies T_X and T_Y from the onset of the stimuli producing the instigating forces for the two alternatives on the first trial to the point of decision favoring one or the other, through the period in which activity X or Y was occurring, then through the interval between trials in which neither activity nor the stimuli for either was present, then again through the interval in which the stimuli for both were once more presented to the second choice, and so on. Now we pursue a similar analysis, but this time we focus on the question of what happens to the strength of $\bar{T}_X$ and $\bar{T}_Y$, the resultant tendencies that are actually involved in the competition for expression in behavior. To do this, we track separately the growth and the decline in strength of the two components of each, namely, T_X and N_X, T_Y and N_Y.

Our earlier conclusion was the following:

$$\frac{\text{Total choice of } X}{\text{Total choice of } Y} = \frac{n(X)}{n(Y)} = \left(\frac{\hat{F}_X}{\hat{F}_Y}\right)\left[\frac{(_gY)_c}{(_gX)_c}\right]$$

Here, once again, we had discovered a *weak ratio rule of choice*: namely, that preference depends on the ratio of the magnitudes of the instigating forces and not on the difference in their magnitude. We also identified conditions under which a *strong ratio rule of choice* would hold true: the ratio of the total choice of X to Y would equal the ratio of the magnitudes of the instigating forces. The latter would be expected when the inertial gap at the end of the consummatory lag following a choice of Y, that is, $(_gY)_c$, was equal to its counterpart $(_gX)_c$, following a choice of X. The conditions under which this might occur would be ones in which activities X and Y were very similar and in which there was no differential knowledge of results. In this case, the parameters uniquely responsible for the level of $(T_X)_c$, namely, c_X and $(t_c)_X$, would be equal to their counterparts for $(T_Y)_c$, that is, c_Y and $(t_c)_Y$.

We might anticipate that our present analysis will produce a similar result, perhaps that

$$\frac{\text{Total choice of } X}{\text{Total choice of } Y} = \frac{n(X)}{n(Y)} = \left(\frac{\hat{F}_X}{\hat{F}_Y}\right)\left[\frac{(_g\bar{Y})_c}{(_g\bar{X})_c}\right]$$

but we must examine carefully the dynamics of a trial keeping alert to the nuances of the theory concerning the dynamics of resistance in this kind of choice situation. We present the derivation with only enough detail to allow an appreciation of the conditions that are assumed and to convey a general understanding of how the final equation is achieved. The detailed derivation is given in the mathematical notes at the end of the chapter.

Conveniently, we proceed by referring to Figure 9.3 which displays the changes in the strength of the various tendencies within a trial for the particular situation under analysis. Figure 9.3 corresponds to Figure 4.7 and is based on the same set of assumed conditions for action tendencies. The

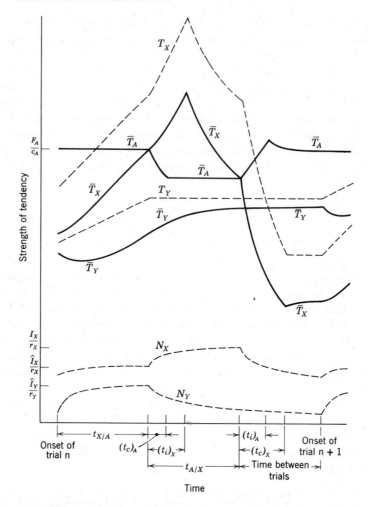

FIGURE 9.3   The details of the changes in the strengths of action and negation tendencies within a trial for a simple idealized two-choice problem.

new figure, however, also includes the changes in negation and resultant action tendencies.

The conditions assumed in Figure 9.3 and for the derivation are as follows:

1. Trials are discrete and sufficiently well-spaced so that the strength of the tendency for the activity preceding the choice of X or Y can legitimately be approximated by its asymptotic value, that is, $T_A = F_A/c_A$, at the beginning of each trial.

2. The sequence of exposure to stimuli is such that: (a) the forces F_A, $\hat{F}_X$, $\hat{F}_Y$, $\hat{I}_X$, and $\hat{I}_Y$ are present when activity A is occurring following the onset of a trial; (b) only the forces F_X and I_X are present (that is, F_A, $\hat{F}_Y$, and $\hat{I}_Y$ each equal zero) following a change to activity X, one of the two alternatives; and (c) only the force F_A is present (that is, $\hat{F}_X$, $\hat{I}_X$, $\hat{F}_Y$, and $\hat{I}_Y$ each equal zero) during the interval subsequent to the resumption of activity A and prior to the onset of the next trial (the time between trials). These three time intervals ($t_{X/A}$, $t_{A/X}$ and the time between trials) with their instigating and inhibitory forces are shown in Table 9.2.[5] Also shown in Table 9.2 is a brief summary of what is happening to the strength of each action, negaction, and resultant tendency within the interval from the beginning of one trial to the next. This portion of Table 9.2 captures the dynamics of a trial under the assumed conditions. We refer to certain of these statements as we proceed with our analysis in conjunction with Figure 9.3.

A comment about activity A and an assumption about the negaction tendencies for the two alternatives X and Y are in order. For the purposes of this analysis, it does not matter whether $\bar{T}_A$, the resultant tendency for the initial and between trial activity, includes an inhibitory component or whether it is based only on T_A, since the asymptotic value of $\bar{T}_A$ is F_A/c_A in either case. Figure 9.3 is drawn as if $N_A = 0$ throughout for simplicity, but Table 9.2 includes I_A in parentheses to show when it would appear under the presently assumed conditions.

The assumption we make concerning the negaction tendencies is that N_{X_F} and N_{Y_F}, the values of N_X and N_Y when a choice occurs, can be approximated by their asymptotic values, $\hat{I}_X/r_X$ and $\hat{I}_Y/r_Y$, respectively, on each trial. This is equivalent to assuming that on any trial, $t_{X/A}$ or $t_{Y/A}$, the time to make a choice of X or Y, is of sufficient duration to allow both N_X and N_Y to approach the limit of their growth. This assumption simplifies the derivation greatly. It is the familiar assumption introduced with Equations 9.4 and 9.5 earlier in the chapter.

[5] An example of the kind of experimental arrangement that corresponds to the conditions assumed in Table 9.2 is to be found in the bead experiment discussed in Chapter 6. When a trial begins, the subject who is seated in front of the apparatus has two alternative containers of beads presented to him. He sees both containers, stimuli that produce $\hat{F}_X$, $\hat{I}_X$, $\hat{F}_Y$, and $\hat{I}_Y$, and the apparatus which, because he is engaged in the choice point activity A, provides F_A. When activity X supplants activity A, that is, when the subject orients himself toward container X, reaches in, takes out a bead and replaces it in the return slot, selective attention operates to confine exposure to F_X and I_X. Finally, when activity A takes over again, the subject sits quietly in front of the apparatus engaged in the choice-point activity with no stimuli for activities X and Y because the next trial has not yet begun. This means that only F_A is operative. With the onset of the next trial, two containers of beads are again presented and the sequence of stimulus exposure is repeated. Of course, if activity shifts from A to Y instead of from A to X, the forces during the middle time period are F_Y and I_Y instead of F_X and I_X.

TABLE 9.2 Summary of the Changing Forces and Tendencies Throughout the Time Interval from the Onset of One Trial to the Onset of the Next as Assumed to Hold True for the Derivation of Proportion of Choices (See Figure 9.3)

	Onset of Trial n ↓ $t_{X/A}$	End of Trial n ↓ $t_{A/X}$	Onset of Trial $n+1$ ↓ Time Between Trials
ONGOING ACTIVITY:	CHOICE POINT ACTIVITY A	ALTERNATIVE ACTIVITY X	CHOICE POINT ACTIVITY A
Forces Present:	$F_A, (I_A), \hat{F}_X,$ $\hat{I}_X, \hat{F}_Y, \hat{I}_Y$	F_X, I_X	$F_A, (I_A)$
Paths of: T_X	Grows linearly with slope $\hat{F}_X$	Initiation consummatory lag; then approach to asymptote $\dfrac{F_X}{c_X} + \dfrac{I_X}{r_X}$	Decreases during cessation consummatory lag; then remains constant
N_X	Rises to asymptote $\dfrac{\hat{I}_X}{r_X}$	Rises to asymptote $\dfrac{I_X}{r_X}$	Approaches asymptote of zero
$\bar{T}_X$	Grows with positive acceleration	Rises; then approaches asymptote $\dfrac{F_X}{c_X}$	Falls during cessation consummatory lag; then grows with negative acceleration toward T_X as N_X is dissipated
T_Y	Grows linearly with slope $\hat{F}_Y$	Remains constant	Remains constant
N_Y	Rises to asymptote $\dfrac{\hat{I}_Y}{r_Y}$	Approaches asymptote of zero	Continues approach to asymptote of zero
$\bar{T}_Y$	Declines initially; grows with positive acceleration	Grows with negative acceleration toward T_Y	Continues negative accelerated growth toward T_Y
$\bar{T}_A$	Approaches to asymptote $\dfrac{F_A}{c_A}$	Decreases during cessation consummatory lag; then remains constant	Increases during initiation consummatory lag; then approaches asymptote, $\dfrac{F_A}{c_A}$

The conditions that we have specified and this assumption concerning the negation tendencies permit us to use Equation 9.5 as the basic equation in our analysis. By rewriting Equation 9.5 in terms of activities A, X, and Y, we can obtain

$$(t_{X/A})' = \frac{F_A/c_A - T_{X_I} + \hat{I}_X/r_X}{\hat{F}_X} = \frac{_g\bar{X}}{\hat{F}_X} \tag{9.6}$$

and

$$(t_{Y/A})' = \frac{F_A/c_A - T_{Y_I} + \hat{I}_Y/r_Y}{\hat{F}_Y} = \frac{_g\bar{Y}}{\hat{F}_Y} \tag{9.7}$$

In these two equations, only T_{X_I} and T_{Y_I} can change from one trial to the next. This conclusion can be drawn from the entries in Table 9.2—specifically, from the statements that in the first time interval, $t_{X/A}$, N_X and N_Y approach their respective asymptotes, $\hat{I}_X/r_X$ and $\hat{I}_Y/r_Y$, and that in the last time interval, the time between trials, $\bar{T}_A$ approaches its asymptote F_A/c_A. Thus, the central task in carrying out the derivation is to calculate the successive values of T_{X_I} and T_{Y_I} over repeated trials. The details of this analysis can be found in the mathematical notes at the end of the chapter. What follows is a synopsis.

On Trial 1 alternative X will be chosen unless $(t_{X/A})'_1 > (t_{Y/A})'_1$. With $(t_{X/A})'$ and $(t_{Y/A})'$ given by Equations 9.6 and 9.7, it follows that X will be chosen unless $_g\bar{X}/_g\bar{Y} > \hat{F}_X/\hat{F}_Y$. This, of course, is the same equation as the one given in the previous section where choice on the first or only trial was the matter of central interest. Let us assume that alternative X is chosen, as shown in Figure 9.3, so that we know $_g\bar{X}/_g\bar{Y} \leq \hat{F}_X/\hat{F}_Y$ initially and that the latency (or decision time) of the first trial is $(t_{X/A})_1$. We also assume, as in Figure 9.3, that $F_X > F_Y$, $\hat{F}_X > \hat{F}_Y$, and $\hat{F}_X/\hat{F}_Y = F_X/F_Y$; and that $I_X > I_Y$, $\hat{I}_X > \hat{I}_Y$, and $\hat{I}_X/\hat{I}_Y = I_X/I_Y$. We can refer to Figure 9.3 to determine what happens to the strength of all tendencies during a trial on which X was chosen, but given the conditions we have assumed, we need only be concerned about the strength of T_X and T_Y.

Consider the path of T_X first. Since $\bar{T}_X = \bar{T}_A$ when X is selected, we know that $\bar{T}_X$ must equal F_A/c_A, the strength of $\bar{T}_A$, at this time. Furthermore, T_X must equal $F_A/c_A + \hat{I}_X/r_X$ at this point because the negation tendency N_X has been assumed equal to $\hat{I}_X/r_X$ at the time of the choice. As may be seen in Figure 9.3, when activity X has run its course and there is a shift back to activity A, the strength of $\bar{T}_X$ again equals the strength of $\bar{T}_A$, but now $\bar{T}_A = (F_A/c_A)[e^{-c_A \cdot (t_c)_A}]$. This is the level to which $\bar{T}_A$ has fallen during its cessation consummatory lag $(t_c)_A$, following the choice of X. Therefore, the strength of T_X at this point in time when activity A resumes is known to be

$$\left(\frac{F_A}{c_A}\right)[e^{-c_A \cdot (t_c)_A}] + \frac{I_X}{r_X}$$

where I_X/r_X is the new and higher asymptotic level to which N_X has increased because of a more systematic exposure (selective attention) to I_X while activity X is ongoing.

When activity A is resumed, T_X decreases in strength during the interval of the cessation consummatory lag $(t_c)_X$, its path determined by the conditions of Case 1a (see Chapter 7) and Equation 7.11. Following the interval of the cessation consummatory lag, the strength of T_X remains constant until the beginning of the next trial.

Despite the several complexities in the path of T_X, and of the sequence of effects on T_X throughout a trial on which X is the alternative selected, one simple and very important property of T_X emerges. *The strength of the inertial tendency for activity X is the same at the beginning of every new trial that follows a trial on which alternative X has been chosen.* Furthermore, this strength is known in the sense that it can be specified in terms of the parameters of the situation. In Chapter 4, where resistance is not a consideration, we referred to the level of T_X at the end of the cessation consummatory lag as $(T_X)_c$ to distinguish it from T_{X_I}, the inertial strength of T_X on the very first trial or on very widely spaced trials. We proceed in a similar way now and use the symbol $(T_X)_c^r$, to refer to the level of T_X at the end of the cessation consummatory lag when resistance must be taken into account. The two values, $(T_X)_c$ and $(T_X)_c^r$, are not the same except under certain special conditions, a point that will have particular significance later in this section when we explore some of the effects of resistance on choice.

Consider now the path of T_Y on a trial when alternative X is chosen. The path of T_Y is considerably simpler than that of T_X. It begins with an initial strength, T_{Y_I}, and grows linearly with slope F_Y for a time $(t_{X/A})_1$, after which it remains constant until the next trial. Since $(t_{X/A})_1$ can be expressed in terms of the parameters of the theory by Equation 9.6, the value of T_Y for any trial following a trial on which X is chosen is known in these terms.

In summary, this analysis of the paths of T_X and T_Y over the duration of a trial on which alternative X is chosen shows that for the next trial both T_X and T_Y can be written as functions of the parameters of the theory, parameters that are assumed to remain constant throughout the period in which choice data is collected. It is easily seen that over a set of successive choices of alternative X, $(T_X)_c^r$ is the same on each successive trial but the inertial strength of T_Y is at a higher level each time. This means that the resultant inertial gap for X, $(_g\bar{X})_c = F_A/c_A - (T_X)_c^r + \hat{I}_X/r_X$ remains constant but that the resultant inertial gap for Y is diminishing and, therefore, that the ratio of these inertial gaps $(_g\bar{X})_c/_g\bar{Y}$ is increasing with each successive trial. As trials continue, a point will be reached where the accumulated inertial strength of T_Y, repeatedly instigated but not expressed, is sufficient to produce the condition $(_g\bar{X})_c/_g\bar{Y} > \hat{F}_X/\hat{F}_Y$, and Y will be chosen for the first time.

The analysis of changes in the strength of T_Y and T_X following the initial choice of Y yields a similar conclusion: that *the strength of the inertial tendency for activity Y is the same at the beginning of every new trial that follows a trial on which alternative Y has been chosen.* This is the strength of T_Y at the end of its cessation consummatory lag, that is, $(T_Y)_c^r$.

As already described fully in Chapter 4, the important implication of finding that a tendency should always fall to the same level following a choice of the alternative supported by that tendency is that there emerges a single value $(t_{X/A})_x^r$, representing the theoretical latency of X on any trial immediately following a choice of X, and a single value $(t_{Y/A})_y^r$, representing the theoretical latency of Y on any trial immediately following a choice of Y. By theoretical latency, we mean the latency that would obtain if that alternative were to be chosen. By using these theoretical latencies, it is possible to write an expression for the number of successive trials on which X will be chosen prior to the first or next Y and another expression for the number of successive trials on which Y will be chosen before a return to X, and so on. From this analysis, a more general one than in Chapter 4, since it includes the effects of resistance, we derive the following conclusion concerning the frequency of choice of X and the frequency of choice of Y in an infinitely long series of trials:

$$\frac{\text{Total choice of } X}{\text{Total choice of } Y} = \frac{n(X)}{n(Y)} = \frac{(t_{Y/A})_y^r}{(t_{X/A})_x^r} = \frac{\hat{F}_X[F_A/c_A - (T_Y)_c^r + \hat{I}_Y/r_Y]}{\hat{F}_Y[F_A/c_A - (T_X)_c^r + \hat{I}_X/r_X]}$$

$$= \left(\frac{\hat{F}_X}{\hat{F}_Y}\right)\left[\frac{(_g\bar{Y})_c}{(_g\bar{X})_c}\right] \qquad (9.8)$$

Again, we recover *the weak ratio rule of choice* and the basic reciprocal relationship of instigating force and inertial gap (this time the inertial gap between resultant tendencies), as in Chapter 4.

Since the proportion of choices of X is given by $n(X)/[n(X) + n(Y)]$, we obtain by substitution:

$$\text{Proportion choice of } X = p(X) = \frac{(t_{Y/A})_y^r}{(t_{Y/A})_y^r + (t_{X/A})_x^r}$$

$$= \frac{\hat{F}_X \cdot (_g\bar{Y})_c}{\hat{F}_X \cdot (_g\bar{Y})_c + \hat{F}_Y \cdot (_g\bar{X})_c} \qquad (9.9)$$

It is clear from Equation 9.8 and Equation 9.9 that an increase in the magnitude of F_X relative to F_Y, or any change that serves to increase $(_g\bar{Y})_c$ relative to $(_g\bar{X})_c$, will increase the choice of activity X.

Having arrived at these preliminary generalizations concerning repeated choices from the same individual, we are in position to ask whether or not resistance makes any difference. How, if at all, does choice behavior with resistance differ from what we otherwise would have observed if I_X and I_Y had been absent, as in the earlier treatment of the problem in Chapter 4?

As can be seen in Equation 9.8, all the effects of resistance are contained in the inertial gaps. Hence, the question of critical interest becomes: How do the inertial gaps with resistance differ, if at all, from those obtained without resistance but under comparable conditions of instigation? We discuss this question in terms of activity X only, since all statements made about activity X hold true equally well for activity Y.

The formal derivation in the notes at the end of the chapter spells out what can be gleaned from a glance at Equation 9.8 and from careful scrutiny of Figure 9.3. *Inhibitory force affects the size of the inertial gap in two distinct ways.* First, as already pointed out in the analysis of single choices from many people, the growth of N_X to its asymptotic level $\hat{I}_X/r_X$, before the choice occurs, has an effect equivalent to an increase in the size of the inertial gap over what it would have been had no resistance been involved. That is, $_g\bar{X} = F_A/c_A - (T_{X_I} - \hat{I}_X/r_X) = _gX + \hat{I}_X/r_X$. Second, as pointed out above, N_X influences the strength of the action tendency for activity X at the end of the cessation consummatory lag on a trial in which X is chosen, leading us to distinguish $(T_X)_c^r$ from $(T_X)_c$. For the same reason, we must write

$$(_g\bar{X})_c = \frac{F_A}{c_A} - \left[(T_X)_c^r - \frac{\hat{I}_X}{r_X}\right] = (_gX)_c^r + \frac{\hat{I}_X}{r_X}$$

for the resultant inertial gap. We look more closely at this second function of resistance, for it leads to a useful summary statement about the systematic effects of inhibitory force for this kind of choice behavior.

Detailed analysis (see Mathematical Notes p. 312) tells us that the strength of an action tendency at the end of the cessation consummatory lag can be separated into two components: $(T_X)_c^r = (T_X)_c + (I_X/r_X) \cdot k_X$. The first component, $(T_X)_c$, is familiar from earlier discussions as the strength of the action tendency at the end of the cessation consummatory lag when there is no resistance present. The second term, $(I_X/r_X) \cdot k_X$, where k_X[6] has a value

[6]
$$k_X = \frac{c_X \cdot e^{-r_X \cdot (t_c)_X} - r_X \cdot e^{-c_X \cdot (t_c)_X}}{c_X - r_X}$$

See the mathematical notes at the end of the chapter for details about k_X and k_Y and their role in choice.

between 0 and 1, specifies the amount of "extra" T_X in $(T_X)_c^r$. The reason that $(T_X)_c^r$ exceeds $(T_X)_c$ is that N_X, in opposing T_X, protects a portion of T_X from being expressed during the interval when activity X is occurring and during the cessation consummatory lag that follows. As can be seen in Figure 9.3, N_X is present throughout and even beyond the cessation consummatory lag for activity X.

By using the relationships $(T_X)_c^r = (T_X)_c + (I_X/r_X) \cdot k_X$ and $(T_Y)_c^r = (T_Y)_c + (I_Y/r_Y) \cdot k_Y$, Equation 9.8 can be rewritten as

$$\frac{n(X)}{n(Y)} = \frac{\hat{F}_X\{[F_A/c_A - (T_Y)_c] + [\hat{I}_Y/r_Y - (I_Y/r_Y) \cdot k_Y]\}}{\hat{F}_Y\{[F_A/c_A - (T_X)_c] + [\hat{I}_X/r_X - (I_X/r_X) \cdot k_X]\}}$$

Furthermore, since $(_gX)_c = F_A/c_A - (T_X)_c$ and $(_gY)_c = F_A/c_A - (T_Y)_c$, we have

$$\frac{n(X)}{n(Y)} = \frac{\hat{F}_X\{(_gY)_c + [\hat{I}_Y/r_Y - (I_Y/r_Y) \cdot k_Y]\}}{\hat{F}_Y\{(_gX)_c + [\hat{I}_X/r_X - (I_X/r_X) \cdot k_X]\}} \tag{9.10}$$

The advantage of Equation 9.10 over Equation 9.8 for our purposes is that Equation 9.10 can be compared directly with Equation 4.11 which, appropriate for conditions of no resistance, states that $n(X)/n(Y) = (\hat{F}_X/\hat{F}_Y) \times [(_gY)_c/(_gX)_c]$. Clearly, the only difference between Equations 4.11 and 9.10 is that a factor dependent on resistance is added to the numerator and the denominator in Equation 9.10.

These factors, $[\hat{I}_Y/r_Y - (I_Y/r_Y) \cdot k_Y]$ in the numerator and $[\hat{I}_X/r_X - (I_X/r_X) \cdot k_X]$ in the denominator, are somewhat complex in their effects, however, since both can be either positive or negative. If both factors are positive, it means that the suppressive effect of resistance is predominant for both alternatives, adding to the inertial gaps to be overcome. A negative value for either factor means that resistance is facilitating the choice of that alternative by reducing the inertial gap. At this point, we proceed with the case in which resistance is acting to suppress the choice of each alternative, the property more commonly ascribed to inhibition. In the notes at the end of the chapter we undertake a more complete analysis of the effects of resistance on choice and consider the paradoxical, facilitative effects as well as the ones that are suppressive.

The case we deal with now is the one in which both $[\hat{I}_X/r_X - (I_X/r_X) \cdot k_X]$ and $[\hat{I}_Y/r_Y - (I_Y/r_Y) \cdot k_Y]$ are positive, and we wish to know what difference it makes in the choices of X and Y that these resistance factors are present. We can proceed most easily by asking when resistance makes *no* difference. The answer to this question is that the choices of X and Y are not affected by resistance if the ratio of $[\hat{I}_Y/r_Y - (I_Y/r_Y) \cdot k_Y]$ to $[\hat{I}_X/r_X - (I_X/r_X) \cdot k_X]$ is the same as the ratio of $(_gY)_c$ to $(_gX)_c$. (See the notes at the end of the chapter for the justification of this statement.)

Although there is nothing especially interesting about the condition per se under which resistance is irrelevant to choice, it provides the reference point for discovering conditions that do affect the choices. A comparison of Equations 4.11 and 9.10 shows rather directly that, *if the ratio of* $[\hat{I}_Y/r_Y - (I_Y/r_Y) \cdot k_Y]$ *to* $[\hat{I}_X/r_X - (I_X/r_X) \cdot k_X]$ *is larger than the ratio of* $(_gY)_c$ *to* $(_gX)_c$, $n(X)/n(Y)$ *will be increased whereas, if the first ratio is smaller than the second*, $n(X)/n(Y)$ *will be decreased*.

Notice that the strong ratio rule, $n(X)/n(Y) = \hat{F}_X/\hat{F}_Y$, derived in Chapter 4 for the case of no resistance, continues to hold true when the implications of the assumed conditions are extended to resistance. The requisite condition is that no differential knowledge of results be provided for the two alternatives. This permits the assumptions $c_X = c_Y$ and $(t_c)_X = (t_c)_Y$. If we go on to assume that the conditions of resistance are equal for the two alternatives, either because resistance is specified as equal or because no mention of negative outcomes is made, it also follows that $r_X = r_Y$, $I_X = I_Y$ and that $\hat{I}_X/\hat{I}_Y = I_X/I_Y$. If activities X and Y have this set of comparable parameter values, $(_gY)_c = (_gX)_c$ and $k_Y = k_X$; these equalities in combination with $I_Y = I_X$ and $\hat{I}_Y = \hat{I}_X$ make $n(X)/n(Y) = (\hat{F}_X/\hat{F}_Y)$, according to Equation 9.10.

In Chapter 6, an experiment that used containers of beads was cited as employing the kind of method that approximates the conditions required for the strong ratio rule to hold true. It is now clear from the derivation just completed that the propriety of analyzing the data from that experiment on the basis of the strong ratio rule requires not a complete absence of inhibition for the alternatives but only that inhibition, if present, is not differential.

We can go one step further in our inquiry and ask how (in terms of Equation 9.10) choice would be affected by multiplying all inhibitory forces by a constant. This is related to the hypothesis advanced in the theory of achievement motivation that the inhibitory force to avoid failure is a multiplicative function of the motive to avoid failure. Data on this point are that individuals high in the motive to avoid failure prefer tasks of intermediate difficulty to very easy or very difficult tasks less often than individuals low in the motive to avoid failure. This finding suggests that the effect of multiplying the inhibitory forces by the same constant should be to reduce the choice of the alternative with the stronger instigating force. By using Equation 9.10, we can phrase this conjecture as follows: Is

$$\frac{\hat{F}_X\{(_gY)_c + M \cdot [\hat{I}_Y/r_Y - (I_Y/r_Y) \cdot k_Y]\}}{\hat{F}_Y\{(_gX)_c + M \cdot [\hat{I}_X/r_X - (I_X/r_X) \cdot k_X]\}}$$

$$< \frac{\hat{F}_X\{(_gY)_c + [\hat{I}_Y/r_Y - (I_Y/r_Y) \cdot k_Y]\}}{\hat{F}_Y\{(_gX)_c + [\hat{I}_X/r_X - (I_X/r_X) \cdot k_X]\}} \, ?$$

The answer to this query is a conditional yes. For the above inequality to hold true, it is necessary to have

$$\frac{[\hat{I}_Y/r_Y - (I_Y/r_Y) \cdot k_Y]}{[\hat{I}_X/r_X - (I_X/r_X) \cdot k_X]} < \frac{({}_gY)_c}{({}_gX)_c}$$

If we assume the same conditions as we assumed previously, making $k_Y = k_X$, $({}_gY)_c = ({}_gX)_c$, and $\hat{I}_X/\hat{I}_Y = I_X/I_Y$, the inequality will be satisfied if $I_X > I_Y$. This last condition, that $I_X > I_Y$, corresponds directly to the hypothesis formulated in the theory of achievement motivation that *both* the instigation to achieve success and the resistance to possible failure are stronger for tasks of intermediate difficulty than for either very easy or very difficult tasks. Although the conditions of the experiments alluded to earlier may not match exactly the ones that we have assumed for our derivation, the data, perhaps, illustrate the predicted relationship.

So much for the problem of repeated choices from the same individual. The role of resistance in choice is complicated. Equations 9.8, 9.9, and 9.10, which emphasize the reciprocal relationship of instigating force and inertial gap for the resultant tendencies, provide useful generalizations. But the complex influence of resistance on the size of inertial gap is, as we have observed, a topic deserving intensive study.

EFFECT OF RESISTANCE ON THE OPERANT LEVEL OF AN ACTIVITY

In Chapter 4, we undertook to show how measures taken from the molar stream of behavior, such as the operant level of an activity and the time spent in an activity, could be derived from the principle of change of activity. The theoretical treatment was confined to the restricted case of alternation back and forth between two different activities X and Y, both instigated by a constant environment that produced neither inhibitory force nor resistance to either activity. Now we return to these measures in order to include the effect of resistance. As before, we shall confine the analysis to the simple situation with only two activities because we have yet to achieve a more general solution. No doubt some of the conclusions drawn for the case of two alternative activities will need to be modified when more activities are involved. Nevertheless, we stand to learn something of the nature of the influence of resistance to one or both activities by examining this simple case.

We begin by recalling that the measure—rate of response—is defined as the number of responses observed divided by the duration of the interval over which the observations are made; that is, $r(X) = n(X)/$Total Time. In addition, however, $n(X)$ is given by the total time of observation divided by the time between successive initiations of the response. For the condition we are dealing with this time is $t_{X/Y} + t_{Y/X}$ where each latency is a constant from cycle to cycle. Thus, we can substitute $n(X) = \text{Total Time}/(t_{X/Y} + t_{Y/X})$ into the expression for rate and obtain $r(X) = 1/(t_{X/Y} + t_{Y/X})$.

First, it is important to observe that this expression for rate depends only on the constancy of $t_{X/Y}$ and $t_{Y/X}$ from cycle to cycle not on whether resistance is involved in their determination. If it can be shown that these latencies remain constant over cycles when resistance is present [let us designate them $(t_{X/Y})^r$ and $(t_{Y/X})^r$ to mark the fact that resistance is a factor], the equation $r(X) = 1/[(t_{X/Y})^r + (t_{Y/X})^r]$ will be applicable. Our first task, therefore, is to establish the constancy of $(t_{X/Y})^r$ and $(t_{Y/X})^r$ from one cycle to the next for the conditions we have assumed. Having done this, our next task will be to compare the magnitudes of $(t_{X/Y})^r$ and $(t_{Y/X})^r$ to those of $t_{X/Y}$ and $t_{Y/X}$ to discover the effects of resistance on the rate of response.

In Chapter 4, when we considered $r(X)$ for the case of no resistance, we assumed that activities X and Y belong to different families to eliminate the complexities imposed by displacement and substitution. We also assumed sufficiently long latencies for activities X and Y so that the final strength of the action tendency sustaining the ongoing activity could be approximated by its asymptotic value. In undertaking the analysis with resistance included, we continue with the first assumption and extend the second by assuming that the final strengths of both negation tendencies can also be approximated by their asymptotic values. Figure 9.4 illustrates these assumptions by showing the course of each of the tendencies, action, negation, and resultant, throughout the period of one cycle, beginning when activity Y has just supplanted activity X and ending when Y is once more ready to take over.

It is apparent from Figure 9.4 that $(t_{X/Y})^r$ and $(t_{Y/X})^r$ are the same from cycle to cycle, but we shall profit from a more detailed analysis, one that starts with our Principle of Change of Activity and carries through to expressions for $(t_{X/Y})^r$ and $(t_{Y/X})^r$ that can be compared to their counterparts, $t_{X/Y}$ and $t_{Y/X}$.

Consider the point in time when activity Y, the ongoing activity at the beginning of the cycle plotted in Figure 9.4, gives way to activity X. The Principle of Change of Activity states that at this point in time $\bar{T}_{X_F} = \bar{T}_{Y_F}$ or $T_{X_F} - N_{X_F} = T_{Y_F} - N_{Y_F}$. By making use of our assumption that N_{X_F}, T_{Y_F} and N_{Y_F} have each had an opportunity to approach its asymptote, this equation can be rewritten as

$$T_{X_F} - \frac{\hat{I}_X}{r_X} = \left(\frac{F_Y}{c_Y} + \frac{I_Y}{r_Y}\right) - \frac{I_Y}{r_Y}$$

This, in turn, simplifies to $T_{X_F} = F_Y/c_Y + \hat{I}_X/r_X$. We have other information about T_{X_F}, namely, $\bar{T}_{X_F} = (T_X)^r_c + \hat{F}_X[(t_{X/Y})^r - (t_c)_X]$. That

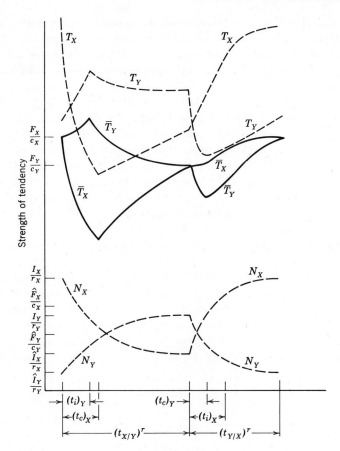

FIGURE 9.4   The details of the changes in strengths of action and negation tendencies in a free operant situation.

is, we know that T_X reaches a value $(T_X)_c^r$ at the conclusion of its cessation consummatory lag and then grows linearly with slope $\hat{F}_X$ over the remainder of the time interval that ends with the initiation of activity X. Since the cessation consummatory lag takes time $(t_c)_X$, the time during which T_X grows linearly to its final value, T_{X_F}, is $(t_{X/Y})^r - (t_c)_X$.

By substituting this expression for T_{X_F} in the equation derived from the Principle of Change of Activity, we obtain $(T_X)_c^r + \hat{F}_X[(t_{X/Y})^r - (t_c)_X] = F_Y/c_Y + \hat{I}_X/r_X$, which can be rearranged to yield

$$(t_{X/Y})^r = \frac{F_Y/c_Y + \hat{I}_X/r_X - (T_X)_c^r}{\hat{F}_X} + (t_c)_X \qquad (9.11)$$

Clearly, $(t_{X/Y})^r$ will be a constant from one occasion to the next if all the terms on the right side of Equation 9.11 are constants, and an examination shows that only $(T_X)_c^r$ is questionable in this regard. Thus, we must look further at $(T_X)_c^r$, the value of T_X at the conclusion of the cessation consummatory lag.

To do this, we note that the cessation consummatory lag begins with T_X at a level given by $F_X/c_X + I_X/r_X$, and during the lag interval T_X remains in Case 1a (see Chapter 7). The equation describing the course of T_X during its cessation consummatory lag comes from Equation 7.11 and takes the form $(T_X)_c^r = (T_X)_c + \hat{I}_X/r_X + (I_X/r_X - \hat{I}_X/r_X) \cdot k_X$ after simplification.[7] Since all the terms on the right side of this equation are constants, $(T_X)_c^r$ must also be a constant. From this we know that $(t_{X/Y})^r$ is constant from one cycle to the next. The same argument can be applied to $(t_{Y/X})^r$ to show its constancy over cycles.

Thus, we have completed our first task, and by so doing have established that $r(X) = 1/[(t_{X/Y})^r + (t_{Y/X})^r]$ is the appropriate equation for rate of response when resistance is involved. Our next task is to investigate what difference, if any, the presence of resistance makes on the rate of response. This requires that the magnitudes of $(t_{X/Y})^r$ and $(t_{Y/X})^r$ be compared to those of $t_{X/Y}$ and $t_{Y/X}$. Once again, it is only necessary that one of the pairs be analyzed since the outcome applies to the other pair as well.

Equation 9.11 for $(t_{X/Y})^r$ and 4.7 for $t_{X/Y}$ are suitable for comparison. They are

$$(t_{X/Y})^r = \frac{F_Y/c_Y + \hat{I}_X/r_X - (T_X)_c^r}{\hat{F}_X} + (t_c)_X$$

and

$$t_{X/Y} = \frac{F_Y/c_Y - (T_X)_c}{\hat{F}_X} + (t_c)_X$$

We have already seen, however, that

$$(T_X)_c^r = (T_X)_c + \frac{\hat{I}_X}{r_X} + \left(\frac{I_X}{r_X} - \frac{\hat{I}_X}{r_X}\right) \cdot k_X$$

[7] It is helpful to recall in arriving at this simplification that

$$(T_X)_c = \left(\frac{F_X}{c_X}\right) \cdot e^{-c_X \cdot (t_c)_X} + \frac{\hat{F}_X}{c_X}[1 - e^{-c_X \cdot (t_c)_X}]$$

Equation 4.5, and

$$k_X = \left[\frac{c_X \cdot e^{-r_X \cdot (t_c)_X} - r_X \cdot e^{-c_X \cdot (t_c)_X}}{c_X - r_X}\right]$$

(see footnote 6).

so that we can rewrite Equation 9.11 as

$$(t_X/Y)^r = \frac{F_Y/c_Y - (T_X)_c - (I_X/r_X - \hat{I}_X/r_X) \cdot k_X}{\hat{F}_X} + (t_c)_X$$

Put into this form it is apparent that $(t_{X/Y})^r$ and $t_{X/Y}$ differ only in the term $(I_X/r_X - \hat{I}_X/r_X) \cdot k_X$ which cannot be negative and, in fact, except under very special circumstances, must be positive. Since $(I_X/r_X - \hat{I}_X/r_X) \cdot k_X$ enters subtractively in the expression for $(t_{X/Y})^r$, our conclusion is that $(t_{X/Y})^r \le t_{X/Y}$. More precisely, $t_{X/Y}$ is greater than $(t_{X/Y})^r$ by an amount equal to

$$\frac{(I_X/r_X - \hat{I}_X/r_X) \cdot k_X}{\hat{F}_X}$$

With shorter latencies predicted for activities X and Y with resistance than without it, the rate of response should be higher with resistance than without it. When this phenomenon of enhanced rate of activity occurs, if it does, it is because the negaction tendency has allowed the action tendency to build up extra strength once it is initiated and this extra strength is then only partially released for expression and reduction during the cessation consummatory lag. After the interval of the lag, when the consummatory force is no longer operative on the action tendency, the continued decline of the negaction tendency, because of continued expression in resistance, releases still more of the action tendency to the resultant tendency. The latter, which is already growing as a consequence of exposure to instigating force, is thus given an additional boost in strength as the resistance declines. This boost reduces the time required for the subsequent change in activity. This will happen, however, only to the degree that the negaction tendency continues to decrease in strength after the interval of the cessation consummatory lag. If the lag itself were long enough for the negaction tendency to have already dropped very substantially and almost to its asymptote within the lag, the implied phenomenon of enhanced rate would be minimal and probably negligible. Put another way, it is only for activities that have relatively short cessation consummatory lags that the paradoxical conclusion should hold true.

The several effects of inhibition are shown in Figure 9.4, representing again the trends shown earlier in Figure 7.7. Notice that N_X continues to decline toward $\hat{I}_X/r_X$ beyond $(t_c)_X$, and $\bar{T}_X$, as a result, shows a somewhat faster rate of growth earlier in this interval than the constant rate of growth shown by T_X from the outset of the interval. Similarly, N_Y continues to decline beyond $(t_c)_Y$ during the residual interval, $(t_{Y/X})^r - (t_c)_Y$, producing a similar early enhancement in the rate of the growth of $\bar{T}_Y$. This paradoxical effect of resistance to an activity on its rate of occurrence in a constant environment is an extension of points introduced earlier concerning the role of cessation consummatory lag and resistance on repeated choice (see pp. 296 to 298).

It should be emphasized that this derivation of the effects of resistance on rate of response pertains to the situation in which the stimulus producing inhibitory force is continuously present and not to one in which such a stimulus is either newly introduced, where there had been none previously, or one in which the magnitude of the inhibitory force is increased. In the latter two situations, the theory implies a temporary decline in the rate of the threatened activity followed by a recovery to or beyond the initial level.[8] For the simple conditions assumed in our discussion, the sequence of decline and recovery following an increase in the magnitude of an inhibitory force would occur in only two cycles, but for more realistic conditions it could be expected to extend over a number of cycles.

Let us briefly consider a case in which the rate of activity X has stabilized before the introduction and continuation of a stimulus that produces an inhibitory force, I_X. Since the rate of an activity is reciprocally related to the sum, $(t_{X/Y})^r + (t_{Y/X})^r$, it will be sufficient to show the expected effect on either $(t_{X/Y})^r$ or $(t_{Y/X})^r$. Notice that in this special case, at least, the ultimate rate of both activities is affected equally by an inhibitory influence on either one of them.

Let us focus on $(t_{X/Y})^r$. We know that when there is no stimulus producing I_X and, therefore, no resistance to activity X, $t_{X/Y}$ is given by

$$t_{X/Y} = \frac{F_Y/c_Y - (T_X)_c}{\hat{F}_X} + (t_c)_X$$

In this expression, $(T_X)_c$ represents the strength of T_X at the end of the cessation consummatory lag that can be attributed to the constant parameters of instigation alone.

Suppose that a stimulus producing $\hat{I}_X$ is introduced after activity Y has supplanted activity X, and subsequent to the cessation consummatory lag for activity X, to make our problem simpler. We know that the effect of $\hat{I}_X$ during the residual interval, $t_{X/Y} - (t_c)_X$, will be an initial increase in N_X toward its limit $\hat{I}_X/r_X$, which must be overcome before activity X can again be initiated. On this particular occasion,

$$t_{X/Y} = \frac{F_Y/c_Y - (T_X)_c + \hat{I}_X/r_X}{\hat{F}_X} + (t_c)_X$$

[8] This phenomenon was reported in Estes' (1944) early study of the effect of punishment on the rate of bar pressing in rats. The enhancement in the rate of response after a temporary suppression following onset of a stimulus previously paired with shock was itself only temporary. We think the reason is that in the Estes study, when bar pressing was re-initiated in the presence of the aversive *CS* but not followed by shock, the magnitude of inhibitory force would begin to diminish as extinction commences (see Chapter 8).

It is the familiar case of a temporary delay in the initiation of an activity produced by the threat of punishment. Now the latency of response is increased.

Finally, assuming that the inhibitory stimulus is maintained to provide I_X when X is occurring as well as $\hat{I}_X$ when it is not, we can expect that the value of $(t_{X/Y})^r$ on subsequent occasions will be given by Equation 9.11 and that this value of $(t_{X/Y})^r$ will be the smallest of the three considered here. This decrease in latency of response implies the highest rate of activity X. In brief, we move from (1) an inertial gap of $({}_g\bar{X})_c = ({}_gX)_c$, with no resistance, to (2) $({}_g\bar{X})_c = ({}_gX)_c + \hat{I}_X/r_X$, when the inhibitory force is first introduced (under the conditions described), to (3) $({}_g\bar{X})_c = ({}_gX)_c - (I_X/r_X - \hat{I}_X/r_X)k_X$ still later on. *The introduction of an inhibitory force produces a temporary suppression of response; its continuation may produce the opposite, an enhancement of the rate of response.*

THE EFFECT OF RESISTANCE ON TIME SPENT IN AN ACTIVITY

The discussion of the effects of resistance on rate of response can be extended to include the measure of time spent in an activity. Of special interest and potential heuristic value are the relationships described in Chapter 4 between the time spent in each of two activities and the latency of each measured when the other is in progress:

$$m(X) = \frac{t_{Y/X}}{(t_{X/Y} + t_{Y/X})}$$

$$m(Y) = \frac{t_{X/Y}}{(t_{X/Y} + t_{Y/X})}$$

$$\frac{m(X)}{m(Y)} = \frac{t_{Y/X}}{t_{X/Y}}$$

Since we have already concluded that the resistance to an activity produced by a constant and continuing source of resistance to the activity will, if anything, shorten the theoretical latency of that activity when the other is in progress, we can see that we are faced with another paradoxical conclusion: *the continuing resistance to one of two alternative activities should tend to increase the amount of time engaged in that activity relative to the other.*

Perhaps this is as good a place as any to terminate an initial effort to use the programmatic Principle of Change of Activity as an integrative bridge between behavioral measures taken from simple incidents and from the molar stream of activity. The direction and the degree of change in the time spent in an activity that is attributable to resistance would appear to depend very much on the nature of the activities involved because the duration of the cessation consummatory lag, and what happens in it, becomes critically important. The whole theory, applied to even this simple instance of free operant behavior, begins to point up possibilities that are intuitively non-obvious. That, in the long run, is the hope of a theory in science, and even more—that these nonobvious implications are sustained empirically when the critical experiment is run.

At this writing, the conceptual analysis of even simple instances of the molar stream of behavior must be listed among the most important items of unfinished business in psychology. We hope that our analysis of change of activity will prove to be a heuristic guide in this endeavor.

SUMMARY

In this chapter we have brought our statements concerning instigation and resistance as determinants of the time to change from one activity to another into summary form. This is as far as we intend to press our conceptual analysis in this book. Guided by a programmatic Principle of Change of Activity (Equation 9.4), which refers to change in the dominance relationship of *resultant* tendencies instead of merely in the action tendencies (as earlier), we have reexamined the problem of choice among alternatives and have pushed farther in our conceptual analysis of the measurable aspects of the molar stream of behavior: that is, the operant level of an activity and the time spent in an activity—at least, for the simple case of two alternatives in a constant environment.

In reference to the question of the determinants of latency, persistence, and choice, we bring the analysis to the point of formulating several rudimentary "laws" describing the systematic effects of the magnitudes of instigating force, inhibitory force, and inertial tendency. They suggest the kind of end product that can be anticipated should an approach like the one that we have proposed be followed systematically in empirical research.

A closer look at the systematic effects following the introduction and the withdrawal of force to inhibit the activity in progress makes it possible to spell out more explicitly than before (Chapters 7 and 8) the implications of our conception of resistance in reference to the effects of punishment and the dynamics of avoidance behavior. The temporary suppressive effect of a punishment, or the threat of punishment, for continuation of an activity in progress produces an interval of increased vulnerability to the interruption of the activity and the change to some other activity for which the inertial tendency and/or the immediate instigation is relatively strong. This, we think, would be enough to account for the initiation of so-called avoidance behavior. And, given our earlier treatment of how inhibitory force is acquired and extinguished, this protects the inhibitory force produced by the punishment or threat of punishment from change in its magnitude on repeated trials.

In the reanalysis of the determinants of choice by many individuals on a single occasion, we again find that the ratio of the magnitudes of forces, and not the difference in magnitude, is what matters in preferential behavior. The presence of forces to inhibit each of two alternatives has no systematic effect on choice when the ratio of the inhibitory forces equals the ratio of the instigating forces. But when the ratio of the inhibitory forces is greater or less than that of the instigating forces, the generally expected differential effects will occur. This focus of interest on the importance of the ratio of forces provides another occasion for discussion of how our conception of the dynamics of action, in this case of resistance, relates to the study of individual differences in personality.

Our further analysis of the determinants of two measures taken from the molar stream of behavior, operant level (or rate) of an activity and time spent in an activity, must be considered exploratory. It leans heavily on the critically important assumptions concerning selectivity in attention and lag in the impact of consummatory force that were introduced earlier as the bridge between the analysis of single incidents of change and the analysis of a sequence of changes in activity.

In order to attain simple mathematical solutions for the several measures, it has been necessary to deal with only two activities and to set one very important condition: that the time taken for a single change in activity is sufficiently long to allow the strength of the action tendency sustaining ongoing activity and both inhibitory tendencies to be approximated by their asymptotic values. It did not seem obviously or grossly inappropriate to do this.

For each of the several measures, the equation which holds true when resistance is a factor can be reduced to one presented somewhere earlier in the book, when resistance was not a factor given consideration, by simply assigning a value of zero to the inhibitory terms.

For all measures based on repeated observations from the same individual, the bottling up of action tendencies by negaction tendencies and the existence of a consummatory lag at the cessation of an activity were found to play a particularly crucial role in the derivation of the effects of resistance.

The introduction of a force to negate an activity already in progress temporarily increases the vulnerability to interruption by some strongly instigated alternative activity. But the suppressive effect on the initial activity is transitory. Before long, in a constant environment, the resultant tendency that sustains activity in progress grows to the same asymptote with and without resistance.

When an inhibitory force for an alternative activity is introduced, and this does not affect the inertial action tendency, there is a delay in the initiation of the alternative activity. In the case of the choice between alternatives, resistance changes the pattern of choice when the ratio of the inhibitory forces departs from the ratio of instigating forces. When the ratio of inhibitory forces exceeds the ratio of instigating forces (favoring choice of the strongest alternative), the choice of the more strongly instigated alternative is weakened.

MATHEMATICAL NOTES

These notes contain certain mathematical details skipped over in the text where we presented derivations for choice with resistance included. The order of topics is the choice paradigm wherein a single observation is made on a large number of individuals followed by the paradigm in which many observations are made on a single individual. For each topic, we carry through the derivation that eventuates in a mathematical statement relating the behavioral measure to the parameters of the theory, and then we make selected comparisons between these equations and the ones of Chapter 4 where resistance was assumed to be absent. In this way, some of the major effects of resistance on these behavioral measures will be brought out.

Just as in Chapter 4 our inquiry is confined to two alternatives. The same simplifying assumptions are made as in Chapter 4, plus several new but corresponding assumptions about resistance.

Two-Alternative Choice with a Single Observation from Many Individuals. Let A be the ongoing activity and X and Y the alternatives. The choice of X or Y is determined by which resultant tendency, $\bar{T}_X$ or $\bar{T}_Y$, reaches the level of $\bar{T}_A$ first. We assume that $\bar{T}_{A_F}$ can be approximated by its asymptotic value F_A/c_A either with or without resistance for activity A present, and that no displacement or substitution is operative.

Alternative X will be chosen if, theoretically, the time required for $\bar{T}_X$ to reach F_A/c_A is less than the time for $\bar{T}_Y$ [that is, $(t_{X/A})' \leq (t_{Y/A})'$] and alternative Y will be chosen if the opposite is true [that is, $(t_{Y/A})' < (t_{X/A})'$]. We assume that $(t_{X/A})'$ and $(t_{Y/A})'$ are sufficiently long that the following approximations can be made

$$\bar{T}_{A_F} = \frac{F_A}{c_A}, \qquad N_{X_F} = \frac{\hat{I}_X}{r_Y} \qquad \text{and} \qquad N_{Y_F} = \frac{\hat{I}_Y}{r_Y}$$

They are the assumptions that turn Equation 9.4 into Equation 9.5 and allow us to write

$$(t_{X/A})' = \frac{F_A/c_A - T_{X_I} + \hat{I}_X/r_X}{\hat{F}_X}$$

and

$$(t_{Y/A})' = \frac{F_A/c_A - T_{Y_I} + \hat{I}_Y/r_Y}{\hat{F}_Y}$$

or, by using the inertial gap notation, $(t_{X/A})' = {}_g\bar{X}/\hat{F}_X$ and $(t_{Y/A})' = {}_g\bar{Y}/\hat{F}_Y$. Thus, those individuals for whom ${}_g\bar{X}/\hat{F}_X \leq {}_g\bar{Y}/\hat{F}_Y$ or, equivalently, ${}_g\bar{X}/{}_g\bar{Y} \leq \hat{F}_X/\hat{F}_Y$ will choose alternative X, and those for whom ${}_g\bar{X}/{}_g\bar{Y} > \hat{F}_X/\hat{F}_Y$ will choose alternative Y. The proportion of choice of X is given by the relative numbers choosing each alternative.

To investigate how the presence of resistance affects the number of individuals choosing alternative X, we rewrite the condition for the choice of X from ${}_g\bar{X}/\hat{F}_X \leq {}_g\bar{Y}/\hat{F}_Y$ into

$$\frac{{}_gX}{\hat{F}_X} + \frac{\hat{I}_X/r_X}{\hat{F}_X} \leq \frac{{}_gY}{\hat{F}_Y} + \frac{\hat{I}_Y/r_Y}{\hat{F}_Y}$$

By rearranging terms, we have

$$\frac{{}_gX}{\hat{F}_X} \leq \frac{{}_gY}{\hat{F}_Y} + \left(\frac{\hat{I}_Y/r_Y}{\hat{F}_Y} - \frac{\hat{I}_X/r_X}{\hat{F}_X} \right)$$

which can be compared to the condition under which an individual will choose X when resistance is absent; namely, ${}_gX/\hat{F}_X \leq {}_gY/\hat{F}_Y$. The condition with resistance will be identical to the one without resistance if and only if

$$\frac{\hat{I}_Y/r_Y}{\hat{F}_Y} - \frac{\hat{I}_X/r_X}{\hat{F}_X} = 0$$

By letting $r_Y = r_X$, this requirement becomes $\hat{I}_Y/\hat{I}_X = \hat{F}_Y/\hat{F}_X$. Thus, resistance has no effect on choosing alternative X if and only if the ratio of the inhibitory forces for Y and X is the same as the ratio of the instigating forces. If $\hat{I}_Y/\hat{I}_X > \hat{F}_Y/\hat{F}_X$, more individuals will choose X whereas, if $\hat{I}_Y/\hat{I}_X < \hat{F}_Y/\hat{F}_X$, more will choose Y as compared to the numbers that would be found if resistance were not present.

Two-Alternative Choice with Repeated Observations from a Single Individual. Again, let A be the ongoing activity with X and Y as alternatives and with $F_X > F_Y$, $\hat{F}_X/\hat{F}_Y = F_X/F_Y$ and $\hat{I}_X/\hat{I}_Y = I_X/I_Y$. The sequence of events assumed to occur on each trial is given in detail in the text of this chapter and will not be repeated here. Summaries for a trial with the negaction tendencies included are presented in Figure 9.1 and Table 9.2. As previously, our aim is to state the total number of choices of X and of Y in terms of the parameters of the theory and to determine the ratio of the two, $n(X)/n(Y)$, in the limit where the total number of trials is allowed to increase indefinitely. The method of proceeding with the derivation is the same as that of Chapter 4, and in order to provide the best opportunity for comparing the two conditions, with and without resistance, we follow the earlier derivation step by step.

The derivation begins on *Trial 1* with the individual engaged in activity A and the critical stimuli for alternatives X and Y presented for the first time. We assume that $(t_{X/A})'$ and $(t_{Y/A})'$ are sufficiently long that N_{X_F} and N_{Y_F} as well as $\bar{T}_A$ can be approximated by their asymptotic values allowing the use of Equation 9.5 throughout. On Trial 1, X will be chosen if and only if $(t_{X/A})'_1 \leq (t_{Y/A})'_1$ where the primes indicate that theoretical latencies are being compared. Since by Equation 9.5

$$(t_{X/A})'_1 = \frac{F_A/c_A - T_{XI} + \hat{I}_X/r_X}{\hat{F}_X} = \frac{{}_gX}{\hat{F}_X}$$

and

$$(t_{Y/A})'_1 = \frac{F_A/c_A - T_{YI} + \hat{I}_Y/r_Y}{\hat{F}_Y} = \frac{{}_gY}{\hat{F}_Y}$$

the condition for the choice of X can be written as ${}_gX/\hat{F}_X \leq {}_gY/\hat{F}_Y$. Let us assume that alternative X was selected on the first trial.

For *Trial 2*, we must know the new inertial values for T_X and T_Y. As previously discussed in this chapter and as discernible in Figure 9.3, the inertial value of T_X is the same on every trial following a trial on which X is chosen. We label this value of T_X as $(T_X)^r_c$ to distinguish it from its counterpart in Chapter 4, $(T_X)_c$. Later in these notes we compare the magnitudes of $(T_X)^r_c$ and $(T_X)_c$ in order to assess the effects of the resistance in choice in this paradigm, but for the present it is sufficient to have determined that $(T_X)^r_c$ is the same following each choice of X.

The new value of T_Y is equal to $T_{YI} + \hat{F}_Y \cdot (t_{X/A})_1$ where $(t_{X/A})_1$ is the actual latency for Trial 1. Therefore, on Trial 2, X will be chosen if and only if $(t_{X/A})'_2 \leq (t_{Y/A})'_2$ where

$$(t_{X/A})'_2 = \frac{F_A/c_A - (T_X)^r_c + \hat{I}_X/r_X}{\hat{F}_X} = \frac{({}_gX)_c}{\hat{F}_X}$$

and

$$(t_{Y/A})'_2 = \frac{F_A/c_A - [T_{YI} + \hat{F}_Y \cdot (t_{X/A})_1] + \hat{I}_Y/r_Y}{\hat{F}_Y} = \frac{{}_gY}{\hat{F}_Y} - \frac{\hat{F}_Y \cdot (t_{X/A})_1}{\hat{F}_Y}$$

$$= (t_{Y/A})'_1 - (t_{X/A})_1.$$

We are able to observe two important points now. First, each time X is chosen following a choice of X, the latency will be the same; let us denote this as $(t_{X/A})^r_x$. Second, in order that Y be chosen for the first time, the original theoretical latency for Y, $(t_{Y/A})'_1$, must equal the total time of exposure to $\hat{F}_Y$ required to bring $\bar{T}_Y$ from its original value to F_A/c_A. We can write this as $(t_{Y/A})'_1 = (t_{X/A})_1 + [n_1(X) - 1](t_{X/A})^r_x + (t_{Y/A})_1$ where $(t_{X/A})_1$ is the latency on the first choice of X, $(t_{X/A})^r_x$ is the latency of each choice of X following a choice of X, $(t_{Y/A})_1$ is the latency of the first choice of Y, and $n_1(X)$ is the number of choices of X prior to the first choice of Y.

As in Chapter 4, we can write $(t_{Y/A})_1 = \phi_1(t_{X/A})^r_x$ where $0 \leq \phi_1 \leq 1$, since we know that $(t_{Y/A})_1 < (t_{X/A})^r_x$ or Y would not have been selected. (It is convenient to use ϕ's and ψ's in this derivation, even though they were used in the derivation in Chapter 4, but it is not intended that they refer to the same numerical values necessarily.) Thus, we have $(t_{Y/A})'_1 = (t_{X/A})_1 + [n_1(X) - 1](t_{X/A})^r_x + \phi_1(t_{X/A})^r_x$ which can be solved for $n_1(X)$ to give $n_1(X) = [(t_{Y/A})'_1 - (t_{X/A})_1]/[(t_{X/A})^r_x] + (1 - \phi_1)$.

We now have the first choice of Y, and we wish to find the number of Y's that will occur before X is chosen again. By using the same argument as before and by noticing that each choice of Y following a choice of Y will require time $(t_{Y/A})^r_y$ because it is based on the recurring $(T_Y)^r_c$, we find that $(t_{X/A})^r_x = \phi_1(t_{X/A})^r_x + [n_1(Y) - 1](t_{Y/A})^r_y + \psi_2(t_{Y/A})^r_y$. This yields

$$n_1(Y) = \frac{(1 - \phi_1)(t_{X/A})^r_x}{(t_{Y/A})^r_y} + (1 - \psi_2)$$

A comparison of this derivation with the one of Chapter 4 makes it apparent that the only difference between the two resides in the values for the latencies, not in the equations obtained. Therefore, we proceed directly to the expression $n(X)/n(Y) = (t_{Y/A})^r_y/(t_{X/A})^r_x$, Equation 9.8, obtained by letting the number of trials increase without limit (that is, let $j \to \infty$) in the expression

$$\frac{n(X)}{n(Y)} = \frac{n_1(X) + n_2(X) + \cdots + n_j(X)}{n_1(Y) + n_2(Y) + \cdots + n_j(Y)}$$

The argument is identical to the one given in Chapter 4 and need not be repeated.

The result of this derivation is the discovery that, for the conditions imposed, the basic form of the equation for choice is the same with and without resistance. Now, we must examine what difference it makes that $n(X)/n(Y) = (t_{Y/A})^r_y/(t_{X/A})^r_x$ when resistance is involved and that $n(X)/n(Y) = (t_{Y/A})_y/(t_{X/A})_x$ when it is absent. To do this, we must go back to the equations for these latencies.

Let us compare $(t_{X/A})^r_x$ to $(t_{X/A})_x$; our findings for these two latencies will be directly translatable for $(t_{Y/A})^r_y$ and $(t_{Y/A})_y$ because the equations are in correspondence. From the notes of Chapter 4 we know that

$$(t_{X/A})_x = \frac{F_A/c_A - (T_X)_c}{\hat{F}_X} \quad \text{with} \quad (T_X)_c = \left(\frac{F_A}{c_A}\right)[e^{-c_A \cdot (t_c)_A}][e^{-c_X \cdot (t_c)_X}]$$

and from the present notes that

$$(t_{X/A})_x^r = \frac{F_A/c_A - (T_X)_c^r + \hat{I}_X/r_X}{\hat{F}_X}$$

In order to evaluate $(T_X)_c^r$, we can pick up T_X at the point where activity A resumes and can follow it through its cessation consummatory lag to $(T_X)_c^r$. When activity A takes over again, $\bar{T}_X = \bar{T}_A = (F_A/c_A)[e^{-c_A \cdot (t_c)_A}]$ and $N_X = I_X/r_X$, so that $\bar{T}_X = T_X - N_X = T_X - I_X/r_X = (F_A/c_A)[e^{-c_A \cdot (t_c)_A}]$ or $T_X = (F_A/c_A)[e^{-c_A \cdot (t_c)_A}] + I_X/r_X$. Thus, as T_X enters its cessation consummatory lag, $N_{X_I} = I_X/r_X$ and $T_{X_I} = (F_A/c_A)[e^{-c_A \cdot (t_c)_A}] + I_X/r_X$. The course of T_X over the next $(t_c)_X$ time interval is given by Equation 7.11 (Case 1a) with $\hat{F}_X$ and $I_X = 0$ and T_{X_I} and N_{X_I}, as specified. When simplified, the resulting equation for T_X at the conclusion of its cessation consummatory lag is

$$(T_X)_c^r = (T_X)_c + \left(\frac{I_X}{r_X}\right)\left[\frac{c_X \cdot e^{-r_X \cdot (t_c)_X} - r_X \cdot e^{-c_X \cdot (t_c)_X}}{c_X - r_X}\right]$$

or, letting the last term be denoted by k_X to simplify the notation,

$$(T_X)_c^r = (T_X)_c + \left(\frac{I_X}{r_X}\right) \cdot k_X$$

An examination of $k_X = (c_X \cdot e^{-r_X \cdot (t_c)_X} - r_X \cdot e^{-c_X \cdot (t_c)_X})/(c_X - r_X)$ reveals that k_X can only take on values in the interval 0 to 1; that is, $0 \le k_X \le 1$ for all admissible values of c_X, r_X, and $(t_c)_X$. As c_X increases in the interval, $0 \le c_X \le r_X$, k_X starts at 1 and declines to $e^{-r_X \cdot (t_c)_X}[1 + r_X \cdot (t_c)_X]$ at $c_X = r_X$. Then k_X goes on to approach 0 for $c_X > r_X$ as c_X becomes indefinitely large. The partial derivative $\delta k_X/\delta (t_c)_X$ is negative for all $c_X, r_X > 0$ and equal to zero for $c_X, r_X = 0$ as k_X goes from 1 for $(t_c)_X = 0$ to a limit of 0 as $(t_c)_X \to \infty$.

Therefore, $(T_X)_c^r$ is greater than $(T_X)_c$ by an amount equal to some fraction $(0 \le k_X \le 1)$ of I_X/r_X. An examination of $(T_Y)_c^r$ and k_Y leads to an analogous statement.

Now, we can return to the comparison of $n(X)/n(Y) = [(t_{Y/A})_y^r]/[(t_{X/A})_x^r]$ to $n(X)/n(Y) = [(t_{Y/A})_y]/[(t_{X/A})_x]$. To do so, let us examine more carefully the difference between

$$(t_{X/A})_x^r = \frac{F_A/c_A - (T_X)_c^r + \hat{I}_X/r_X}{\hat{F}_X}$$

$$= \frac{[F_A/c_A - (T_X)_c] + [\hat{I}_X/r_X - (I_X/r_X) \cdot k_X]}{\hat{F}_X}$$

and

$$(t_{X/A})_x = \frac{F_A/c_A - (T_X)_c}{\hat{F}_X}$$

or written in simpler form, between

$$(t_{X/A})_x^r = \frac{(_gX)_c + [\hat{I}_X/r_X - (I_X/r_X) \cdot k_X]}{\hat{F}_X}$$

and $(t_{X/A})_x = (_gX)_c/\hat{F}_X$. First, notice that $[\hat{I}_X/r_X - (I_X/r_X) \cdot k_X]$ can be either positive or negative depending on the relative magnitude of the selective attention parameter relating $\hat{I}_X$ to I_X and the k_X parameter. If the drop from I_X to $\hat{I}_X$ is less than the fraction (k_X) of I_X involved, then the term $[\hat{I}_X/r_X - (I_X/r_X) \cdot k_X]$ will be positive, otherwise it will be negative. Second, notice that, if $[\hat{I}_X/r_X - (I_X/r_X) \cdot k_X]$ is positive, $(t_{X/A})_x^r$ is longer than $(t_{X/A})_x$ and the effect of resistance on the X alternative could be described as suppressive. If, however, $[\hat{I}_X/r_X - (I_X/r_X) \cdot k_X]$ is negative, $(t_{X/A})_x^r$ is smaller than $(t_{X/A})_x$, and resistance imposes a paradoxical facilitative effect on alternative X. The source of the latter effect is to be found in the protection from expression that the negaction tendency affords the action tendency, so that under the proper conditions an excess of action tendency can be attained.

To assist in considering the way in which resistance might affect choice, the comparison between $n(X)/n(Y) = (t_{Y/A})_y^r/(t_{X/A})_x^r$ and $n(X)/n(Y) = (t_{Y/A})_y/(t_{X/A})_x$ can be written as the comparison between

$$\frac{n(X)}{n(Y)} = \left(\frac{\hat{F}_X}{\hat{F}_Y}\right)\left\{\frac{(_gY)_c + [\hat{I}_Y/r_Y - (I_Y/r_Y) \cdot k_Y]}{(_gX)_c + [\hat{I}_X/r_X - (I_X/r_X) \cdot k_X]}\right\}$$

when resistance is involved and

$$\frac{n(X)}{n(Y)} = \left(\frac{\hat{F}_X}{\hat{F}_Y}\right)\left[\frac{(_gY)_c}{(_gX)_c}\right]$$

when it is not. When will resistance have no effect on choice? This will be when

$$\left(\frac{\hat{F}_X}{\hat{F}_Y}\right)\left[\frac{(_gY)_c}{(_gX)_c}\right] = \left(\frac{\hat{F}_X}{\hat{F}_Y}\right)\left\{\frac{(_gY)_c + [\hat{I}_Y/r_Y - (I_Y/r_Y) \cdot k_Y]}{(_gX)_c + [\hat{I}_X/r_X - (I_X/r_X) \cdot k_X]}\right\}$$

or simplified if and only if

$$(_gY)_c \cdot \left[\frac{\hat{I}_X}{r_X} - \left(\frac{I_X}{r_X}\right) \cdot k_X\right] = (_gX)_c \cdot \left[\frac{\hat{I}_Y}{r_Y} - \left(\frac{I_Y}{r_Y}\right) \cdot k_Y\right]$$

Correspondingly, we find that resistance will decrease the choice of X, presumed to be the alternative with the greater instigating force if and only if

$$(_gY)_c \cdot \left[\frac{\hat{I}_X}{r_X} - \left(\frac{I_X}{r_X}\right) \cdot k_X\right] > (_gX)_c \cdot \left[\frac{\hat{I}_Y}{r_Y} - \left(\frac{I_Y}{r_Y}\right) \cdot k_Y\right]$$

When conditions are such that resistance functions suppressively on both X and Y (that is, the bracketted negaction terms are both positive), resistance will have no effect on choice when

$$\frac{(_gY)_c}{(_gX)_c} = \frac{[\hat{I}_Y/r_Y - (I_Y/r_Y) \cdot k_Y]}{[\hat{I}_X/r_X - (I_X/r_X) \cdot k_X]}$$

For ratios of inhibitory effects less than $(_gY)_c/(_gX)_c$ the choice of alternative X will be less than it would have been without resistance, and for ratios greater than $(_gY)_c/(_gX)_c$ the choice of alternative X will be greater.

When conditions are such that resistance exerts a suppressive effect on alternative X but a facilitating effect on alternative Y (that is, the bracketted negaction term for X is positive and that for Y is negative), resistance can only decrease the choice of X, since it must be that

$$(_gY)_c \cdot \left[\frac{\hat{I}_X}{r_X} - \left(\frac{I_X}{r_X}\right) \cdot k_X\right] > (_gX)_c \cdot \left[\frac{\hat{I}_Y}{r_Y} - \left(\frac{I_Y}{r_Y}\right) \cdot k_Y\right]$$

where the left-hand term is positive and the right-hand term negative. Similarly, when resistance provides a facilitative effect on alternative X and a suppressive effect on alternative Y, resistance can only increase the choice of X.

Last, when conditions are such that both alternatives are facilitated by resistance (that is, the bracketted negaction terms are both negative), choice will be unaffected if, and only if,

$$\frac{(_gY)_c}{(_gX)_c} = \frac{[\hat{I}_Y/r_Y - (I_Y/r_Y) \cdot k_Y]}{[\hat{I}_X/r_X - (I_X/r_X) \cdot k_X]}$$

However, the choice of alternative X will be less than what it would have been without resistance for ratios of inhibitory effects that are greater than $(_gY)_c/(_gX)_c$ and greater than what it would have been for ratios less than $(_gY)_c/(_gX)_c$.

CHAPTER 10

OVERVIEW AND AMPLIFICATION

In this final chapter, we review the basic assumptions and concepts of earlier chapters, but from slightly different perspectives, in order to amplify the earlier treatment of selected issues. We say enough about some implications of the analysis to point out possible directions for further development. We also enlarge and qualify our earlier discussion of certain important topics about which our views are very tentative, at best, as a preliminary to more intensive study. In place of a tough-minded appraisal of the scheme in relation to the details of factual evidence about the variety of topics in reference to which it has some particular testable implication, a task that we hope to encourage among others who know the evidence concerning particular problems best, we end with a description of some innovations in our own empirical research that are explicitly related to the conceptual analysis of a change in activity. This will suggest the kind of specification concerning conditions that the new conceptual analysis demands and which we have sometimes found lacking in preliminary considerations of the contemporary fund of empirical findings.

We realize that we have made so many guesses in this effort to develop a coherent view of the dynamics of action that we must be wrong on some or even many of them. But, also, we realize that the whole theory of behavior, not just some limited hypothesis, is on the line in any confrontation with factual evidence and that unless a theory is developed to the point that many or most of its implications can be determined and appreciated, there is very little basis for self-correction through experimentation.

A theory of motivation and action has an unavoidable requirement to meet the demand of generality. We have sought to identify the fundamental behavioral problem and to advance a conceptual analysis that would have a substantial degree of generality. Perhaps, more important, we have attempted to convey the promise of interest in the *dynamic* processes of motivation and action by pushing this far toward completeness and coherence.

315

It is, we realize, no more than a plausible beginning. Hence, in this final chapter we continue the exposition of the directions of our thought instead of initiating a tough-minded appraisal and the inevitable repair of deficiencies. That will become a common enough endeavor if the proposals have heuristic value.

THE FUNDAMENTAL PROBLEM OF BEHAVIOR:
A CHANGE OF ACTIVITY

One striking feature of the molar stream of behavior of an individual under natural conditions is that change from one activity to another often brings about a substantial change in the immediate environment of the individual. Consider, for example, a typical day in the life of a working man. He awakens in his bedroom but leaves it almost immediately to wash, shave, and then to eat his breakfast. From the kitchen table he moves outside to his automobile for the drive to work. He leaves his automobile in the parking lot and walks into the factory or office to spend most of the day in one place except, perhaps, to go to a lunchroom at midday. At about 5 P.M. he leaves the plant for the parking lot, enters his automobile to return home, eats dinner in the dining room, and later falls asleep in his bed. On holidays and weekends, the several different environments that define his behavioral possibilities are different, but the pattern of a change in environment correlated with a change of activity continues. The immediate consequence of a change from one activity to another is, as often as not, a substantial change in the immediate stimulus situation. The changing stimulus situation has such an obvious selective effect on subsequent behavior that it has encouraged the now traditional view of sensory dominance in the control of behavior—the notion that every change in behavior must be attributed to some prior change in stimulation. This view is challenged directly by our conceptual analysis.

To proceed, we must work back from this natural stream of behavior to something more amenable to conceptual and experimental analysis. We produce the first simplification by limiting the interval of observation to a period in which the immediate environment of the subject seems constant to an observer. Given an adequate taxonomy of behavior in this situation or, at least, an adequate definition of one activity, the observer can record the rate of an activity in a constant environment (Skinner, 1938) or the time spent in various activities (Allison, 1963). It is less obvious to the observer, when the immediate physical surroundings of the subject are constant, that a change from one activity to another still normally produces a change in the immediate environment as it actually exists for the subject. The orienting of receptors toward the aspects of the immediate stimulus situation that provide the supports and guides for the particular activity that has been initiated suggests that *selectivity of attention must be the general rule.* This reduces the time of exposure to other potential goads to action that are present in the immediate surroundings.

The effect of restricted attention can often be nearly equivalent to what is produced by an actual change in the physical location of the individual. The subject, as we conceive him, is always more or less deeply involved in a particular activity, depending on the strength of the tendency that is sustaining it. It is not difficult to conceive of selectivity in attention as something that varies in degree and to imagine that in some circumstances there is an almost exclusive and prolonged restriction of attention to guides and goads for the activity that is in progress, even though the environment contains goads for other activities. Thus, even in a constant environment as defined by the observer, there exists a more or less serious departure from the ideal case of constant exposure to *all* the potential goads to action, that is, all the potential instigating forces, that are present in the immediate physical surroundings.

It is not surprising, then, that we should seek further simplification of the behavioral problem of motivation. We notice that the rate of a particular activity and the time spent in that activity are indices that depend on the willingness of the subject to initiate the particular activity when he is already doing something else, and to persist in that activity once it has been initiated. In taking the next step toward simplification of the problem, our interest focuses on the simple change from one activity to another during an interval of observation in which the physical environment of the subject, as defined by the observer, is constant. This does not overcome the complication of selectivity in attention, however, and we still fall short of the simple ideal case that was imagined and exploited in Chapter 1. Nevertheless, this simple ideal case can serve as a standard from which the actual conditions of behavior may be said to depart in particular ways with certain clearly implied effects.

Perhaps, some useful cautions are suggested in this explicit consideration of the continuum of possibilities that range from the simple ideal case of Chapter 1 to the complexities arising in any attempt to account for the rate of an activity or the time spent in an activity on a typical day in the natural and frequently changing environment of an individual. In the absence of any better guide as to how to interpret molar behavioral data of the latter sort, we would apply the Principle of Change of Activity for the ideal case and then would expect the greatest departures from theoretical expectation to occur (a) when the magnitude of the instigating force for particular activities is very strong, implying concentrated attention for prolonged periods to stimuli that are relevant to the ongoing activity, resulting in extreme restriction of the time of exposure to other goads for action, and (b) when the various places to and from which an individual moves are highly differenti- ated with respect to the kinds of activities that can occur in them. In the latter case, when there are few goads to any activities other than the one in progress, the change to some other activity is much less dependent on the instigation of new alternatives than in the ideal case. It is much more dependent on the consummation of the tendency sustaining the activity in progress and on the hierarchy of inertial tendencies within the individual.

Selectivity in the Observer

The initiation of an activity and the persistence of an activity are clearly not isolated motivational problems but are interrelated aspects of a change of activity. Nor is choice among alternatives a separate and distinct behavioral problem. It, like the others, is distinguished by what an observer is prepared to record when a change of activity occurs. It seems highly unlikely that an individual will ever find himself engaged in an activity in an environment that admits of only one other possibility or when motivated to engage in only one other activity. The immediate environment will almost always be richer in its goads and guides to action. And the individual's repertory of inertial tendencies will normally include more than one alternative. What seems like a simple change from one activity to another can as readily be viewed as a choice of one from among the set of instigated alternatives. Whether this change of activity yields a measure called persistence (of the ongoing activity), or latency (of the alternative that is initiated), or choice (preference from among a predetermined set of alternatives) depends on the interest of the observer. Has he stopped his clock at the cessation of the initial activity and then looked away? Has he ignored what has been happening until a particular activity is initiated? Has he waited only long enough to see which of three specified alternatives was chosen (that is, initiated before the others)? Whichever it is, we apply a single Principle of Change of Activity to the same stream of behavior but adapt it to the particular behavioral event *defined by the observer* as the persistence of activity *A*, the latency of activity *B*, or an instance of preference for activity *C* (see also Barker, 1963, Chapter 1).

Theoretical Basis for Correlations among Different Behavioral Measures

This single principle provides the theoretical ground for expecting correla- tions among the several measures that have traditionally constituted the behavioral definition of the problem of motivation, that is, willingness to initiate an activity, to persist in it, and to prefer it when given a choice among alternatives. And the measures taken from the molar stream of be- havior in a constant environment—the operant level of an activity and the time spent in that activity—can now be added to the list.

The Principle of Change of Activity can provide the integrative thread, the conceptual bridge, and the logical necessity so often lacking in reference to the matrix of correlations among various response measures that is of central importance in the study of individual differences in personality. It, at least, can perform this function with respect to the measures of latency of response, persistence, choice, the rate of response, and the time spent in an activity. And it is but a small step from having the theoretical expectations of correlations among various measures in reference to a specific activity to having equally sound theoretical expectations of correlations among the various measures in reference to different activities that belong to the same family (Chapter 2). By these steps, we can move easily from the conceptual analysis of the *process* of motivation in terms of specific forces and tendencies to the study and description of the relatively general individual differences in *personality* in terms of motives.

Implications of the Simple Change of Activity

The simplest change of activity in a constant environment implies a change in the dominance relations of tendencies during the interval of observation. This is the premise on which our theoretical analysis of the dynamics of action is based. We then consider the several ways in which the tendency expressed in behavior can be weakened relative to the others, and the ways in which the originally subordinate tendency can be strengthened relative to the others. We search for the proximate causes of changes in the relative strengths of tendencies. Here, at the very outset, is the assumption that tendencies would persist in their present state unless subjected to some external influence, that is, unless acted on by some force. The persisting tendency, the *inertial* tendency, is the cornerstone in our theoretical account and, because of it, we claim to have a theory of the behavior of an *active*—instead of merely a reactive organism. The individual is conceived as motivated to engage in various activities at a particular time even without the consideration of the *immediate* stimulus situation.

The mere fact that an activity in progress at the beginning of the interval of observation is replaced by another activity implies, at the very minimum, a change in the relative strength of two behavioral tendencies. That, in a nutshell, defines the problem for a theory of motivation.

THE INTERRELATED PROCESSES OF MOTIVATION

We account for *changes* in the relative strength of tendencies in terms of three interrelated dynamic processes: *instigation*, *resistance*, and *consummation*. These processes occur simultaneously to control the relative strength of the resultant action tendencies and, thus, to control the content of the stream of an individual's behavior.

Very simply stated, we view the activity already in progress when an interval of observation begins as the expression of the then dominant (or strongest) behavioral tendency in the individual. The strength of this tendency is the algebraic resultant of the conflict between an action tendency, that is, a tendency to engage in the activity, and a negaction tendency, that is, a tendency not to engage in the activity. A change in activity occurs when the resultant action tendency for some other activity attains dominance.

Our conception of the instigation of action is an account of how the strength of an action tendency is increased and sustained by the instigating force of the stimulus situation for that activity. Instigation affects both dominant and subordinate action tendencies.

Our conception of resistance to action is an account of how the strength of a negaction tendency is increased and sustained by the inhibitory force of the immediate stimulus situation, how the negaction tendency functions to resist the behavioral expression of an action tendency, and how this resistance dissipates the strength of the negaction tendency.

Our conception of consummation is an account of the functional significance of behavior itself: its role as the proximate cause of reductions in the strength of action tendencies that are being expressed in behavior. We refer to this function as the consummatory force of an activity.

We have redefined the functional significance of the stimulus and the response. The stimulus does not elicit nor cause the response tendency, as we conceive it. Nor is the behavior inducing property of the immediate stimulus situation considered sufficient to define the nature and the relative strengths of the then active response tendencies. Instead, the stimulus situation functions selectively *to produce changes* in the strength of action tendencies that are already present. The hierarchy of "active" inertial tendencies includes many that are unrelated to and unaffected by exposure to the immediate stimulus situation. In view of this, we are led to ask: How essential is the stimulus situation for action? We consider this topic in a subsequent section.

We have also assigned a functional role in the dynamics of behavior to the behavior itself. In traditional S-R theory, the response functions in a critically important way by producing distinctive cues that can influence the chain of stimulus-controlled events. We have already referred to this typical effect of many changes of activity and certainly do not intend to minimize its importance. But the concept of the consummatory force of an activity elevates the response itself to a position of importance equivalent to that of stimulus as a selective influence on behavior. The consummatory force of an activity is the capacity of the activity in progress to produce a certain rate of reduction in the strength of the tendency then being expressed. This might be viewed as a quantified catharsis theory of the role of the response. We have found it helpful to our understanding of the concept to consider the rather sudden reduction of anger immediately following a hostile remark or some other overt aggressive reaction as illustrative of consummatory force.

Our initial guess as to the determinants of the consummatory force of an activity is commonsensical and yet deductively fruitful. There is little novelty in the idea that eating certain foods slackens the appetite more rapidly than eating others—to say, in other words, that activities may differ in consummatory value. And the notion that one violent burst of aggression will appease anger more rapidly and thoroughly than the same action moderately done seems equally close to the level of everyday observation. This is the notion that the *intensity* of the activity influences consummatory force. The combination of these two ideas yields the path for the strength of a tendency as a function of the duration of the activity and defines the limit toward which the strength of a simultaneously instigated and consummated action tendency moves as F/c. This stabilization in the strength of a tendency sustaining ongoing activity implies variability in behavior without any appeal to a change in the stimulus situation. The variability in behavior is deduced from the conception of the inherent dynamics of the behavior and not from an appeal to a change in the stimulus situation.

We have had little that is new to say about the processes of displacement and substitution. We have been guided by the development of these concepts in psychoanalytic theory and by Lewin's early attempt to sharpen their conceptual status (see Lewin, 1938). If the instigation or the consummation of one particular action tendency can have the more general effects referred to as displacement and substitution, the amount of this spread of effect from one action tendency to another defines the degree of the relatedness of the two activities. The evidence is so clear that the desire to eat one kind of food can be whetted by instigation and can be satisfied by consummation with respect to another kind of food that we habitually think of the term "appetite" in reference to the family of functionally related action tendencies we here refer to as the tendency to eat. These concepts and the use of descriptive terms for families of functionally related tendencies (for example, motives) is an essential simplification for the study and the description of individual differences in personality. Throughout the book, we have repeatedly tried to illustrate how one can move back and forth between the conceptual analysis of the process of motivation to the description of individual differences in personality. We have referred to the concepts of motive to achieve success and of motive to avoid failure as equivalent to statements about a family of instigating forces (to achieve success) and a family of inhibitory forces (to avoid failure). The concepts of displacement and substitution, referring as they do to the common fate of functionally related tendencies, allow the transition from references to specific instigating forces and to specific action tendencies to the description of persons as differing in strength of motive.

Our conception of resistance, in a sense, is arbitrary. We might have treated the tendency *not* to engage in a particular activity as another action tendency, a tendency to engage in *activity not X* where activity *not X c̄* activity *X*. The resistance to an activity would then reduce to the familiar competition for dominance among tendencies to engage in activities that are incompatible. The inhibitory force of the stimulus then would be viewed merely as the instigating force to engage in the activity of doing activity *not X*. It is a viable alternative and one to be thoroughly explored in the future.

Instead, we decided to be guided by the suggestion for a different conception of inhibition of action that is inherent in the logic of the current cognitive theories of motivation (Tolman, Lewin, Decision Theory) that derive the tendency to do something or not to do it from the multiplicative combination of certainty that an act will produce a given consequence and the value of the consequence. When the consequence is negative, a negation tendency is implied (Atkinson, 1964, Chapter 10). We have pursued the implications of an opposing or resisting tendency that specifically functions to block the expression of some other tendency but, in doing so, does not consume (that is, reduce) the strength of the original action tendency. The idea that resistance constitutes an expression of a negation tendency and that this is the way in which a negation tendency is reduced (or dissipated) emerged as we were guided by the analogy already provided in our treatment of the rise and fall in the strength of an action tendency.

It was our original intention to examine the issue of displacement, substitution, and compatibility relations among negation tendencies. It remains as unfinished business. Instead, we have decided to become familiar with some of the thus far important implications of the concept of resistance: that the effect of punishment and/or the threat of punishment is transitory; that as a result of resistance, the action tendency that is opposed will become even stronger than without resistance; and that the sudden withdrawal of inhibitory force should produce a transitory surge in the level of expression of the tendency that has suffered resistance. They open up new avenues for the discussion and investigation of the role of punishment and of threats of punishment when employed to suppress or otherwise control behavior.

We have just arrived at the point of being able to formulate some reasonable questions about resistance. For example, what would be expected if the analogy with action is incorrect and the negation tendencies are not reduced in resistance and do not persist like action tendencies but are completely dependent on the presence of the inhibitory force of a stimulus? Here, we think, is an example of the kind of change in the theoretical conception that may be forced by confrontation with the details of factual evidence. But that confrontation will be more profitable if there is a coherent development of the suggested alternatives in advance.

The interrelatedness of the three dynamic processes of motivation is nowhere more obvious than in the final treatment of the consummatory force of the activity in progress. The consummatory value of the activity is a factor. That much is simple and straightforward. But the consummatory force also depends on the intensity or the degree of the involvement in the activity in progress, which is assumed to be a function of the strength of the *resultant* action tendency being expressed. But the resultant action tendency depends, in turn, on the strength of the action tendency relative to the strength of the negation tendency, and the strength of the former cannot become stable until the strength of the latter has become stable, etc. We either accept the challenge of these complexities in the dynamics of action, or we avoid the task of attempting to explain a change of activity in all of its various possible guises.

THE PRINCIPLE OF CHANGE OF ACTIVITY

Major Determinants of Selectivity of Behavior

The Principle of Change of Activity identifies the major determinants of selectivity in behavior. It implies that there is *always a hierarchy of inertial tendencies*, reflecting the balance of instigation to action and consummation in past behavior, there is *always the selective impact of the immediate physical surroundings*, represented in the potential set of instigating and inhibitory forces to which an individual may be exposed, and that there is *always the selective effects of the reinforcement and punishment histories of particular activities in similar situations* which define the relative magnitudes of those forces.

The inertial tendency represents the present effect of previous deprivation, whether it results from the external imposition of control over the opportunity for expression of some tendency, as when animals are deprived of food or water for a certain number of hours, or from a self-imposed time of deprivation. The latter typically occurs when an individual's own resistance to some activity functions to suppress expression of the action tendency. This is one of the important selective influences on behavior that has been given special emphasis in the clinical study of personality dynamics. A similar self-imposed deprivation is also implied whenever an individual is exposed to instigating forces for incompatible and nonsubstitutable activities and makes a choice. There remains always the persisting tendency (the unfulfilled wish) to be reflected in the hierarchy of inertial tendencies on a subsequent occasion. We refer now to what in another theoretical context is treated as post-decisional dissonance (Festinger, 1957).

The inertial tendency, in its selective priming or tuning function, embodies the properties of "set" or "readiness to respond." We represent, in the concept of a hierarchy of inertial tendencies, the already active and differentiated state of motivation of an individual which is antecedent to the effect of the present stimulus situation. This concept suggests the possibility of spontaneous activity, that is, the emission of a particular activity in the complete absence of an appropriate stimulus.[1]

The second obvious source of selectivity in behavior is the immediate physical environment, since it defines the instigating forces to which the individual will be exposed. Here we refer to the effects of the manipulable stimulus situation which has been the center of interest in traditional experimental psychology. We have attempted to develop a conception of the role of the stimulus that is consistent with the contemporary conception of the brain which "places emphasis on an active organism that controls the stimuli to which it is sensitive and upon which it acts" (Pribram, 1960, p. 32).

The actual physical environment of the subject, that is, the environment as defined by an observer, provides guides and goads for a limited set of activities. The goading function of the stimulus situation (that is, its instigating force property) influences which tendency will be expressed. The guiding function of the stimulus influences the form, organization, and efficiency of the activity.

Except in cases of unconditioned instigating force, the previous history of the individual when exposed to a given stimulus situation is critically important. The life history of the individual, the topic of interest in the study of learning and development of personality, comes into the determination of behavior in two ways. In addition to its influence on the inertial level of behavioral tendencies, an effect that is quite independent of the present stimulus situation, it has the effects represented in the concepts of instigating and inhibitory forces. The reinforcement and punishment histories of activities account for the magnitudes of instigating and inhibitory force for the different activities.

The distinction between the strength or level of a tendency and the magnitude of instigating force corresponds to the distinction between "arousal"

---

[1] The time to change from activity A to B, when there is no instigation for B, depends on the time it takes for $\bar{T}_A$ to diminish so that $\bar{T}_B = \bar{T}_A$. When resistance is present for activities A and B, Equations 7.7 and 7.12 can be used to obtain the paths of $\bar{T}_B$ and $\bar{T}_A$, respectively. However, these two equations do not yield a solution for $t_{B/A}$, the time required for the change in activity. For the special case of no resistance,

$$T_B = T_{B_I} \quad \text{and} \quad T_A = T_{A_I} \cdot e^{-c_A \cdot t} + \frac{F_A}{c_A}(1 - e^{-c_A \cdot t})$$

over the interval of observation. This yields the solution

$$t_{B/A} = \frac{1}{c_A} \ln \left(\frac{T_{A_I} - F_A/c_A}{T_{B_I} - F_A/c_A} \right)$$

where $T_{A_I} > T_{B_I} > F_A/c_A$.

and "arousability" made by Whalen (1966) in a treatment of sexual motivation. "Sexual arousal" refers to "the momentary level of sexual excitation." "Sexual arousability" refers to "an individual's characteristic rate of approach to orgasm as a result of sexual stimulation." We make the same distinction between the state function (tendency) and the rate function (force). And we would tend to agree with Whalen's conclusion "that these two dimensions of sexuality comprise sexual motivation" (Whalen, 1966, p. 152).

How Essential is the Immediate Stimulus Situation?

Quite apart from its being the source of instigating forces or *goads to action*, the immediate environment of an individual provides supports and *guides for action*. Yet neither the goad to action nor the guide for action is essential. An activity can occur without an instigating stimulus and without the usual environmental cues and supports that function mainly to enhance the internal organization and efficient performance of the activity.

Let us consider, as an example, the activity of having a conversation with a friend. This activity can be initiated even though the friend is not present. One does not need the environmental goad or instigating force. Inertial tendency is sufficient. Actually, talking to a friend requires very little in the way of environmental guides for action, particularly if one has a lot to say. Sometimes one does not even look at the friend even when he is physically present, to say nothing of listening to what he might have to say. The activity can occur without the usual goads and guides and be nearly a replica of the real thing.

Walking to the bathroom in the dark of night is another matter. Here there is no goad to action from the immediate *external* environment, and because it is dark, there are none of the reliable visual guides. What happens? The individual steps away from his bed with great hesitation, groping for the wall that is imagined in a certain place. This provides a substitute for the usual visual cues in terms of which the activity of walking to the bathroom is organized. The activity can occur without the usual guides, but it is performed less smoothly and less efficiently than normally. It is obvious that normally this activity involves a fairly continuous interaction with a changing sequence of visual cues. Plug the ears and hold the nose but leave on the lights, and the efficiency of walking to the bathroom is unaffected. Walk across a familiar room in daylight, but with eyes closed, and the meaning of guides to action is apparent. They are the cues and supports, the discriminanda and manipulanda, with which an individual has a particular kind of commerce while engaging in an activity.

In hallucinatory activity, the individual interacts with imagined cues and supports. The inertial tendency is so strong that it is expressed both overtly and covertly. Once the activity is initiated, there follows—fullblown—the expression of an elaborated tendency with both the usual covert imaginal and usual overt motoric manifestations. This kind of "break with reality" is a matter of degree. It should occur most readily in a constant and impoverished environment, that is, when the immediate environment does not force on the individual any particular kind of perceptual and imaginal activity. Such is the character of the realistic dream in which the visual content is accompanied by some incipient motoric expression, talking, turning, etc. There is continuity between the commonly accepted instances of misperceiving and acting congruent with the misperception, for example, waving to a familiar face in a crowd that soon is recognized as that of a stranger, and the more obvious break with reality that is evident in the behavior of a psychotic person. Here there is hallucinatory activity, unsupported by the goads and guides provided by the environment for most individuals. We view this hallucinatory activity as directly comparable to the so-called vacuum activity of lower animals that has been described by ethologists. An example of the latter is the performance by gulls and geese of an integrated series of actions that constitute raking in an egg to sit on, but when there is, in fact, no egg (Tinbergen, 1951).

The unfolding of a fairly well-organized activity without environmental guides illustrates a property of an elaborated tendency. Neither goads nor guides to action are essential when the tendency is well elaborated and the inertial tendency is very strong. An habitual activity, which seems to run off automatically with little if any conscious awareness, approximates hallucinatory activity, although it is guided by the immediate stimulus situation.

The theory about the dynamics of action is not concerned with the form of an activity or how well or efficiently it will be done. It is concerned with *when* the activity will be initiated, how involved the individual will become in the activity, and how long it will continue. Thus, in the case of playing the piano, our present interest is in when it will be initiated given that a child is now eating his supper, how vigorously it will be done, how long it will go on, and not in how pleasing it will sound to an audience. The stimulus as a goad to action influences when, how vigorously, and how long. The stimulus as a guide to action influences how well an activity is executed.

When a four-year-old child pounds mercilessly on a piano, he is probably expressing a tendency to play the piano. The critical reaction of an unsympathetic parent (or teacher) to excessively loud and irritating sounds is a reaction to the quality of the performance. The question of playing the piano well is a motivational question only to the extent that the answer to the question makes reference to the time spent playing and the willingness of an individual to initiate and persist in practice. The explanation of the organization and efficient performance of this or any other activity goes beyond the specific province of motivation.

Possibility of Nonspecific Parameters

It was suggested quite early (Chapter 4) that even though the Principle of Change of Activity does not include a variable that has nonspecific effects comparable to those of D (drive) in S-R behavior theory, such a possibility is not systematically ruled out. The argument advanced then was that the multiplication of all the terms in the Principle of Change of Activity by a constant would not affect the measures of latency, persistence, or choice, but would affect the level of ongoing performance. This argument was made before the treatment of resistance, and it needs to be reexamined.

Equation 9.5, which gives the programmatic Principle of Change of Activity when resistance is included and, therefore, serves as the referent for this discussion, is

$$t_{B/A} = \frac{F_A/c_A - (T_{B_I} - \hat{I}_B/r_B)}{\hat{F}_B}$$

Consider the effect of a nonspecific multiplicative influence D on all tendencies, action, and negaction in Equation 9.5. Since the multiplication of each tendency by D implies the multiplication of the corresponding force by D, each term of Equation 9.5 is affected, and we have

$$t_{B/A} = \frac{(D)F_A/c_A - [(D)T_{B_I} - (D)\hat{I}_B/r_B]}{(D)\hat{F}_B}$$

It is apparent that, as before, the time taken for a change in activity remains unaltered by such a totally nonspecific multiplicative influence on all tendencies. For $D > 1$, however, the level of performance and/or the degree of involvement of the individual in the ongoing activity is enhanced just as was the case when resistance was absent. The latter squares with the behavioral evidence that has been introduced to illustrate the effect of conditions thought to produce drive on the vigor of response (Brown, 1961). In addition, our conjecture earlier in this chapter that restriction of attention might be a function of the strength of tendency that sustains activity in progress leads to Easterbrook's (1959) argument concerning decreased cue utilization and, consequently, decreased efficiency of behavior under conditions of very intense drive. The restriction of cue utilization might also imply less effective instigating force for alternative activities implying, in turn, that latency might increase, rather than decrease, as a result of a nonspecific excitant.

But there are other possibilities to consider. What if the nonspecific influence D affected all forces, instigating and inhibitory, but did not affect any tendencies? Then the programmatic Principle of Change of Activity would read

$$t_{B/A} = \frac{(D)\,F_A/c_A - [T_{B_I} - (D)\hat{I}_B/r_B]}{(D)\hat{F}_B}$$

with the implication that latency would be longer for larger values of D. This effect would be over and above the longer latency that might be expected because of more selective attention associated with the increased level of ongoing performance.

Another set of possibilities arises if it is hypothesized that the multiplicative influence is nonspecific *within* the instigation process or the resistance process but does not extend across the two. If, for example, all action tendencies, and therefore their corresponding instigating forces, are multiplied by D but the negaction tendencies are not, we obtain

$$t_{B/A} = \frac{D(F_A/c_A) - [(D)T_{B_I} - \hat{I}_B/r_B]}{(D)\hat{F}_B}$$

Now, larger values of D should result in shorter latencies. This effect, however, would be opposed by the conjectured selective attention effect arising from the heightened level of ongoing activity.

On the other hand, D might affect only the rates of change (or arousability) of action tendencies, that is, only instigating forces. Then,

$$t_{B/A} = \frac{(D)\,F_A/c_A - (T_{B_I} - \hat{I}_B/r_B)}{(D)\hat{F}_B}$$

Again, an increase in the level of tendency expressed in the ongoing behavior is implied with its conjectured effect on selective attention, but whether or not D in the above equation functions to lengthen or to shorten latency depends on the relative magnitudes of T_{B_I} and $\hat{I}_B/r_B$.

Nonspecific multiplicative effects that apply to resistance but not to instigation produce

$$t_{B/A} = \frac{F_A/c_A - [T_{B_I} - (D)(\hat{I}_B/r_B)]}{\hat{F}_B}$$

whether negaction tendencies and their corresponding inhibitory forces or the inhibitory forces alone are affected by D. In this case, the strength of resultant tendency expressed in the ongoing activity is not altered by D but, as is easily seen in the equation above, longer latency results from larger values of D.

In summary, a nonspecific excitant, acting on both action tendencies and instigating forces or on instigating forces alone, can be expected to produce a greater intensity of performance and/or degree of involvement of the individual in the ongoing activity, but no such general statement about effects on latency can be made. The direction of effects to be expected from a nonspecific depressant (that is, when $0 < D < 1$) is, of course, opposite to that from a nonspecific excitant.

An Alternative Principle of Action

We have identified the activity in progress with the dominant or strongest resultant action tendency. We have assumed that the activity for which the tendency is strongest will occur and, with it, any other mutually compatible activities. The individual, as conceived, would express all of his action tendencies simultaneously if all activities were compatible. But since this is impossible, the conflict is resolved, we have assumed, in favor of the strongest among the competitors.

The rule deserves special comment. It states that the strongest tendency will be expressed in action but also that, if several activities are ongoing simultaneously (certainly the most likely state of affairs), the configuration of compatibility-incompatibility relationships among activities as well as the strengths of the tendencies determine the particular set of activities that occurs.

It is an interesting and possibly very important facet of this rule that compatibility-incompatibility relations can sometimes override strengths of tendencies in determining the set of ongoing activities. A simple example, using three activities, illustrates this. Assume for activities X, Y, and Z that $X\bar{c}Y$, XcZ, and $Y\bar{c}Z$. Even if $T_Y > T_Z$, activity Z will occur if $T_X > T_Y$, since the occurrence of activity X prevents the occurrence of activity Y and permits the occurrence of activity Z. For example, activity X might be socializing with visiting relatives, activity Y reading a book, and activity Z watching television. An individual might very well have a stronger tendency to read a book than watch television but, because he had an even stronger tendency to socialize with his relatives, he would watch television rather than read. One might legitimately cite this as an instance of the individual engaging in a "nonpreferred" activity.

To pursue this particular example further, consider two young husbands each of whom is entertaining his mother-in-law. When Mother first arrives, T_X is strongest for both but for one the dominance order is $T_X > T_Y > T_Z$ and for the other $T_X > T_Z > T_Y$. Both young men would spend time visiting with Mother and watching television. As the attractiveness of the visits begins to pale for the young men (that is, as T_X declines in strength), however, the first begins to read because $T_Y > T_X > T_Z$, whereas the second continues to socialize and to watch television because $T_Z > T_X >$

T_Y. It would look as if the first young man had changed his preference from watching television to reading whereas, actually, all that has happened is that his tendency to socialize with his mother-in-law had weakened. Interestingly enough, the second young man would give the appearance of enjoying his mother-in-law's company more than the first because he was spending more time than the first socializing with her. But, in fact, he should have a weaker T_X because of his continued expression of that tendency. The bookish son-in-law could be expected to welcome another visit from Mother more readily than his counterpart because he is left with a stronger inertial T_X.

Our assumption about the relationship of tendencies to action extends but does not break with tradition in psychology. But we can conceive of an alternative. The alternative we have in mind is suggested by Festinger's theory of cognitive dissonance (Festinger, 1957): the behavior in progress at a particular time represents that set of mutually compatible activities for which the summation of the separate resultant tendencies is greatest. According to this alternative Principle of Action, the single, strongest resultant action tendency might be subordinate to a set of tendencies for which the sum of the resultant tendencies was greater.

Consider the case in which $T_Q > T_X > T_Y > T_Z$, activity Q is incompatible with all the other activities ($Q\bar{c}X$, $Q\bar{c}Y$, $Q\bar{c}Z$), the other activities are compatible (XcY, XcZ, YcZ), and $T_X + T_Y + T_Z > T_Q$. Given the alternative Principle of Action, the multiple activity XYZ is expected even though T_Q is dominant. In the language of dissonance theory, the cognitive correlates of doing Q are dissonant with cognitive correlates of doing X, doing Y, and doing Z. There is less dissonance when the mutually compatible activities X, Y, and Z occur (with their consonant cognitive elements) than should activity Q occur.

Our Principle of Action, as it stands, would seem to permit the initiation of a dissonance-increasing activity. Perhaps, this is enough to suggest the need for a more discerning analysis of the gap between action tendencies, however conceived, and behavior with much more explicit attention given to the effects of compatibility relations among activities.

Another way of relating the present scheme to the theory of cognitive dissonance is to view the action tendency that sustains activity in progress and the negaction tendencies for all the incompatible subordinate activities as defining consonant cognitive elements and to view the negaction tendency opposing activity in progress plus all the subordinate action tendencies as defining the dissonant cognitive elements.[2] The strength of a tendency corresponds to the dimension of importance that is included as a weighting factor in the calculation of cognitive dissonance.

---

[2] Suggested to us by Robert Parnes (private communication).

LEARNING IN RELATION TO THE DYNAMICS OF ACTION

Learning, as conceived in Chapters 5 and 8, has to do with the elaboration of tendencies and the growth and the extinction of the force properties of the stimulus situation. The position adopted, although not an inherent part of the theory concerning the dynamics of action, does illustrate how a theory of learning can (and we think should) be developed in terms commensurate with those of the logically prior conceptual analysis of the contemporaneous determinants of behavior. That, more than the details of the particular learning theory presented, is our point of emphasis.

Learning, as conceived, has to do with changes in the dispositional properties of the individual. The change in him is a change in the *content* of his behavioral tendencies (elaboration) and a change in their arousability (Whalen's term) in certain situations (that is, in the magnitude of instigating and/or inhibitory force of a stimulus situation). To say that the arousability of a tendency has changed is equivalent to saying that the magnitude of instigating (or inhibitory) force of the stimulus situation has changed for the individual. The former language seems more congenial when talking about how a subject has been affected by training. It reminds us that the individual is somehow different. The latter language is more useful when the functional significance of what has been learned by a particular individual in a particular stimulus situation is the matter of central interest.

Additive and Nonadditive Combinations of the Effects of Inertial Motivation and Training in Principle of Change of Activity

In the earliest formal version of S-R behavior theory (Hull, 1943), the effect of time of food deprivation (hunger drive) and reward training (habit) were presumed to combine multiplicatively in the determination of the latency of response. The Principle of Change of Activity (Equation 1.12) also posits a nonadditive combination of the effects of deprivation (inertial tendency) and the effects of reward training that are mediated by exposure to the stimulus (instigating force). On the other hand, the Principle of Change of Activity with resistance included (Equation 9.5) posits an additive combination of the effects of deprivation (inertial tendency) and the effects of previous punishment of a response (negaction tendency produced by inhibitory force) in the determination of latency of response. They are two examples of specific hypotheses about the mathematical combination of the effects of training and the inertial tendency embodied in the Principle of Change of Activity.[3] As suggested in Chapter 1, these hypotheses are

[3] See Birch (1961) and Birch, Clifford and Butterfield (1961) for an example of a test of the additivity of the effects of an aversive stimulus and the effects of deprivation on the vigor of response.

amenable to experimental test by using the techniques and theory of conjoint measurement as developed by Luce and Tukey (1964), Krantz (1964), and Tversky (1967).

Reinforcement. Our interest in change of activity, when applied to those behavioral events considered the primary reinforcements in theories of learning, has helped us to separate the properties of instigating force of the stimulus and the consummatory value of the activity. The former accounts for reinforcement (strengthening) of the instigating force of the stimulus situation—the learning effect. The latter accounts for the immediate diminution in the action tendency, that is, the consummatory character of the event, and the typical change in the content of activity immediately thereafter that is probably responsible for eating, drinking, sexual activity, etc., having been easily discriminated by common observation as primary ends of behavior. In the Principle of Change of Activity we find a reasonable explanation of why behavioral events of great adaptive significance (the so-called biological need-reducing events) tend to be characterized by both strong unconditioned instigating force and substantial consummatory value. The argument developed in Chapter 5 provides, we think, an understanding of how completely divergent theories of reinforcement such as drive-reduction and drive-induction could be advanced. The identification of reinforcement with the magnitude of the instigating force of the stimulus is more like the drive-induction theory of Sheffield, Roby, and Campbell (1954) and Spence (1956) and is consistent with the empirical generalization of Premack (1959).

Unfortunately omitted, at this writing, is an attempt to use our conceptual analysis in reference to the behavioral effects of intermittent reinforcement. We believe that it is important to the solution of this problem to appreciate that a nonreinforced trial may weaken the instigating force of the stimulus (implying lower probability of future response) but does little or nothing to reduce the strength of inertial tendency (implying higher probability of future response). The greater resistance to extinction following intermittent reinforcement may be coordinate with the increased level of performance immediately following nonreinforcement (Amsel, 1958). In one interpretation of this performance-enhancing effect of frustration, Bower (1962) called attention to the possibility of the perseveration of the fractional anticipatory goal reaction and its function as a source of drive (incentive motivation) in the S-R behavior theory (Spence, 1956). This idea corresponds, in its implications for immediately subsequent behavior, to our general assumption of inertia applied to behavioral tendencies. Preliminary efforts to isolate the learning and immediate motivational effects of "reinforced" and "non-reinforced" trials will be described in the final section of this chapter.

THE RELATION OF THOUGHT AND ACTION RECONSIDERED

In the preliminary discussion of the relationship between overt and covert activity (Chapters 2, 6, and 8), the point given special emphasis was the *correlation* between the content of thought and action engendered by the fact of their common origin. Cognitive expectation of reward is the covert correlate of instigation of an activity that has previously been followed by reward. Cognitive expectation of punishment is the covert correlate of resistance to an activity that has previously been punished. This conception justifies the consideration of covert activities as diagnostic but not causal when the primary concern is the explanation of overt behavior. One can describe the cognitive structure of the individual in terms of his verbal reports about expectations and preferences and can predict action because a particular cognitive structure implies a particular dispositional structure. One could presumably go the other way and can describe the dispositional structure of an individual (that is, the relative magnitudes of the instigating and the inhibitory forces of various stimulus situations for an individual) and can predict his cognitive structure. In a sense, this is what happens when one makes inferences about a subject's subjective probabilities and utility functions from his overt choices and then looks for confirming evidence in the verbally reported expectations and ratings of the relative attractiveness of options.

The view of the content of covert activity as diagnostic but not as causal provides a possible basis for the integration of cognitive and behavioral theories. But is it an adequate conception? We think that it probably is not in light of other discerning treatments of the same issue (for example, Campbell, 1963).

Let us proceed indirectly to another possible conclusion: that covert activity plays an important selective role in the determination of behavior. This means that the individual who has a conscious expectation of reward or punishment will behave differently because he does, and the effect on his behavior is more than can be explained by reference to the process by which the mere activated tendency for a certain covert activity functions as the source of the instigating force for the related overt action.

How can we demonstrate the functional significance of conscious thought? Perhaps, we can do this most easily by imagining a group of primitive men in a situation of danger. Suppose all of them were unaware of the danger. All would succumb. Suppose one of them consciously anticipated the actual threat. If he could convey to the others the nature of the anticipated threat by gesture or by language, each of the others would be provided with an additional environmental cue having the functional significance of an instigating or inhibitory force. One or more of their overt behavioral tendencies would be affected by this additional goad to action. And they would behave differently than if there had been no utterance about the anticipated threat.

If the behavior of others to whom one communicates the content of one's own conscious thought is affected, why should not the behavior of the individual who gave the utterance be similarly affected when he, alone, is privy to his own covert activity? Why should the conscious expectation of a particular reward, for example, not function as the source of an additional instigating force to overt action in the subject?

Viewed in this way, the expression of a tendency covertly, in conscious thought, should normally function *to amplify an effect that is already implicit in the conditions of a given situation*. In an earlier discussion, the ticking metronome in Pavlov's experiment was conceived as producing an instigating force to hear a metronome and to taste food in the mouth after several classical conditioning trials. This increased the strength of the tendency to hear the metronome and to taste the food. The strength of the tendency for covert activity was assumed to be the source of instigating force to salivate that strengthens the tendency to salivate. The latter, when dominant among its competitors, produced the overt response of salivating. All this could occur, as described, without the covert expression of the tendency to hear the metronome ticking and to taste the food. But if the latter were sufficiently strong to be expressed in the covert activity of hearing the metronome and of imagining the taste of the food, and if this, in turn, functioned as the source of an additional instigating force to action, the result would be an amplification of an effect that is already implicit in the instigating force of a ticking metronome whether or not it is heard, namely, an increase in the magnitude of the tendency to salivate and the concurrent salivary reaction mediated by the mere perceptual tendency.

This, in brief, is a conceivable function of covert activity—to provide the additional instigating and inhibitory forces that affect the strength of action and negation tendencies. Conscious thought about the positive and negative consequences of actions, however engendered, could then play the same kind of selective role in the determination of overt action that we have assigned only to the immediate stimulus situation.

Often the content of the covert activity would be instigated by the immediate stimulus situation. But there remains another potent influence on the content of an individual's stream of thought—his own inertial tendencies. The latter, although conceivably too weak to produce effective control of overt activity, might be sufficiently strong to be expressed covertly in thought. This, in turn, might then function as the instigating force to action, thus, strengthening the action tendency enough ultimately to bring about the initiation of an overt activity. Here, then, is a different conception of the functional significance of covert activity. It goes beyond the mere emphasis of the diagnostic implications of the content of thought and identifies the covert activity as potentially an additional amplifying source of the instigating and inhibitory forces for overt action.

In verbal discourse between individuals, a speaker often stands in the same temporal relation to his own words as the listener. And then the effect on both listener and speaker is the same. If Patrick Henry had uttered his classic remark spontaneously, and without conscious aforethought, we might suppose that his ringing declaration, "Give me liberty or give me death!" would have produced an immediate effect in him no less than in his audience. This frequently happens in the rapid interchange of a conversation among individuals. An individual emits a verbal statement without any prior aforethought, hearing the statement for the first time at the same instant as his listeners. This is most obvious when the utterance is a spontaneously humorous remark. Both speaker and audience laugh together in sudden reaction to the unwitting joke or pun. The speaker is hearing his own words, and he is *conscious of what he was going to say* for the first time at the same instant as the listener. It is like the creative process so frequently described by artists, scientists, writers: one does not know what it will be until it is out. In this case, the informational content or the tone of the utterance can function as an instigating or inhibitory force for both listener and speaker. If the same words were spoken privately, the informational content and the implicit tone of the private utterance would function as a force to action or negation in the speaker alone, comparable, in effect, to that of the immediate environment. All of this description suggests that talking to oneself can have substantial motivational significance. Thinking positively can enhance the instigation of action and thinking negatively, the resistance to action.

In this way, provision is made for the control of overt activities by the products of covert activities such as remembering, calculating, visualizing, and planning. These and other cognitive activities can yield the contents of consciousness that selectively instigate and inhibit tendencies for overt activities. Such an interpretation was given to the results obtained in an experiment on verbal control in children (Birch, 1966) which showed that older children persist longer than younger children in an activity instigated by a single external command. The younger children were the equal of the older children, however, when the external command was given repeatedly. It was suggested that the older children, who are presumably more skilled in verbal self-instructions than the younger children, received instigation from their own covert activities in the single command situation—instigation that was lacking for the younger children.

It is but a small step to still a third position concerning the function of consciousness. Having admitted the possibility that a conscious thought could function as a force to action or negation, one must consider again the pre-Freudian alternative: the possibility that all instigation and resistance is mediated by conscious thought. This is to say that it is not the perceptual tendency to hear the metronome that mediates conditioned instigating force to salivate but, instead, the conscious awareness of the click that constitutes the instigating force for overt response. Given this general view, one could say again that an action is merely a reaction to an internal stimulus but mean by internal stimulus, *a conscious thought.*

We shall endeavor to evaluate these and other possible relations between thought and action in future work. Presently our objective is limited to their exposition as possibilities within the framework of our conceptual analysis. The three views are shown graphically in Figure 10.1.

Alternative A views thought and action as correlates and emphasizes the

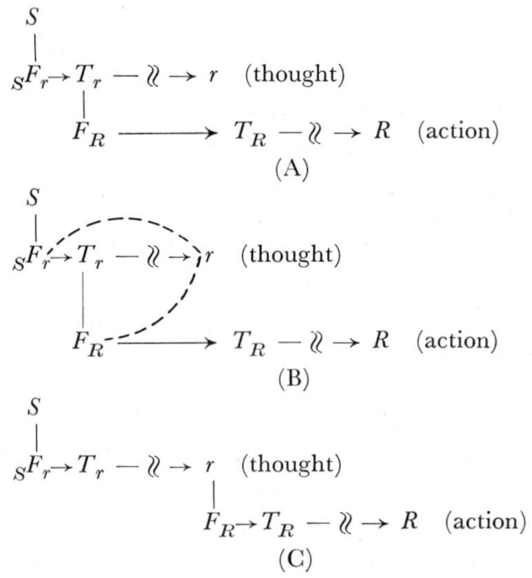

FIGURE 10.1   The graphic representation of three possible relationships between conscious thought (r) and action (R), treated as covert and overt activity in the text. In (A) instigation to action is mediated by the perceptual-imaginal tendency (T_r) which, when dominant, is expressed in thought. The content of thought and action are correlated and so the content analysis of thought is diagnostic of action. In (B) conscious thought is considered an additional source of instigating force for both covert and overt activity. It, thus, functions *to amplify* trends that are already implicit in the unconscious process. In (C) all instigation and resistance to overt action is mediated by conscious thought. The unconscious perceptual-imaginal tendency (T_r) does not mediate instigation or resistance to overt action.

diagnostic significance of covert activity without positing any causal significance.

Alternative B considers the covert expression of a tendency, that is, conscious thought, as an additional and, therefore, amplifying source of instigating and inhibitory forces for subsequent thought and action.

Alternative C claims that all instigation and resistance to action is mediated by the instigating and inhibitory force of covert activity, that is, conscious thought.

In the graphic representation of all three of the alternatives, the typical temporal relation of thought and action is suggested. In A, action normally follows thought because T_r, which is immediately antecedent to r, is the natural event producing F_R to change T_R. The magnitude of T_r may be sufficient to dominate competitors and to produce the covert activity r before this magnitude of T_r, functioning as a source of F_R, has produced the change in T_R needed for it to dominate its competitors and to be expressed in overt activity. In alternative C, the conscious thought r is both the necessary and sufficient condition for F_R that causes the change in T_R, required for its overt expression.

We hope that our analysis of the dynamics of overt action will provide the conceptual tools needed to identify and to specify the functional significance of conscious thought. Until we can do this more confidently, we shall attempt to exploit the implications of alternative A which, at least, identifies the potential diagnostic significance of information about the subject's conscious beliefs and values. This conception of the correlative relationship between these dimensions of covert activity and instigation, or resistance, to action has provided the basis for relating the present scheme to, for example, the theory of achievement motivation that is stated in terms of the cognitive correlates of overt action (Atkinson and Feather, 1966).

Affect and Emotion

Our discussion of covert activity has emphasized the content of thought in relation to the content or the nature of the overt activity. We have tried to justify the view that the cognitive expectations that acts will lead to certain consequences and the cognitive evaluation of those consequences are to be considered diagnostic, covert correlates of action tendencies instead of causes of those action tendencies. What about feelings and emotion? Without attempting to specify here either the physical source or the potential functional significance of various affective reactions that are familiarly called hope, frustration, disappointment, satisfaction, dread, relief, etc., we can specify, in the language of the theory, the conditions that seem to be associated with these various affective states. Intrinsic enjoyment or pleasure seems to occur when an activity is produced by the exposure to the unconditioned instigating force of a stimulus, as in eating or sexual activity. Affectively positive anticipation (appetite or hope) occurs as one moves toward an opportunity for an intrinsically enjoyable activity. This anticipatory emotional state occurs in the phase of instrumental pursuit of a goal (as one approaches the goal) and as there is an increase in the strength of the action tendency that is attributable to an increase in the magnitude of the instigating force of the stimulus situation in relation to the relative constancy of the consummatory value of the activity in progress. This is shown in Table 10.1. The table includes several other tentative identifications of familiar

TABLE 10.1   Positive and Negative Affective States Are Associated with the Nature of Changes in the Magnitude of Instigating Force of the Stimulus Situation Relative to the Consummatory Value of the Activity in Progress

AFFECTIVE STATE	CRITICAL DETERMINANTS		STRENGTH OF ACTION TENDENCY
	F	c	
Hope ($+$)	Increase in magnitude	Relatively constant	Increase
Satisfaction ($+$)	Relatively constant	Increase in magnitude	Decrease
Disappointment ($-$)	Decrease in magnitude	Relatively constant	Decrease
Frustration ($-$)	Relatively constant	Decrease in magnitude	Increase

affective states with increases and decreases in the magnitude of the instigating force or the consummatory value of the activity which constitutes the behavioral expression of the tendency. One can surmise from the table that the various affective states are associated with different phases of the traditional sequence of instrumental activities that culminate in some kind of consummatory activity or frustration. They are related in some way to changes in the two critical determinants of the strength of action tendency that sustains the ongoing behavior—F and c. Our analysis parallels an earlier one by Feather (1963) in terms of the cognitive correlates of action.

It would appear that *whenever one or the other of these factors (F or c) is increasing in magnitude faster than the other, and there is a change in the F/c ratio, there is also positive affect.* Thus we find the *hope* or *anticipation* of pleasure correlated with an increase in T when F increases but c is relatively constant, and we find *satisfaction* correlated with the decrease in T attributable to the more dramatic increase in the magnitude of c than F in the so-called consummatory activity.

On the other hand, *negative affect occurs whenever one or another of the two factors* (*F* or *c*) *is decreasing more rapidly than the other.* Thus we find loss of hope or *disappointment* accompanies a reduction in *T* produced by a decrease in magnitude of *F* with relatively constant *c*. This occurs when, for some reason, there is a decrease in the certainty or the promise of reward, that is, an extinction of *F*. And irritation, or the feeling of frustration, occurs when the consummatory value of ongoing activity diminishes more rapidly than the magnitude of the instigating force. The increase in the strength of action tendency associated with the delay often confronted while waiting for a slow moving elevator, as compared with the alternative of continued walking toward one's destination, is perhaps an adequate example.

It is particularly interesting to observe that the organizing principle is not simply the direction of the change in the strength of an action tendency. It has often been argued that negative and positive affect (pain and pleasure) merely reflect increased excitation (drive) or decreased excitation (that is, drive-reduction). In our view, the nature of the affective reaction is uncorrelated with the direction of the change in the strength of an action tendency. Increases and decreases in the level of arousal can be affectively positive or negative, depending on the conditions responsible for the changes. The idea that the key to affective reactions is the change in the magnitude of the instigating force of the stimulus situation relative to the change in the consummatory value of the response clearly implies that the affective reactions are usually related to the actual changes in the stimulus situation and/or the change in the nature of the ongoing activity rather than the static conditions of stimulus and response. When, in other words, the magnitude of action tendency is changing, and perhaps as a function of the rate of the change, there is an accompanying affective reaction.

Essentially the same method of analysis can be undertaken to identify the theoretical conditions associated with fear, anxiety, dread, and relief, the several emotional reactions associated with aversive behavior. This is done in Table 10.2. The feeling of dread, called fear, when its object is known to

TABLE 10.2   Dread (Fear and Anxiety) and Relief Are Associated with Presence or Increase and Reduction of Resistance

EMOTIONAL STATE	CRITICAL DETERMINANTS
Dread	Presence or increase of negation tendency and resistance
Relief	Reduction of negation tendency and resistance

an individual, and anxiety, when it is not, is associated with the presence or the increase of resistance to an activity. When there is the kind of covert expression we call expectancy of a particular punishment (or of failure, etc.) that implies a correlated negaction tendency, the description fear of punishment or fear of failure seems to provide an adequate description of the emotional state of the subject. When there is resistance to an activity, attributable to the inhibitory force of the stimulus situation, but no covert expression to identify the object of dread, that is, no cognitive expectation of the nature of the threat, the term anxiety is traditionally employed. The emotional state called *relief* is very obviously correlated with *reduction* in resistance—the diminution of negaction tendency that soon occurs when an inhibitory force is withdrawn. This most typically occurs when the stimulus situation no longer implies the threat of punishment and the covert activity called expectancy of punishment has ceased.

The conscious emotion called fear, as here conceived, involves sensations (that is, covert expressions) having their origin in an autonomic reaction, coupled with the cognitive content that defines the threatening object. Take away the latter and you have anxiety. The physiological reaction is, in our view, one aspect of the inhibitory process or, perhaps, of the unconditioned instigation to flight produced by the same stimulus situation that produces inhibitory force. Fear and fear-reduction are closely correlated with the genesis of avoidance behavior, as explained in Chapter 8, but they are not considered causal variables in the present scheme.

NEW INTERPRETATIONS AND GUIDING HYPOTHESES

At various stages in the development of the ideas discussed in these chapters, we have confronted the relevant details of available empirical evidence in order to appraise the value of our assumptions to that point. Almost invariably we have found that the question of interest could not be answered until we completed the specification of some other neglected aspect of the theory. It becomes very apparent that in most confrontations with behavioral data, it is not simply one or another isolated assumption that is put to the test. The whole set of assumptions about the dynamic processes of motivation are on the line because their implications are so generally interrelated. Faced with the choice between less than definitive attempts to appraise some part of the theory in reference to the most relevant fund of evidence or a continued effort to sharpen the specification of the nature of the several interrelated processes that control the change of activity, we have consistently followed the latter path. We have opted for the coherence and the scope of the conceptual scheme first, guided, of course, by our knowledge of the gross features of empirical evidence. This book, therefore, represents only the creative or opening phase of a dialogue. Now, in the final sections, we begin the critical corrective phase that we hope this book will encourage among others who best know the evidence on certain problems. We consider some new interpretations or guiding hypotheses that concern familiar behavioral problems and some of the innovations in our empirical research at Michigan that have begun to concretize important implications of the scheme. Our aim is to provide directions for empirical inquiry.

Phenomena Related to Inertial Tendency

The assumption of inertia that is applied to behavioral tendencies is heuristic in its integrative implications. It embraces, as coordinate phenomena, the effect of the time of deprivation (the traditional way of controlling motivation in animal research), the well-known reciprocal relationship between the effects of reward training (however conceived) and the latency of response, and the kind of stupidity in behavior that is apparent when humans fail to maximize expected utility in choices and animals prefer the alternative for which less adequate training has been given. To this varied set of phenomena (now to be viewed as the effects or illustrations of inertial tendency) can be added still others: many or most of the Freudian instances of persistence of the unfulfilled wish, the Ziegarnik effect, the effects of experimentally induced human motivation on thematic apperception, and the differential effects of success and failure, to name a few. We consider three of these behavioral phenomena that have been of particular interest to us.

The Effect of Time of Food Deprivation. As pointed out in Chapter 2, the critical condition defining a period of deprivation is that the subject is not permitted to engage in a certain kind of activity (in this case eating) over a specified interval of time. This means that no direct expression of the tendency (in this case Tendency to Eat) is allowed. Hence, the consummatory force operating during this interval should ordinarily be quite small. It is able to arise only as a consequence of substitution. This implies little or no reduction in the strength of the tendency for the activity in question. But the tendency can increase in strength during the deprivation interval and should do so if the organism is subjected to the appropriate instigating forces from time to time. In the case of food deprivation, external (environmental) stimuli, internal stimuli (drive stimulus and the sensory return from overt activity), and covert activities (discussed earlier in this chapter), all are potential sources of the instigating force to eat. Few experiments on the effects of time of deprivation have minimized the exposure to the instigating force from environmental stimuli, to say nothing of attempting to rule out instigation from the other potential sources. Thus, there is ample reason to suspect that, in practice, a period of food deprivation includes repeated exposures to the instigating force to eat under conditions that do effectively prevent the direct expression of the tendency to eat in an activity having substantial consummatory value.

Rats deprived of food are prevented from eating but are not necessarily shielded from the sight and the smell of food and from other cues associated with eating nor from the internal stimuli that may be a consequence of their deprivation. This condition, given our additional assumptions about displacement, is well designed to build up the inertial tendency to eat. And within limits, the longer the deprivation interval is, the stronger should become the inertial tendency to eat. The latter encompasses a large number of specific food-related activities. This strengthened tendency to eat can be manifested in any one of the specific activities belonging to the family—in instrumental elaborations of the tendency as well as eating itself.

Consider the results of two experiments that were particularly concerned about the possible role of stimuli, external and internal, in producing the effects of food deprivation on food-seeking and eating behavior. Neither of the studies was explicitly designed to explore the concept of inertial tendency, as here defined, but both of them—Birch, Burnstein, and Clark (1958) and Brown and Belloni (1963)—were concerned about the adequacy of an explanation of the behavioral phenomena of hunger strictly in terms of stimuli and previous training.

In both experiments, a strict food maintenance schedule was imposed under which rats, housed in individual cages, were without food for 22 hours and then allowed to eat for 2 hours. Birch, Burnstein, and Clark conducted their experiment in the basement of a classroom building and relied on the noise from the ventilating system and constant illumination to minimize changes in the environmental stimulation over the deprivation period. Brown and Belloni placed their animals in cages inside a room that provided constant illumination and was well-insulated against any outside auditory stimuli. It seems almost certainly true that they achieved a more nearly constant external environment for their rats than did the first experiment.

Another important difference in method is that in the Birch et al. experiment feeding troughs were continuously present in the cages and simply were filled with food at feeding times. A running record was made of the depressions of the empty food trough throughout the deprivation interval for each of the rats. In the later experiment, the food troughs were removable. This permitted them to be placed in the cages only at feeding and testing times. The number of empty trough·depressions was recorded for each rat during the one-hour test period.

Figure 10.2 presents the results for the corresponding deprivation times obtained in the two experiments when the animals, all of which had been trained on a 22-hour maintenance schedule, were now deprived of food for

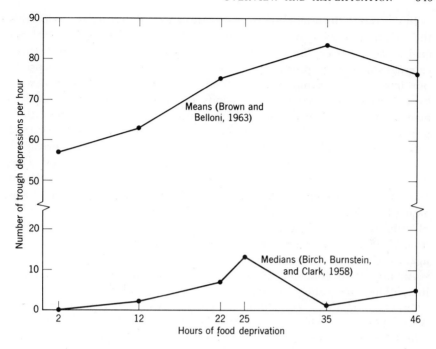

FIGURE 10.2   The data from two experiments showing the strength of the tendency to eat as a function of the time of food deprivation.

longer than 22 hours, for the first time in their lives. Both sets of data suggest that the tendency to eat, identified with the number of trough depressions given in an hour, grows to a maximum and then declines with the increasing time of food deprivation from 2 to 46 hours.

The initial segments of the two curves in which the tendency to eat is growing steadily in strength is a good example of the buildup of the inertial tendency to be expected under deprivation conditions. The decline in the curves, following their maxima, means either that the consummatory value of the trough-pressing activity has increased or that the instigating force of the stimulus situation has decreased or that both changes have occurred. Since there is no reason to think that the *nature* of the food-related activity engaged in by the animals varied with the time of deprivation, there is no basis for assuming a change in consummatory value. The decline that can be observed in the curves probably represents, then, an effect attributable to the occurrence of the same food-related activities but in the presence of stimuli having a weaker instigating force. Recall that the strength of a tendency being expressed in behavior approaches a limit defined by F/c.

In the Birch, Burnstein, and Clark study, such a difference in the magnitude of the instigating force could result from the lack of a constant external environment during the experiment. If, as seems likely, some distinctive external stimuli were present each day at different times within the deprivation interval (for example, sounds produced by students changing classes, by security officers making their rounds, etc.), they would be expected to acquire differential magnitudes of instigating force as a function of their proximity to the activity of eating each day. Because of the daily cycle of activities in the building, external stimuli from 24 to 46 hours deprivation would be the same as from 0 to 22 hours. The decline in the tendency to eat from 25 to 35 hours deprivation, thus, could be attributed to the continued expression of the inertial tendency in combination with the minimal instigating force from the external stimuli in that interval. This conjecture gains plausibility when we observe that the number of trough depressions increases from 35 to 46 hours deprivation, that is, as the time of feeding approaches again.

An appeal to changing external stimuli with different magnitudes of instigating force cannot be made in the Brown and Belloni study. The external environment was held much more nearly constant for their animals. Assuming that the shape of the Brown and Belloni curve is reliably non-monotone, we are required to look elsewhere for a change in the stimulus situation. One possibility, long assumed within the S-R tradition, is that certain internal stimuli change systematically with time of deprivation (that is, the drive stimulus). The instigating force acquired by the drive stimulus for 22 hours deprivation (the normal time of feeding) would generalize to other similar drive stimuli, including the ones produced by the greater than 24 hours of deprivation imposed in the test. The generalized instigating force could maintain and even increase the tendency to eat for a time following the 22-hour deprivation point but would fail to do so when the internal stimuli became sufficiently dissimilar to the ones present during conditioning (that is, at 22 hours food deprivation). If future experimentation establishes that in a constant external environment the curve defining the strength of tendency to eat levels off rather than declines as deprivation continues beyond the regular feeding time, the need to appeal to the presence of these internal stimuli will be removed. A monotone growth to asymptote (F/c) for the tendency to eat is derivable directly from the combination of a constant instigating force (F) from the environment and a constant consummatory value (c) from food-related activities (see Figure 1.6).

It is apparent from Figure 10.1 that the data from the two experiments are different in certain respects, although alike in basic form. The overall level of activity is appreciably higher and the point of maximum activity is somewhat later in the deprivation interval in the Brown and Belloni study.

In evaluating these discrepancies, it is important to notice that Birch, Burnstein, and Clark report results in terms of medians (because of the markedly skewed distributions obtained), whereas Brown and Belloni report means (presumably because skewing was not a problem). The different summary statistics employed could conceivably be responsible for the differences in the curves, but there are psychological as well as statistical reasons for the two sets of results to differ in the ways they do. As observed earlier in this section, Birch, Burnstein, and Clark left the food trough in the rat's cage continuously. Brown and Belloni inserted it into the cage only at the time of feeding and testing. Thus, in the former study, there was ample opportunity for some magnitude of instigating force of the empty food troughs to have extinguished, as a consequence of nonreinforcement (see Chapter 5). In the latter study, the food troughs were present only at the time of eating during the training period and so should have retained strong instigating force for the testing period. This presumed difference in the magnitude of the instigating force of the empty food troughs is sufficient to account for the difference in overall level of reported activity.

The point of maximum activity appears at 25 hours deprivation in Birch, Burnstein, and Clark's study and 35 hours in Brown and Belloni's. Such a discrepancy is to be expected if, as hypothesized, external environmental stimuli are the predominant source of instigating forces to eat in the former experiment and internal, drive stimuli the predominant source in the latter. The reason is that instigating force would be expected to drop off dramatically for environmental stimuli following the regular time of eating but would be expected to do so only gradually for the internal stimuli. Support for the tendency to eat, thus, could be maintained by the drive stimuli but not by the environmental stimuli.

In sum, both sets of data can be given a reasonable interpretation in terms of the assumptions of the present scheme. In giving our account, no appeal is made to a nonspecific energizing factor such as the D of Hullian theory. We have discussed in Chapter 4, and again in the present chapter, how such a nonspecific multiplicative factor could enter into the theory of action. If it can be shown that the effects of deprivation require such a factor, the conclusions reached in those theoretical explorations will become most relevant.

This discussion of the time of deprivation has stressed the growth in inertial tendency during the deprivation interval. However, under some conditions, an inertial tendency can be expected to decline in strength over a time interval even while occasionally being instigated. An inertial tendency not being expressed directly can nevertheless dissipate over time as a consequence of substitution. One can imagine a phenomenon opposite in direction but analogous in process to the growth of an inertial tendency over time as a consequence of displacement. This would be the case if the individual were *stimulus deprived*, that is, kept from exposure to stimuli that functioned as instigating force for some activity but not deprived of the opportunity to engage in the activity itself or in various substitute activities. Then the effects of aperiodic exposure to direct or indirect consummatory force would be cumulative, and the strength of the tendency would be reduced.[3]

Consider again the reduction in an inertial tendency that should occur when the tendency is expressed in behavior but is supported by weak or even decreasing instigating force, so that its strength is falling to an asymptote defined by (F/c). The decline in the tendency to eat when deprivation of food was extended beyond the regular feeding time was interpreted in this way in the preceding discussion. This also must be the case when a golfer, after hitting an errant shot, begins to look for his lost ball with strong inertial tendency but then gradually loses hope as the search behind each bush or clump of weeds is futile and, hence, each new bush or clump produces even less instigating force to sustain the search.

Immediate Motivational Effects of Success and Failure. Another important inertial effect, discussed in Chapter 6, is Weiner's separation of the immediate motivational effects of success and failure from their effects on cognitive learning, namely, the differential effect on the subsequent subjective probability of success. This work, described by him in the language of the theory of achievement motivation, was treated in Chapter 6 in terms of the distinction between an effect on inertial action tendency and a change in the magnitude of instigating force. Since we had yet to present the theory of resistance, we could not in the earlier chapter consider his additional argument that success and failure have similar effects on the strength of the inertial tendency to avoid failure which functions to resist subsequent achievement-oriented action.

Weiner (1970) has collated scattered evidence from earlier studies (Weiner, 1963; 1965; 1966; Weiner and Rosenbaum, 1965) which shows that some individuals—those who score high on tests of anxiety—typically show a decrement in level of performance after failure and enhanced level of performance after success. This is directly opposite to the typical pattern of results for less anxious or more positively motivated individuals that has been attributed to differential inertial action tendency. Weiner has explained this consistent trend among anxious individuals by assuming that success reduces both the tendency to achieve success and the tendency to avoid failure but that failure reduces neither. Hence, when individuals are classified by personality tests into subgroups according to which of the two tendencies is predominant in them, the net effects of success and failure respectively are (1)

---

[3] Perhaps, the functional significance of the behavior that constitutes mourning the loss of a loved one is to be understood in these terms.

the reduction versus persistence of a resultant tendency to avoid failure (that is, resistance) among more anxious individuals, and (2) the reduction versus persistence of a resultant tendency to achieve success among less anxious and more positively motivated persons.

Of immediate interest is the concept of inertial resistance following failure which Weiner has suggested. Can we account for this in terms of our present analysis of the dynamics of resistance?

It is important to observe, at the outset, that success and failure are mutually exclusive outcomes of achievement-oriented activity. It is as if an animal had learned to expect either food *or* shock at the end of the alley on each trial. This means that during the instrumental phase of an achievement-oriented activity, the stimulus situation is the source of both instigating force (corresponding to expectancy of success) and inhibitory force (corresponding to expectancy of failure). But, when the individual succeeds at some task, there is a change in the stimulus situation. This change in the stimulus, which defines the outcome of the activity as successful (for example, the visual stimulus of the thrown ringer in a ringtoss game), constitutes at the same time a removal of the stimulus situation which, until that moment, had produced an inhibitory force. The individual who has just succeeded is no longer threatened with failure on that occasion. Thus, as the stimulus situation defining success produces instigating force which boosts the strength of the action tendency, the avoidant or negation tendency, now no longer sustained and supported by the exposure to an inhibitory force, should begin to diminish immediately as a result of the continued force of resistance. As the individual engages in the consummatory activity of succeeding, the action tendency is then also reduced.

In brief, the negation tendency (to avoid failure) is reduced by success because the inhibitory force sustaining it until that time is withdrawn, but the force of resistance, responsible for reduction of a negation tendency, continues. The action tendency (to achieve success) is reduced by the consummatory force of succeeding.

What about the effect of failure? Again, there is a change in the stimulus situation. The change in the stimulus situation that defines the outcome as failure (for example, the visual stimulus of a miss in a ringtoss game) produces the strong inhibitory force of failure which should boost the strength of negation tendency. But this also constitutes removal of the stimulus which until then had sustained an expectancy of success on that occasion, that is, the instigating force. Thus the magnitude of negation tendency is immediately increased by failure but there is no comparable increase in the action tendency. The latter persists unchanged when the instigating force to achieve success on that trial has been withdrawn.

The immediate consequence of this difference in the two conditions should be a reduction of resistance immediately following success and increased resistance immediately following failure, as Weiner has been led to assume. Weiner's general hypothesis, developed in terms of a preliminary treatment of the concept of inertial tendency (Atkinson and Cartwright, 1964) but before the present theory of resistance had been clarified (Chapter 8), is that success reduces the characteristic achievement-related motivation of an individual but failure does not. For some individuals this is primarily and most noticeably a reduction in action tendency, for others in negaction tendency. The diametrically opposite observed effects on the level of performance follow from this.

The details of the process described above may be more easily understood if we consider an analogous problem in the domain of animal behavior. Let food-seeking and shock-avoidance constitute the content of the action and negaction tendencies instead of success-seeking and failure-avoidance. And to complete the analogy, the food reward and shock punishment must be mutually exclusive outcomes of a simple instrumental activity like running in an alley. What happens to the tendency to eat and the tendency to avoid the shock on the reward trials (that is, when the outcome is food–no shock) and on the punishment trials (that is, when the outcome is no food–shock)?

After some preliminary training with both outcomes, the stimulus of the start box and alley will be the source of both the instigating and the inhibitory force. But the change in the stimulus situation following the run on the reward trials constitutes a strong instigating force to eat and the removal of the inhibitory force, since the animal has never been punished while or immediately after eating the food. The stimulus of food in the goal box immediately boosts the action tendency, and then the activity of eating reduces it. Meanwhile the negaction tendency, no longer sustained and supported by inhibitory force, should be diminished by the continued force of resistance. Both tendencies, in other words, are reduced on the reward trials.

In contrast, the change in the stimulus situation following a run on the punishment trials constitutes a sudden increase in the magnitude of inhibitory force and the withdrawal of the instigating force, since the animal has never eaten while or immediately after being shocked. The negaction tendency is given an immediate boost. The action tendency persists unchanged. Both tendencies, in other words, should be stronger immediately after the punishment trial than immediately after the reward trial.

It could be expected in both this animal case and the human case of achievement-oriented behavior that the persistence of a negaction tendency following punishment (or failure) should be more transitory than the persistence of an action tendency. The negaction tendency should diminish when the subject leaves the situation because it is continually expressed in resistance. A comparable reduction in an action tendency requires that it be directly expressed in activity or in substitution.

In the animal case described above, it is obvious that the kind of outcome that reduces the inertial action tendency (that is, food reward) meets the condition for reinforcement of the instigating force. The kind of outcome that does not reduce the inertial action tendency (no reward) meets the condition for extinction of the instigating force. The implications for behavior on an immediately subsequent trial are just the opposite for the two effects.

But this is not also true in the case of negation and punishment. The kind of outcome that boosts the negation tendency and allows for persistence of resistance is punishment, and this also strengthens the inhibitory force for a subsequent occasion. And the trial without punishment is the one that produces reduction of the negation tendency and the extinction of the inhibitory force. The effect of the change in force and the inertial effect are supplementary in the case of resistance.

Perceptual and Cognitive Activities.   There is a considerable body of data from diverse sources such as after images, brightness and color contrast, the Zeigarnick effect, functional fixedness, and the analysis of dreams for which the concept of persisting tendency should be readily applicable. In fact, a concept of persisting tendency in one form or another has been used in separate accounts of all of these perceptual and cognitive phenomena in the past, suggesting that persistence is a fundamental characteristic of tendencies for covert activities.

In applying the present theory to perceptual and cognitive activities, we have adopted the hypothesis that the laws governing the occurrence of covert activities are not different from the ones that govern the occurrence of overt activities. That is, we propose that the action and negation tendencies for covert activities persist unless operated on by forces, that there is competition among tendencies for covert activities with the strongest resultant tendency expressed in consciousness, and that the resultant tendencies for covert activities reflect the excess of action tendencies over their corresponding negation tendencies. Issues of compatibility and incompatibility are assumed to arise and the processes of elaboration are expected to apply.

The conception of perception and cognition as activities engaged in by the organism is in the tradition of Kant and coordinates with much contemporary theorizing in these domains both in the United States and the Soviet Union (see, for example, Neisser, 1967; and Cole and Maltzman, 1969). It remains to be seen whether our hypothesis that what is perceived and what is thought about at any given moment can be accounted for in terms of force and tendency for covert activities, as specified in the theory, but there is some supporting evidence.

For example, the empirical generalization that the physical intensity and the duration of the exposure to a spot of light combine multiplicatively in their relation to the detection of the spot can be interpreted as an instance of the tendency to perceive the light growing in strength as a function of the magnitude of instigating force of the light operating over time. Similarly, the sequence of perceiving first one figure and then another when fixating a reversible figure can be viewed as repeated shifts in covert activity, amenable to the analyses of Chapters 4 and 9. A detailed examination of the implications of our assumptions for the analyses of covert activities is, however, work left undone in the present book.

Effects of Punishment and Avoidance Behavior

The framework we offer for explaining the facts of avoidance behavior rests on interpreting avoidance in terms of punishment. Our theory of punishment, in turn, is developed out of the hypothesis that noxious stimuli function as inhibitory forces to increase the strength of negation tendencies which resist the expression of action tendencies.

Since negation tendencies are "consumed" by their resistance to action tendencies, all punishments are necessarily temporary in their effects. This is true even for the special conditions in which a negation tendency nullifies an action tendency. Ultimately, *unless there are strong substitution effects*, the action tendency will regain dominance. The derived transitory nature of punishment is a prominent feature of this theory. That action tendencies will grow to a higher asymptote when expressed in the face of resistance than in the absence of resistance, implying that punishment can actually result in a stronger tendency for an activity rather than a weaker, is another notable feature.

In using the theory of resistance to analyze avoidance behavior, we first should notice that every avoidance situation is a punishment situation in which all activities except the one selected as the avoidance response are punished. The punishment occurs in the presence of a warning signal, allowing that stimulus to acquire inhibitory force properties for each of the punished activities. This means that the avoidance response first appears and then continues over trials solely by default, that is, because all activities with stronger action tendencies are held in check by resistance. Each time the warning signal comes on, it increases the strength of the negation tendencies for all nonavoidance activities and, by preventing their occurrence, permits avoidance.

Each avoidance trial is one on which the organism does not receive the noxious stimulus, but it is also one on which he does not engage in the punished activities. This is the second important point to notice because without the occurrence of these activities a critical event for the conditioning of inhibitory force is missing, and there is no reason that the inhibitory force of the warning signal should change. Thus, avoidance can be maintained over many trials, and it is irrelevant whether or not punishment would have been administered had the organism engaged in the nonavoidance activities.

Determinants of the Operant Level of an Activity

The operant level of an activity refers to the number of times that activity occurs over some interval of time. This means that at least one other activity is also engaged in during the interval, and it is apparent that the operant rate of any activity is a function of the strengths of the tendencies for all the activities being engaged in. This can be seen particularly clearly in our derivation (see Chapter 4) where for the case of only two activities the operant rate of the one is identical to the operant rate of the other.

In analyzing the operant behavior of an organism, it is important to distinguish the intensity or vigor of an activity as it is ongoing from the operant rate of the activity. Theoretically, the former is identified with the absolute strength of the resultant action tendency being expressed, and the latter with the relative magnitudes of the resultant action tendencies for all the activities engaged in. An adequate account of the stream of behavior requires a theory that integrates these two, quite separable, aspects of operant behavior.

INITIAL THEORY-GUIDED RESEARCH

We have begun to pursue the implications of this conceptual analysis in experiments on animal and human motivation. Recent doctoral studies by Allison (1963), Weiner (1963), Brown (1967), Karabenick (1967), Valle (1967) and other interrelated experiments, some preliminary ones (Atkinson and Birch, 1966) and more recent ones by Timberlake and Birch (1967) and Birch (1968) have begun to concretize the implications of our analysis for the design of research and the method of study and to yield results that are directly relevant to the theory. We shall review them briefly in closing.

Studies of Animal Motivation

A good case can be made that many of the basic aspects of the theory of action are more readily investigated by using animals than by using human beings because more lifelike situations can be arranged for animals in the laboratory and because the tendencies to action are more simply related to observable activities in lower organisms. Mainly, for these reasons, new research with rats has been undertaken on problems related to changes in activity, consummatory effects, and inertial tendency.

We have engaged in a continuing endeavor to devise a method for studying changes in activity that will permit the systematic analysis of factors affecting the tendencies for both the ongoing and alternative activities. An apparatus called the Hex Maze, pictured in Figure 6.5, which allows the rat to move freely from one activity to another throughout a testing period was designed and used to demonstrate that the latency of response is a function of the characteristics of the ongoing as well as the alternative activity (Birch, 1966). The Hex Maze was also employed by Allison (1964) to assess the motive to eat in rats and in a series of experiments reported in Timberlake and Birch (1967) and Birch (1968) in which a single shift in activity was studied. In two of these experiments it was demonstrated that, consistent with the primary implication of the Principle of Change of Activity, the time taken for a simple shift in activity is related to variables that affect both the tendency for the ongoing activity (hours of food deprivation) and the tendency for the alternative activity (complexity and novelty of the exploratory chamber). In a third experiment, the shift in activity was between eating in the goal box of a runway and exploring an adjacent chamber. The amount eaten and the time taken to change activities from eating to exploring increased with training on the runway and were greater after training on trials for which the rats were placed into the goal box than when they ran into it. Considerable progress has been made in solving the methodological problems associated with research on the Principle of Change of Activity and, hopefully, additional improvements will allow a thorough investigation of all factors of interest.

A dissertation by Karabenick (1967) reported the results of an extensive investigation of the consummatory effects of the magnitude of food reward in a double runway of the type used by Amsel and Roussel (1952). During the first stage of his study, Karabenick employed four groups to combine exhaustively the number of food pellets (15 or 1) in the first and second goal boxes of the alley. Subsequently, he shifted the reward magnitude in the first goal box to the other value for half the animals while he continued the original conditions of reward for the remaining animals. Numerous and sometimes complex consummatory effects were found. It can be concluded from these data that consummatory behavior affects the immediately subsequent strength of tendency and that the effects are a function of the strength of the tendency prior to the consummatory event. These are characteristics of behavior that emphasize the continuity of its underlying processes and invite analysis in terms of the theory of action, a task also undertaken by Karabenick.

The concept of inertial or persisting tendency, based on the hypothesis that a tendency retains its strength over time unless altered by forces, is uniquely important to the theory of action. It not only provides the basis for certain explanations from the theory but is also responsible for its dynamic nature. More generally, the concept of persisting tendency offers a viable alternative to the stimulus-bound conception of behavior that ties each response of an organism to its immediate stimulus environment.

We began the research suggested by the concept of persisting tendency with the three experiments reported in Birch (1968).[4] We directed our attention to the following three characteristics of persisting tendencies as represented in the theory of action:

1. Exposure to stimuli with appropriate instigating force value will increase the strength of an action tendency for an organism.

2. Unless subjected to consummatory force, an action tendency will maintain its strength even though the organism is no longer exposed to the instigating stimuli for that activity.

3. The longer an organism is exposed to an instigating stimulus the stronger his action tendency should become.

The same method was used in all three experiments. Rats were housed in a room well removed from the place in which their regular feeding occurred each day for 90 minutes in distinctive cages. This procedure was intended to minimize the instigating force for eating associated with the stimuli of the living cages and to maximize it for the stimuli of the feeding cages. The amount of food eaten in a test period was compared among groups identical with respect to time since last eating but different with respect to the duration of the exposure to the stimuli of the empty feeding cages. Our purpose was to check whether exposure to the instigating stimuli increases the strength of the tendency to eat and, if so, whether these increases are related to the duration of exposure. In one experiment some of the animals were given a 30-minute delay period between the exposure to the empty feeding cages and testing, during which they were returned to their living cages. This was done to discover whether the effects of the instigation from the empty feeding cages would persist over a 30-minute interval of little or no instigation from external sources.

The three experiments combined yield results as follows.

1. The exposure of rats to instigating stimuli for eating does increase the strength of the tendency to eat.

2. The tendency to eat retains its greater strength gained from the exposure to the instigating stimuli over a 30-minute interval at least.

3. The greater duration of exposure to instigating stimuli for eating produces a stronger tendency to eat, but this conclusion must be offered more tentatively in that satisfactory statistical significance among exposure durations was not attained in any single experiment; yet, the rank order of the effects is as expected in each.

[4] Fred P. Valle and Guy J. Johnson assisted in these experiments.

More recent evidence on the third point is contained in a dissertation by Valle (1967). As a consequence of greater precision in this experiment, statistical significance was attained for the amount of food eaten in the test attributable to the duration of exposure to the instigating stimuli. Valle also demonstrated that stimuli resulting from handling the animals at the time of feeding could acquire instigating force for eating and that these effects could be eliminated by providing nonfeeding related handling for the animals also. ·

Studies of Achievement Motivation.   After a number of unsuccessful, or at best, only partially successful attempts to provide an empirical demonstration of the primary implication of the Principle of Change of Activity (summarized in Atkinson and Birch, 1966), M. Brown (1967) studied the time taken to change from an achievement-related task to a subsequent task in a long series of activities in which the next task available to the subject was under direct experimental control. His results confirm the general expectation that the time taken to change from one activity to another (whether it be viewed as the persistence of the one or the latency of the other) will be systematically influenced by two classes of variables—the one affecting the resultant tendency sustaining the initial activity and the other affecting the resultant tendency that is expressed in the subsequent activity. Brown's subjects took significantly longer to begin to put away unsolved anagram tasks than solved ones following a signal to move on to the next activity, and significantly longer when the next task was a different kind of activity (rating the social desirability of a list of traits) than when it was another test of skill in solving anagrams. The results demonstrate that the time to change from one activity to another is affected by both the outcome (success or failure) of the initial achievement-oriented activity and the nature of the subsequent activity. The shorter time to change following success than failure implies that the consummatory value of success is greater than that of failure as was assumed previously (Chapter 2) in reference to the greater expression of n Achievement in thematic apperception immediately following failure than success and in the Weiner experiment (Chapter 6). The study was also designed to show, but did not, that individual differences in strength of achievement-related motives (n Achievement and Test Anxiety) would affect these time measurements in predictable ways.

In some of our preliminary efforts to establish a method for studying molar changes in human activity, for example, from achievement-oriented activity to affiliative activity, we sought to demonstrate that the time to change would be influenced by the relative strength of the two kinds of motive (that is, n Achievement versus n Affiliation) within the subject. In successive attempts that involved the kind of highly contrived conditions that are sometimes required in experimental social psychology, we found some suggestive evidence that individual differences in first one of the motives and then the other were related to the time to change from an achievement test to an affiliative activity. But the definitive demonstration that this kind of molar change of activity depends on the hierarchy of motives within individuals (that is, personality) has thus far eluded us (Atkinson and Birch, 1966). It is one of the fundamental implications of the Principle of Change of Activity and one demanding a great deal of experimental ingenuity to demonstrate.

The conceptual analysis of the several motivational effects of success and failure among individuals who differ in strength of achievement-related motives, provides an adequate test of anyone's understanding of this theory concerning the dynamics of action. The requirements of research design and in method of study for this problem illustrate the upgraded demand for training in personality methods, for the understanding of the relation between personality and basic behavioral process, and for skill in experimentation that is now more obviously required for systematic research on human motivation. Let us consider again Weiner's (1965) effort to disentangle the immediate motivational effects of success and failure (that is, differential inertial tendency) from their effect on learning (that is, change in magnitude of instigating and inhibitory force).[5]

Our discussion of the two kinds of effects contingent on success and failure, in the preceding section, draws attention to the key experimental problem if one is primarily interested in studying the differential inertial effects of success and failure. It is to control and to hold constant the magnitude of instigating force and inhibitory force on the test trial that immediately follows the critical success and failure experience. Otherwise, there is a complete confounding of effects attributable to differential inertial tendency and effects attributable to the forces.

Weiner assumed the logic of the theory of achievement motivation (see Atkinson and Feather, 1966) to achieve this kind of experimental control. We follow his justification of the design of the experiment but with comments that give our new interpretation of the conditions and results.

First, he assumed that the conditions of achievement motivation would be equivalent for a task undertaken with the initial subjective probability of success of 0.70 or 0.30. We now would consider these two conditions as equivalent in magnitude of instigating force (to achieve success) and inhibitory force (to avoid failure). Second, he assumed that repeated success when initial probability was 0.70 would produce successive increases in subjective probability having motivational implications equivalent to the ones that

---

[5] A preliminary discussion of the procedure and results for individuals high in *n* Achievement but low in Anxiety is given in Ch. 6, pp. 189 to 193.

were produced by the successive decreases in subjective probability caused by repeated failure when the initial probability was 0.30. We recall our treatment of the change of instigating force and inhibitory force (Chapters 5, 6, and 8). Third, he assumed that persons appropriately classified in terms of relative strengths of motive to achieve success and motive to avoid failure as given by the conventional diagnostic personality tests would yield results following the success and failure treatments that were either primarily indicative of the inertial tendency to achieve success or the inertial tendency to avoid failure. We consider his classification of subjects into a high *n* Achievement–low Anxiety group versus low *n* Achievement–high Anxiety group as essentially equivalent to control of the relative strength of the instigating force to achieve versus the inhibitory force to avoid failure among his subjects. The results of the former group should approximate the ones expected with minimal resistance. The results of the latter group (that is, the more anxious subjects) should provide the clearest information concerning the proposed concept of inertial resistance.

The results reported in Chapter 6 for those highly motivated to achieve—a higher level of performance and a greater persistence following failure than following success—are consistent with theoretical expectations concerning the inertial action tendency.

Among the more anxious subjects, the result was different. The level of performance measured on the trial immediately following the first success and first failure was significantly lower following the failure. This much is consistent with the assumption that the tendency to avoid failure, responsible for resistance, would persist following failure. But there was no evidence of less persistence in the achievement-oriented activity following failure than following success when those anxious subjects continually had the opportunity to change to another kind of task, one that did not require skill nor involve the evaluation of performance. This other expected behavioral manifestation of inertial resistance was missing.

This, like most of the other empirical implications of our conceptual scheme that have been suggested in our discussions, must be considered an open question. With a nod of special gratitude to Freud and Zeigarnik, we hope that the inertial effects of these unresolved questions will be expressed in the stream of future empirical research.

GLOSSARY

action tendency   An impulse to engage in an activity, T.

activity A The name of the initial, ongoing, overt activity in an interval of observation.

activity a The name of the initial, ongoing, covert activity in an interval of observation.

activity AX The name of an ongoing, multiple activity; compatible activities A and X are occurring simultaneously.

activity X The name of an overt activity.

activity x The name of a covert activity.

c_X The consummatory value of activity X.

C_X The consummatory force of activity X.

C_{XY} The indirect consummatory force of activity X for activity Y.

c_{XY} The substitute consummatory value of activity X for activity Y.

cessation consummatory lag   The delay between cessation of an activity as defined by an observer and the termination of the consummatory force of that activity, (t_c).

change of activity   The simultaneous cessation of one activity and initiation of another.

compatible activities   Activities that can be engaged in simultaneously, for example, XcY.

compound action tendency   A composite of elemental action tendencies all of which instigate the same activity; for example, $T_{X:J,K}$.

conditioned inhibitory force   The acquired capacity of a stimulus to increase the strength of a negaction tendency, $_{cs}I$.

conditioned instigating force   The acquired capacity of a stimulus to increase the strength of an action tendency, $_{cs}F$.

consummatory force   That which defines the rate at which the strength of an action tendency diminishes, C.

357

consummatory value   A determinant of consummatory force which refers to the effect attributable to the nature of the activity as distinct from its intensity, c.

direct consummatory force   A consummatory force that depends only on the tendency being expressed in action.

displacement   The indirect strengthening of the inertial tendency for one activity that is attributable to the instigation of some other activity.

dominant tendency   The strongest among a set of tendencies to engage in mutually incompatible activities.

e The base of the natural logarithms.

effective instigating force   The sum of direct and indirect instigating forces for a particular activity.

elaboration   The broadening of a family of tendencies to include new and additional components of activity as when the tendency to eat becomes elaborated so as to include also the instrumental act of running to the food.

elemental action tendency   When the strength of the tendency to engage in a particular activity is attributable to the strength of a single action tendency.

F Instigating force for an activity that is occurring.

$_{cs}F_X$ A conditioned instigating force for activity X when continuous exposure to the stimulus can be assumed.

F_X The effective instigating force for activity X when activity X is occurring.

F_{XX} The direct instigating force for activity X when activity X is occurring.

F_{YX} The indirect instigating force for activity X resulting from direct instigation of activity Y.

$F_{X:G}$ The effective instigating force for activity $X:G$ when activity X is occurring.

$F_{X:J,K}$ The total effective instigating force for activity $X:J, K$ when activity X is occurring.

$F_{X,Y:G}$ The effective instigating force for activity $X, Y:G$ when activity X is occurring.

$_sF_X$ The effective instigating force of a stimulus for activity X when activity X is occurring.

$_{us}F_X$ The effective instigating force for activity X produced by an unconditioned stimulus; an unconditioned instigating force for activity X.

F_x The effective instigating force for activity x when activity x is occurring.

$\hat{F}$ The instigating force for an activity that is not occurring.

$\hat{F}_X$ The effective instigating force for activity X when activity X is not occurring.

F_X/c_X The asymptotic value of the action tendency, T_X, when there is simultaneous instigation and expression of T_X and no resistance, I_X.

$F_X/c_X + I_X/r_X$ The asymptotic value for an action tendency when it is subjected to instigation, resistance and consummation under ideal conditions.

family of tendencies   A class of tendencies for functionally-related or functionally-equivalent activities defined in terms of the displacement (δ) and the substitution (γ) among the several activities.

force of resistance   That which defines the rate at which the strength of a negation tendency is reduced by resistance to an action tendency, R.

$_gX$ The inertial gap for activity X, given by the value of the difference between the final strength of tendency sustaining the activity in progress (T_{A_F}) and the strength of the inertial tendency to undertake the alternative activity X (T_{X_I}).

$_g\bar{X}$ The effective inertial gap for activity X, given by the value of the difference between the final strength of effective tendency sustaining the activity in progress ($\bar{T}_{A_F}$) and the strength of the inertial effective tendency to undertake alternative activity X ($\bar{T}_{X_I}$).

$(_gX)_c$ The inertial gap for activity X under the special condition where $T_{X_I} = (T_X)_c$; see also $_gX$.

$(_g\bar{X})_c$ The effective inertial gap for activity X under the special conditions where $\bar{T}_{X_I} = (\bar{T}_X)_c$; see also $_g\bar{X}$.

heterogeneous activity   A succession of different activities during an interval of observation.

homogeneous activity   An activity, unitary or multiple, that continues throughout an interval of observation.

I Inhibitory force.

I_X The effective inhibitory force for activity X when activity X is occurring.

$_sI_X$ The effective inhibitory force of a stimulus for activity X when activity X is occurring.

$I_{X:P}$ The effective inhibitory force for activity $X:P$ when activity X is occurring.

$\hat{I}_X$ The effective inhibitory force for activity X when activity X is not occurring.

I_x The effective inhibitory force for activity x when activity x is occurring.

I_X/r_X The asymptotic value of the negation tendency N_X when it is being simultaneously affected by an inhibitory force and the force of resistance.

incompatible activities   Two activities are incompatible if one, and only one, can be engaged in at any given moment in time, for example, $X\hat{c}Y$.

indirect consummatory force   The substitute consummatory force—a consummatory force that depends on the relationship of one activity (for example, Y) to another activity (for example, X), C_{XY}; the fundamental process underlying the phenomenon of substitution.

indirect instigating force   The displaced instigating force—an instigating force that depends on the relationship of one activity (for example, Y) to another being directly instigated (for example, X), F_{XY}; the fundamental process underlying the phenomenon of displacement.

inertial tendency   The strength of a tendency at the beginning of an interval of observation, T_I or N_I or $\bar{T}_I$.

inhibitory force   That which defines the rate of increase in the strength of a negation tendency, I.

inhibitory tendency   Negation tendency, N.

initiation consummatory lag   The delay between the initiation of an activity as defined by an observer and the beginning of the consummatory force of that activity, (t_i).

instigating force   That which defines the rate of increase in the strength of an action tendency F.

interval of observation   The time interval begun arbitrarily by an observer and terminated by either the initiation of a particular activity or the cessation of an ongoing activity depending on the interest of the observer.

multiple activity   An individual is doing more than one thing, that is, he is simultaneously expressing the tendencies for two or more compatible activities, for example, activity AX.

$m(X)$ The proportion of time spent in activity X.

N Negation tendency; the tendency not to engage in an activity.

N_X The negation tendency for activity X; the tendency not to engage in activity X.

N_{X_I} The inertial negation tendency for activity X; the inertial tendency not to engage in activity X.

$N_{X:P}$ The negation tendency for activity $X:P$; the tendency not to engage in activity $X:P$.

$\bar{N}_X$ The effective negation tendency; the magnitude of N_X expressed in resistance to T_X.

$n(X)$ The number of times that activity X has occurred.

negation tendency   Inhibitory tendency, a tendency not to engage in a particular activity, N.

$p(X)$ The proportion of choices of alternative X.

R The force of resistance.

R_X The force of resistance produced by the opposition of N_X to T_X.

r_X The parameter representing the extent to which the negaction tendency N_X is reduced per unit of time in resistance to the action tendency T_X; the analog of consummatory value.

$r(X)$ The rate of activity X.

resistance   Opposition to an action tendency by a negaction tendency.

resultant action tendency   The algebraic sum of the strengths of action and negaction tendencies for a particular activity, $\bar{T}$.

substitute consummatory force   Indirect consummatory force, for example, C_{XY}.

substitute value   Indirect consummatory value, the capacity of one activity (for example, X) to reduce the inertial tendency for another activity (for example, Y), c_{XY}.

substitution   The indirect weakening of the inertial tendency for one activity that is attributable to the consummatory force of some other activity.

T_X The action tendency for activity X; the tendency to engage in activity X.

T_{X_F} The final strength of T_X in an interval of observation.

T_{X_I} The initial strength of T_X in an interval of observation; the inertial tendency.

$(T_X)_c$ The strength of T_X at the end of the cessation consummatory lag for activity X.

$(T_X)_c^r$ The value of T_X at the end of its cessation consummatory lag when resistance is present (used only in derivation on pp. 311–314).

$T_{X:G}$ The elemental action tendency to engage in activity $X:G$.

$T_{X:J,K}$ The compound action tendency to engage in activity $X:J, K$; $T_{X:J,K} = T_{X:J} + T_{X:K}$.

$T_{X,Y:G}$ The elemental action tendency to engage in activity $X, Y:G$.

T_x The action tendency for activity x.

$T_{x:g}$ The elemental action tendency to engage in activity $x:g$.

$\bar{T}_X$ The effective action tendency for activity X; $\bar{T}_X = T_X - N_X$; the equivalent of resultant action tendency.

t Time.

$t_{B/A}$ The duration of an interval of observation that begins with activity A in progress and ends with the observation that activity B has just supplanted activity A; time to initiate activity B given the initial activity A.

t_c The duration of the cessation consummatory lag.

$(t_c)_X$ The duration of the cessation consummatory lag for activity X.

t_i The duration of the initiation consummatory lag.

$(t_i)_X$ The duration of the initiation consummatory lag for activity X.

$(t_{X/A})'$ The theoretical latency of activity X given an initial activity A; the time it would take for activity X to be initiated if X were the only alternative activity being instigated.

tendency to eat   A class term embracing all the specific action tendencies belonging to the family of functionally related activities called "eating"; see also *elaboration* and *family of tendencies*.

unconditioned inhibitory force   The property of a stimulus to increase innately the strength of a negaction tendency, $_{US}I$.

unconditioned instigating force   The property of a stimulus to increase innately the strength of an action tendency, $_{US}F$.

unitary activity   An individual is doing only one thing, that is, he is expressing the tendency for only one activity, for example, activity X.

XcY Activity X and activity Y are compatible; XcY is equivalent to YcX.

$X\bar{c}Y$ Activity X and activity Y are incompatible; $X\bar{c}Y$ is equivalent to $Y\bar{c}X$.

α The average rate of change in T_A during the interval that begins with the observation that activity A is in progress and ends with the observation that activity B has just supplanted activity A.

α' The average rate of change in N_A during the interval that begins with the observation that activity A is in progress and ends with the observation that activity B has just supplanted activity A.

β The average rate of change in T_B during the interval that begins with the observation that activity A is in progress and ends with the observation that activity B has just supplanted activity A.

β' The average rate of change in N_B during the interval that begins with the observation that activity A is in progress and ends with the observation that activity B has just supplanted activity A.

γ_{AB} A parameter of substitution ($0 \leq \gamma \leq 1$) that represents the degree of relationship between activities A and B and the degree to which the direct consummatory force of activity A gives rise to an indirect consummatory force on T_B.

δ_{YX} A parameter of displacement ($0 \leq \delta_{YX} \leq 1$) that represents the degree of relationship between activities Y and X and the degree to which direct instigation of activity Y gives rise to indirect instigation of activity X.

θ A parameter in the conditioning of inhibitory force that denotes the fraction of the strength of the negaction tendency expressed in the resistance to an activity in progress that becomes the magnitude of conditioned inhibitory force of the stimulus on the next occasion.

λ A parameter in the conditioning of instigating force that denotes the fraction of the strength of the action tendency expressed in an activity that becomes the magnitude of the conditioned instigating force of the stimulus on the next occasion.

BIBLIOGRAPHY

Allison, J. Strength of preference for food, magnitude of food reward, and performance in instrumental conditioning. Unpublished doctoral dissertation, University of Michigan, 1963. Also in *J. comp. physiol. Psychol.*, 1964, **57,** 217–223.

Allport, G. W. *Personality.* New York: Holt, 1937.

Allport, G. W. The ego in contemporary psychology. *Psychol. Rev.*, 1943, **50,** 451–478.

Amsel, A. The role of frustrative nonreward in noncontinuous situations. *Psychol. Bull.*, 1958, **55,** 102–119.

Amsel, A., and Roussel, J. Motivational properties of frustration: I. Effect on a running response of the addition of frustration to the motivational complex. *J. exp. Psychol.*, 1952, **43,** 363–368.

Atkinson, J. W. *Motives in fantasy, action and society.* New York: D. Van Nostrand, 1958.

Atkinson, J. W. *An introduction to motivation.* Princeton, N.J.: D. Van Nostrand, 1964.

Atkinson, J. W., and Birch, D. Determinants of human choice. Unpublished final report, NSF Project GS-9, University of Michigan, 1966, pps. 31.

Atkinson, J. W., and Cartwright, D. Some neglected variables in contemporary conceptions of decision and performance. *Psychological Reports*, 1964, **14,** 575–590.

Atkinson, J. W., and Feather, N. T. (Eds.) *A theory of achievement motivation.* New York: Wiley, 1966.

Atkinson, J. W., and Litwin, G. H. Achievement motive and test anxiety conceived as motive to approach success and motive to avoid failure. *J. abnorm. soc. Psychol.*, 1960, **60,** 52–63.

Atkinson, J. W., and McClelland, D. C. The projective expression of needs: II. The effect of different intensities of the hunger drive on thematic apperception. *J. exp. Psychol.*, 1948, **38,** 643–658.

Atkinson, J. W., and Reitman, W. R. Performance as a function of motive strength and expectancy of goal attainment. *J. abnorm. soc. Psychol.*, 1956, **53,** 361–366.

Barker, R. G. *The stream of behavior*. New York: Appleton-Century-Crofts, 1963.

Birch, D. A motivational interpretation of extinction. In Jones, M. R. (Ed.) *Nebraska symposium on motivation*, 1961. Lincoln, Neb: University of Nebraska Press, 1961.

Birch, D. Verbal control of nonverbal behavior. *J. exp. child Psychol.*, 1966, **4,** 266–275.

Birch, D. Shift in activity and the concept of persisting tendency. In Spence, K. W. and Spence, J. T. (Eds.) *The psychology of learning and motivation: Advances in research and theory*, Vol. II. New York: Academic Press, 1968.

Birch, D., Burnstein, E., and Clark, R. A. Response strength as a function of hours of food deprivation under a controlled maintenance schedule. *J. comp. physiol. Psychol.*, 1958, **51,** 350–354.

Birch, D., Clifford, L. T., and Butterfield, Julie. Response latency as a function of size of gap in the elevated runway. *J. exp. Psychol.*, 1961, **62,** 179–186.

Birch, D., and Veroff, J. *Motivation: A study of action*. Belmont, Calif.: Brooks/Cole, 1966.

Boe, E. E., and Church, R. M. *Punishment: Issues and experiments*. New York: Appleton-Century-Crofts, 1968.

Bower, G. H. The influence of graded reductions in reward and prior frustrating events upon the magnitude of the frustration effect. *J. comp. physiol. Psychol.*, 1962, **55,** 582–587.

Brown, J. S. Gradients of approach and avoidance responses and their relation to level of motivation. *J. comp. physiol. Psychol.*, 1948, **41,** 450–465.

Brown, J. S. *The motivation of behavior*. New York: McGraw-Hill, 1961.

Brown, J. S., and Belloni, Marigold. Performance as a function of deprivation time following periodic feeding in an isolated environment. *J. comp. physiol. Psychol.*, 1963, **56,** 105–110.

Brown, J. S., Kalish, H. I., and Farber, I. E. Conditioned fear as revealed by magnitude of startle response to an auditory stimulus. *J. exp. Psychol.*, 1951, **41,** 317–327.

Brown, M. Factors determining expectancy of success and reaction to success and failure. Unpublished project report, University of Michigan, August 15, 1963.

Brown, M. Determinants of persistence and initiation of achievement-related activities. Unpublished doctoral dissertation, University of Michigan, 1967.

Burdick, H. The relationship of attraction, need achievement and certainty to conformity under conditions of a simulated group atmosphere. Unpublished doctoral dissertation, University of Michigan, 1955.

Campbell, B. A., and Church, R. M. *Punishment and aversive behavior.* New York: Appleton-Century-Crofts, 1969.

Campbell, D. T. Social attitudes and other acquired behavioral dispositions. In Koch, S. (Ed.) *Psychology: A study of a science,* Vol. 6, *Investigations of man as socius.* New York: McGraw-Hill, 1963.

Church, R. M. The varied effects of punishment on behavior. *Psychol. Rev.,* 1963, **70,** 369–402.

Cole, M., and Maltzman, I. *A handbook of contemporary Soviet psychology.* New York: Basic Books, Inc., 1969.

Cotton, J. W. Running time as a function of amount of food deprivation. *J. exp. Psychol.,* 1953, **46,** 188–198.

Easterbrook, J. A. The effect of emotion on cue utilization and the organization of behavior. *Psychol. Rev.,* 1959, **66,** 183–201.

Edwards, W. The theory of decision making. *Psychol. Bull.,* 1954, **51,** 380–417.

Ellison, G. D. Differential salivary conditioning to traces. *J. comp. physiol. Psychol.,* 1964, **57,** 373–380.

Ericksen, C. W. Unconscious processes. In Jones, M. R. (Ed.) *Nebraska symposium on motivation,* 1958. Lincoln, Neb.: University of Nebraska Press, 1958.

Estes, W. K. An experimental study of punishment. *Psychol. Monogr.,* 1944, **57,** Whole No. 263.

Feather, N. T. Persistence in relation to achievement motivation, anxiety about failure, and task difficulty. Unpublished doctoral dissertation, University of Michigan, 1960.

Feather, N. T. The relationship of persistence at a task to expectation of success and achievement-related motives. *J. abnorm. soc. Psychol.,* 1961, **63,** 552–561.

Feather, N. T. The study of persistence. *Psychol. Bull.,* 1962, **59,** 94–115.

Feather, N. T. Mowrer's revised two-factor theory and the motive-expectancy-value model. *Psychol. Rev.,* 1963, **70,** 500–515.

Feshbach, S. The drive-reducing function of fantasy behavior. *J. abnorm. soc. Psychol.,* 1955, **50,** 3–11.

Festinger, L. *A theory of cognitive dissonance.* New York: Harper and Row, 1957.

French, Elizabeth G. Some characteristics of achievement motivation. *J. exp. Psychol.,* 1955, **50,** 232–236.

French, Elizabeth G. Motivation as a variable in work-partner selection. *J. abnorm. soc. Psychol.,* 1956, **53,** 96–99.

French, Elizabeth G., and Thomas, F. H. The relation of achievement motivation to problem-solving effectiveness. *J. abnorm. soc. Psychol.,* 1958, **56,** 45–48.

Freud, S. Instincts and their vicissitudes (1915). In *Collected papers,* Vol. IV (Riviere, Joan, transl.). London: The Hogarth Press and the Institute of Psychoanalysis; New York: Basic Books, 1949.

Haber, R. N., and Alpert, R. The role of situation and picture cues in projective measurement of the achievement motive. In Atkinson, J. W. (Ed.) *Motives in fantasy, action and society*. Princeton: D. Van Nostrand, 1958, Ch. 45, pp. 644–663.

Hebb, D. O. *The organization of behavior*. New York: Wiley, 1949.

Horner, Matina, Karabenick, S. A., and Atkinson, J. W. A nontraumatic analog of traumatic avoidance learning. Presentation to Michigan Academy of Science, Ann Arbor, Michigan, 1965.

Humphreys, L. G. Acquisition and extinction of verbal expectations in a situation analogous to conditioning. *J. exp. Psychol.*, 1939, **25,** 294–301.

Hull, C. L. Special review: Thorndike's *Fundamentals of learning. Psychol. Bull.*, 1935, **32,** 807–823.

Hull, C. L. Mind, mechanism and adaptive behavior. *Psychol. Rev.*, 1937, **44,** 1–32.

Hull, C. L. *Principles of behavior*. New York: Appleton, 1943.

James, W. *The principles of psychology*, 2 vols. New York: Henry Holt, 1902.

Karabenick, S. A. The effect of consummatory behavior on the strength of an immediately subsequent instrumental response. Unpublished doctoral dissertation, University of Michigan, 1967.

Koch, S. Behavior as "intrinsically" regulated: Work notes towards a pretheory of phenomena called "motivational." In Jones, M. R. (Ed.) *Nebraska symposium on motivation*, 1956. Lincoln, Neb.: University of Nebraska Press, 1956.

Krantz, D. H. Conjoint measurement: The Luce-Tukey axiomatization and some extensions. *J. math. Psychol.*, 1964, **1,** 248–277.

Lawrence, D. H., and Festinger, L. *Deterrents and reinforcement*. Stanford: Stanford University Press, 1962.

Lewin, K. *Principles of topological psychology*. New York: McGraw-Hill, 1936.

Lewin, K. *The conceptual representation and the measurement of psychological forces*. Durham, N.C.: Duke University Press, 1938.

Lewin, K., Dembo, Tamara, Festinger, L., and Sears, Pauline S. Level of aspiration. In Hunt, J. McV. (Ed.) *Personality and the behavior disorders*, Vol. I. New York: Ronald Press, 1944, pp. 333–378.

Litwin, G. H. Achievement motivation, expectancy of success, and risk-taking behavior. In Atkinson, J. W., and Feather, N. T. (Eds.) *A theory of achievement motivation*. New York: Wiley, 1966.

Lowell, E. L. The effect of need for achievement on learning and speed of performance. *J. Psychol.*, 1952, **33,** 31–40.

Lucas, J. D. The interactive effects of anxiety, failure and interserial duplication. *Amer. J. Psychol.*, 1952, **55,** 59–66.

Luce, R. D., and Tukey, J. W. Simultaneous conjoint measurement: A new type of fundamental measurement. *J. math. Psychol.*, 1964, **1,** 1–27.

Mandler, G., and Sarason, S. B. A study of anxiety and learning. *J. abnorm. soc. Psychol.*, 1952, **47,** 166–173.

Marzocco, F. N. Frustration effect as a function of drive level, habit strength and distribution of trials during extinction. Unpublished doctoral dissertation, State University of Iowa, 1951.

McClelland, D. C. *Personality.* New York: William Sloane Associates (Dryden Press), 1951.

McClelland, D. C., Atkinson, J. W., Clark, R. A., and Lowell, E. L. *The achievement motive.* New York: Appleton-Century-Crofts, 1953.

McDougall, W. *An introduction to social psychology.* London: Methuen, 1908.

Miller, N. E. Liberalization of basic S-R concepts: Extensions to conflict behavior, motivation, and social learning. In Koch, S. (Ed.) *Psychology: A study of a science*, Vol. II. New York: McGraw-Hill, 1959, 196–292.

Miller, N. E. Studies of fear as an acquirable drive. I. Fear as motivation and fear-reduction as reinforcement in the learning of new responses. *J. exp. Psychol.*, 1948, **38,** 89–101.

Mischel, T. Pragmatic aspects of explanation. *Philos, Science*, 1966, **33,** 40–60.

Mischel. T. (Ed.) *Human action: Conceptual and empirical issues.* New York and London: Academic Press, 1969.

Montgomery, K. C. "Spontaneous alternation" as a function of time between trials and amount of work. *J. exp. Psychol.*, 1951, **42,** 82–93.

Moulton, R. W. Effects of success and failure on level of aspiration as related to achievement motives. *J. personal. soc. Psychol.*, 1965, **1,** 399–406.

Mowrer, O. H. A stimulus-response analysis of anxiety and its role as a reinforcing agent. *Psychol. Rev.*, 1939, **46,** 553–566.

Murray, H. A. et al., *Explorations in personality.* New York: Oxford University Press, 1938.

Neisser, U. *Cognitive psychology.* New York: Appleton-Century-Crofts, 1967.

Ovsiankina, M. Die wiederaufnahme unterbrochener handlungen. *Psychol. Forsch.*, 1928, **11,** 302–379.

Pavlov, I. P. *Conditioned reflexes* (transl. by G. V. Annep). Oxford: Clarendon Press, 1927.

Premack, D. Toward empirical behavior laws: I. Positive reinforcement. *Psychol. Rev.*, 1959, **66,** 219–233.

Pribram, K. H. A review of theory in physiological psychology. In Farnsworth, P. R. and McNemar, Q. (Eds.) *Annual review of psychology.* Palo Alto: Annual Reviews, Inc., 1960.

Raynor, J. O. The relationship between distant future goals and achievement motivation. Unpublished doctoral dissertation, University of Michigan, 1968.

Raynor, J. O. Future orientation and motivation of immediate activity: An elaboration of the theory of achievement motivation. *Psychol. Rev.*, 1969, **76,** 606–610.

Schneirla, T. C. An evolutionary and developmental theory of biphasic processes underlying approach and withdrawal. In Jones, M. R. (Ed.) *Nebraska symposium on motivation*, 1959. Lincoln, Neb.: University of Nebraska Press, 1959.

Sheffield, F. D., Roby, T. B., and Campbell, B. A. Drive reduction versus consummatory behavior as determinants of reinforcement. *J. comp. physiol. Psychol.*, 1954, **47,** 349–354.

Sherrington, C. S. *The integrative action of the nervous system.* New Haven: Yale University Press, 1926.

Skinner, B. F. *The behavior of organisms: An experimental approach.* New York: Appleton-Century, 1938.

Solomon, R. L. Punishment. *Amer. Psychol.*, 1964, **19,** 239–253.

Solomon, R. L., and Brush, E. S. Experimentally derived conceptions of anxiety and aversion. In Jones, M. R. (Ed.) *Nebraska symposium on motivation*, 1956. Lincoln, Neb.: University of Nebraska Press, 1956.

Solomon, R. L., Kamin, L. J., and Wynne, L. C. Traumatic avoidance learning: The outcome of several extinction procedures with dogs. *J. abnorm. soc. Psychol.*, 1953, **48,** 291–302.

Solomon, R. L., and Wynne, L. C. Traumatic avoidance learning: The principles of anxiety conservation and partial irreversibility. *Psychol. Rev.*, 1954, **61,** 353–385.

Spence, K. W. *Behavior theory and conditioning.* New Haven: Yale University Press, 1956.

Stellar, E., and Hill, J. H. The rat's rate of drinking as a function of water deprivation. *J. comp. physiol. Psychol.*, 1952, **45,** 96–102.

Strong, E. K. An interest test for personnel managers. *J. person. Res.*, 1926, **5,** 194–204.

Thorndike, E. L. *Animal intelligence.* New York: Macmillan, 1911.

Timberlake, W., and Birch, D. Complexity, novelty, and food deprivation as determinants of speed of a shift from one behavior to another. *J. comp. physiol. Psychol.*, 1967, **63,** 545–548.

Tinbergen, N. *The study of instinct.* Oxford: Clarendon Press, 1951.

Tolman, E. C. A behavioristic account of the emotions. *Psychol. Rev.*, 1923, **30,** 217–227.

Tolman, E. C. *Purposive behavior in animals and men.* New York: Appleton-Century, 1932.

Tolman, E. C. The determiners of behavior at a choice point. *Psychol. Rev.*, 1938, **45,** 1–41.

Tolman, E. C. Principles of performance. *Psychol. Rev.*, 1955, **62,** 315–326.

Tversky, A. A general theory of polynomial conjoint measurement. *J. math. Psychol.*, 1967, **4,** 1–20.

Valle, F. P. Effect of feeding-related stimuli on eating. Unpublished doctoral dissertation, University of Michigan, 1967. Also in *J. comp. physiol. Psychol.*, 1968, **66,** 773–776.

Weiner, B. Effects of unsatisfied achievement-related motivation on persistence and subsequent performance. Unpublished doctoral dissertation, University of Michigan, 1963.

Weiner, B. The effects of unsatisfied achievement motivation on persistence and subsequent performance. *J. personal.*, 1965, **33,** 428–442.

Weiner, B. The role of success and failure in the learning of easy and complex tasks. *J. personal. soc. Psychol.*, 1966, **3,** 339–343.

Weiner, B. New conceptions in the study of achievement motivation. In Maher, B. (Ed) *Progress in experimental personality research*, Vol. 5. New York: Academic Press, 1970.

Weiner, B., and Rosenbaum, R. Determinants of choice between achievement and nonachievement related activities. *J. exper. Res. Personal.*, 1965, 1, 114–121.

Wendt, H. W. Motivation, effort, and performance. In McClelland, D. C. (Ed.) *Studies in motivation.* New York: Appleton-Century-Crofts, 1955.

Whalen, R. E. Sexual motivation. *Psychol. Rev.*, 1966, **73,** 151–163.

Woodworth, R. S. *Dynamic psychology.* New York: Columbia University Press, 1918.

Woodworth, R. S. *Psychology: A study of mental life.* New York: Holt, Rinehart and Winston, 1921.

Zeigarnik, B. Das Behalten erledigter und unerledigter Handlungen. *Psychol. Forsch.*, 1927, **9,** 1–85. Translated and condensed as "On finished and unfinished tasks" in Ellis, W. D. *A source book of gestalt psychology.* New York: Harcourt, Brace and World, 1938, 300–314.

Zeller, A. F. An experimental analogue of repression: III. The effect of induced failure and success on memory measured by recall. *J. exp. Psychol.*, 1951, **42,** 32–38.

INDEX

See Glossary on pages 357–363 for definitions of technical terms